HAL BROOKS

Clown etc

HAL BROOKS

Clown *etc*

www.halbrooks.me

Matador
5 Weir Road
Kibworth Beauchamp
Leicester LE8 0LQ, UK
Tel: (+44) 116 279 2299
Fax: (+44) 116 279 2277
Email: books@troubador.co.uk
Web: www.troubador.co.uk/matador

ISBN 978 1848763 142

British Library Cataloguing in Publication Data.
A catalogue record for this book is available from the British Library.

Typeset in 12pt Perpetua by Troubador Publishing Ltd, Leicester, UK
Printed and bound in Great Britain by TJ International Ltd, Padstow, Cornwall

Matador is an imprint of Troubador Publishing Ltd

To all the family

Contents

Chapter 1

Early Days

What a time to begin anything. It's 5.12 am on a November morning, sitting on the side of my bed in a motor caravan. I have been tossing about for hours with my mind going twenty to the dozen. It's the morning of the 17th November 1976.

Yesterday was my anniversary, thirty years married to my darling wife Deena. Whilst on the phone to her last night she had to remind me what the date was. I had made myself a cup of tea and it was very cold. My only heating was from a gas ring on the stove, and whilst drinking the tea I suddenly thought to myself, what the heck was I doing sitting here, a well-nourished fifty-five year old male, freezing cold, sipping a hot cup of tea whilst the London traffic rushed by a few yards away.

It occurred to me that others, my family included, might also be interested in the answer. So I decided to get it all down. Making a start in an out-of-date RoSPA diary that was to hand, I wrote a beginning to this saga. Just a couple of pages before I got back to sleep for another hour. Pleased at my decision and quite confident that I could do it, although I had not written at any length before.

I was parked outside the Ladywell Centre in Lewisham, London, whilst touring the local schools with my school road safety shows. About nine o'clock I would be joined by a local Road Safety Officer, RSO, to accompany me on my day's work.

Working the schools took me all over the country and so after doing four shows a day, having cooked and eaten my meal, I was ready, after a sleep, to write all evening. I was surprised to discover how much I enjoyed it.

During these tours I was able to get permission to park in a secure overnight place provided by the local authorities employing me. Mostly these were council premises of all kinds, very basic.

In Southwark I parked in the Peckham Highways depot. In Greys, Essex, it was a disused fire station. Refuse collecting and lighting depots, gritting departments, driver training establishments and in some parts of the country in the garden of the RSO himself. It was not safe to be in car parks or open spaces, as the Police were most likely to move you on.

In the schools I am introduced as 'Kerby Drill', the Road Safety Clown. My real name is Harry Dennis Brooks, and my stage name is Hal Brooks. I am a member of the entertainer's union Equity and have been so since the fifties. Before that I was a member of the Amalgamated Society of Woodworkers, The ASW, and had been so since I was fourteen and on the bench learning my craft from dad, who was at the other end of the bench. Which conveniently brings me back to where this grown-up clown started.

I remember 1927. It was the year when I grew up into childhood. I was six years old. I can recall earlier memories but these, I think, have been helped along the way by relatives. But when 1927 came along I distinctly remember saying to myself 'I am definitely not going to be able to get used to this'. I had the same feeling at the turn of this century, saying the year 2000 sounded ridiculous, but by then I was nearly in my eighties.

I don't remember much about living in 19 Rackham Street, North Kensington, London W10, where I was born. I do remember trundling the piano across the road when we moved to No. 24. The small iron castors of the piano were no match for the tar macadam of the road surface. This was when I was six. We always had a piano, and I'm told I could play God Save The 'You Know Who' when I was five.

I was the baby of the family. Mum, Mary, Dad Henry (always called Harry), Charlie, Fred, Floss, Rose, Lily, Rene and me. An ordinary working class family that in the twenties, owing to carpenter dad having a steady job, we were a little better off than some. An indication of this was dad had rented No. 19 but was buying No. 24 through a building society mortgage.

Dad did his service in the 1918 war making aeroplane propellers. When he married mum, he was still an apprentice to Green and Abbots, Builders etc. One of the jobs he was on was the building of Selfridges, in Oxford Street. He told me that his first job in the morning was to get the beer for the men's breakfast. Each man's can was hanging on a broom handle he held to manage them all.

There were five children in dad's family. I know there was an Albert and sisters Liz and Rose. His father was a tall, bent figure with a large nose. A retired bricklayer. Dad used to relate that he'd worked on the convent that was halfway down the Portobello Road. He pointed out the red brick arches that were all hand-rubbed (shaped) by him years ago. A nice reminder, even today, of the old boy's skill. He fell off a ladder once for which he got some compensation. Some of it found its way into the Eagle Public House in Ladbroke Grove. To counteract the brick dust no doubt!

Dad's mother was of slighter build. I remember her with beautiful white hair. I'm sure someone mentioned that in her youth it was bright ginger. It probably accounts for the colour of mine, Rose's and Floss's auburn locks. I didn't go into their rooms much. They lived on the ground floor that you had to go up steps to reach, as there was also a semi-basement level below.

The pungent smell of wintergreen ointment was always present. It was then a popular remedy for ageing and painful limbs. It was different from the smell of camphorated oil I got doused with whenever I was chesty.

Mum of course was over forty when she had me. I never knew her as a young person, but I'll bet she looked more like Sister Rose than Floss, Lily or Rene. I must have been fussed over a lot when I was young. Five ladies seeing to one baby. I'm not aware of it though. Mum and dad, fully protective as they were, were not ones to kiss and cuddle openly. I don't remember ever seeing mum and dad kiss each other. Things were a lot different then.

We took for granted total security in the family. Mum was one of a larger family. Her dad worked in the gasworks in Kensal Rise. A thicker set figure than my dad, with a bald head. The family name was Wingrove. His wife's maiden name was Gardener, and they lived in the Portobello Road next to an off-licence.

I was very young at the time when Gran Wingrove died. Standing by the edge of her bed whilst all her girls were taking turns rubbing her legs to fight the cramp. That isn't an assisted memory. I really remember that. Her children were Emma, Mary, Ann, Nell, Rene, Arthur, John and Charlie.

Mum and Em were 'in service' in Dorset. So it was easy to see where she got the skills to be able to take in a bit of washing and ironing to help keeping her own family. She was a good cook too. Seeing to us lot was a full time job. Getting all the family off to work in the morning before seeing to Rene and me had to be her first chore. We were all very different. I think only Rose used to talk to her at this time of the day, except for dad who always said 'toodle-oo' before cycling off. The others were not very talkative whilst preparing to go to work.

Having a large family it came to pass that mum was taken pity on by the local school head in Barlby Road. I was accepted at four when five years was the norm. I cried all day. So I was sent back home for another year. Rene must have been attending school at this time.

Although I cannot see it in my mind's eye I remember dad had made a wooden steam engine for the family. One big enough to climb on, and for a child to bestow the rank of engine driver in the pretend games of childhood.

I was aware of the Fuller family who lived opposite. One of the sons had two thumbs on one hand. That was something in itself, but more important to me was Eva Fuller, his younger sister. My first love for sure.

My first teacher was a Mrs Bedwood . She was a kindly motherly person but not like my mum. She wore perfume. One afternoon when mum came to collect me I was not to be found. After a search someone discovered me in toilets. I'd had an 'accident' and wasn't quite sure what to do. Mum knew though. Don't we take Mums for granted.

The infants' playground in Barlby Road had an asphalt surface. I don't remember any grass about. In the corner, adjacent to the main road, was a building containing the woodwork class. I was to have a closer association with this and the teacher, a Mr Pearce, later on. Our wickets and goalposts were painted on the high walls

Infants ran into juniors and events are hard to separate. The home scene is more vivid to me. In No.19 when we lived there, an old lady, Mrs Bloomfield, was living in a first floor room. Mum had befriended her then and now kept an eye on her. Since we had moved into No.24 I used to visit her on a Sunday morning to fetch her a pint of porter, a weekly amount, from the local off-licence.

I understood that this treat was solely due to the half crown (25p) that a Mrs Store allowed her. Colonel & Mrs Store were a kindly caring upper class couple, (whatever upper class meant in the context of a young child) who did charitable works, with their own money, in our neighbourhood.

I never saw the Colonel but I do remember his wife. A tall regal figure always dressed in black with a wide-brimmed hat. To me she reminded me of Queen Mary. All this knowledge of course, was what I gleaned from hearing my parents talk. I also think my Mum benefited from her influence a little later on.

There's a photograph of me and mum on the beach at Herne Bay. Mum had been poorly and we were staying in a convalescent home for a short while. I can't be sure but looking back it seemed the sort of situation that Mrs Store's kindly influence was highly probable in bringing about.

Once when I returned from one of my regular Sunday visits to the off-licence, Mrs Bloomfield was preparing her dinner. I can still remember the aroma of the rasher of bacon frying in the pan along with three or four mushrooms. We never had mushrooms. It probably accounts for the deep and abiding memory I have of this. Plus the fact that Mrs B more than likely gave me a taste as a reward for my errand running.

One of the first things that happened when we moved over to No.24 was dad started re-pointing all the brickwork on the house front. The bricks were stocks of some kind. These were all shades of yellow ochre. A beautiful natural clay streaked with greys.

No.24 wasn't 'vacant possession' when dad bought it. A Mrs Williams and her son Alfie lived on the top floor. They were there for quite a while but then suddenly moved out. It was probably the pressure of the Brooks' family growing into adulthood and requiring more room.

The house was one of thirty terraced-joined houses that made up the street. No.1 bordered Ladbroke Grove, and Raymead Street was at the bottom end. The ground floor was three steps down to a semi-basement, and there were steps leading up to the front door. Our coal cellar was beneath the front steps. A coalhole, with cast iron cover, was situated so that coal could be shot into the cellar from the street outside.

There was a passage with a door to the front room on the right and a straight staircase up to the inside lavatory. There weren't referred to as 'loos' then. The bottom of the stairs, with a cupboard under complete with gas and electricity meters, also showed the entrance door to the living room, our kitchen.

Further along the passage was the wash house. In the left corner was a brick-built water heater with a fireplace under its iron tub to heat the water. In the right-hand corner was a sink and tap. We all washed there. Sometimes a little uncomfortably for a certain young person. I remember Rose 'assisting me' to wash my neck!

A door from the wash house led to the back yard. We had an outside WC and shed the same size leading up to a nine-inch brick wall that separated us from St. Charles Square, the houses of which backed on to ours. We were lucky. There was a tree in the garden over the wall. Not many Rackham Street back yards had that novelty. I remember how handy that wall was too. During bonfire night we could walk along it to where we saw the glow of another family's bonfire.

Going up the stairs there was a borrowed light over the WC door. This pane of glass saved the passageway from being all doom and gloom. There, two rooms followed the contours of downstairs. The front bedroom was mum and dad's where I slept until the Williams family moved from the top floor. I have no family left to ask now but it seems the boys must have been bedded downstairs and the girls in the middle room upstairs. It must have been quite a crush.

Anyway, we all spread out when Mrs Williams left with Alfie. Two boys in the back, three girls in the front, parents beneath them, Rene and me 'neath the boys. It remained like that until Fred got wed to Cis. Then Rene moved up with Lil, Rose and Floss, I moved in with Charlie, and Dad turned the middle room into a bathroom. Rather like a game of chess on going without any checkmate. I remember the gas boiler used to supply the hot water. We used an enamel bucket to transfer the hot water over the short distance to the bath.

Dad was into doing a bit of home brewing at this time. Vigormalt it was called. A tin of something resembling black treacle was tipped into a large container of water and a supply of dried yeast added. When the mixture stopped doing what it had to do, dad bottled the results. It was sometimes disconcerting whilst bathing, to hear a few loud pops emanating from where the brew stood in bottles on top of a cupboard. None of it was wasted I gather. It was also beneficial for a side effect, regularity!

Dad also set to work downstairs by punching a doorway through from the back to the front room. The door and the upper part of the frame were glazed with obscure glass, so turning it into a borrowed light.

Ingenious dad made a plywood '21' shape with small bulbs outlining the numbers. These were wired together and connected to an accumulator battery for illuminations when we all reached twenty-one years. The piano was in the front room behind the panel and so standing the '21' on its lid, the lights were seen in both rooms.

The piano at that time was a Cramer, later on we had a Boyd. Mum put us all to the instrument. (It has just occurred to me as I write neither parent played themselves, so it's an indication that they were determined to do all they could manage for their family). It couldn't have been easy. It's no good saying pianos were cheaper then, it still must have been a bit of a sacrifice on their parts for the betterment of their family.

I remember when I bought our first piano. We went into Swansea looking for a cheapy, and came back owning an upright Challen, costing an enormous one hundred pounds. So it seems I've a lot of my parents in me, music-wise at least. When it was my turn mum asked a cousin, Elsie Chaplin, if she would take me on as a pupil. Elsie was a piano teacher with umpteen certificates to her name.

It started well, but later on she told Mum I would not get anywhere if I didn't stop playing by ear. How I wish she had persisted. Eventually the music would have become dominant and I would have had the best of both worlds. Now I have to be satisfied with my own rendition of tunes, instead of what the composer actually wrote. There is one compensation though, having worked at it all my life I developed my own style. A not very complicated one, but tuneful. It seems to work.

The next few years were spent consolidating our youth. Rackham Street had three gangs in it. Top, bottom and middle, and ne'er the trio would meet. It seems strange now to think back, but there couldn't have been more than a dozen children in each gang and I was in the middle one. We all played together as though it was all predetermined. Saturdays were the magical ingredient. After inspection from Rose I was out of the house like a shot.

According to the time of year certain games would be all the rage. Summer would bring out a flush of cherrystones. Cherry hogs we called them. We would all be collecting these cherry centres, and a couple of the gang would be out on the pavement with a shoe box with little doorways cut in one side, with a number above it. From a distance chalked on the pavement you then rolled your stones into the box. If it went in you received the number of stones that the number over the doorway stated.

Autumn time it was conkers. There were lots of trees producing the horse chestnuts we used. Drill a hole through the centre, generally with a meat skewer, to provide a hole to put your string through, already knotted. These were offered to an opponent passively to enable him or her to knock the living daylights out of your dangling target.

Whichever conker survived gained a number each time it won. A oncer, or a niner, whatever. All sorts of curious schemes were afoot to toughen up these targets. Soaking in vinegar was one I know. The wily one with the most successful never let on what they used. In the oven for a quick bake was another treatment, if mum let you.

'Pin a Go' was a very busy time indeed. Each of us had a book that hid items hidden in its pages, mostly cigarette cards. You put your pin into a closed book and opened it at the page where you inserted it. You then kept anything on that page. We never thought how easy it would have been to buy a strip of pins from a shop. I can only imagine we must have got our supplies from our mum's needlework boxes. Such were loyalties to the game.

Sometimes we actually played cards using cigarette cards as currency. Mostly it was Banker. Rarely we played Pontoon. I don't remember playing card games like Donkey, in the street. They were kept for indoors and in our house, mainly over Christmas.

The more physical games also had their spasmodic periods of popularity. 'Cuttey' was a leap frog game played across the street from kerb to kerb. One of us formed a 'back' for the rest of us to sail over, legs astride using the hands as a support. The last one over then formed a back about a yard from the kerb. You then had to get over using only one step to do so. The next back was formed two yards away. Two steps were allowed for this one. You drop out if you can't manage it, and so on until you cross the road. It took about four or five steps to cross our street.

Warney Echo was another favourite. This was more rough and tumble. Five or six a side, one team to form up against the railings. Number one holds on tight and lets the head of the next one go between his legs, and so on. The game commences when all the team is bending down forming a tunnel of backs. The opposing team's first member then has to leap astride onto the backs as far as he can reach, and so on until all the players are accommodated.

As soon as they are all on the chant goes 'Warney Echo, one two three, 1-2-3 1-2-3, Warney Echo 1-2-3, my fair lady'. Then it's the other team's go. Much more than rarely, the whole caboodle collapses. Either because the first jumpers didn't get on far enough for the rest of the team to get a safe resting place or the weight of them all did the trick. Mostly it was because the last couple of 'fliers' had only their team-mate's backs to cling on to. So looking like a drunken camel sprouting a multiplicity of humps, the mass of writhing juniors would sink like a weak blancmange long before the song finished!

In the Autumn when it got dark comparatively early we played a version of hide and seek. 'Reeleeso,' it was called. For the purposes of this explanation a bit more of our immediate neighbourhood has to be sketched in. Rackham, our street, then a quieter street, Hewer Street, running parallel to each other. This street, however, wasn't full of houses. The ones that were there were of a better quality than ours. On one side was a warehouse and a funeral establishment. They made coffins there. Opposite was a Post Office sorting centre, so the two streets could be turned into a roundabout, sort of.

Two teams were made up, and I rather think it was mostly boys for this game. Most folk marking out a rectangle ten feet long, by the pavement width, would have used chalk or something. Our something was a moist mixture of marking fluid that all the team, if only the boys were there, could be relied on to contribute to with their fly buttons open. You can see why this is a fair weather game. A shower would soon render the marking out lines invisible.

On with the game. One team went off leaving one member in the box. His team's job was to get another of his mates to run through the box shouting, you've guessed it, 'REELEEESO!' If he got caught doing it he was captured also. One run through the box equals one let out. So it was a hunt and be hunted sort of game. Trying to get to the middle of the street and through the box with the opposing team after your blood, was quite something.

It was strange in those days; some of us never saw our friends' parents. The Loders for instance. Great pals, but their dad worked on the railway. The work shift kept him out of our sight in daylight hours. So we wouldn't have recognised him even if we saw him. We were strangely isolated from anybody but ourselves, and of course, the gang.

When I was a little older I don't know what caused it, but it came about that I had to fight Jacky Munn from the bottom gang. I was lording it about a bit as to what I intended doing, and the time arrived to deliver. After a lot of sparring about the lad bonked me one. I must say no-one was more surprised than me. It hurt and I didn't like it. Take no notice what you'd seen Tom Mix or Buck Jones do in the threepenny Saturday morning cinema show in the Playhouse, this was too real. Anyway I lost, and I became best friends with my attacker. A lesson was learned all round I think.

One year mum's Christmas present to me was a pair of roller skates. I was eleven at the time. I became quite proficient. In the past I'd had a chemistry set, another year there was a conjuring outfit, but I had never actually blossomed into either of these professions. But I wasn't bad on the skates. Skating on the pavements with the constant jarring of the paving slabs jerking you about. Hewer Street was heaven. It was a smooth asphalt surface, unlike my road, which was tarmac. I wasn't to know then how important skill at skating was to be in the future.

The No. 15 bus from the East and West Ham terminated in Ladbroke Grove. Top of our street. Behind the actual parking place and turnaround point, was the fire station. It made up a roundabout convenient for going back on the return journey. They always slowed down a bit to do so. It was a grand opportunity to grab the buses back bumpers for a lift. Being pulled behind the bus was quite something, especially with skates on.

One day my luck ran out. The road was pockmarked and rutted, what with the buses and fire engines constantly going over it. I came a cropper. My right kneecap lost a bit the size of a half-crown, as big as a two pound coin now. It didn't heal, festered, and I was admitted to the infirmary, now St. Charles Hospital, right at the bottom of our street.

Before the advent of antibiotics I was put on three-hourly poultices to the knee. In conjunction with these was the use of a rubber bandage. Nurse Cory, a formidable-looking but motherly woman wearing the dark blue belt of a staff nurse, tended me. I was very lucky. Everybody was kind and friendly during my stay.

I had blood poisoning and was subjected to all sorts of tests. One strange result was that mum was told her son had rheumatism. It was to be many years before it really caught up with me. I was put on beef tea. I loved it, still do, and am always on the lookout for it. As I am grasping my pen to write this, it can be safely presumed I survived.

Before I was discharged the gang soon found out where I was. My ward was adjacent to the bottom of the street. With the window opened up a bit we could shout to each other. A matter of twenty feet or so. One day there was great excitement amongst the tribe. They knew all about babies! Older boys from another gang had told them quite explicitly how they came about.

The mind boggles when you think of what some passers-by must have thought to have such stop-press news hollered across the pavement. Most of it went above our heads as to the significance of its nature. We were still very firmly being allowed to grow up in our own time. There was no pushing and shoving by such forces as television then.

Chapter 2

John

By the time I left hospital I was quite used to large wards with high ceilings, so, upon returning home it was a shock to realise how small our rooms were. There was another kind of shock too. I was no longer the baby of the family. Whilst I was in being cared for, the local newspaper carried the headline 'Tragic death of young mother, leaving two children, after dying of peritonitis'. The result of a back street abortion, so the papers said.

The young mum was my auntie Dode, mum's younger sister. The two children, Audrey and John, were then about three and one years old. Audrey was being cared for by the sister of the father, George. They lived near Southend. Mum had taken John, the baby. So after a twelve-year break from nappies, mum was at it again.

They were beautiful children, both with fair hair. I should think that my four sisters must have thought, 'here we go again, another Harry cometh amongst us'. There's nothing like a baby to set things alight in a household. It was very sad to think that it had to come about this way.

Mum and the family just could not understand what drove Dode to consider the action she took. I was not old enough to understand all the circumstances surrounding the case. The twenties and thirties saw many people in desperate situations. It was so different then. The young arrival made quite a difference to my life. I don't remember all the details, but I'm sure I had my share of the pram pushing and minding 'his nibs'.

So mum now started caring for her ninth child. She had lost her first born, Henry, so after bearing eight of her own, this young one, my cousin John, came into the fold.

This fold was very interesting. From my perspective Charlie, my eldest brother, always seemed grown-up. At fourteen he started to buy books. I presumed he was facing dad on the bench learning to be a carpenter, earning money and contributing to the family pot. That meant at last he had pocket money he had earned himself.

He must have been a studious lad. He taught himself, Spanish, German and French, wrote plays and songs and taught himself the piano. I remember him being competent enough to play Liszt Hungarian Rhapsody No.2. He had a friend Bert who worked in Boots the Chemists, who was a pharmacist.

Dad had built a shed in the back yard for its whole length. It ran down one wall. His bench was nearest the house and mum's mangle was housed at the other end. Bert and Charlie used to work in the shed on a Sunday morning. I can't remember us not having a shed. I was always being turfed out of it by someone or other. One Sunday when they were out there, something went bang and they both came out dazed with their hair singed. They showed me how magnesium ignited once. Just like fireworks.

Charlie's room was quite something. He'd decorated it himself. It wasn't a very large room. Just really room for two single beds, Fred's and his. The walls were panelled by using a narrow moulding stuck on the wallpaper. The panels were shaded in pale green with gold paint on the moulding. The ceiling was also so decorated. It shows you the patience of the man when I tell you the mouldings on the ceiling were only about an inch long, spaced an inch apart.

A bookcase spanned the wall to the door with his writing bureau and drawers etc. in the middle. It was all oak with glass panels, stained a light green with the grain filled up with plaster to show white flecks in contrast. He had a large oak wardrobe in the chimney breast nearest the windows. He would be writing all night.

He smoked De Reske minors with a cork tip. His ashtrays were small Bakelite barrels, almost always full. He never inhaled, just puffed. He always signed himself Charles E. Brooks. The 'E' was for Edward. I moved in with Charlie when Fred got married.

After a while we nearly started conversing with each other. I'm afraid I wasn't quite out of the stage where my elder brothers could tolerate me. They would complain to mum about my sniffing amongst other things. But it was a beginning. Charlie taught me how to write my name in German. He also showed me the word anti-disestablishmentarianism. He said you could also put a 'pro' in front of it. A spelling gem I still remember.

Over the mantelpiece hung a round mirror. The wood frame was carved and surmounting it was an eagle with wings outstretched. On the mantelpiece was an oak clock he'd made with the top adorned by a similar-sized eagle. He had made this copy in papier mache. He showed me the wire skeleton of the bird's shape that he'd built it upon.

I wondered why he had made a small model of a dome. It was about eighteen inches in diameter, and it showed three stages of completion. Main timber construction, with a third revealing intermediate timbers, and the rest showed it fully boarded. It was the sort of thing you'd make prior to going in for a City & Guilds examination. I think he was going for a Clerk of Works certificate.

Charlie tried to join the police but he wore glasses sometimes, and they weren't acceptable then. Today, these establishments do accept less than perfect specimens. I'm sure a person of his intelligence and drive would have done the force proud.

Before the advent of electric pickups on gramophones, he built a cabinet in oak about two foot square and thirty inches high to house a wind-up clockwork mechanism and turntable. He experimented with different shaped horns to amplify the music. These were made from thin plywood and followed many weird shapes before he was satisfied. Al Jolson was all the rage, bringing tears to everyone's eyes with his singing of 'Sonny Boy'.

Charlie had one love, his Norton motorcycle and sidecar. He used it to go to night classes and work. One day he was involved in an accident and died shortly afterwards. Mum never got over it. It was traumatic for all of us. He was the first dead person I had seen. Lying in bed, for all the world, asleep. Such a loss at twenty-seven. I have often thought how different my future might have been, growing up with him keeping an eye on me, during my post sniffing years. Those two words of monumental proportions rise in my thoughts as I write. 'If only.'

Later in my life when it became my business to seek humour in all sorts of situations, I did manage to make a clown prop that evolved around the word and poem 'If'. That comes later though.

Fred was quite a different person. A carpenter like all of us men, and a great mixer. I never knew him without his pals. A grown-up gang sort of thing. His closest friend was Georgie Arnold who lived a few doors away. They were both keen footballers. Fred was a goalkeeper. His team, St. Swithin's, was in a league that played weekends.

They played their home games on Wormwood Scrubbs. It was a big park stretching from Scrubbs Lane over to Acton. The Acton side housed the buildings of Wormwood Scrubbs Prison. A rather grim place, I thought. Nearer our side was a large area without grass and covered with a sort of black ash. This was a fairyland that came to life when a bank holiday brought a visit from the swings, roundabouts and showmen of a travelling fair.

Looking back I can only think that the Scrubbs was too long a walk for us young folk, because I never saw Fred play. Once whilst playing he suffered a severe accident and hurt his knee and leg. It was mum who told me this.

The time I am relating to now was a very hard time on the building site. Unemployment was rife. There was always a small queue of hopefuls outside every building site, hoping to be taken on.

Fred had a pal, Jackie Cox. They went from job to job together. Piecework was all the rage then. This way of earning wages meant each item on a job would be priced and the more you did the more you were paid. Put like that it sounds eminently sensible. But of course it had a downside.

Example. To hang a door, put the hinges on, fit lock and door handles, cost say two pounds. A jobless man outside, desperate, would volunteer to do it for one pound ninety, and so on. Cut-throat was a mild term to describe this practice. The unions fought it tooth and nail because of its effects on the slower worker and the old. Fred told me there were often occasions on some sites when the tea boy came around the brew was left to get cold. The foreman was in sight. The threat of the sack had always to be considered.

I remember Charlie walking to Reading in search of work. He wrote home asking mum to send his fare back. He also used to varnish the soles of his shoes to get more wear out of them. This was about the time imitation leather showed its head. Charlie bought a pair. It seemed to me to be a cross between real leather and cardboard. The main consideration then being affordability. They were a lot cheaper.

One day Fred and Jack struck a really bad job. The foreman was a bully and the prices were down to a minimum. They were to hang so many doors in such a time. When the foreman was hailed to say they'd completed the task, 'all fixed', they were too. The doors were in their openings; well and truly fixed, with four inch nails. Carrying their toolboxes Fred and Jack marched off the site.

Fred also had a motorcycle. His was a Douglas. I remember mum's consternation once when one of his crowd of friends won a motorbike in a raffle. It was an Indian. I knew not whether it was in need of repair, but they decided to strip it down anyway. I expect you can gather which household bore the brunt of the operation. There were bits of machinery all over the place until they were finished.

The period before the lads started to get fixations with all the girls they attracted, are times I love to remember. Party times. What with Auntie Em's family as well, we always had a house-full. One time there was a punchball in the passageway at the foot of the stairs. With a stout screw eye in the ceiling and a removable one in the floor. The ball itself was a lovely soft leather inflated sphere suspended between two strong rubber straps, each about three feet in length. It was a wonderful way for the chaps to reveal their manliness. When the girls had a turn it was hilarious.

Games after tea. Here the men were out in the passage to be let in one at a time for the girl's game. Afterwards, the girls came in for the men to get their own back. I used to sit on the stairs listening to their shrieks. There was a main meal about suppertime. The young ones ate in the front room, the aunts and uncles in the back room. Mum made sure I was in with her.

There was always something to drink, supplied by dad. Sometimes it ran out and then one or two of the men would go round to the off-licence, the Earl of Granville, for more. So different today. The new habit seems to be everybody meets in the pub and then goes onto someone's house. All our festivities went on in the house. There was only one person who always went over the top; it was auntie Em's husband Fred. He was well-managed though by dad.

Inevitably then, a game of cards was started in the back room and the others were dancing and singing in the front. I learned how to play Whist from these sessions. It was wonderful whilst I was winning, but ever since then, the losing bits have stayed with me. Gambling has never had any attraction for me.

When everybody was worn out all the men slept in one bedroom and the girls in another. The grown-ups cleared away and all fell silent. The mornings were quite serene. Tea, coffee, eggs and bacon, all to each one's preference. I loved our parties. Even today I'd rather have a crush in the house than all the room of a hired hall.

A little bit more about our patch. Next to Hewer Street was Treverton Street. Whereas Hewer Street was quieter than Rackham was, Treverton was anything but. Whether the people there would agree is open to argument. Treverton Street held a family who had relatives opposite us. The Bloomfields. A hard-working family, and the elder boys gained popularity and local fame in the boxing game.

It was on a Saturday night that things livened up. It was always after the pubs were closed. It might have been just family differences but they seemed to occur pretty regularly. It also seemed that the nastiness seemed to break out in our street. Punch-ups were a feature, alongside a lot of noise and I expect, swearing. It was the peacekeeper who was interesting though. After keeping the street awake it was a girl, or actually a teenager, Liza Bloomfield from our street's family, who sorted them all out. She was well-liked and popular and if I had to choose an ally in any trouble I'd choose Liza.

Treverton Street never lacked entrepreneurial spirit though. Someone used to hire out cycles from there. Ladies' and gents' bikes. The tariff must have been in the region of tuppence an hour or we children couldn't have afforded it. But what wonderful freedom it gave us. As I remember no safety checks were ever made on them, and the brakes were dubious to say the least. But that wouldn't have deterred us. We could always scrape our shoes on the ground or run into something to stop!

There was also a shop in the short road that connected Rackham, Hewer and Treverton to the road where our school was. So we passed it daily. It was not a real shop but in someone's front room. Up a few steps, it sold a variety of goods, including sweets and coal. Not the bagged fuel that we are used to today, but sold by weight. So you took your own sack for it to be shovelled into. I hardly think buying sweets and loose coal from someone's front room would be allowed today. I can still remember the invasive smell of that coal.

Most sweets could be purchased for a halfpenny or a penny. There was one hygienic comfort; they were kept in glass jars with round lids. I never wrote down the shop talk at the time but it could have been something like 'let me just shovel this coal before I get you the gob stoppers'. It's a good job that the patent medicines would have come in their own bottles!

After I'd written this I realised I was thinking in the distinctly cynical modern way. But I know the sweets might have tasted all the better for it, from a young purchaser's point of view. And gob stoppers. What an evocative term. How many licks before this multi-coloured sphere changed colour?

One day there was a stir in our street. A removal van was parked halfway down on the other side. The family, I remember, were the Branwhites. They were moving to Slough, Bucks. It was when the new town was providing employment. Word soon got around; it didn't require much advertisement. Jobs were the lubricant needed to make people move from our street.

Our street had its own shop. Lallems was its name. It was a corner shop, at the beginning sort of thing. Number two it must have been, as it was on our side. It was well stocked and well used. One memory about the shop sticks in my mind. During one of our naughty periods I remember pinching some biscuits from there. I'm sure that the owners must have known and made allowances for us children not knowing any better and held off from taking punitive action. They were loose and kept in deep tins, a glass lid had to be lifted to get at them. Youngsters today would have probably been caught on CCTV and the course of their lives entirely changed.

Once I was having a look over the Convent wall in St. Charles Square. A copper saw me and I ran. He chased me out of the square and into Ladbroke Grove and down Rackham Street to number twenty-four. He caught me just as I was going down the three steps into the house. He gave me a good talking to. Mum came out just then and I don't remember the wallop, but as sure as 'eggs is eggs' I must have got one. Mum used to chastise us. I remember sister Lily came flying in once. The fact that she'd dived under the kitchen table didn't help her a bit. I don't remember dad ever laying hands on us but mum wasn't one to say 'you wait till your father gets in'. Her response was instant. On the whole though we were all well behaved, most of the time.

I'd have been scarred for life if she'd known of some of the things we got up to. Running behind lorries for instance. Once I ran behind a United Dairies milk lorry. It wasn't going very fast and I made myself comfy underneath the body where the spare wheel was usually kept. But it picked up speed and it took me right out to its depot at Park Royal, about five miles, before I managed to get off. It was only the fact that the Grand Union Canal ran close-by and I knew it was the same stretch of water we used to call The Cut. It ran under a bridge further along Ladbroke Grove. So I walked back along the towpath. If mum had found out I was due on two counts for trouble. One for doing such a dangerous thing in the first place, and two for going by the canal in the second place. It was always a no-go area for us children then.

I once had a Diana air rifle. I aimed it at a sparrow in our neighbour's tree. When I fired the pellet the bird fell to the ground, dead. The awful feeling between pretending and for real. I changed and grew up very quickly in those few moments. When I picked up the bird it struck me how final it was. I was very sorry and never aimed at a bird again. I'm not very good at killing things.

A few years after that I wonder what my poor mum would have thought if she had known that we used to go to the Seven Arches, Stonebridge, and fire at each other across the canal, playing cowboys. We only stopped after being chased by a bargee who, on coming out of the tunnel, found himself amongst whistling lead pellets. Someone did get hit on the forehead. A small bump came up above his eye. He could so easily have been blinded. These memories caused a lot of heart searching for me as a parent. Knowing how we lay down the law to our own children.

Most of our action was to take place much nearer home. Near the Eagle Public House in fact. There were generally three or four buses lined up whilst the drivers and conductors were in a cafe for a break before returning to East Ham. As the buses were empty we used to board them for a look around. In the first instance we were looking for empty cigarette packets to get the cards. Sets of ciggy cards were much sought after. Often small albums were given to encourage smokers to use their products. In fact time has demonstrated how attractive and collectable some of these little gems could become.

Then we kids started smoking. Probably from the age of nine or thereabouts. There were plenty of cheap cigarettes that we children could afford. Crayol brand cost three a penny. Turban brand, which we children knew of and declared pretty awful. It was decided by the majority of us to be made of camel dung, but they were in our price range.

Then someone invented a larger-than-life home-made variety. By picking up all the dog ends, cigarette butts, and collecting the tobacco, we made our own. Stripping the backing tissue from the silver paper we used this as a cigarette paper. Ours were not slender items as was originally in the packet, but much larger. So it was common to see ciggys about one inch in diameter and four inches long being puffed at by us 'little angels'. How I got to be my age I don't know.

The Eagle Public House faced Ladbroke Grove. Its side entrance alongside where the buses stopped housed a urinal. A smallish door opened on to a glazed wall that could accommodate four grown males. The fact is it was more public than private. I'm thinking the bus company may have had an interest in the facility in some way, for use by their bus personnel. It was all-male then.

What was less appreciated was that it was commonly used by us as a comfort station. We were all past the age of our mums letting us wee in the gutter. We all lived within two hundred yards of the pub, as a crow flies. We were definitely not crows. So however busy this little haven was, we could always dart in, push through a couple of legs, and complete our mission before the grown-ups would even loosen their flies. Oh the speed of youth!

After dad had built the shed he filled in the yard with a glazed roof for about eight feet to form a covered area for mum to do the washing under. The glass used was reinforced with small chicken wire, clearly visible but not interfering with the light flow. Should it get broken, pieces could not drop on to any one.

It also housed a wooden trough on four legs, about eighteen inches from the ground to enable a bucket to be put under to draw off the used water. Dad had lined the trough with zinc. A plughole was used to drain off the water. Mum's rubber rollered wringer, an Acme, was screwed onto one side of the tub. Acme, there's a name to conjure with. This would give your age away!

Dad had done this to lighten the load for mum on a Monday. Washing for all of us, what a hard day it must have been. She would light the boiler, a brick built affair, for boiling the whites. This was also the source of her hot water. The only water softener at the time was soda and Sunlight soap. She would use a corrugated scrubbing board and a flat length of scrubbing wood that used to slope into one of her galvanised baths. These were about two-foot wide with a handle at each end of an elliptical top. The sides sloped down about fifteen inches, and all day Monday she would be at it.

I hated being ill and away from school on a Monday. I didn't get half the time spent on me as on another day. I remember how mum coped with feeding the lot of us on wash days. A large saucepan would be on the stove bubbling away. I specially remember the day it was boiled fish by the constant presence of the cat in the kitchen. Mum always had a cat. It was never fussed over. The only concession allowed it in the realm of food was fish, otherwise it ate what the family ate. It was always a she cat and of course the neighbourhood had to put up with all the romancing noises of all the toms in the district, at regular intervals. Mum always managed to find a home for all her kittens.

When the contents of the bubbling saucepan wasn't fish it usually was rabbit. The liquids of both dishes were white and well laced with parsley. The mind boggles at the problem of getting all that washing dried in a small back yard. You can also detect how we were becoming different from the neighbours, though. I'm sure most mums would have loved to have had that covered way out the back.

The back room downstairs, our living room, we called the kitchen, had a cooking range and coal fire. A large cast iron boiler, with two handles, was always on the stove hob for hot water. We had a table in the window with a stool that spanned its length. We all got round the table on Sunday. How, I don't remember. I mean none of us were of a slight build. But on Sundays I think we managed it.

Ah Sundays! I remember a Lyons chocolate Swiss roll being cut up, a piece each, what heaven! With mum's rock cakes and bread pudding, we fed well. She was a good cook and had a big round biscuit tin for her cakes. She baked about forty to fifty a week. I can remember the solid small currants and sultanas sticking out of the sides, burnt slightly to make them chewy. Ends of cakes are still liked by me.

Mum's bread puddings were always spicy and dark brown. They never hung about for long. She used to swear by her oven and cooking range. When it was black leaded and brushed it always looked a treat. The product she used I remember had black stripes on its yellow wrapping. It was called Zebo.

Time progressed and dad finally persuaded her to have a gas cooker installed. There were rumblings of dissatisfaction for days. She wouldn't get the same work out of this new grey intruder. It was not like her coal fired range.

When she'd mastered it, however, and made it do what she wanted it to do, you'd have thought it was mum that pleaded with dad to get her one, not the other way round. Both my mum and dad were a bit cantankerous and stubborn, in a nice sort of way. My wife Deena says I take after them both!

Dad of course, being a maintenance carpenter in a large factory, E.N.V. Engineering, was often called in to work on a Sunday when the machines were silent, or most of them anyway. The work's furnaces weren't allowed to go cold over the weekend. Hence weekend work.

The firm made crown wheels and pinions for cars, lorries, and any sort of petrol or diesel driven engines. These two items could change the circular motion of a driving shaft into the force that turned the wheels of any vehicle.

They were made from steel that is comparatively soft to shape into gears, which is then case-hardened by heating to make them very strong, enough to do the job. This was done in the hardening shop where the furnaces were. All the departments were called 'shops'.

Once dad took me in to see the place. The smell of the cutting oil that was used on the gear cutting machines was all pervasive. I was not to know then that one day, just after my fourteenth birthday; I'd be accompanying dad as his apprentice.

One person I met that Sunday was a Mr. Armstrong. He was the firm's chief accountant. A wizard with figures so dad said. He had a club foot and was a very kindly person. How do I remember all this from so far back? I wasn't very old, but my likes and dislikes were more mature. Especially in the sweets line. He presented me with a Turkish Delight bar. I remember the make, Rowntrees. It was a little firmer than the modern variety and not quite so sweet. So for over eighty years I've been on the lookout to renew my acquaintance with this delightful sweetmeat.

E.N.V. Engineering Ltd. was also responsible for some very well known people visiting the works. Dad met Sir Henry Seagrave, who with his car 'The Golden Arrow', held the world speed record for a time. One of dad's first jobs for Mr Hewkins, the owner of E.N.V., was to make the man's furniture.

To do this he went down to the docks to select the mahogany boards needed and did it all from scratch. My dad was a very resourceful person and while I was growing up he seemed rather quiet and not at all 'pushy'. But in his later years, relieved of the burden of providing for us all, he showed that he had a keen wit and personality that was more than a match for all his children.

Mum was all for us spreading our wings. Many's the time we children were allowed to go to the Scrubbs for a picnic on our own. She let us have an old tablecloth or sheet for a 'tent' and gave us an egg to cook. A tall order as our 'frying pan' was an Oxo tin. Not the large variety with a hinged lid, but the smaller one that just held six cubes. As mum would have been worried if we had been away for much over two hours, and the grass was over a mile away, our picnics must have been more walking than eating.

There was another occasion though, when a visit to the Scrubbs had a more serious outcome. I loved school and there was no difficulty in getting me to go. But once I was persuaded by one of the others how exciting it was to 'hop the wag'. Play truant. Inevitably we ended up playing over the back of the Scrubbs. Iron railings with spikes on top marked the boundary. On the other side were allotments. These were portions of ground let to people who grew flowers and all manner of foods for their own use.

I remember it was very windy and chilly so we lit a fire for warmth. Anyway, with all the larking about we let the fire get too large. The wind took the flames under the railings. We were powerless to get to them. Panic. We all scooted. As well as the railway that ran along the back of the Scrubbs, there was also our lifeline, the canal. We beat our retreat along the towpath to home. We never did learn the extent of the damage and we didn't ask. I never skipped school again.

My eldest Sister Floss was rather a quieter person than the rest of us. Dark auburn hair and rather slight of build, I can imagine her taking after dad's mum. Ever since I can remember, she was a seamstress. She made dresses for all the family. Her and her Singer sewing machine. In the kitchen we had a chest of drawers. Two large drawers at the bottom, two small ones at the top. Mum let me have the top right one for all my bits. Mostly scraps of materials Floss let me have.

One of Floss's friends, a girl from work, Doris Burns, was a small minefield of chatter and exuberance. Great fun at parties. Fred's crowd loved her. I think she would have liked to have seen more of our Charlie. But the feeling was not mutual.

What happened early morning in our house was usual I suppose in most homes. Floss was a no talker in the morning. Not so sister Rose. As soon as she got up she and mum were talking with each other nineteen to the dozen. This continued until she left the house to become a shop assistant. Rose's hair was lighter than Floss's, a lovely gold colour. All my sisters were good-looking and attractive.

Chapter 3

Rose

Rose was radiant but shy. Her first job was in the West End store, Peter Robinson's. It was while she worked there that I have my most abiding memory of her. She had joined the store's dramatic group. The play I saw her in was 'The Last of Mrs. Cheney'. She had about two lines of dialogue in her part. When her time came, she stepped forward, said her lines, and blushed a beautiful pink. Most of the audience was relatives of some sort, and it was noticed in that kindly way of a shared trauma.

It was from Rose I learned about the pecking order in the West End shops. She, being a junior, had to wait for her seniors to become engaged with a customer before she stepped forward to serve. Years later TV's 'Are You Being Served?' exploited the humour of this custom to the full.

Rose was a great knitter and her crochet work was excellent. She played the piano and had a good voice. I always envied her ability to do them both at the same time. I only played by ear and had to watch the keys. She read music so it seemed easier for her. She was always looking at the music, and belting it out verbally at the same time. She was great friends with Charlie and at one time they shared the cost of a Hohner piano accordion, a 120 bass instrument. We still have it.

Rose left Robinson's and became an assistant in the Irish Linen Depot in Ealing. She soon became very knowledgeable about the cloth. A few years on she took on an insurance round. A highly intelligent person was Rose, really bright all round. It was she who kept the back of my neck the cleanest in the street!

Next down from Rose was sister Lily. I never called her anything but Lil. She was the only member of the family to go on to a polytechnic. She was excellent at embroidery with silks. One of her pieces was a lady in crinolines. Learning to become a tailoress, she eventually worked at Bradleys, the fur people in Westbourne Grove.

Lil worked in the mantle department, working on gowns that were in excess of one hundred pounds. A fair price in the thirties. She was very particular about her work. If mum ever bought a coat, invariably Lil would be on hand to make it fit properly. Once having to attend a wedding, and not having enough time to make a suit herself, bought one, but wasn't happy until she took most of it to pieces and re-made it to fit her properly.

Lil also played the piano quite well, and had also been taught by cousin Elsie who gave me the ultimatum, 'Stop playing by ear or else!' I was one of her 'or else's'!

I think that Rose would have loved to have gone onto further education, like Lil, but it was a bit early in the family's financial position. When Lil's position was reviewed, dad, Charlie, Fred, Floss and Rose were earning and her chance came because all the extras could then be afforded. Uniform, gym gear, etc. She was also let off earning her own living for a time.

I was very fortunate to be a boy who certainly was not an academic. When the eleven-plus came round it kept on turning as far as I was concerned. I never knew if I'd passed. I rather think I didn't! My parents never thrust a school report under my delicate nose that said 'He could have done better'.

It was the same with sister Rene. In modern parlance we were both late developers. How thankful I am now that it were so. My only regret is mum never lived to see what her youngest got up to later on. Dad came to see me when I got a week's work on stage in Collins Music Hall as a lightning sketch artist.

Rene with her fair hair cut in a fringe followed mum in her choice of career. She was working in a laundry and doing housework, and as a carer and home help later on. We were all hard workers and no pressures were put on us to be high fliers. We all had a good and protected childhood. A very precious thing indeed.

When Fred brought Cis home to meet us we all thought how quiet she was. Our house was always full of opinions, sometimes noisily put across. Cis was pretty, and slight. We all took to her right away. Charlie and Lil were often at loggerheads, so it was a great change to have someone in the family mix who was a little quieter.

I remember the wedding. Cis was waiting on the first floor to come down to the car to go to church. Charlie was also there. He was best man. She looked lovely and the day went off well. It was more than likely she had made all the wedding clothes. She was a seamstress like Floss.

It happened that Charlie had also had a previous job, for a short time, working for Chibnalls, the bakers. So Charlie made the trifles for the wedding feast. Cis's father was also a baker. When the couple left to settle into their own place, number twenty-four Rackham Street became a little quieter. But the trifles made in large containers by big brother kept the little brother very happy for a couple of days afterwards.

I was a big lad. Fat they said. What with a mop of ginger curls, I was a target for a few uncalled-for remarks. Charlie Powell from over the road was a bit of a bully and used to do this. But he kept well clear of my mum. She wouldn't put up with any of his remarks and wasn't averse to chasing him down the street.

One thing I never liked was going out to buy new clothes. Gardners was the name of the outfitters in The Edgeware Road. It meant a bus ride to get there but mum had difficulty finding short trousers with large enough seats for me anywhere else!

Our front room at number twenty-four was a semi-basement with a small paved area outside the window and a small garden a yard away from the house. A patch of earth about ten feet square. Dad was very fond of his garden just like most of our neighbours.

He spent quite a bit on plants. The seed catalogue was a frequent visitor to our letterbox. The garden had a small evergreen hedge bordering it, but it was the soil I remember mostly. It was black and gritty. Dad used to buy fresh topsoil to try to raise its standard, but it was an uphill struggle. It must have been the amount of soot and pollution from the atmosphere that was constantly settling on his roses, and throttling them.

Around the garden was a kind of railing with a pointed upper edge. Once when a load of earth had arrived, Rene and the other girls were helping dad carry it in from the road in tin baths and basins when Rene slipped. She fell forward and a spike impaled her under the chin. How it missed being fatal, I don't know, but it certainly upset us all. She must have been about twelve at the time.

The railings that bordered the pavement were made of cast iron. These became casualties of the impending war when the Government ordered their removal for melting down. A few years before this I remember one naughty thing we did sometimes. The railings had a kind of barley twist stem, with a floral ornament on top. We would run down the street with an iron bar or heavy pipe knocking against these tops. Mainly to make a clattering noise as we ran. Many a top was knocked off this way; it certainly wasn't deadheading as the gardeners knew it.

Highlight of my week then was the Saturday morning film show at The Playhouse. Westerns were my favourite. They still are. Then I was always trying to copy my film heroes of the time by making wooden guns, and cowboy trousers. These were sacks with a cut down the middle to form legs, and sewn with not very small stitches. The scar on my upper lip is a reminder of when I used to imagine doing a bit of rock climbing and suspending myself from the front steps balustrade on the sort of cord one used to wind round spinning tops.

There has not been much mention of holidays so far. I was wonderfully placed here. Mum's sisters Ann and Nell now lived in the Somerset area of Minehead and Alcomb. Mum would never visit them without taking Rene and me along.

When we got older I went on my own. Being seen off at Paddington Station by my elders, I loved it. Ann had a guest house but we rarely we stayed there, unless it was out of season. She was a widow, and she and her daughter Elsie Reed relied on the earnings from summer visitors.

Nell was different. Her husband, Sid Swanger and daughter Joan lived a few miles away in Alcomb. It was also a little bit in from the coast. But Sid had his own taxi, and plied for hire locally. These customers mostly were holidaymakers, whilst I was visiting.

Often there was a spare seat and my uncle would see if they minded his young nephew occupying it, should they be going farther afield. I must have been well behaved then, and who could resist a good-looking lad with his mop of ginger hair, and freckles! So Lynton, Ilfracombe and other coastal resorts had, unbeknownst to them, also been graced by my presence, albeit for a short time, by a future memoir writer.

Most of these coastal resorts had a building called the Winter Gardens. A kind of large public greenhouse, pleasantly appointed, with live music being provided by a pianist, or sometimes a trio. I loved the music. They were nice places to be in when the weather wasn't at its best.

Another source of holidaying came from an unusual relationship. Opposite us in Rackham Street lived dad's sister Liz. I never knew why but Liz and mum never spoke to each other. Liz had married Tom Groves and had only sons in her family. There was the eldest Tom, next Fred, and I think a Charlie came later. I was not encouraged to play with them. But whether parents liked it or not, both families' children were the best of friends. Mum used to say they ate their bread and jam without butter. This lad liked it all the more for that. I could mop it down with the rest of them.

Tom had a mop of curly hair and Fred was blonde. From an early age Fred had more than a bit of a temper. A long time after this, his wife told me and Deena how he very nearly threw one of their children out of the window because it wouldn't stop crying. In an adjoining street lived their auntie Edie. The relationship between us all was never quite clear to me, but one thing for sure was auntie Edie liked me, and must have got on well with mum.

Auntie Edie had relatives in the Folkestone area. She never had a family of her own. She often took me to Folkestone, not right in the town, but by Shakespeare Cliff amongst the cornfields and cliff tops. There was a tunnel under the cliffs and the ventilation shafts were clearly visible, giving the impression of large chimney pots sticking up amongst the grass and chalk cliffs.

One abiding memory was of the poppies in the ripe cornfields. The red of those poppies with their intense black centres has stayed with me all these years. There are many more modern varieties about these days, but they do not affect me in the way the colours of those plants of the past did.

There was another route to holidays, this time from the school. It was a charity called the Country Holiday Fund. There was a sort of means test for selection, but mum always paid the full amount towards my going. Fifteen shillings.

There were lots of children who paid less. The whole idea was, and still is, a means to give the less well off youngsters the chance of a two weeks' break away from home. Now, whenever I go to the Ideal Homes exhibition, I always seek out their stand for a chat and to make a donation.

We were lodged for the two weeks with a family who looked after us. I went to Chew Stoke, near Bristol, Brightlingsea in Essex, and Ross-on-Wye in Avon.

In Chew Stoke, a stone bridge with a clear water stream flowing under it, and looking down over its wall comes to mind. By the river in Ross, we used to cut withy branches to use as rods for fishing. It was a fast flowing river and very clear. Where we did best was a spot that had a deep hole in the riverbed. Someone had thrown a white enamel bowl in and it landed upside down. The bowl bottom acted as a kind of reflector and illuminated any fish that swam over it. We only caught small stuff but every now and again a whopper passed over our window into the deep.

Both those holidays passed by without much stress. Not so the seaside town of Brightlingsea. It seems that the year before a very different ginger-haired boy stayed there. The local boys called him Red Checker. I've no idea what he got up to make them angry, but when I came onto the scene the erroneous word got around that Red Checker was back. I was taunted and bullied for two weeks.

The weather that year must have been very good and I got sun burned. It's all right being ginger with freckles but you have to be careful in the sun. Not being used to the sun and sea air, I suppose, I got really burnt. I remember the pain on top of the persecution. And mum wasn't there to defend me. I returned home a little lighter, having peeled and shed a lot of skin in the aftermath. I don't know what Red Checker did, but my double has a lot to answer for.

Apart from Mrs. Bedwood, my first teacher, I haven't mentioned subsequent mentors. Mr. Patterson was a music teacher. Tall, slight stoop, wore glasses. He had cause to chastise me one morning and I got the cane. Mr. Yates, my first art teacher, also had cause to do the same. I'd just drawn a glass tumbler in pastels. I can't think that it was for the drawing, more likely for playing up in class.

Then there was Mr. Tyler. A strict but fair person, with a ruddy complexion. Although he wasn't a music teacher, he had a piano in his classroom. Normally pianos were only found in the assembly hall. Sometimes he would allow his pupils who could play to have a go.

By this time I had developed a style of playing that could be described as reasonable. Tunes were easily recognisable and the accompanying left-hand was a sort of vamp. But it was very monotonous. Thump-tee-thump sort of thing. I can still hear Mr. Tyler say, 'Brooks, if you want to improve your playing, you will have to vary your left hand'. Later I took his advice very much to heart.

Sitting next to me in class was a lad named Albert Lilley. My drawing skills up to then were nothing to write home about. One day it was quite different. The subject to be drawn was a half-glazed terracotta jug, a favourite subject of all known art teachers at that time.

Albert did a lovely outline drawing leaving the glazed top half of the jug empty of shading. It was very good and was highly praised, and rightly so. But hold on a minute. I suddenly thought, if he can do it, so can I. So, at the princely age of nine, my artistic abilities stepped up a few notches, and have continued to do so ever since.

Another person who was to be very important in shaping my future was a head teacher Mr. Keates. He had friends in the artistic and entertainment circles of the time.

One Christmas he introduced to the whole school, assembled in the hall, an entertainer friend. This man said to us, 'Now boys and girls, I want you to shut your eyes and imagine I have my family with me. There is Horace, Winnie, and the Baby'.

It was the famous Harry Hemsley, and most of us were familiar with his 'family' from his radio programmes. We sat enthralled through his gentle and funny act, being performed for our Christmas treat.

A few weeks later Mr. Keates introduced us to another friend's work. An artist this time. He showed the school a drawing this friend had done using the word Keates. It showed a yokel farmer with a straw sticking out of his mouth. I never forgot it.

Over the years it stuck with me and I became quite practised at doing this with people's names. I later called them 'face names' when I used them many years later as a basis for my stage act as a lightning sketch artist.

Another major influence on me was Mr. Pearce, our woodwork teacher. I was more used to this subject than a lot of boys because I could get at dad's tools and bench. Mr. Pearce was very particular about how we sharpened our pencils, always using the chisel to provide a point by shaving the wood away from us and most importantly, to use the chisel set aside for the job. 'Don't blunt your own chisels by cutting through the pencil lead'.

In one of these lessons I made an elliptical bracket with a small shelf. I was very pleased with it and was looking forward to taking it home to show it off. Alas, my elation must have led to a bout of misbehaviour. The next thing I knew, Mr. Pearce had grabbed my wooden work of art and had thrown it the length of the classroom, disarranging it somewhat. Anyway, dad never saw his son's minor masterpiece.

It was years afterwards when we met up again. I had started evening classes to try and better myself when, lo and behold, the principal was our same Mr. Pearce. We got on well. He was a very clever person as well as being highly skilled. I have always been of the opinion that to be trained as a carpenter does nobody any harm, and is a complete balance to the sometimes isolation of academia.

There is still a vital person to be mentioned in my schooldays. Mr. Huggett. He was also an artist. A short broad shouldered man with a bald head, a real father figure to us young tearaways.

It was his custom to select from the whole school any youngster whom he considered showed artistic promise. We would all assemble in the school hall every Friday morning to draw and paint for the whole day. To me it was a real treat. Often the subject would be a bowl of fruit.

After drawing the subject onto cartridge paper, we would soak the sheets in the wash basins, then carefully spread them flat onto wet blotting paper placed on our drawing boards.

Once Mr.Huggett said to me, 'Brooks, you see that crinkly effect you get when painting, rather similar to the ridges of sand left after the tide has gone out. Well, I have friends in the Royal Academy that strive to get that very effect'. How it used to come about I don't know, but he was always very interested when it did happen.

At the end of the day Mr.Huggett would come round to make a final comment on our efforts. Sometimes he would stop by me and say 'You've done very well today Brooks, so you go first'. I would then get first pick of the contents of the fruit bowl. There were always a few nuts left for the last ones out. What a man! I consider myself very lucky indeed to have been taught by such kindly, dedicated and perceptive teachers.

Why I should remember a Mr.Seagrove, a well-liked man, was for a delicately different reason. He had a habit of getting attention from a noisy classroom by banging on the blackboard. It was only the fact that he occasionally followed the same procedure when we were relatively quiet. It was rumoured it was a cover up for him breaking wind! It seems as though we were already sussing out a few grown-up foibles, even then!

Chapter 4

Leaving School

Nearing fourteen, and getting ready for the wide world outside school, I was encouraged to do some artwork to show any future employer. The testimonial I got from the head teacher on leaving, it was known by us then as a character, made a point of saying I had artistic potential.

It was the practice on leaving to be given these pep talks about going out to get a job. In later life it struck me that the emphasis was always on finding an employer. It was never thought that us working class children should ever expect any other solution to earning a living except by getting a job. There was never any suggestion you could be self-employed and work for yourself. Yet for the majority of my working life I have done just that.

Mum had seen all her family off to work and now it was her youngest's turn. She wanted me to be apprenticed to a trade or something of that sort. (Seemingly not another carpenter!) She approached an agency that specialised in this very thing. The first job I got from them was in a jeweller's establishment in Hatton Garden. I was to be a diamond setter. The starting salary was seven shillings and sixpence a week.

The place of work could have been taken right out of a Dickens story. Slum dwellings being used as a workshop. Worse than Rackham Street. Up two flights of unlit stairs to the workplace. The furniture consisted of a circular workbench that looked as though someone had taken a few bites out of its circumference. In each bite was a stool, upon which a person was seated. From the bench stretched a leather apron into the occupant's lap. This was to ensure no trimmings of precious metal would drop to the floor.

I was instructed how to hold a short piece of wood that had a strip of metal embedded in something like pitch, or cement, into its end. The procedure of seating a gemstone into a pre-drilled hole in the metal began. A cutting tool, the size and shape of a bradawl, was used to pare away the sides of the hole until the stone fitted snugly in the metal. In a few years time I would be doing this in real rings and brooches etc, and then not in brass, but in gold or platinum.

As with beginners anywhere, whilst learning, there's tea to be made, sweeping the floors, running errands, being a dogs body in general. At the end each day I had to go through the sweepings up, rubbish and what have you, to see that nothing of value got thrown away. I lasted a week. Back to the agency.

The next outing was to Regent Street. This was as an apprentice jeweller's designer. This was a very up-market establishment where pieces of jewellery were made to order. The fact that we were dealing in precious metals again meant there was an amount of similarity in what the lowliest of the low was called upon to do. As it was a more publicly orientated workplace and showroom, it meant there was a lot more rubbish and sifting to do. Males and females here, whereas the Hatton Garden was not.

The bit I was learning about as an apprentice, was of other people's work. How it was recorded for future reference after the sale had left the shop. A customer wants a ring made. She, or he, is seen by the designer. Coloured drawings are produced for their consideration. A choice is made and the ring or piece of jewellery is mocked up in candle wax. If all is approved the item is made up.

When it is made, I would produce a plaster mould to be stored in the archives. With a slab of plasticine and strips of zinc, the piece is pressed into the slab. The zinc strips are then stuck around the impression, and the plaster poured in. When set hard, I coloured the representation to look like the real thing. I gained more knowledge about their rubbish and sifting than designing in the month I was there. For this the starting wage was five shillings per week.

I have lots of memories about this job. The going to work by the tube was a new experience, the walk to the workplace. All were eye-opening things for a youngster used to a biking mode of travel. At lunchtime I would scoot out with mum's packed lunch to a cafe a few minutes away behind the main streets for a cup of tea and a bun. I am addicted to buns. Even now as an older than average adult, whenever I am in a new location that has a baker's shop, I sample their bun-making capacity.

When out shopping, if I can purchase a bun loaf to nibble whilst perusing the local shops, I am indeed a happy man. Especially if there's a few currants overcooked around the edges. These are so chewy! A memory that will never die gleaned from mum's rock cakes.

This period, the mid-thirties, was a hard time. The depression was not immediately felt in the plush environs of the West End shops, except for the seemingly endless voices of groups of unemployed miners or North Country folk seeking to ease their shortage of work or cash. They continually traversed the edge of pavements singing for their everything. It was all the more sharply in focus when one worked in a place of luxury items for sale.

One thing I can't remember about my becoming a teenager. Getting into long trousers! It must have been very near to getting a job. The age difference from Fred and I meant there were no hand-me-downs available. I am reminded of this because John was a very late walker. Once he did walk, he never sat down again.

He had a novel way of motion. He kind of sat sideways on his bottom whilst he threw a leg in the direction he was aiming for. Mum used all the girls' old knickers on him to ease his passage, and keep him warm. Anyway, next I found myself on the end of dad's bench, working in the E.N.V.

I suppose it was inevitable that that's where I would end up. After all, I was only following in Charlie and Fred's footsteps. So instead of my trip on the Metropolitan Line each morning, I got on my bike for about a mile and a quarter to the E.N.V. engineering works in Willesden. A learner chippie. So mum didn't get her wishes for little Harry in the end. It was not the articled apprenticeship that she so sought after. And there was another carpenter's apron in the wash!

To say I was upset about it all, however, was so far from the truth. I was in my element. So now, instead of being chased out of the shed, I was to be shown how to use all the lovely tools that had been such an attraction to me during my formative years.

I must mention about the bicycle. It was for my thirteenth birthday. It was a Mohawk, costing three pounds, nineteen shillings and nine pence. A roadster. Heavy, but rugged and comfy.

Once, eager to explore its possibilities, I joined a few of us from the street on a jaunt to the seaside. Southend-on-Sea, Essex, to be exact. About thirty-five miles. We did it, and of course it was a great adventure, but the cost on our bottoms was something out of this world. We never trained for it of course! 'Let's go to Southend', and we went. The very fact of being able to describe it after seventy-two years so indelibly, indicates the lasting impression it made on my rump. The saddle maker had fitted a small brass tag on the saddle with their name on it. We shared the same name, Brooks.

There was another time when cycle wheels came to the attention of our family. Sister Floss came home with George Rolfe, who was also a two-wheeler, plus another saddle. George was a fireman who rode a tandem. Floss was definitely not a cyclist and was fair skinned like me.

So when, one Sunday afternoon, she arrived back home after an afternoon's ride, she had double trouble to contend with. Sunburn and saddle soreness. Poor girl. I don't know whether or not the fact that she was not even a cyclist made it worse, or not. The weather had been very sunny and she was sort of emulating a beetroot, colour-wise. However, later on she and George married and had two lovely girls.

During my first days in work I was the subject of much kindly curiosity by the firm's workers. Dad, being the maintenance carpenter, ranged over the whole factory in the course of his work, so he was very well known. 'Oh, that's Harry's boy!' Also only dad wore a carpenter's apron, but now there was another one, albeit a few sizes smaller.

Dad was a very likeable and friendly person and so I greatly benefited from the cloak of this affection. It was more than likely I was dubbed 'young 'Arry'. There weren't many spare aitches about in the works then.

So now I was a member of the maintenance department. There were several such groups that kept the works going smoothly. We were the woodworkers. The engineers were called the wheelwrights. There were the electricians and toolmakers, plus a few security people and sweeper-uppers.

The office staff were quite separate. They had their own entrance out in the main road, and some of the workers there never saw much of the inside of the factory. Neither did the overall-wearers see much of office life. Dad and I catered for both. The difference in noise levels between the two places of work was very marked. In the works shouting was common. If you shouted in the other place you'd be having a go at someone.

Dad had other members on his staff apart from me. The most memorable was Jack Coleman, the painter. He was an old sailor who had served his time before the mast. He must have been close to retiring. His walrus moustache was stained heavily from the juices that spurted out occasionally from his pipe. I didn't ever see many teeth, but that might have been due to his rugged appearance. He always wore a cap. I still don't know whether he was bald or not. He always mixed his own paint. It was mostly grey in colour, a mixture of white lead undercoat and black in oil.

These colours in oil were just that. Dense pigments in small tins, in no way as runny as undercoat paint. Then there was turpentine and terebine, a drier. The white lead was mixed with turpentine and linseed oil and took a long time to dry on its own. The driers were added to speed this process.

A film I remember of years ago was of Boris Karloff playing 'The Mummy'. This character had gnarled, cracked and claw-like hands, just like Jack's. It was through the association with white lead. It's a very dangerous substance, especially on contact with the skin. And over the years it had taken its toll on Jack's hands and digits, as it had done so in the past on queens' and courtiers' faces when used innocently as a beauty aid.

The other member of our department was a labourer, one Nobby Holloway. A highly interesting and intelligent man who chose not to take up the tools himself, but to help others carry out their work. I asked him about this, and he was quite frank about it. He was not interested in taking responsibility. He'd had a hard life. A Barnardo's boy, he was used to looking after himself and was content with his lot. Dad and I were fortunate to find a helper like Nobby.

His hobby was a motorcycle and sidecar. With this, his favourite trips were to the seaside in Littlehampton, Sussex. Bognor Regis's neighbour, where I am writing this, just three miles away. When aged fourteen I knew not of either place. Nobby looked after me, I know.

Some of my fondest memories of this time were when we were all working over a weekend. The machines were shut down, and a few wheelwrights were also in. Apart from the occasional clang of hammering, the air was alive with sound. Everybody singing the latest song at the tops of their voices. The roof girders were alive with the sound of music, so to speak. We were up in the air but not quite so high as the Alps. We were not to know a Julie Andrews of the future would attempt to steal our thunder.

One thing about leaving school was there wasn't a convenient place to meet up after work. The gangs of earlier times had dispersed, and the most central meeting place had moved out of the street. The Eagle Public House, where the buses turned round, was on one corner of Telford Road. Opposite was a coffee stall. This was a mobile eating place built on a horse-drawn wagon. It was never hauled by one though. The owner and a helper man-handled it into its evening workplace, pushing on the shafts of the cart to do so. Where it went in the daytime I don't know, but there was a mews nearby that also stabled horses. So I might be mistaken about the hauling business.

Anyway, that stall became the magnet for us teenagers. A cup of tea, coffee or Bovril could be stretched out if you were short, or with money, hot meat pies and cheesecakes were there to be scoffed. It was standing room only. You could sit down on a fine night, as long as it hadn't been raining. I don't remember many girls being drawn there, because the novelty soon wore off for me, and I rarely went. It was soon apparent to me that this was one adult pastime that was overrated.

There was a lot of unemployment amongst us school leavers. Great efforts were made to get us to night school. These classes were held in Warnington Road School. This was where I completed my school days. It was an old-type establishment even then. Indeed, it was completely rebuilt after I left.

One feature keenly remembered was that opposite the front gate was a sweet shop. It was here that I remember the advent of fizzy drinks. Fantas it was called. The machine had a water container shaped rather like a large light bulb on end. A gas cylinder was under the counter. Different flavourings were added to the water as it was given a great burp of this gas, producing all the bubbles that ran up your nose. Delicious to all these small possible future elder statesman, plumbers or carpenters.

A short distance from the school's entrance was Golborne Road. This road was at right angles to Ladbroke Grove into which it ran. Before then it reached and passed over Portobello Road, the same road that housed my mum's family over the years, and my own very young family was to also make its acquaintance later on. I remember it being a very long road. At its other end was Notting Hill Gate. One day to be made well-known by Hollywood. In the middle bit, the antiques market of world renown.

These two roads held lots of memories from my childhood. It was Golborne Road that had in its confines one pie and eel shop. We kids would line up to visit for a bowl of soup. There was not a lot of taste in it until you added lashings of vinegar. Mum always used to scoff at it from the point of view of actual nourishment value. However, it used to vie with the fish and chip shops for popularity. The main thing was it could be afforded within the confines of our pocket money. 'It's only fish heads stewed up', she maintained. But I liked the white sauce and parsley bit.

We could never afford a pie unless mum subsidised us. I don't think we would have touched the eels even if we could have afforded them. They were kept in white enamel bowls and cut into one-inch pieces. The transparent gel surrounding it made me feel queasy. The bones were clearly visible, sticking out of the ends!

A few doors away was the shop where mum went to buy her tea. It was sold loose and was weighed up while you waited. Further down still was a music shop. Harpers, it was called. It sold records and sheet music. The records were ten inches and twelve inches. Plum coloured labels were less expensive than red labels. Red coloured were usually classical music and plum more general like the latest songs and dance music.

Two purchases stick in my mind. Fingal's Cave and Gigli singing, 'Your Tiny Hand is Frozen'. The records stood upright in cardboard sleeves on shelves across the width of the shop, numbered for ease of selection. Most were decorated with the portrait of HMV's dog listening to its Master, wondering I suppose, how the Dickens did he get in there?

Rose, Charlie and Lil bought the latest numbers from Harpers. Charlie and Rose started collecting records, of a mainly classical type. A few years later after Charlie had died; I also started sharing the cost of building up a collection with Rose, some of which I still have. A very important purchase also was of gramophone needles. How strange that sounds nowadays?

At the junction with Portobello Road was a lavatory in the middle of the road. Both sexes had to go underground for relief. Its glass tiles in the roof helped to illuminate the interior. We always had an attendant then. The ladies were charged a penny, the gents went free. Why that was was always a mystery to me.

Thompson's, the shop on the corner was a cut-price sweet shop. Many's the Sunday evening I would be sent there for a large slab of Cadbury's milk chocolate. Mostly it was one of the boys, Charlie or Fred, who would pay for this treat. A half-pound bar usually cost a shilling, but it was only ten pence in Thompson's.

A few yards round the corner was Elphick's. We always got our bacon from there. Mum did a weekly shop there too. It always had clean sawdust over its boarded floor. Mostly we knew all these shop people quite well. Much later on when we moved out to Greenford, mum still liked to shop there, making the longer journey by bus.

The appeal of attending evening classes had to be strengthened with more than the thought of bettering oneself. As with young people at any time in history, we always 'knew it all,' so where was the carrot?

The session that attracted us lads was about one and a half hours on selected evenings. Obviously the classes were there most weekday evenings for those who wanted to study, but to entice those round the edges, films were used. Short films about twenty minutes in duration. Say five films in all. We would have travel pictures and popular general subjects, but all evenings were well-laced with comedy. Chaplin, Walter Ford, Chester Conklin, Buster Keaton, and Harold Lloyd to name but a few.

One offering was entitled 'The Inventor', star unknown. Alarm clock rings and wakes up chicken perched on a sloping surface. Chicken lays egg which trundles down to saucepan of water on gas ring. This is automatically ignited by the same contraption that also lights the ring under the kettle. Inventor rises from bed and steps into trousers laid out on floor. Stepping into the legs, he pulls a cord attached to the trousers' waist, and up they go with a slight shiggle. He slips braces over his shoulders. Egg done, water poured in teapot, he has his breakfast. Prepares to go to business

Under the stairs he goes to cupboard and brings out very large magnet. Bringing his very streamlined small car from the garage he waits by the gate for a limousine to come by. He points magnet at larger cars' bumpers and cadges a lift to work etc, etc.

We saw very many famous clowns and funnymen. All were silent and in black and white. I was not to know then that I would be travelling a similar path. Using a car very similar to the Keystone Cops automobiles, and in later years making and planting a 'sausage tree', building a large 'atomic egg' and even constructing an 'anti-aircraft cow' called Bamber.

In the meantime I had to learn to be a carpenter. That the strategy to lure us to learning may not have produced academics; it did get us off the streets.

With regular earnings come choices of what to do with all this 'wealth'. Attending Burton's the gentleman's tailors without mum was high on the list. Grey flannels and sports jackets were in fashion then. Not as though they were ever out of it, mind you. The staple diet you might say. The explosion of ideas, colours and styles was not due until much later. Unless of course you had the wherewithal.

Cycling was of course still very popular. With money you could buy all sorts of accessories for your wardrobe. Apart from cycle shorts I did make an effort to look right about the feet. Cycle shoes with large tongues in various coloured leathers were all the rage. My solution was to make large tongues out of leather belting from work, used in driving the machines, and simply slip them under the laces of my normal shoes. I like to think they were undetectable from the real things. Some hope!

I remember at this age friendships were more enduring. One such friendship was with a Ronald New. His was a remarkable family, very left wing politically and unconventional to say the least. All could swear like troopers. The Brooks's never swore. Mr. New was a plumber and played the accordion. His mop of hair was whiter than white. He suffered from neurasthenia, a kind of shell shock. He shook constantly. This gave his playing a unforced vibrato that was somehow very pleasant.

Ron's mother was so different. She could have been very Spanish in skin colour, and compared to the size of her family could be described as tiny. Wonderfully kind people, very Christian in habits, but all professed to be atheists.

Jack, Ron's older brother, was a keen rower on the Thames. It always tickled me when boat race day came around to hear his scathing remarks about all the hype that was filling the airwaves concerning the accomplishments of the two Blues teams. 'Any of the Thames Clubs I know could take them on any day of the week'. If there had been a more proletarian feel to the two crews, he may have been less critical.

Rose, the daughter, was just like her mother. If there was a hint of injustice about they fought like tigers. A younger brother, Basil, was very artistic. Beautiful with the pencil.

They lived in Lancaster Road. This road also held a very well-used public baths facility, and a swimming pool. The cubicles were the size of our scullery with one bath in each, with one tap to each bath. The water was controlled by the bath's attendant from outside. You shouted your likes and dislikes and he sent in hot or cold water as per instructions. The one tap on the end looked rather like a blunt bird's beak the size of your fist. All the folk working there wore clogs.

The man in charge of the pool was a well-known boxer whose family, the Bloomfields, lived in Rackham Street. He was a heavyweight with bulging muscles showing through his vest. It was always warm in there so he needed no more than that. A very friendly and well-liked person, he was a fatherly figure to us youngsters, although only in his twenties. He brooked no nonsense. It was a very responsible job.

The noise in the swimming pool was deafening. The tiled surfaces sent the sounds of the young at play reverberating everywhere. The shallow end was three feet deep going down to six foot six. You could see the bottom quite clearly. Growing up and getting used to this, I have never felt comfortable swimming in the sea or rivers where the bottom didn't show itself. It could be slippery too. You were out in an instant should you be caught pushing someone in.

It was a boys-only pool, ours. There were dressing cubicles around the bath. Most of us swam in the nude. There were slips for hire though. It was here that the local school children came and learnt to swim. Different classes at different times. Just as you went to woodwork lessons at a certain age, so you did with swimming lessons.

The area where the pool was situated also housed a well-known musician at the time, a trumpeter, Nat Connella. A local boy who became a national figure. The New family was great fans of his. A darker side of the district was also to become well known. Only a couple of hundred yards or so from the pool was a small cul-de-sac called Rillington Place. Later, the scene of many murders. The murderer concealed his victims behind panels, under floors and all sorts of gruesome remains were revealed when he was finally caught.

The other end of Lancaster Road joined Ladbroke Grove. Also at this end was a cinema, The Royalty. Very plush. It was at this junction that I remember some of the first traffic lights in London being installed.

I was getting on well at work. Amongst the first jobs I was given was making duck boards. The floors around the factory machines were often littered with bits of metal called swarfage. As the cutting tools bit into the metal, flakes could fly off and they could be sharp and dangerous to the feet. My duck boards elevated the workers two inches off the floor and were constructed to allow any swarfage to fall through spaces between each strip of timber, from which they were constructed. They looked exactly like the boards used in parks to enable the wildfowl to waddle down from the bank to the water. Hence the name, duck boards. They also were easier on the feet than concrete.

This was an ongoing job for dad and me. Each machine had to have one and there were plenty of machines around. So we used plenty of 'three by ones', as we called the wooden slats. In repairs, making new, or replacing them. To get the longest of wear out of them the nails used to make them had to be punched well below the surface so as not to trip the workers as the wood wore down.

All the factory workers had to record when they got to work by clocking in. A wall cabinet displaying a clock face had a handle that had to be depressed after you'd inserted your work card. This printed the time of the clock onto your card. The card also showed the day and date with the time. You did this each morning, dinnertime, after dinner and after work.

Every Wednesday the cards were sent to the pay office who tallied up how many hours you had worked all week. Being paid an hourly rate, so much an hour, that was the amount you had in your weekly pay packet, after stoppages. This process had a warming effect on two people, mum and me.

Three minutes were allowed to show you were there on time. After that you lost a quarter of an hour's pay. This takes in the fact that there might be a queue trying to punch their cards. On a Friday afternoon a person from the pay office came and handed you your wage packet, for a signature. This person was not the one you railed against if you didn't agree with the amounts in the packet. All complaints had to go through the shop foreman.

Mostly all the machines needed two hands to work so there was no smoking whilst doing so. The men who wanted to do so went for a 'spit and a draw', the parlance used when retiring to the lavatory for a smoke. In the WC there were about twelve cubicles. Sometimes when a lot of them were going there for a smoke, an urgent request for the toilets genuine use resulted in the said urgent one having to bang on all the doors to alert the insiders to get a move on.

Also, first thing in the morning some of the men went there to pick a couple of horses for the three-thirty. I tried nipping off once, only to have dad come in banging the doors saying 'Arry, you in there?' None of the other foremen sought their underlings this way. I only did it once.

Betting was endemic throughout the works. A lot had a flutter each day. Dad included. Someone in the works must have been running a book, or bets were being placed outside, I don't know. Gambling has never interested me.

Dad encouraged me to start buying and building up my own tool kit. He let me get on with making a tool-carrying chest in preparation for this. In doing so I was taught the use and care of them.

In the beginning I used his tools until I had my own. One of my first buys was a metal Stanley smoothing plane. One of the machines in the works was used to engrave parts numbers onto all the manufactured items. I had my plane marked H.D.Brooks. I still have it in general use, although now it has a second or third cutting blade, called a plane iron.

Some of the wooden planes I made myself. One of these was a rebate plane, commonly called a rabbit plane. I also made its plane iron, from an old one-inch file. I heated the hardened steel and let it cool slowly. This was called annealing and it took the hardness out that was used to do the filing with originally. I then shaped it and sharpened it before re-hardening it again. I still have this also.

One of my first memories about the cupboard under the stairs, apart from that being where the gas meter generally was, were shelves full of dad's wooden moulding planes. Beautifully made hardwood tools that housed different shaped cutting blades, for working different patterns along the edges of lengths of timber. Be it for skirting boards or picture rails. Each cutting iron was a different shape, so a number were needed to work the different designs and sizes. Dad had about fifty of them.

Each carpenter usually had a steel punch made that bore his name. He would mark all his tools with this. These planes were never used to the extent of them wearing out, so each could have had many owners during their lifetime. Three or four names on each plane sometimes.

I remember when metal planes came on the market. You could use a variety of irons in the one plane. It was a great saving of space in the toolbox. Strange then how these wooden tools became collectors' items after gracing many benches over many years. I still have most of dad's. They came down to me via Brother Charlie, then Fred. We all used them.

In the works we had an amateur photographer who used us all as his subjects. Having a shot of yourself in the workplace was a novel idea, and he did well. His name was Tojo and was reckoned to be Japanese. His looks suggested this to be true. I suffered from a crowded mouth when young. One tooth got neglected being behind another, decayed, and it had to come out. So on Tojo's visit I had a gap in the front of my mouth.

Teenage years bear heavily on one's appearance, so I made a wooden molar to fill the gap, slotting it in between the teeth either side. It was almost secure enough to eat with, though it was never tested. But for posing purposes it served me well. Arms folded and wearing a clean apron and with my hair combed I came out a treat. With my shirt sleeves rolled up, and not afraid to smile widely, I was most presentable, according to my estimation.

I was encouraged to go to real evening classes to further my skills in woodwork and metalwork. So much was happening about this time, there was lots of disturbing news coming from the Continent. I was enrolled in the Amalgamated Society of Woodworkers by dad when I joined him at work. I was becoming politically conscious and taking far more note of happenings, both locally and nationally.

Being working class we were used to tub thumping from a very early age at local elections. Banging on dustbin lids and chanting 'vote, vote, vote, for mister who ever the Labour candidate was at the time, and throw old so-and-so out of doors'. 'Of course old so-and-so was the opposition, whoever that was. Also from an early age it struck me that whoever was elected it didn't seem to make much difference. The girls didn't argue much but I had a few set-tos with dad. He was always telling me to slow down a bit. At Union branch meetings the atmosphere was also often highly charged.

The nearest school for night learning was just as far away as the other school but in another direction. Away from the streets I was used to. A quieter area all told. There were quite a lot of council houses about, semi-detached, with decent gardens.

The curriculum was as if you'd just carried on at school after your fourteenth birthday. The principal was Mr. Pearce, my old woodwork master. English and all the other bits and pieces were there if that was your wish. Also woodwork and metalwork. I remember I tried to write an adventure story. It was packed full of action. The grammar was not so hot, but we were really encouraged to spread our wings.

I remember my first lesson in metalwork. We had to make a nail punch. I shaped the metal, which was carbon steel, and then hardened it by using the blowtorch to make it a red-hot. Cherry they called it. Then I plunged it into cold water to harden it. The sizzling over, I cleaned the punch until it gleamed its natural colour. Then with a more gentle approach with the blowtorch I waited until the metal turned a straw colour and plunged it into the water again. So now, after annealing it, I had then taken the brittleness out of it and I could safely wallop it with a hammer, and it would not shatter in my hands.

This simple experience made a very deep impression on this would-be carpenter. If I'd had the opportunity throughout my life to have a forge as well as a workshop, I would have jumped at the chance. I would not have wanted to become a blacksmith as such, just be able to marry the advantages of the two skills. The strength of steel plus the warmth and beauty of wood.

During this period I met a lad my age, Reg Clowes, who was also a trainee chippie. We became firm friends. His was a lovely family. Mum, dad a milkman, and younger daughter Violet. Very caring folk.

Another ongoing task for the works was the making of containers for finished products to travel in. Each car has a crown wheel and pinion. Although made in different departments, before they left the factory they had to be matched to work 'as a team'.

We had a very large order going to the Volvo car factory in Sweden. Dad had devised a plywood container that carried two pairs at a time. They had hinged lids, the hinges being strips of hessian glued firmly to them. After delivery in Sweden the containers were returned to be used again. They took a lot of wear, so repairs and replacements were the order of the day.

I got this job. It was the hinges that brought me into looking after the glue pot. Scotch glue came in looking like thin slabs of toffee. After breaking it into small pieces it was soaked in cold water overnight. It was a double cooker sort of arrangement. The softened glue was then liquefied by heating it in hot water. It was not usable until it was very hot and runny. So the bottom container holding the water had to be watched to see it did not boil away.

Both top and bottom of the glue pot were made of cast iron and with the water in it was quite a weight. As the heating was supplied by a gas ring, should the water boil away or if the glue was burnt in any way, what a stink it made! You had to be some way away not to notice it.

This was the only glue I knew about then. It was made from animal skins and bones. To do a big job you needed to keep the workshop warm to keep the liquid runny. Today there are so many different types of adhesives about; one can be spoiled for choice.

When ships were made of wood a ship's carpenter was a very important person. If the boat was holed it was his job to stop the water coming in and he could be using the same very large timbers as the carpenters who built the huge docks and jetties. Cabinet-makers using rare woods and thin sheets of veneers, on the other hand, were at the other end of the scale.

The term woodworker has such a wide remit, but some of its individual names have always given a clue as to what in particular was going on. The term joiner generally indicated someone working on the bench. Joinery. That's the key.

Woodworking was and is still mostly all about joints. Whether using mortise and tenon, spikes, dovetails or the like. However, in modern times the necessity for the joint is increasingly being eroded by modern adhesives. Some of these bonds are stronger than the material that is being joined. Will there be a day when the joiner comes to the job fully loaded up with tubes of this and that, ready for any eventuality? Some might say the joiner would then be stuck on his own petard! Old tools will become even more collectable.

We were not the only ones with problems of making packing cases. Some of our big machines were made in Europe and America and weighed tons. They were as big as a large garden shed. They were bolted to a base that was sometimes made of very thick oak planks. They were then encased in beautiful wide boards of lovely pine timber. We used to de-nail these with care and use the wood again.

Dad ordered our timber from Davies's of Hayes. They were by a canal so the bulk of it came by barge. We usually ordered a variety of timber sizes needed to do all our work, in one load. Plywood and other boards were ordered specially. Hardboard was not invented then.

I made myself a dartboard once. I cut short pieces of wood and glued them together to form a board of end grain timber. I shaped this into a dartboard, about twenty inches in diameter. The reason why I did this was to enable the darts to strike the board in end grain wood. Ordinary dartboards were usually made out of a cross cut section of a tree trunk for the same reason.

To stop drying out and splitting, these boards would usually have been kept submerged in water until needed. My novel idea was to avoid the soaking by giving my board a coating of creosote. This also preserved the timber. There was only one snag. Creosote is a derivative of tar and remains active for a long time. When I thought my stuff had dried out we began to use it for a game. The darts responded very well to the end grain. They penetrated the fibres perfectly with no dropouts.

However when the darts were extracted they also brought out a film of creosote on the points and we rapidly began to smell as though we'd been painting the garden fence. It was a bit of a disaster. The stuff got everywhere. I can't remember what I did with it afterwards, but I know it won't have rotted away wherever it is! Someone might also ponder why the heck somebody glued all those blocks of wood together to form a circle? I hope they read this.

Another job I had to learn was how to make the trolleys the metal blanks were sent around the works in. These were very strongly made wooden containers on trolley wheels. To stand the wear of having very heavy pieces of metal thrown into them, they had to be covered with thin sheet steel to protect the wood.

To fix this metal with nails required a sharply pointed tool and a large hammer, to make holes for the nails to go through. Excellent exercise for a young lad who aspired to look like Charles Atlas. This Charles chap advertised weekly in all the popular journals saying how 'You too can have a body like mine!' Perfect torso, bulging muscles and standing poised like a great Adonis. He was the envy of most fourteen to twenty-year-olds with an eye on impressing the fairer sex.

The drawing that accompanied the advert was of a well-built lad, surrounded by admiring females, kicking sand at a weedy looking youth lying on the beach. Very emotive indeed. Supposing the sand got in the sandwiches? Anyway, day dreaming could easily be rudely interrupted if my hammer slipped.

These heavy metal blanks were made after another woodworker had done his job by producing a similar shape in wood. This shape was used to make the mould for the molten metal to be poured into. This person was a pattern maker. He would be working from plans issued by the drawing office. Whereas I used a three-foot rule, and rarely worked to less than a sixteenth of an inch, these plans were mostly in thousandths of an inch. 'Thous' was the term used by these people.

Sometimes dad was asked to make a pattern outside the normal run of the mill. Whenever he thought it was within my capabilities he always let me tackle it. One thing I had to make was a small impeller pump blade about six inches in diameter. I managed it to my intense satisfaction. After giving it a couple of coats of flat black paint it pleased me enough to be remembered by me after seventy or so years!

A very important part of the works was the tool making section. The head toolmaker was a very clever Czechoslovakian, a Mr. Haubner. Just as our own department was to look after the fabric of the works, so his domain was seeing that each machine was tooled up for the production. The millwrights kept the machines running, but the cutting edges, so to speak, were the job of the toolmakers.

By now war clouds were gathering over Europe and plans were afoot to build a shadow factory away from Willesden. Shadow was the term given to a duplicate facility built some way away to ensure continuity of production should one or the other be bombed.

Apart from motor vehicle parts we were heavily engaged in aircraft work as well. The gear wheels for this work were beautiful to see. They were to me. Gleaming metal works of engineering art.

Each year, a most important job for us was to erect and maintain our stand in the annual motor exhibition held in the Olympia, London. It used to involve three or four days work getting everything ready for our sales people to show off our products to the World's buyers.

Our stand was on the first floor of the Olympia, one of many stands that made up a kind of balcony to the big halls below. It was the size of a large room. Another kind of carpenter was responsible for its erection. Their job was called exhibition work. Short stay building you might say.

Apart from the timber used for the sides and back of the stand the main covering components were Essex board and fabric. The board was a multi-layered paper product that achieved similar results to the plaster board of today. The ceilings were normally stretched white fabric. From above it resembled a sea of white. Exhibition workers were always under pressure to get in and get out. Olympia was a very popular venue and as soon as the last visitor left from the car exhibition, these boys would be back tearing it all out ready for the next occupant's use.

We would come with all the stand's furniture and erect it for the period of the show. The sign writers had done their job for our fascia board, and when dad and I left, the firm's salesmen and technical staff got to grips with getting orders for the works that eventually resulted in us getting a pay packet each Friday.

Before the show opened only one or two bars and cafes were open, serving the workers' needs. My self-appointed task on the first day was to sort out where the tea was being sold. The building housed many kinds of food outlets and when I first went with dad I was not at all good at locating where the food was. The building seemed enormous and it took a few visits to get used to its complexities.

It was the same when the exhibition moved to Earls Court but I remember it didn't hold the same number of halls. One thing both venues had in common was the price of everything. They never made many concessions to us workers. It was always top whack. What was also common to both places was the display of up-to-the-minute cars, vehicles and anything that enabled people to get out and about without walking. Beautiful products, presented in a way to display their utmost wantability to the customer. A World show, and dad and I were a part of it.

Chapter 5

Learning the Trade

We had some big jobs to do during these of formative years. One of these was to increase ventilation in one of the roofs. We had to cut an opening in the roof timbers to house the metal cowling that was to let more air in. This new cowling was as large as this learner carpenter was himself. But Nobby, dad and I managed its size and weight, although the job was not helped by the slope of the roof. Or the fact that I didn't like heights.

The main learning bit from this job was not the woodwork but the plumbing. After the cowl was installed, our woodwork had to be made waterproof. A thin sheet of lead had to be dressed over it snugly to throw the rain off onto the roof, hence into the guttering, and away. To make it easier for ourselves we mocked up a similar shape on the bench and did the shaping below. Dad let me have a go at the easier bits. Lots of tap-tap-tappings to move the lead where we wanted it go. A painstaking task. It took four separate pieces to keep the rain out all round.

Apart from pinions and crown wheels we also made complete back axles for all types of vehicles. Another of our products was the 'Wilson pre-selective gearbox'. Dad had met the inventor, Wilson. I only met his son. I didn't understand all the technicalities involved, but we did have to cater for its testing rooms. We built a soundproof test bed inside the works.

This structure had timber framing and was covered with an insulation boarding, made from compressed sugar cane, and called Celotax. Completely cutting out the sounds of the factory, the testers could listen to the sound of the gearbox running under normal operating speeds. These gearboxes were being used in the racing cars of the time, and also the upper priced cars, Alvis, Bentley, etc. Another test was in an actual car travelling on the roads. The car used for this job was a large Bentley open tourer. I was a friend of the test driver who sported a very distinctive moustache. He let me accompany him once on a test run. He wore a leather helmet and goggles. All exciting stuff to a not a long owner of a pedal cycle. I don't think there was much of a speed limit then, and belting up the Western Avenue caused a few heads to turn. This type of car was not known for its silent approach.

The foreman of each department had a kind of office on the floor of the factory. These were open top affairs about 7 feet high with a window all round from about 4 feet up, and the bottom part being covered with tongue and grooved matching timber. The first one I worked on, after erecting all the framing, dad left me to finish nailing the bottom boarding. I was in my element here. Plenty of nails and a two-pound claw hammer, I made short work of it. I was pleased with my dexterity and speed. Not so dad. In my enthusiasm I was a bit heavy-handed. The unbounded joy of belting in all the nails was plainly evident by the hammer marks I left on the surface of the wood.

I was to have hammered the nails nearly level with the wood surface, then punched them below the surface using a nail punch. The surface of my nailing resembled the Mountains of Mourne. I spent the rest of the afternoon dousing these ups and downs with hot water, Dad's remedy to make the wood swell back to its original flat surface. I was beginning to learn. We then moved out of the way for old Jack to come in and finish the job. First filling up the nail holes with putty then giving all the knots in the wood a coat of Shellac, called knotting. This sealed in any resin that might be lurking in the wood, preventing it from seeping out and leaving a sticky mess after painting.

This resin was an amazing substance. Produced by the tree for whatever purpose, I only knew it as a tacky fluid. It did solidify in time and become amber. This substance was to become the final resting place of insects and the like over millions of years. Beautifully preserved in a transparent grave, where each was captured in the stickiness of the moment, and transformed into a visual spectacle for future generations to wonder at.

If Jack didn't do his job properly, the resin would plague anybody who got it on their hands or clothes. Even now I don't know of a simple solvent that gets it off. This tenacious quality is made full use of by the varnish manufacturers who use resin in their products. Then Jack with his gurgling pipe would seal it from sight with a coat of grey paint.

Shortly after joining E.N.V. I became a member of the work's darts team. My game was nothing to shout home about. The fact that I was now drinking in between throws of the darts indicates I was of a legal age to indulge. Once after a match that saw me down three pints of bitter, I was horrified when I got home to discover I felt numb all over. It really put the wind up me. There was hardly a mention of lager beer at this time. A darker beer called mild and was less potent seemingly. A popular call in those days was a mixture of both. A mild and bitter please!

I also started playing tennis. Sister Lily was also keen and we played a lot together, mostly on public courts in the parks. I bought an instruction booklet on serving. It had a clever photographic sequence showing a certain service in great detail. The effect was the same as if you were watching a slow motion film. I'm sure it helped our game.

Lily always attracted a crowd of friends, and often on Sunday mornings we would all go to the Ducane Road open-air pool for a swim. In the summer sunshine it was heaven. The water was always cold. The unheated pool took a lot of sunshine to take the sting out of it. Once diving into an unheated seawater pool in Southend, it literally stopped me breathing. And after a dip we all gathered in the pub opposite for a drink. Mostly a bitter shandy.

I was still attending evening classes. My friend Reg became a member of the gang also. Lil also started taking up skating. There was a roller skating rink at Cricklewood but it was not until they started ice skating that we joined them.

I was already proficient on rollers so ice-skating caused me no sleepless nights. The main difference between ice and rollers is, when falling on ice you mostly slid and got wet. With roller skates you come to an immediate and sometimes bruising stop on the unforgiving floor. Mind you, at most times the ice was always doing its best to behave like very moist rock whenever I fell down.

At first we hired skates 'til we could afford our own. They weren't cheap either. Earls court was our first ice rink, being the nearest. There was another in Richmond and one at Wembley Stadium. Then to our delight a new outdoor rink opened not far from the stadium. This was a revelation, being in the open air. It was the nearest we were likely to get to the frozen pools glamorised by film stars Sonja Henie and the like.

It was a wooden structure with bare trimmings. The ice was sound though, and skating outdoors on a moonlit frosty night took one's breath away. It also had something lacking in indoor rinks. A club house. The décor was that of a shack in the mountains, Rockies or the Alps. After a spell outside, to go in for a hot drink, mainly chocolate, Ovaltine or Bovril was to us ' the bees knees', a saying of the time, meaning the very best. If it snowed it really seemed like an alpine adventure. Our band of enthusiasts grew somewhat when mates from E.N.V. joined us. It made things a bit easier getting about then, because some of these owned cars.

Then things really began to change at the works. A shadow factory was being built in Perivale, about six miles from the main works in Willesden. It was comparatively rural to us. I knew it as a day out for picnics when younger. I also knew its canal led back to North Kensington. It was a bit further on even than when I sneaked lifts on the backs of lorries, only being able to get off when the lorry slowed down, miles away. Then I had used the towpath to guide me home.

The A4 was close by. We knew the A4 as the Western Avenue then. One of its landmarks was a very famous Art Deco building. Perivale was the home of Hoover, the vacuum cleaner manufacturers. It was set back from the road with beautiful green lawns. A perfect setting for the lovely decorated factory. The industrial estate age was still in its infancy then, and our factory was one of a number starting to spring up on this green field site. The building was nowhere near as big as the parent company. It was however, large enough to duplicate many departments, though in a representative way only. Should the Willesden site be damaged, all would not be lost.

As well as all the machines and processes being set up so were the maintenance departments. Ron Haubner, the eldest son of the head toolmaker, was sent to represent that department. I, the youngest son of the carpenter, was sent to do the same for dad. The two of us now had someone else to answer to. The works manager. He was a man in his 40s, called Tommy Blackwell. He didn't interfere much. Ron and I simply carried on doing our jobs but in a different place, without the comfort of having a fatherly eye watching over us.

Being a new building there were hardly any repairs, only additions and alterations. I ordered what I wanted through dad and it was usually brought out by a works lorry. I can remember more of the social side of working there than what and how I did it. Being in my late teens might explain that. The activities outside works time were far more interesting I think.

I had been awarded a small weekly sum to help with the fees to further education. I enrolled in the Lime Grove Building College in the Shepherd's Bush area to gain a City and Guilds certificate. With this I aimed at either becoming a clerk of works, or a teacher.

The person teaching the woodwork was obviously very knowledgeable about the course being taught, but in my eyes seemed lacking in real experience of the conditions of working on a building site, or in a factory like mine. Also the majority of the class were not carpenters, but office bound students from architects and surveyors businesses. Their homework was obviously done in works time. Anyway I think I had a chip on my shoulder about this. It wasn't the only thing that was different about this growing lad. I was becoming more politically minded and very much aware of the changing times. Terrible tales were coming out of Germany then. It was the time of a build up of forces that led to the outbreak of the war that was destined to come a couple of years later. Instinctively, I took the opposite position and got more involved by joining forces against the official line.

Often, whilst coming home from evening classes, I would be passed by a group of Black Shirts walking in the gutter opposite, pushing a green-grocer type barrow loaded with fly posters, buckets of paste and whitewash. They were supporters of Oswald Mosley, a man that praised Hitler and was right wing enough I thought to want to spread his racist doctrines by force, if given the chance. Ugly times just beneath the surface. Anyway, I did not proceed with my building studies.

Now working at the new shadow factory, instead of a leisurely ride to work of about ten minutes duration, I had six miles to cycle every morning. There was an immediate need to solve the problem of keeping me comparatively dry in the rain whilst doing so. I tried a cape and leggings first. They were sufficient for leisure cycling but had limitations when you had to do it to secure your wage packet. My cycle had changed too. From a heavy roadster to a light sports frame. The handlebars were also more in keeping with the smart set.

The old dependable Sturmey Archer three speed hub was changed to a longer chained system, where you actually saw three different sized sprockets that when each engaged altered the strain on tired limbs. Nowadays this system is used on most bikes, then, it was new. So, however you tried to cover up, either the rain made you wet from outside, or perspiration soaked you from the inside. Both ways were pleasant enough in the summer but during the winter months you were very pleased to get to the end of your journey.

Once I was given a lift to work by one of brother Fred's friends, Jimmy Saunders, who owned an Aerial motorcycle. A foursquare engine developing goodness knows how many horsepower. It was a very powerful motorcycle of its time. We ripped up The Avenue with me clinging on for dear life.

Jimmy was an ex-army man with a grand set of teeth. It fascinated me to see him eat an ice cream. He just bit chunks off with relish. At the time I must have had something not quite right with my mouth. I just couldn't do such a thing. It gave me the quivers to watch. Now, with a much-reduced battery of molars, through age and wear and tear, I might manage it.

Lunch breaks were somewhat different in the new works now. We had a bit of grass down one side of the building. It was on the rough side to say the least, but when the weather permitted, we often put up stumps and played a little cricket. It was during a brief session one day that I was put off the game for life. A fast ball bounced and parted my auburn locks, ridding the parting of every particle of dandruff. It frightened the life out of me, although the procedure was entirely painless.

Increasingly now we had new friends from Perivale joining our weekend pursuits. Two of these, Vic Smart and Fred Herbert were machine operators. Vic was as rotund as Fred was a beanstalk. They were not turners as such. Their machines did a series of pre-set operations. Known as capstan operators, they were on piecework and were well paid by our standards. Vic ran a Jaguar, and Fred also had a car. Increasingly now after a Saturday night out we all went to Leicester Square to the Lyons Corner House for a meal.

Mostly we paid a set price for a course of food that gave you a choice of the menu. Or you could have a la carte. The food was good and inexpensive and of course it rounded off the evening perfectly. We all worked hard and got on together and so during these unsettled times it was the kind of haven for a few hours that was very much looked forward to.

Vic Smart had a relative who was interested in spiritualism. So as with any other activity being suggested as requiring inspection by the gang, some of us got involved. The 'relative' fixed up a meeting with a medium. It was in the Holland Park area and we all trooped down the steps to the basement of a large house to see what was on offer. At this time I was definitely not of any religious inclination. To say I was at least sceptical was to put it mildly.

I forgot what we each paid, but I'm quite sure it wasn't free. If the medium was a professional we were paying her wages. That first meeting attracted quite a number of our gang. Vic and Fred were there, Reg Clowes, Ron New, Lily, members of the relatives' family including an attractive girl about our age, a daughter, and me.

It was a large carpeted room with chairs all around, and by the number I saw meant a sizeable reimbursement to the organisers if everybody paid. It was a solemn feeling that bounded the group. Soft lights and music must have been a regular expectation to those guests who could have been sincere believers and regular visitors. The medium, a woman, was introduced to us along with a kind of a CV of herself. She took a seat and relaxed, closing her eyes.

Seventy years have passed since I sat there but I remember the scene very clearly. The lights lowered until complete darkness became the norm. Very soft music continued. The dark was tangible, you could cut it. A few sighs coming from where I thought the lady was and a little later a voice was enquiring 'is anyone there'? If there was then they could have been waving something like a cone about, because a ghostly cone was jigging about. It was definitely visible in the darkness.

Then I was very much aware of a tall presence in front of me. I remember more about the cold feeling I got. The voice was saying it was from a person of some antiquity, a Far Eastern type or a Red Indian. I gathered that I was being told I had great healing qualities. So here was I from what I thought and unbeliever of all sorts of things being told I had great potential in the realms of alternative medicine

Other things were moving about and other figures as well. The hairs on the back of my neck were still in a vertical position and the excitement from the other visitors could also be felt. Other members of the group also received various pronouncements regarding their futures, then the session came to an end.

The lights came on to reveal the medium just coming out of her trance and a wide variety of expressions on other faces. Everything was as before the lights went out and darkness engulfed our world. Well, what did we all think about that?

Vic's relative, a brother, and he were believers, as were some of his family. It wasn't easy to express a friendly view of the goings on so as to keep everybody happy if you took a sceptical view of all of it, as I did. To fight your corner you would have to say we'd all been taken for a ride and it was all a fraud. Not very friendly that. So keep your mouth shut.

What surprised me was the outcome. A little later Ronnie New, an avowed atheist and politically left wing minded young man, took up with the pretty daughter first seen at the séance. So a perfect example of the attraction of the opposites?

Ron Haubner was a toolmaker and music lover. He was a Strauss waltz fan.

Johann Strauss and his son had composed so many fine waltzes and Ron liked them all. It was maybe that his father was a mid-European and his mother a Scottish woman, that sowed the seeds of this love. Anyway a Czech and a Scot had produced a very good friend for me. I somehow sensed there was more to come of this friendship.

So when Ron became a keen skater and I cajoled sister Rose to get some skates to join the gang, it was no surprise to me that after a very short time, the gang wondered what stopped them from accompanying us of a weekend. I don't think Rose used her skates more than two or three times, I definitely know she never learned to skate properly before they got married.

He was a good looking man and Rose, also a Strauss fan, with her golden hair, made them both a handsome pair. I've always thought my instinct that the ending would be like that was right. And so it was. I had been sizing up Ron for a few years now, and I was very fond of Rose. How she hadn't been snapped up before was a mystery to me.

Apart from the waltzes there was one piece of music that united the three of us, it was Fingal's Cave from the Hebridean overture by Mendelssohn. When she went her own way with Ron of course, our collection of gramophone records had to be divided. I'm not sure who got Fingal's Cave. If it was me it's still in my collection out in the back garden. A black record case filled with twelve-inch vinyl records. It doesn't get moved much owing to it weighs a ton. Now I'm reminded of it, I'll seek it out just to set my mind at rest as to who got what?

When they started their family it was then they bought a house in Perivale. Percy Bilton was the builder who built their semi-detached property. That was the hallmark developer of those times. Percy Bilton populated the semi-rural Perivale with hordes of these dwellings. The prices of which ranged around £450 to £650 freehold.

I visited them once in the winter. There was no central heating then. The fireplace in each room was meant to suffice. It certainly contained the fire safely but it seemed as if all the heat went straight up the chimney. They let me, a visitor, have pole position in front of the grate, and I warmed my face and hands. But my back was freezing. We had a laugh at it in between shivering. The situation did not improve until the country's building regulations were altered to counteract the jerry building, as it was known at the time, and minimum standards were introduced. Mind you it was probably pleasant living there in a hot Summer.

Things were worsening on the home front. War clouds were gathering. Reg was now working on bomb shelters. Getting full money too. I approached our works manager on the matter of wages. He insisted I was not old enough to warrant a full rate. Of course I disagreed, and thought I was worth more being the only person looking after the whole works, in the woodwork line. I suppose it was an indication of my becoming more militant at that time. My politics were definitely of the left at this age.

All the more surprising then, when I found that I was developing a religious bent. This was a revelation to me, and although I cannot put a finger on why it was, it could have been influenced by the spiritualism episode. Exactly how long it lasted I'm not sure, what I do know, and remember vividly, was how much I was affected by it, hook line and sinker. Even to this day I can understand people with deep feelings of faith, believing with such intensity. It alters your whole world.

I found myself walking on air. I'm sure the feeling I had was not of church dogma and the like, but a feeling of how right the teaching of Christianity was, as a solution to man's aged old problems. Getting on together and looking after each other. Simplistic perhaps, but in line with my political feelings that reckoned bread should be free and nobody should be deprived of water.

Each person should have shelter, and housing must be made a non-profit making business. This I thought could be achieved if each were entitled to one house/shelter, but not own two. This of course was before the National Health Service came about. These feelings and arguments would be the basis of my politics for a while yet.

To me these views at that moment were compatible with the feelings that Jesus was advocating in his time. Of course the difference between having ideas of this nature and putting them into practice, needless to say, bears a marked similarity to the reactions he got in 20 AD to those I got in the nineteen thirties

Also in this supernatural period of mine, I did once visit a spiritualist church. It had welcoming messages on its walls inviting visitors. My own assessment of this visit was of the feeling I got afterwards, it was, watch out, strangers!

I am even tempered, and would like to be a pacifist in the true meaning of the word, but, one of the foremen in the machine shop was in the habit of smoking his fags smaller than the virtual dog end. One day I saw him put this measly wet butt, no longer than a half inch long, on his index finger and flick it at an animal's face. I realised then my brotherly feelings were not all encompassing.

I was in a park one Sunday watching trenches being dug. A message had gone to Hitler saying stop it or else. The 'or else' bit was the order of the day. The war was declared and shortly afterwards the sirens went off. It wasn't long before the all clear sounded; it was a false alarm. But I don't think anybody out there had much of an idea what to have done if it had been a real warning!

The radio became a part of life then. With bulletins and instructions on behaviour in this new situation, it came into its own. Blackout, air raid wardens, shelters and shortages. Collecting aluminium, garden railings disappearing, and rationing. Ration books, coupons, identity cards and the wondering when it was all going to start. The rough stuff that is!

The evacuation of the children. Up 'til now John, my younger brother, has barely had a mention. Now, he was in the front of it all. Mum must have had a hard time letting him go. We were all still waiting. When are the bombs going to drop? Some uneasy months followed. The blackout and the restricted headlights of cars and lorries all deepened the gloom. Air raids had commenced and the anti-aircraft guns went into action. It was a while before you could recognise nice from nasty sounds.

I was out whilst a raid was on and the guns were going hammer and tongs. Next to the coffee stall at the Eagle was an air raid shelter. I went down into it. It was early morning before the all clear went. Venturing out I realised it was the noise of the guns that had kept me down there. I was only about five hundred yards from home. Later on we got used to the different sounds and could then respond in a more rational manner.

In the cupboard under the stairs was our only shelter. It depended who was home if it was used at all. With our size of family if an emergency came, the ones under the stairs were far better off than whoever was plugging the doorway. Being of a noble character it would have been me who would have had his bottom shot off. Bombs were falling and sometimes you got to know where. Also you might see some of the actual damage done. But London is a big place.

Life was still going on. We were able to get about. Jobs were changing gradually. What were mostly male situations in the job market were being blurred by the call up. Sister Lil, an expert tailoress, became a bus conductress. She looked very smart in her uniform. Mum was surprised, but Lil loved it, even when on early shift. A little in the way of perks came our way with used tickets she had to dish out. Large numbers of anything like that always fascinated me. Similar with cigarette cards earlier.

It was around September time. It was dark by six in the evening and the sirens were sounding soon afterwards. Mum was ironing in the kitchen. I was sitting by the stove, reading. We had a nice fire going and I was right up on the fireguard. There was a curious whooshing sound and the entire soot contents of the chimney came flying out of the grate like a train. A muffled bang and the lights went out. Amidst the coughing and spluttering we were so disoriented it was difficult to say just what had happened.

We were in pitch-blackness and we smelt gas. None of us were injured, thankfully, but we had to spend a very uncomfortable few hours 'til dawn before we could see the damage and get ourselves sorted out. Our street had suffered three bombs. Top, bottom, and, our one, near the middle.

There were no casualties. When daylight came we saw that our faces were blackened with soot, except for the bloodshot rings around our eyes. What was interesting and uncomfortable was we found ourselves on show. Curiosity we take for granted sometimes, but when you are the objects of that curiosity and become the peeped at, it's so different. Just then, we had become the targets of the curious. Once we'd washed and changed our clothes, we slipped back into anonymity. But the house couldn't do that. Windows were broken, the doorframe of the wash house was displaced, but structurally the building was sound.

So after the cleanup we carried on as before. I remember one house was damaged in a way which even my later building experience would suggest was highly unusual. Through the broken windows we could see what looked like a white tepee, a Red Indian dwelling. The plaster ceiling had come down except that the central electrical fitting had stayed up. It was a lathe and plaster ceiling of those earlier times, so all round the sides of the room had been shaken loose and fallen down, but were being held at up in a cone like position, by the ceiling rose.

Shortly afterwards the bombing tactics changed to firebombing and instead of high explosives dropping, thousands of incendiary bombs rained down. These missiles were a lot smaller, but of course could start large fires if not put out. One fell in our backyard and dad and I put it out with a stirrup pump. Before we went back into the house we both noticed a glow in the top floor of next door. An incendiary had come through the flat zinc lined roof, and was burning on the floor. This was serious, as we knew nobody was in. We knew the people that lived there were away for a few days.

A Mr Tomkins lived next door to them. He was an amiable man of about 55 who liked a drink. When told of the trouble he agreed to help dad carry buckets of water up three flights of stairs to feed me, lying on the floor pointing the hose at the flames. I had read leaflets explaining what should be done in the circumstances. Lie on the floor, hold hose over the head and direct water onto the incendiary. There was no moon and with the raid still on we couldn't put the lights on. It was quite dark. Dad did most of the pumping and poor old Tomkins, puffing and wheezing, kept the buckets of water coming. Eventually we put out the fire.

Next day in the light we went up to inspect the damage. The blaze had been caught before any major damage was done. That was good. We also saw that there was a sink and water tap in one corner of the room! I never heard if Mr T ever passed any comments about our timely action the night before. The only consolation being he had a very good excuse to down a few pints afterwards in an attempt to forget the incident. Shortly afterwards the council officers declared the street a disaster area and we were advised to move.

Dad owned our house and I never knew what arrangements were in place that eased the business of moving and renting other accommodation but pretty soon we found ourselves in rooms in a house about half a mile away, nearer the Scrubs. One thing sticks in my mind about this event. I met a nice girl who lived about four doors away. We got on well together. Her father was an undertaker. I sensed from the beginning that he wasn't very keen on me.

Whether it was my politics or his religion that caused the indifference, I don't know. The family were Catholics. My religious episode was well over by this time so I never had the chance to debate the subject.

We moved again soon afterwards, this time to a basement flat. Leaving Rackham Street after the bomb affair was of course a wrench to all of us. When Charlie died and I had the room to myself, there was never much effort or desire to change anything much. His furniture and large wardrobe were still there. I don't think Mum wanted the upset of much change. So although I used the top part, the deep drawer at the base of the wardrobe was untouched. Charlie was a man of many parts and his interests were wide. One of these was geology.

The amounts of specimen rock, metals and the like were considerable. Also he had an ingot of silver there. It was about six inches long, three inches wide, and an inch thick. It was very weighty. Dad had it assayed to gauge its value before he sold it. The money must have come in very handy indeed. Dad's chemist friend Bertie Eel took possession of the rest of the collection. The wardrobe disappeared at around the same time.

Rose and Fred had Charlie's bookcases and books. The piano accordion that Rose and Charlie bought together finally ended up in my possession. The procession of all these events are very difficult to visualise now. The air raids were going on most of the time. Rarely did a night go by without one. One Sunday we went to see a film in the Shepherd's Bush Pavilion Cinema. Whilst queuing to get in there was a constant stream of fire engines passing by. It was the Blitz raging at the time. The docks were ablaze then. The firemen looked exhausted as they went by. Then they rode in the open air, not like today's vehicles that afford them some cover.

The battle raging overhead was the subject of much radio news. The scores of planes downed that day or night were regularly put out in the programmes. We never came nearer to all the action going on than that night we were bombed. It was very apparent lots of folks were having an awful time. A bomb or successful incendiary left awful scars for all to see.

I had another go at Tommy Blackwell about upping my wages. He wasn't having any. I was still too young to warrant full pay. Reg was working hard putting bunks up in the air raid shelters, and getting proper rates doing it. I decided an ultimatum was in order. It didn't work. Next thing I was out of E.N.V., but free to get the work I was hearing about.

Hey Ho, what next young Sir?

Chapter 6

The Army Beckons

Mum and dad didn't get at me for the way I left E.N.V. They must have been secretly worried. I had come out of a reserved occupation and everybody knew what happened to men of my age who were fit and able . They were called up. But I found work building bomb shelters. I had never gone for a job before, I'm sure Reg must have had an input here. There may have been more money, but in the process I got a taste of working on a building site. Not so cosy as the E.N.V.. I was really my own boss in Perivale. Quite different outside. It was all a bit of a culture shock, but the novelty made up for the change I suppose. And of course the money.

What alarmed me was the quality of the shelters we were constructing. Very, very basic. The colour of the mortar did not give the impression of containing much cement. I suppose I was naïve about many things then. The Parthenon had been built long before this war started and much of it is still standing. And I don't think our cement had been about then, just a lime mix. Tommy Blackwell was probably right in stating I still had a lot of growing up to do. Anyway in four or five weeks an official buff coloured envelope came with my name on it. My calling up papers. First there was a trip to Hounslow for a medical. The verdict was A1. What did I want to do? I didn't fancy doing anything, but the official had heard that joke many times before. So back I went to tell mum that at least her son was fit to travel!

The time came when I was accompanied to Paddington Station by mum and dad. It was so strange. Knowing now what it's like being a parent, it must have been hell for them to see their youngest go off to war. Fred had started with dad again in the Willesden works, so probably did my old job whenever required. I never knew if a new carpenter ever replaced me when I left. There's no one left to ask.

So horf we went to a North Wales holiday resort, Rhyl. About thirty-five of us got out onto the station platform that day. Our destination, The Thirty Fifth Signal Training Establishment, Royal Artillery, Sunnyvale Holiday Camp, Rhyl. We three, Bill Smith, Bob Sessions and I were given a wooden chalet to look at, and if we didn't like it, it was not policy to say so. We were lucky we got on well together and Bill, a lad from Cheriton, Folkestone, was a gem.

He looked like the proverbial farm worker. Ruddy complexion and a decent nose. We became buddies at once. Bob was of a restless nature and very much a ladies' man. He was out in the town at any opportunity. Secretly, the fact I was a skilled person I did think there might be a soft maintenence job vacancy awaiting in camp for which I was admirably suited to fill. Then it came out. Thirty-five joinees and twenty-eight of us were carpenters. It seemed that the War Office thought, 'these people have already been trained in one profession, they are just ripe to learn another'.

What happened in the next few days isn't easy to place in order of actual happenings. We had a meal. Why it should be remembered I think is because the carrots were greasy. Everybody was called to the playground then. Oh dear, what a mistake that is, I mean, of course, the parade ground. Our overall boss was a major. He outlined briefly the programme in front of us. In twelve weeks we would be shown how to behave like a British soldier in bearing and drill.

We would learn the Morse Code and be able to send and receive it at twelve words a minute. The ways of doing it. By flags, Morse key, blinks of light, telephone and signal flag. We would learn all about the field gun, known as the twenty-five pounder. How to deploy it, fire it and get information to the gunners from the observation officer who had the enemy in view, called an OP observation point. Learn how to ride and service a motorcycle and how to master a Bedford lorry and keep it in running order.

Of course our major didn't actually go into so much detail then. What he did say in so many words, with a smile on his face, and in a friendly sort of way, was that he was going to knock seven different kinds of s**t out of us in the course of our stay with him. To aid and abet him he attached one lance bombardier, (the artillery word for corporal). Lance means one-striper, a two-striper was called a bombardier, and a three stripe non-commissioned officer a sergeant.

These three people were the ones who barked out orders that were best obeyed. Altogether we made up a unit called No. 30 Squad. The major omitted to say he hoped we would all get on well together.

The chalet contained three bunk beds and we each drew three blankets from the quartermaster's store. This N.C.O. (non-commissioned officer) was in charge of all items of importance on the camp. Uniforms, food, guns etc. It was September, so it was a pleasant place to be, for that time of the year. The holiday camp would have probably been closed in the winter months. Then we collected our uniforms and equipment. Everybody was a little unsure about what happened to our civvies. In fact they would be sent back home by the Q.M's staff, post paid sort of thing. But it wasn't exactly made clear at that precise moment. I suspect quite a few bob exchanged hands to ensure somebody's suitcase really did wend its way home to mummy. Well, we were rookies. Our uniforms were stiff and made very unforgiving by an anti-gas rinse after manufacture.

The puttees, a kind of old fashioned spat, were more so. It took quite a few battles getting them on and buckled before they were at all friendly. Balancing the hat went off without a hitch. The steel helmet required no balancing. The two pairs of boots looked very formidable and shouted blisters from a long way off. Yet after a couple of weeks everything had mellowed and become very comfortable. I think that was due to having a few sharp edges being knocked off ourselves.

Later we saw the M.O., medical officer. We were asked to drop them, (trousers), and enable him to gain an accurate view of our potential. Preparations were there and then put in place, mostly on your bum, to protect you from diseases you'd never heard of.

We were then allowed the rest of the day to recover. Most of us were flat out on bunks. Some didn't manage that, they were on the floor. It was generally agreed it wasn't at all pleasant to be a person with feelings for a few hours.

One non-holiday camp feature was our Naafi. This semi-official section of the army had sought to offer some degree of relaxation and succour to the troops. A sort of cafe come meeting place for off-duty moments. Prices were reasonable and the cigarette ration was dished out from there. There were some obscure brands amongst the issue sometimes. I was on about ten a day then. One thing comes to mind. It was right at the beginning of becoming a multiple group of people. As in civvy street we handed our fags around, and around, until you ran out. It then dawned on you it wasn't civvy street. No fags were coming back your way. Very sad. Perhaps things would improve later!

The jolt from one culture to another caught me by surprise. At home splinters, cuts and bruises caused me hardly any trouble. I must have come in with a splinter or something because the wound festered in the course of the week. It gave me a bad time and I experienced sick parade through it. Fortunately it did heal, and in time my body became more friendly to the army food and a new way of living.

The real instructions started with weaponry. This young NCO showed us how to dismantle a Bren gun and reassemble it in such a way that the speed at which he did it was breathtaking. You could almost feel like applauding the effort, except he wasn't a friendly sort of chap. I don't know whether they had been instructed to behave like that. To emphasise the difference between the army way of doing things and what we were used to in civilian life.

The sergeant was a kinder person. One thing was very clear from the beginning. The Army was the boss. I remember the feeling whilst out of camp, that we had towards the civilian police. They didn't matter so much now. The military police were our new and real masters. A one-striped NCO had real power. Backed up by the Army book of regulations, better do as you're told, as distinct from being asked to do it!

We had one recruit who was from a university and he was not so malleable as the rest of us. In the end he was sent elsewhere. Time was not on the side of the Army when it came up against someone who knew how not to learn. We just shut up and got on with it.

The drill bit I found easy. I could bang my feet with the rest of them. One of the first things that we did when getting to camp was to watch No. 29 squad pass out after their initial training. It was incredible to think these lads were only a few weeks ahead of us. When it was explained that we too would pass out in the same way in time, well!

It happened though, and to cap it all, Bob Sessions and I were promoted to be unpaid, local lance bombardiers and given one stripe for the Battery tailor to sew on our uniforms.

Learning the Morse Code was a real challenge. Made up of two elements, dots and dashes, one was only distinguishable from the other by sounding twice as long. The system invented by one Samuel Morse was a sound alphabet. He designed it so that the most used letters in our daily lives were the shortest sounds. The letter E was one dot, the letter T one dash, and soon we were dot dashing all over the place. Grimly squeezing them out of our mouths with a sound like, de equals dot, dah equals dash, hoping they'll nestle in our civilian brains in good old Army fashion.

With hindsight, Jerry must have thought to himself 'I've got a right lot here. Thirty or so young potential enemies going around repeating de da de da dits as though their lives depended on it.' In fact it was far more serious. Misunderstood signals in the field could result in catastrophy. We learnt how to send it by using a Morse keyboard. A short-stemmed instrument with a little knob on the end. When depressed it made contact with a second terminal resulting in a dot or dash down sent down the telephone line, or over the airwaves. When the inventor Marconi sent a message across the Atlantic in the shape of a spark in times earlier, radio telephony was set to become commonplace.

To be able to send and read twelve words a minute was a big task for us. We, in the artillery, were small fry though. The Royal Corps of Signals were the masters. They sent at speeds in excess of twenty words a minute. They also sent language in code. These codes are sometimes groups of random letters. How important a phonetic system was here. Each letter was given a name. A, B, C, D, became ack, beer, charlie, don. So much easier to follow whilst being jammed by the enemy!

We sent messages visually too. With an ordinary flag a message could be sent and received. Short wave dot, longer stroke dash. Being the army this also was taught in the way of drill. 'Dot two three, Dash two Three'.

Then there was the Aldis lamp. This sent flashes of light to a recipient. Short and longer dashes did the trick. Another version using the sun as the bulb, was called a Heliograph. It was quite tricky to send the flashes where you wanted them to go. I know there was a little siting hole in the mirror but I never managed to work it properly.

After this attempt at showing us some of the new things we had to get under our belts, I had better mention semaphore and international code flags that the Navy used to communicate with as well as all our stuff. They also used megaphones and ships' whistles. I suspect that should we have had a battalion of Red Indians, such as we had from the colonies, the War Office might have gone up in smoke signals!

Come Saturdays it was recreation time. Not ours, but the Major's. Mostly it was a five mile run. More than mostly, because I can't think of anything else we ever did for those first few weeks. Come rain or shine, daps on, shorts and vests and away you go. At first it was pretty hard, six words meaning agony. Then after we shed our civilian outlook, the aching joints were receding fast, eyes were brightening and we still had some puff left at the end of five miles, we realised we were pretty fit.

After a hot shower, change of clothes, we were ready for tea and they could have served any sort of meal and not a scrap would be left. We were ravenous. And so it was, our desire to be always of a critical nature, of everyone and everything, gradually subsided until we were quite comfortable with our lot, and looked forward to when we would be let out to have a look at Rhyl.

Showing ourselves to the outside world meant, of course, looking like a real soldier. When we first arrived we thought we were the bees knees, and twice as good looking. Now we realised what we must have looked like then when we saw No.31 Squad showing itself for the first time in their awkward looking still stiff suits, ill-fitting caps and boots still not having enough work done on them to produce a glimmer of a shine. We must also have stood out like sore thumbs.

We were having gun drill now. Not on the modern gun but the eighteen-pounder that preceded it. The drill was the same, so why not. The newer equipment could be better used elsewhere.

Every day now we were in the classroom with pencils and notebooks taking down this and that. How the field telephone works. Setting up a field telephone exchange. Writing it all down dilligently. I am not a person who understands these things, and I must admit some of the words I wrote down never contaminated my brain. I still don't understand much where electrical circuits are concerned. I do know how to change a fuse and how to switch the light on or off, and I must have learned enough for the Army bods to have been satisfied.

There was one lesson I just could not get my head around. It was a word called deployment. The phrase that really bugged me was 'B echelon'. To deploy! In the Army it meant where everyone was either on the move or in a static position. But it didn't register with me. Imagine an army strung out along the road. Headquarters personnel, fighting units, supply units, then come the odds and sods. All the bits that have a place in the scheme of things but they are the smaller bits. Cooks, pay clerks, that was the 'B' echelon. What a good job I understand it now! I'm past calling up age so it really doesn't matter, unless they invent a Royal Corps of Ancients!

Our three blankets issued when we arrived were not going to see us safely through the winter. Eventually I could make a very snug hibernation for the night from the eight blankets I'd managed to amass. You form a secure tunnel of several layers of blanket in the form of a long envelope. You then slide in from the pillow end and leaving a decent flap to cover your head with. A decent nose was handy just to poke out with to stop suffocation. We were no longer rookies. I expect deals were made to secure extra goods when required from the upright keepers guarding the stocks of articles that bore the government identification symbol of an arrow! I'm sure we didn't pinch them.

Anyway, it was a question of survival. Our pretty Summer chalets were no match for the North Wales winter snows and winds. After one blizzard the door blew open and as nobody volunteered to get out of their cocoons, we had about three feet of snow in with us when we did get up.

Things were going pretty well now. Learning to slow march was fascinating. The use of slowing down the action in films was just accepted by filmgoers for effect, but doing it in real life, walking half speed sort of thing. But once I got the hang of it, I liked it.

Then it arrived. Our passing out parade. Watched by the eagle eyed instructors and goggle eyed potential No. 31 Squad, we surprised ourselves with our performance. Our reward, because of the time of year when we got called up, was leave. Home for Christmas. We had done twelve weeks so I think someone higher up must have thought we deserved a break.

Clutching our passes and train tickets we headed for the Smoke. A Cockney term for London. I remember walking up the slope from Paddington Station. After three months by the seaside, the blackout and the weather was not very nice. I decided I didn't like London.

But the family had moved to a new home in Greenford, Middlesex, not far from Perivale and next door to Fred and Cis. It was very different from Rackham Street. A semi-detached property with a front and back garden. Greenford then was very easy to get on with. This was before the explosion of development that came after the war.

Leave over, it was back to the learning process army-style. The subject was motor cycles. How to ride them, service them, and try to keep safe whilst doing so. Out of all of the group only one had any experience with the machine in civvy Street. So back to the classroom with exercise books at the ready.

On Monday we wrote down all the bits and parts of the said steed, plus all the things one has to carry out to maintain mobility. These are called tasks.

Tuesday, we were issued with leather jacket, crash helmet, and one 240cc. BSA motor bike. Remember what you wrote down yesterday well, there's a field, go and do it. So hanging on for grim death we kick start the thing and whoosh, we were off.

Wednesday, more practice but on the beach. Thursday, we were out on the road in single file. Friday morning those that passed the inspection and were deemed to be able and fully functional motorcyclists. Friday afternoon, return the bike, jacket and helmet to the stores. Keep the notebook and be prepared. Oh, and on Monday you are going to learn to drive cars and lorries. (Who's on guard duty this weekend?)

The process was very similar but with one significant difference. This time we were awarded an instructor to be a mentor for us. My chap was called a driver instructor and although he had no stripe he virtually had the same powers. He was stripe-less, I had one. He let it be known he was boss, and I wasn't encouraged to believe he was going to make it easy for me. I didn't care for him either.

The vehicles we used to learn on was a Bedford lorry and Guy pickup truck. We were allowed two weeks to accomplish this mission. On the whole I enjoyed this period. The lorries caused less trauma than the pickup. The gearbox was the enemy. You needed to double de-clutch. On the Bedford we could change from one gear to another reasonably easily in one go. The Guy arrangement was to get out of one gear first before attempting to enter another.

At first it seemed impossible, with our inexperienced actions, to get any sort of sequence going. The agonising sounds coming from the gearbox whilst learning was beyond belief, and that was getting out of gear. Getting into another gear was worse. The Guy trucks were very tough and durable, but not at all friendly.

But there, it came about a second time, we passed the test and were qualified to be in charge of a vehicle on His Majesty's Highway. (As history was to reveal when we left the services we clutched our pink slip and in exchange for it we were granted a civilian driving licence). I have often wondered since being de-mobbed, if I would have passed the normal test!

Sad news came from the home front. Lily and her driver Bert on the normal number seven bus route to Acton, became war casualties. The bus caught a direct hit as it just passed the roundabout at Western Avenue. Bert and six passengers were killed. Lil had extensive injuries caused by the blast and flying glass and I was granted a few days compassionate leave to visit her in Harefield Hospital. It was not the first time I had been to Harefield. The time before was attending a celebratory weekend under canvas, a present to mark an anniversary of a Royal personage. That also was not a visit with happy memories.

It was a very distressed sister I found when I arrived. Lying in bed, cuts and bruises all clean and dry, but exposed. To help keep the scarring to a minimum the wounds were left uncovered. It was clear that the loss of Bert was causing her far more pain than her injuries. They had been a crew for a long time and for their working lives to be so cruelly marred was going to take some time to get over, as future events were to reveal.

All the NAAFIs I knew always had a piano on site. This pleased me immensely. I can't remember not being able to get a tune out of one. Once or twice I volunteered to play at a camp concert but I wasn't very pushy about it. Playing by ear had many pitfalls and I was wary about playing for an audience. The film of the moment was called 'Dangerous Moonlight'. It concerned a concert pianist and the theme music was the Warsaw Concerto.

I could give a fair rendition of this and I was endlessly asked to play it by another squaddie. He also asked me if I could teach him to play. I very much doubted if I was a person able to teach anything, let alone a piano. But he wasn't to be put off. It's strange, I can visualise his face quite clearly even now. His name was Frank.

I suggested I could teach him how to pick out the notes of this concerto. He jumped at the chance. So began the saga likened to the blind leading the blind. It worked though. Such was his concentration and his determination on the one tune he not only mastered it but went on to develop his talents to grasp a very reasonable ability to play other pieces as well. This was not the actual piano concerto, only my rendition of it, but, nevertheless I was truly astonished that he'd done it. Being able to get some sort tune out of the instrument had never been easy, to my lights, anyway.

About this time we really were getting hands on learning. On one adventure I was a wireless operator in a big Humber snipe saloon. This type of vehicle was used a lot by top brass. It was a Brigadier on this occasion. The way this man read a map was to me quite amazing. Sitting with his map on his lap he was giving orders to his driver in the most explicit way. This was while we were going as fast as the road would allow. As we were in the North Wales area of the Conway Valley, it was no mean feat.

Another time I was signaller to the Captain of a battery up in the OP (observation post), looking over a large plain of countryside near Trawsffynwyd.

We were high enough for him to observe and send back orders to the gunners.

Shortly afterwards we could see their shells bursting about the target. 'Traverse left, up two hundred'. On his instructions I was sending his signals back to the battery commander. It was all eye-opening stuff. This was what we'd been cramming up on the past few months. This was what being a signaller was all about, in actual action. After all this preparation it was not to be for me though.

At the end of training comes the time when we we're being allocated to various regiments. One chap was sent to an air observation battery . His venue was to be up in the air, balloon-wise. When it came to my turn they told me I was being transferred to a coastal regiment.

We were to operate the guns pointing out to sea. We would be helping the Navy carry out the examination service of all vessels approaching our shores. Our patch was guarding the River Ribble, Fort Crosby, Liverpool.

About three miles out to sea the examination vessel would intercept all ships wanting to come in. After inspection, the ships would be told what flags to hoist to ensure an unmolested journey. Should they not be welcome the sea defences would deal with them. That's what I had been sent to do. No twenty-five pounders here. Fixed guns of a much larger clouting potential

It soon became clear this was a whole different kettle of fish. I was attached to headquarters staff and my main function would be as a telephone exchange operator, starting that night. The sight of the exchange frightened the life out of me. Our field sets were portable and could be carried on our backs. This one took up the side of the room. There were so many plug-holes I daren't count them. I was petrified all night in case a call came in. Fright must have deleted the memory of how I coped.

Next day I was told I was to go to Lytham St Anne's to join a battery there. This certainly was different. The battery was based on a local boating pool. So from holiday camp chalet to boating pool, you can't get more holiday than that, can you?

I wonder why it didn't seem as though I was enjoying a seaside jaunt! It must have been the army influence, and the prevailing colour of khaki.

The hard training period at Rhyl certainly had a few advantages here. The signals training kept me from being a gunner. I was on the battery staff. A four-day routine. Three days manning the telephone exchange, four hours on, four hours off, with the fourth day off. I did no guard duty. The gunners had a five-day routine. Four days on fifth day off. During their spell on duty they also did a guard duty.

One other job that was their lot was known as 'dawn patrol'. The boating lake was not on main sewage. We had army latrines, the bucket type. The gun watch doing the four to eight morning shift also emptied these receptacles. A large container on wheels also had a tipping facility. They trundled this out to a manhole and disposed of the contents.

The young girls of the village of Lytham St Anne's were much impressed by the title 'dawn patrol', I am reliably informed. It had such a noble ring about it. As well as managing the telephone exchange the battery staff had to man the B.O.P. (battery observation post). Our BOP had an elevated position enabling us a clear view of the coast and the mouth of the River Ribble. It was this river that the examination services' job was to check all ships coming in to.

When on duty in the BOP, we entered each vessel's name and time of entry into the logbook. A few vessels we saw often. Dredgers for instance. All were booked in and out as they dredged according to the tides.

The other jobs and duties were regulated by the C.O., Sergeant Major and any other bod who was of a higher rank than you. My unpaid stripe didn't last long. It was agreed by the higher non-commissioned officers I couldn't have been all that good because I'd never put anybody on a charge. The moment that clinched it though, was one night coming into camp after my pass had expired, the other person coming in following my passage was the CO. So I reverted to the honourable rank of gunner.

Our Sergeant Major was a regular soldier. Strict, but fair. Unfortunately, I think it was a flaw in his features that earned him the name of Whackeye. Not out loud mind you. He and the other NCOs did a reasonable job overall. But the camp being small with monotonous duties sometimes seemed oppressive. This was the early part of the war. Invasion was a possibility so we were on constant alert.

I developed a skin rash and after reporting sick I also changed colour, that being gentian violet. This prescribed treatment by the medical officer was dished out by an elderly member of the R.A.M.C., Royal Army Medical Corps.

My mauve period was of a prolonged nature so I was seen by a specialist who said it was a kind of dermatitis. The treatment was varied according to the MO who was seeing me on morning sick parades. I know there were other colours of balm that followed, I just can't remember all their names. Meanwhile life, I mean army life, went on. Now and again we saw top brass. Recognisable by the red band around their hats, ours were gunnery officers who put the gun crews to test.

Once I was out on the launch that towed the target that the guns ranged on. It was a safe distance to our rear when they let go. My job was to signal by Aldis lamp to the emplacements on shore how they were doing. Camouflage was all the rage then and unless I saw the flash of the guns I didn't know where to point the lamp. I was keenly aware of the blank shells being fired though if they got too close.

There was another occasion when I was at sea. We B.O.P. lads were known by the pilot vessel's crew, who let us go out with them sometimes, to give us experience working back to shore through the vessel's radio. I am not a good sailor. Sitting out in the mouth of the Ribble, down below working the radio, in a stuffy warm atmosphere with the whole craft going up an down about six feet was definitely a memorable occasion by army standards. I was always busy elsewhere when further invitations were offered.

The village of Lytham was a nice size for our outfit. On our days out on a pass a local dance was often on hand. We were also in striking distance of Blackpool. One of my pals in camp, Eddie, lived there. His parents had a shop and they were very hospitable to us whenever we went to see them. I remember locally caught hake for tea especially. In fact I developed a taste for it then that has stayed with me over the years.

The swimming baths were also an attraction I remember, very modern at that time. Our HQ was in Crosby and covered a very wide command. Once I found myself in Barry, South Wales, Nell's Point to be exact. It was the jumping off place for an island in the middle of the Bristol Channel, name of Flatholme. A sister island called Steepholme was a mile or so away.

My first visit to the island was a memorable one. There were plenty of troops there and it also had a NAAFI. Although I don't remember seeing any women on it, dances were held in the place. The two individuals who ran the establishment had an array of female attire that they wore on these occasions. They also used to quarrel quite fiercely.

There were two other things on the island that marked it out. Apart from its lighthouse it had for the purposes of marine safety something resembling a giant gramophone horn. This was for use in fog. When it was working you may not be able to see it but you knew it as a signal to stop talking, because you'd be wasting your breath. At night, its sound was able to lift you off your mattress. Its signature was one long and one short blast.

The other interesting thing on the island had four legs and looked like a donkey. It was given away by the size of its ears. Oh, and I nearly forgot, there was a dog too. These animals apparently belonged to the lighthouse community. Once having a dental appointment I was transported across to the mainland by launch with other appointees to the dental chair. We obediently opened our mouths for surveying as per normal practice.

One chap, though, was very unconventional. He wouldn't even go into the surgery. I have never seen such a commotion. He was threatened with everything the Army could throw at him. He never budged. Strange that. He was more than terrified. I wondered how he coped with the toothache.

My skin condition did not improve at all, so I was sent to Fulwood Barracks Hospital in Preston. There was a grim humour that abounded when you said you were going to Preston for treatment. There were two Army places of healing in the area, the other was at Sheroe Green. My one was for skin problems, the other was for VD.

My experience of Army hospitals could only be set against what happened to me when I hurt my leg at twelve years of age. Then, the matron and ward sister were all-powerful. The discipline in Fulwood was quite different. Our ward orderlies were squaddies like ourselves. It was similar to the gunners who taught us to drive. They were the same rank as us but were bestowed authority over us to do the job. It often happened that when they came on their rounds at night and were in a hurry to get away, they'd leave us to apply the balm ourselves.

The food wasn't all that hot. We all grumbled and threatened to do this and that. So one day I suggested we complained to the duty officer. Everybody was enthusiastic. Next day when asked 'Any complaints'? I spoke up. The silence of the rest of the patients was deafening. I was left in no doubt as to who might not be in the best books of all the accompanying NCOs on the ward round that day.

I wasn't getting better anyway. It seemed that wherever I sprouted hair so the rash followed. In the end I was prescribed an ointment that burned off the top layer of skin. This was only to be applied for a limited period. A few hours only. Such was the enthusiasm of the patient and the lax method of nursing, I nearly burned holes in myself. It took the troublesome skin off, and when the wounds had healed I was up for discharge from the hospital.

There were a few of us awaiting inspection by the specialist. He was an officer of upper rank, middle aged and of the old school. Whilst we were waiting, one chap was doing his best to worsen his condition, he was hoping for his ticket. Getting your ticket was the Army's phrase for discharge from the services.

Then it was my turn. There were three or four people in the room. The specialist said 'Ah, Brooks, it seems as if your condition might reoccur, so to keep you away from extremes of heat I have adjusted your fitness rating from A1 to C2. I'm sure you wouldn't want the disappointment of a complete discharge'!!!

I was bowled over. Wouldn't I indeed. I had no idea that I had been anywhere near being considered for such a tragedy!!! And so C2 meant I was in a holding grade, British Isles only. I realise now that this news must have been welcomed by mum and dad in one way at least. For their son wasn't being sent abroad. But he was no longer as fit as when he joined the Army.

After a couple of years in Lytham I was transferred up to the coast to Fleetwood. This battery was also on a boating lake. We were on the other side of Blackpool here. The trams ran along the seafront from the Blackpool Tower into Fleetwood. I was similarly engaged as before in Lytham. There was quite a gulf between the two establishments though. There was very little friendliness about. It was because of the Sergeant Major. He was known by us all as Snaky, a very fitting description. He was of the lowest common denominator. He soured the whole camp. He was particularly hard on the gun teams.

While I was in Fleetwood a glut of fish came into the docks and the Army was asked to help out. A fatigue party was sent to ease the load on the dockers. When I did my stint we were at the docks early when the tide was in. The trawler's decks were level with the quayside. I was amazed at the variety and different sizes of fish we unloaded in wicker baskets.

As the day wore on, so the tide started to drop. In a couple of hours the vessel's decks were about twelve feet below the landing stage. I might have referred to my dislike of heights before, so you can imagine my discomfiture at this turn of events. We had to stand on the dock edge looking down ready to guide the baskets safely ashore from the swinging crane rope. Not my idea of fun, I can assure you.

Also helping was a unit of American soldiers. At the end of the day we journeyed back to camp via their place. Our officers had mixed with theirs throughout the day. The outcome was, through the generosity of our hosts, our officers mess received a little help with some goods that were rare sights to us squaddies. Like a side of bacon?

We got to see inside one of the American equivalents of our NAAFI canteen. We were in the presence of a superstore as compared to our corner shop, sort of thing. All very interesting. In contrast, I think the small amount of wages accrued by our efforts were used to help with the Battery's fund. I don't remember seeing any of it anyway.

The days dragged on, became weeks, then months, then years. There really did not appear even a glimmer of hope that it could end. I never thought much about the fact that it was so, as distinct from the boys not serving in the UK. I'm sure they never thought of it as boring. There must have been literally millions who would not give a second thought to changing places with us. But we were isolated from their reality. We were high enough up on the map to be unaware of all the preparations going on all around the coasts lower down.

It came out of the blue. About seven one morning the lads in our hut were still rubbing their eyes when a voice on the radio announced the D-Day landings in France. It was the sixth of June, early summer to us, a fine morning and the difference from the day before, 5th June, was quite amazing.

The excitement was even then being tempered with our thoughts of how lucky we were to be still guarding a boating pool. Our situation had not changed. What had changed was the news that somehow 'things' were on the move. In fact things were going quite fast on the coastal defences front. In a few months lots of my mates were transferred from the coastal batteries. My C2 grading parted me from them.

I found myself being used more as a member of a fatigue party than as a telephonist. Also it never occurred to me when the temporary coastal defences lost all their personnel who looked after everything? I soon found out. I became a caretaker.

Two of us would be sent to an empty battery site to look after the guns and premises until further orders. One would look after the guns, the other would do the cooking. We would be registered locally for our rations, like everybody else had been all along.

My alloted partner in this first caretaking venture was called Bill, and we were sent to Portishead, near Bristol. We got on well. Him the guns, me the cook.

It soon became clear that all the time I had watched my mum do the cooking I had picked up quite a lot, and surprised myself how competent I felt. I could cook greens and other veg. A pinch of bicarb worked wonders here. In

Portishead the water was as hard as nails. Before the days of washing-up liquid and shampoos, we only had soda, and soap which always separated in the wash basins. Mind you, it was wartime soap.

The most annoying thing though, was having a shower and trying to rinse your hair. It just could not be done. Our locks stuck up towards the stars, stiff as a board.

I may have known how to make rice pudding but I was lacking in other things. I had full use of a pantry that used to cater for the whole battery. Cubbyholes abounded with the label announcing contents stuck above.

Most had remnants of former contents in them still. Especially the rice. I was puzzled about the flecks of brown rice in with the rest, but was not unduly perturbed. It was later when the penny dropped and it became clear what they were. I never told Bill, and we both had our digestive systems fortified by years of digesting Army cooking. It never harmed us, but I looked very carefully for evidence of other intruders elsewhere in the cook house after that.

The village of Portishead was a lively place and Bill and I soon became honorary inhabitants. They had a youth club that was run by a man called Alan. There was always something going on there and plenty of grown-ups accompanied their children in the activities. Every Sunday afternoon, Alan would place a large enamel basin full of milk on a low gas and make cream for teas. Gradually the milk separated and he then skimmed the cream of the top in a very handy looking bowl to be dished out with any fruit that was available.

As I was a regular visitor he didn't charge me much, and his food was inexpensive as well. He was very friendly, nearly bald, and had a bird like manner. He tolerated no nonsense though, and I was a frequent visitor. I made friends with a Dick Chapman who with wife Gladys and son John, aged about 10, were also friends of Alan.

Dick was an engineer in the nearby Portishead power station. He took me to see the place one Sunday. It was enormous. On the ground floor were the steam turbines that generated the electricity. Vast pipes and conduits were rampant. The sound was never to be forgotten.

The building itself was very tall. There were lots of floors, not concrete and solid, you walked on metal gratings. So when you were well up you could still see right through to the ground floor. I was very uncomfortable until I was back on the terra firma.

The station was coal fired and Dick's job was to do with the boilers.

Afterwards I went to their house for tea, and many times afterwards. Also in the household was a middle-aged woman who I knew as Auntie. She had severe rheumatoid arthritis. Her hands were clenched painfully tight with it. She loved crochet but could barely manage to hold the crochet hook.

This is rather poignant to me because about the same age as her I developed the same disease. It also attacked my hands but, and it's a big but, I respond to modern medicines, unheard of then in the forties. I consider myself a very lucky man.

Chapter 7

On the Move

After Portishead I was posted to Tynecastle. I have looked carefully at the map and can find no such place in the Newcastle area. It was probably the name of the Army establishment I was posted to.

It was about this time I think that I became mobile again. I was in charge of a fifteen hundredweight Chevrolet pickup truck. I remember delivering rations to the men manning the Bull forts that were mid-Channel in the River Humber. Man-made steel forts, they guarded the area around Cleethorpes, in the mouth of the river. Talk about memories of landing fish in Fleetwood, this was worse. The quays in the docks were stationary, the decks of the ration boat were anything but. Needless to say I was glad it was short-lived.

I had a spell in Grimsby and Hull. It was an experience in Hull I remember most. Whilst driving behind a bus, it pulled up at a stop in a main shopping area. I edged out to go round. It was a long time since learning to drive and having my own wagon, and I didn't go wide enough. I caught his rear offside corner. It wasn't a bad misjudgement but the bus driver had a duty to report any damage. Even slight.

Names were exchanged and licences passed back and forth. When I got back to camp everybody told me not to get too bothered, the Army would look after me. So anticipating help from the aforesaid 'looker afterer' I duly went to court on a charge of driving 'without due care and

attention'. Not ever owning a vehicle, or indeed having to fork out for insurance before, I was to put it mildly, somewhat naïve.

With best suit on and buttons a-gleam, I stood before the Beak to learn what the next step was. In about thirty seconds flat a solicitor representing the bus company started taking my good name to pieces. He passed these enormous beautifully clear photographs of the bus showing a bump this side, and the another from underneath, then kerb side. All the while this was going on I was desperately seeking out a friendly face, in a khaki uniform, that might also be in court.

There was none. I was shaken out of my stupor when I heard the judge ask 'if I had anything to say'? I rallied and put up the best defence I could. Anyway a guilty verdict was delivered and I was fined four pounds. Also being told where to find the clerk who would accept payment.

In the forties, four pounds represented a week's wages for a carpenter. Getting over the shock I went to make arrangements with the clerk only to be told my fine 'had already been paid'. Was this the Army indeed 'looking after their own' or had someone in the court room taken pity on my obvious distress. I never found out but I'm pretty sure it wasn't the Army.

I remember being in Newcastle for a short while. Probably en route to somewhere. What comes to mind was a new kind of NAFFI was being opened there. It was a new concept for the forces. The battle was still raging on the continent but politically positions were being jockeyed for with the post-war elections in mind and looking after the returning troops who were also voters.

The shiny new building was called the Services Club. The taste of things to come for a modern Army. I'll bet the Colonel Blimps of this world had apoplexy when the idea was first mooted. It was quite different from what we were used to. It was more like the stage door canteen you saw in the films. I'm sure the Yanks were quite used to this sort of service being offered to us other ranks, but for us it was a revelation. It was great.

Another incident sticks in my memory. I was in a fatigue party doing chores once, attached to a unit of Pioneers. These were men called up over a certain age. There were some unique characters amongst this lot. They were all fans of big Bill Campbell. Billed as a cowboy type entertainer of that era specialising in sentimental ballads and yearning for the wild days of the west to return.

His radio programme was extremely popular. He came out on a Wednesday afternoon. After lunch that day work came to a halt and we all sat on our bunks listening to the latest offering to be broadcast. Anyone who didn't incurred the wrath of the whole outfit, and some of these men were very large and strong, and all had a purposeful glint in their eyes. My C2 grading led me into some very interesting situations.

Then I was posted to east Yorkshire, Kilnsea to be exact. I was billeted with a Yorkshire lady called Carrie. She ran a café, had bantam chickens, and was an excellent cook. She was a proper mother figure to me. Not many people had egg on toast for breakfast then. They weren't large eggs but the chicks did their best. Carrie used to eke out the fat situation in cooking with liquid paraffin. Her cakes were fantastic all day but next day they would have made excellent missiles. Not many got through to the next day though.

She looked after her elderly mother too. A farmer on an adjacent farm let me trawl his fields for mushrooms. I did well. The arrangement was he could have a picking from them. He took his pick and left me with all the ones I didn't want, mainly the horse mushrooms Carrie and I both agreed he was a mean old B! One thing though, I learnt the difference between the two kinds.

It was here I gave up my 15 cwt truck for a motorcycle. It was a Norton, a beauty. Just like my brother Charlie had. My journey this time was an adventure for this boy from the Smoke, into the Yorkshire wilds.

My first journey out on the road through the sand dunes found me at a loss as to why the bike was red hot. I had forgotten all about retarding the engine once you'd kicked-started. So I was running with the equivalent of a choke full out.

Same as the pickup, it was years since I was taught and had been astride a motorcycle. It was very eerie going out in the dark. I was on Spurn Point, a spur of land that juts out into the North Sea. It is also bounded by the River Humber. It is a couple of miles long and I was helping removing the guns and ammunition from there.

The strip of land isn't very wide and the waves lapping the beach on either side of you at once was a bit unnerving. Especially in the murky weather.

I did love it though. In the daytime you constantly disturbed the families of birds out with their families trailing behind them. It was here I realised the strange thing about appearances. The Sergeant Major wore a moustache when I first saw him. He was young, agreeable, friendly and was no bother. Then he shaved it off, and immediately revealed his real age, which was a good few years older. Quite the reverse to what you would normally encounter.

I enjoyed my stay with Carrie but then I was called back to Wales. The job this time was in Mumbles, on the Gower coast. A party of us was sent to unload the ammunition off an island that also had a lighthouse. Earlier it had a complement of men to operate the two guns on the place. The Army had built a causeway from the island to the mainland that was only open at low tide.

The observation and HQ post for the guns was situated in a house called Hilltop, up Thistleboon, on the mainland. The big house was in fact on top of a very large hill. The first time we went there the NAAFI was still open in the village. We stayed in Hilltop whilst we did the job.

I haven't mentioned my friend Reg Clowes for a while. We managed to get leave together once or twice during our call up. He was in the RAF. As befits a carpenter he also had a job out of the normal run of RAF service. He was engaged in tidying up after plane casualties. They were notified with the map references of any crashes and looked after the interests of our boys and the RAF.

It took him into Europe following the flow of hostilities. Once on leave I was in his home when his mum was railing off about some butcher she knew who was doing a bit on the black market. In no uncertain terms she let him know what she thought of him. A very courageous and Christian lady was Reg's mum. The whole family was quite exceptional.

We had our photographs taken together in uniform. I remember our side hats looked as ridiculous on the one as the other. Large greatcoats that seemed to dwarf our faces and these hats were largely dominated by our badges. And us pretending we were grown-up in our twenties. Reg saw some awesome things doing his job.

I think it was about the time I was in Portishead that, still being troubled by the reason for my downgrading, I was referred to a Doctor Kingston Hardy in the Bristol General Hospital. I remember little about the man except that he wore a white coat and sat astride a chair. Also he was the only doctor to get down to have a real close look with a magnifying glass.

He pronounced eczema. I was prescribed an ointment called Sicolam Cream. From then on I very gradually improved and continued to do so. My saviour indeed. As I improved I took on a different hue. I was now a pleasant pinkish colour.

I was still based in Mumbles when V.E. Day was declared. It wasn't long afterwards the first returning troops started coming in, and their dates of release issued. Units were being disbanded. There were lots of odd bodies about. I went over to Flatholme to help extricate armaments and ammo.

There were about twenty of us in the party. I was the only gunner. The rest were men who had put down to stay for a while. They were all Sergeant Majors of some sort. It was pandemonium. It was also very dangerous. These guns were in positions of tactical advantage and none were easy things to shift. I kept a very low profile.

When I got called back to Mumbles, Swansea, I was relieved. There were a dozen of us in the party this time, and we were back to continue unloading the shells. Back up at Hilltop, the weather was fine and we got on well together. Coming back after a drink one night someone suggested we climb up to Hilltop from the village. It was very dark, very steep, and we were the worse for wear.

Once we left the street lights behind, it was pitch black. The only thing we knew was that we had to continue going up. Scuffs, grazes and cuts were our lot during that ascent. Most of us were thoroughly sober by the time we reached the summit. When we reviewed what we did in the cold light next day, most of us were horrified.

One day whilst out on the island, Ossie Morris, the island caretaker, had his demobilisation papers through. He lived in Swansea and was home most of the time anyway. He just used to take a chance. Whoever was in charge of the group baldly stated one of us must now take over from him.

We would cut cards for it. My hand revealed me as the new caretaker of Mumbles Island. So when our gang departed saying fond farewells to the new lord of the manor, it was time to take stock. No mate this time as there wasn't an awful lot to protect. We had taken a large part of it off ourselves.

The first night was not very nice. All the different levels and gun emplacements were new to me. Large water tanks, very slightly salted, were a constant reminder you were at sea. Even if it was only a quarter of a mile or so.

I had two companions, they were a mum and son, black and white cats. She used to catch fish in the pools for him. He was a magnificent specimen. Whether they ever went off to shore I never found out.

The lighthouse itself was fully automatic. I only knew if it wasn't working by the arrival of the keepers who came and looked after it. I rarely saw them. They had a reserve light that could be switched on from shore should they have a breakdown.

I duly presented myself at the local grocer with my ration book and registered with him. The NAAFI had closed by then. His daughter was a nice girl a bit younger than me, Maureen was her name. She kept an eye open for any extras to the usual for me. So I settled in.

I soon got to know the rhythm of the tides. When the causeway would be open, flooded, or too rough to venture out onto. It could be, and was, quite rough at times. Swansea Bay was a large, sandy, beautiful beach. I saw a ship war damaged, and to prevent its sinking, it was beached safely in the Bay. Many damaged ships must have been similarly treated over the war years.

The island was quite high and rocky with the light perched on top. Steps lead down to the concrete causeway that was at least six feet wide. It led to a set of wooden steps up from the beach to the promenade.

Up on top, the first thing that caught your eye was the Mumbles Pier ballroom. Regular dances were held there. I could imagine the gunners on duty during an early watch hearing the strains of dance music wafting across the waves when the wind was right. All gone now, just me.

My first weeks of being there were pretty uneventful, then something happened. A Saturday night dance was on. I had locked up and paid my money to get in for the evening. I had a drink or two and went to the dance floor. The girl from the shop was there and I went over to ask for a dance. She was spoken for so I turned to a girl she had been talking to and asked her. Off we went. Oh dear, what have we here. She was fair and a far better dancer than I. In fact I didn't know I could dance until then.

But there I was gliding over the polished floor as though I knew what I was doing. I took a closer look at this slim figure in my arms. I couldn't see any eyebrows, she was so fair. She was home from college for a short holiday.

I remember talking about Shakespeare, and other subjects close to my heart and found we had lots of interests in common. Was I wearing boots or did I have a pair of civvy shoes on. I don't know. But anyway I managed to get permission to walk her home when the strains of the last waltz had died away. So I venture to say my whole life changed there and then.

Waiting for the tide to drop low enough for me to get across that night was quite a different affair. I still had to watch for pockets of seaweed and slippery patches on the pitted concrete but now I had quite a spring in my step.

Did I make a good enough impression for another meeting? Before she returned to teacher training college I knew I had. We went to the local cinema together, the Tivoli. I didn't put my glasses on and I found out afterwards, she hadn't either, so I leave you to guess how much of the film we actually saw. She was Enid Leach, (also known as Deena), the owner of beautiful dark blue eyes. Then we only met each other when she was on holiday in Mumbles, or I was on leave in London.

Whitelands, her college, was situated in Putney, quite a way from Greenford where I lived then. We used to catch up with each other on Earl's Court station. But we corresponded every day.

On being called up at Rhyl I had often wondered what the married men of our group found to write home about every evening. I was doing it myself now. It might have been the original flexing of the muscles I am now using in writing these memoirs. I know my mum rarely got a letter from me. Mostly it was to say the postal order had arrived, and thanks for the cake!

On one leave I attended a dance in the college. I was shown to all her friends. What they thought of the attendee I really don't know. I could look a very scruffy individual sometimes. But I did my best to make a good impression. The uniform helped no doubt. After one leave I was being seen off at Paddington Station and it was very tearful. We were very much in love. This ginger-haired soldier and distressed lovely young girl prompted kind words from a motherly person. Was he destined for the Far East dear? Our lads were still out there! No, to Mumbles!

The big occasion when I took 'my girl' over to meet mum and dad, was a great success. They liked my Welsh young lady and her different accent very much.

How I fared down her end in Mumbles was more difficult to gauge. One night I was invited round for a cup of tea to this big house on a road that was as high as Hilltop. It had a large basement and four floors, and was built in the grand manner. It was not in its prime but was still a substantial dwelling. Up two flights of stone steps to the front door. In a large room with deep skirting boards and lovely cornices I sat holding my cuppa.

The tea was contained in a bone china Wedgwood decorated cup and saucer. Me in khaki and on my best behaviour. There was a piano in the room and that caught my eye. Not since the canteen in Rhyl had I been in close proximity to one, except on leave.

I was well attended by my fair maid. I have no recollection of the daft things I might have said. Every now and again the door would open enough for me to see someone peering in to see who it was ' Our Enid' had brought home.

Eventually on being introduced it was clear there would be difficulties. They sounded to my ears very Welsh. A while later I was told that the young Cockney soldier in the front room needed a bit of getting used too, speech wise.

The whole family had not long come to Mumbles from the Welsh valleys. Tredegar to be exact. My thoughts were, as long as we all remained patient, we'd get by. I only had to learn another method of exchanging messages as well as all the ones I used as a signaller.

I was invited to have a play on the piano. The evening went well and I didn't overstay my welcome. The tides were such that I could get straight back on the island and to bed.

Later on, I realised I had been given the once over by a very talented group of people. Amongst them, a carpenter, bricklayer, dance teacher, singers and actors, violinist and sax player. A very talented group indeed. It put my own playing of the piano by ear on the black keys in perspective somewhat. Ah, well!

As time will, it carried on. VJ Day came and went, leaving all of us with the knowledge that science had changed the world for good. My group was coming into the frame now. Nearly six years in meant it was my time to say goodbye to khaki.

The days went by in a jumble in those last weeks. I don't remember giving the island keys to anyone. Did the cats also get de-mobbed? And I think it was Watford where I was finally transformed. Brown pin striped suit, brown shoes, (keep the socks and underclothes), and a trilby, in exchange for the 303 rifle and other Army gear. I took great care of the pink form that could be exchanged for my civvy driving licence.

I was assessed on de-mob for a pension. After all, I had gone in A1. My new pink dressing was speedily bringing me back to normality, Whatever that is? I was awarded a limited run of so many weeks at such a rate in a final settlement. I just wanted to get home. After the Blitz even Paddington Station looked positively inviting.

Mum wasn't the sort of person who expressed her feelings in a grand manner but I know she was very pleased to have her son back in the fold. Meanwhile I was on de-mob leave with the benefits of the government's generosity, if not in my pocket, at least available and at hand. I forgot how much we got to go home with. It must have been quite something to utter those three figures '838, Sir!' for the last time. Each pay day, since joining up, after coming smartly to a halt, that was the routine for collecting your money, just the last three figures.

The full number of this now retired gunner was 1129838. It doesn't have to be tattooed on me to remember it. I wonder if there had been any other conscripted men in history with the same number? Did they also come out in one piece, albeit slightly altered, older and much wiser, as I had just done?

One thing was for sure, I didn't come out of it alone. A little something in Putney was destined to have to be taken into consideration from now on. And little old selfish me had to adjust.

I wasn't ready to face the tools yet. It was a paid holiday we were on so let's enjoy it. Except that my own company was not so acceptable now. It was nice to be in proper clothes again. I was never one for fashion so the dated pre-war stuff suited me. Provided it fitted and I hadn't changed much in stature, only in years.

Greenford was still new to me and there was a lot to take in. We had a park close by and a bottle making factory within breaking distance. Greenford Road was a main thoroughfare so it was nearly always busy. It was nice living next to Fred and Cis and their children. Lil was still at home. Fred was still working at E.N.V. with dad.

I set myself up in dad's small shed to gradually ease me back into the trade. Most of my time was spent on the Underground, and Earls Court in particular. I suppose the attraction was obvious.

I drew out fifty pounds to buy a moped. A Vespa. It didn't get bought. It was used to lubricate plans I had with this girl of mine. I can't remember formally asking for her hand, we just both knew. Mum wasn't a bit surprised. She'd known, seeing us both together on visits since de-mob, how the wind was blowing. Also the thought must have been with her, here we go again, he's only been home a couple of months in five years and he's going off again. But nobody could have had more supportive folks and family.

Once the decision had been arrived at, things went swiftly. We had been meeting also at Turnpike Lane Station at the time. So it was from that area we bought a ring. A slim gold band with a many faceted surface. I got us a special licence and a date was set for November 16th, 1946 at the Brentford Registry Office. I was twenty five, and Enid was just twenty years old.

Why we had switched courting stations was because Enid was now working in Enfield as an infant teacher in Brick Lane School. Since qualifying she had also been in digs there.

Sister Lily was a great help in making the arrangements and booked a photographer. Somehow or other I had grown myself a taz (moustache) on the upper lip. The photographs of it showed me looking rather like the Red Shadow in the Desert Song, rather mysterious.

The only real mystery was how the Dickens I managed it without causing an uproar in the family. It was very short lived. We were so naive. We didn't think anybody would want to come all the way from Wales to see us wed. So we didn't invite anybody. It's a wonder they ever spoke to us again.

I must explain that it was an unusual situation down in the Mumbles. Enid with her two sisters, Betty and Coral, were orphaned whilst very young. The two sisters were brought up by an uncle's family and Enid was brought up by the Stocktons. Two sisters, Eunice and Muriel, married two brothers, David and Bryn. The mother of these two girls took Enid in but had died a while ago.

So in the big house I had had a cuppa in, Dave and Eunice with their son Bernard lived in a ground floor flat. Muriel, Bryn and their son Carl lived in the first floor flat. In the top floor flat lived Rhyce Morgan and Doreen, with their son Ralph. Rhyce was the two sisters' brother. And none of them got an invite. All I hope is that they knew we were getting tied up. I was told by my future wife that she'd asked Bryn's permission. Good for her. We were so unthinking. We might have looked grown-up but there!

Lil also ordered a car to take us to do the deed. A college friend of Enid's, Mary, came to look after her mate. Mum had cooked a lovely dinner for us, parsnips as well, which awaited our return. One of us newlyweds wasn't keen on them at the time but she likes them now!

We had decided to honeymoon in Richmond, Surrey. Nothing booked. We got there by Underground and looked around for a place to stay. We found one at the Malvern hotel. A whole weekend. One of the first presents I bought my new wife was on that occasion. It was Beethoven's Moonlight Sonata. We loved that record.

After booking us in and showing us our rooms the owner of the Malvern, a man, went out for the evening. We both enjoyed a hot bath. The water coming from a monstrous contraption masquerading under the grand title of a gas geyser. It roared and spluttered but delivered the goods eventually. We enjoyed our stay there.

Next morning at breakfast everybody was charming and we were quite unaware we must have stuck out like sore thumbs as we tucked into our tinned tomatoes.

On Sunday we went to the pictures. It was about the Oakifanoki swamps in Florida. What a marvellous word to remember from your honeymoon. Oakifanoki. Oh, and the bill for the stay. We still have the receipt, two pounds, four shillings and seven pence. Two pounds 87p. What a fortune and what value!

On Monday morning with all our belongings in two suitcases, we came up the steps from Manor House Station. It was drizzling with rain. We started looking in shop windows for any signs of accommodation to let. We didn't see much in the way of encouragement to home hunters on the notice boards. The morning passed.

In the afternoon we saw an advert in a shop doorway 'Furnished room to let'. It was in Northumberland Park Road, Tottenham. Hotfoot, we went to enquire. A Mrs McDonald answered our knock. She seemed slightly confused with our enquiry and asked how we knew about her house. It turned out, so she said, that it must have been an old card left in the window after the paid period had expired.

But she did have a room. It only had a single bed in though. We were not to be put off and agreed to pay two pounds ten shillings per week in advance. It was a great deal of money then, but we couldn't believe our luck. Rooms were very scarce in 1946.

This particular one was an upstairs front bedroom in an ordinary semi-detached house. The room's content consisted of a single three-foot bed, a small chest of drawers and an orange box standing on end. In pre-war days oranges used to come to shops in wooden crates. The bare wood was covered with crepe paper and coloured orange too. It was supposed to resemble a small nest of shelves.

We were to share the kitchen downstairs. We were in this part of the world because Enid's job was close by. I could work anywhere as a carpenter so it seemed sensible to live near the job of the one member of the family who was earning our living at the moment.

My new found employment was to get her off to work in the morning, do the shopping, and meet her from school. Our initial enthusiasm about the room was slightly dampened by further experiences of living in the house. We learned that Mrs M. was in business in a big way. In the front room downstairs was a young couple like ourselves. Up stairs in the back bedroom was a further young married pair. The front upstairs box room had as occupants a father and son about eight years of age.

In the back room downstairs where the landlady lived, was a curtained-off section that was her domain. On the other side of the curtain she boarded three men who were working on the roads locally. We all had to use the one kitchenette and WC, so it was not surprising that most of us were taking the local papers to study other accommodation prospects.

Our task was made all the more urgent after an incident that happened one night after the pubs were shut. Mrs McDonald, after knocking on our door,

The Many Faces of Hal Brooks

With sister Rene in Herne Bay

Mum, Mary

Dad Henry

With Deena, sons and parents

Our family before Rene and me

Brother Charlie and sister Floss

Sister Rose

Brother Fred

Michael and Jim

Floss, Rene, Lily, John amd Rose

Pre-war Rackham Street

John Brooks

Brother Charlie

*Mum, Lily and cousin
Joan Swanger*

Left: Me Climbing
Right: Young me outside E.N.V

Left: Mum and Dad in the backyard, Rackham Street
Right: In Minehead with auntie Anne

The houses Les and I built in Potters Bar

Wednesday 20th March 1991

end on Clown Town

● Clowns president Ron Moody is pictured with two local favourites Kerby Drill (Hal Brooks) left, and Bingo (Trevor Pharo) during the reception at the Bognor Regis Centre

With Ron Moody and Bingo at the first convention

Our registry office wedding with Dad, Lily and Deena's friend Mary

*Gunner Brooks RA,
sporting army haircut*

Wearing a clean apron

Me in Portishead Youth Club 1944

Throwing a party in Mumbles

Me, Daisy and Podgy

On the bill at Collins Music Hall

Deena and me in Dick Whittington

Fleurette, Jack, and me, Giant, 1953

On stage at Butlin's 1958

*With some young campers,
Pwllheli 1958*

*Enjoying a drawing
game*

My stage quiz Your Number's Up

Deena in a consoling role

In the Children's Theatre

Junior Talent Show 1958

*Chidren's Redcoat team,
Bognor camp 1961*

As Uncle Hal and Auntie Deena

Pierre and Co, London Easter Parade 1962

With Pierre and Deena on the Esplanade Stage

A gala date in Southampton

Our first Road Safety show 1963

With Pierre in the Model T Ford

Jersey Battle of Flowers

Outside the Olympia motor show

stood swaying on the landing outside. Using filthy language she was accusing the previous occupants of the room for having the nerve to take her to the rent tribunal. These bodies had been set up to place a fair rent on furnished properties and give a slight protection against eviction by unscrupulous landlords.

Alternating between abusing the previous couple she was wheedling me to write a letter stating I had not paid her more than so much rent for our room. I had no intention of being conned into making such a statement.

She accepted some writing by me that appeared to relieve her of the chance of prosecution. It did no such thing, but she was so very fuddled with gin, I think, and accepted the note. Another thing that concerned us was the safety of the lovely blankets the girls had given us for wedding presents. We wondered if they would somehow get lost in our absence!

Shortly afterwards, we received an answer to a letter we had written about two furnished rooms to let in Enfield. We couldn't believe our luck. We were invited to an interview in Faversham Avenue by the advertiser.

She was also a teacher, with a son away at Christ's Hospital,

The Bluecoat School. A widow, she was a Mrs Munday, and was struck by the letter we'd sent her. In this I said I was able and willing to do odd jobs about the house. I expect that, plus Enid also being a teacher, meant she took to us. We got the two rooms. Two pounds per week.

Later we heard the heartbreaking story of her having to decide about how to choose which of the letters to answer. It gives a good indication of the housing shortage at that time. She chose us out of eighty seven letters. She was very kind to us and we moved in at once.

Two rooms and sharing kitchen and bathroom. What luxury. We lived there for two years and we both kept busy. When my beloved cooked her first dinner it had never occurred to me she might not be able to cook. She just got on with it and cooked a lovely meal. We both enjoyed our first real Sunday dinner together.

Shortly afterwards, Reg, who had also got married to Ruth, was invited round for Sunday breakfast. It was a very happy foursome that day, all were experts at handling a knife and fork and very appreciative of efforts made by others, over a hot stove, on their behalf.

I had got a job a few miles away in Potters Bar. We were building bungalows for a builder, Ron Clark. His dad had been a developer before the war and now he was carrying on finishing off the estate. The materials situation and weather were against us, and it was a real struggle to keep working.

I made a good friend on this job. Les Harris. He had been in the RAF, so we had our service experience to bind us together. He was a bricklayer, and a good one too, and was already working on his own account when possible. The outcome was that we approached Ron Clark to sell us a corner building site to enable us to put up a pair of houses for ourselves. One each. The piece of ground cost us £500. £250 each, and so No.1 and 1A Allandale Crescent were born.

It was Enid's money that enabled us to raise this amount. Her parent's house in Tredegar was left in trust for the three girls when their parents died. Betty, the eldest, was already married. Coral, the next sister, was about to get wed, so they decided to sell the house to help them all. It was this share of the proceeds along with our savings that enabled us to go in with Les and his wife, Rose.

There was a system of granting licences to build then. With both our service records Les and I were granted a licence to build. The weather intervened about this time. 1947, a terrible winter, was upon us. The building industry lost more workers that winter than any I can remember.

From about November to March not many bricks were laid or plastering done, for Ron. Walls were put up one day and overnight the frost would pull them down again. The mortar used to lay the bricks was responsible. Overnight, before it had a chance to set and solidify, the water in the mix froze. This causes water to expand and can easily make a row of bricks unstable, so it topples.

The plasterers were vainly trying to board up windows and door openings to let them get at the walls inside. Lighting fires all over the place. It was no use. Gradually all the men were laid off. Only I remained. I wasn't building either. I was making furniture for the boss in his garden shed workshop.

Talk about history repeating itself, my dad had done something similar himself for his boss at E.N.V. My furniture was not a great success though. I had some good ideas but the timber at hand didn't help me. My modern pieces, full of curves and places for glass shelves weighed a ton. The quality of post war timber did not help either As a furniture maker I had a lot to learn. The real reason why I was retained these few months was moored on the River Lee, not very far away.

To enable Ron to have me help him convert a fire float he had bought himself into a floating home the following Spring, the vessel, 52-feet long and 12-foot beam (wide), was moored at Waltham Cross.

Ron Clark was an amazing person. He really was a builder. A carpenter himself he could turn his hand to any trade. He had more drive than most men

I knew then. He reckoned it would take us a year to complete. He was the finest saw sharpener I ever knew. When we extended and developed the curved ribs of the boat, to raise the deck height, we used two inch thick planks of pine, nine inches wide, (probably potential floor joists)!

His rip saw was about three-foot long and I could saw all day, non-stop, on the tough timbers. It became the first boat I'd seen with a fireplace, ideal boiler and a hot water system including radiators. We built the lot. It wasn't only to be a moored house boat either. It would be seaworthy and he was going to travel all over the world in this, with his family, wife and one child at that time. I don't know if he managed this in the end. I do know that when we'd finished, although he married late in life, his family grew by leaps and bounds. I'm sure it went past the capacity of the boat.

Whilst working on the river I collected quite a bit of driftwood. This I dried out and made a cabinet for a record player we'd had built for us by a friend. Not having any plywood at this time, and hardboard hadn't been invented, I used asbestos sheeting for the sides, back and shelves.

It looked very good, but like my previous furniture efforts it weighed a ton. This time I didn't mind because it acted as a wonderful baffle for the speakers, and the records sounded marvellous. This was before the latent dangers of using asbestos was known about.

To hold the fuel for his planned marine travels Ron bought a large tank that had come from a motor torpedo boat. This war surplus material had a great fascination for Ron. It was available and cheap. The tank was wrapped in layers of thin rubber to protect it from enemy fire. Bullets would simply pass straight through with the layers of rubber which would re-seal the holes against leaks. We got enough rubber from this protective idea to cover all the decks of our fire float.

He also acquired a very dubious looking block and tackle. We spent a very hairy afternoon with the tackle lashed to a overhanging branch, hoisting this enormous copper tank aboard. This ex-artefact of war had probably seen many of the perilous situations we now faced getting it comfy in its new home. When the project was completed I moved on. The experience of working a year with such a man was worth its weight in gold.

Mrs Munday had decided to move to Esher in Surrey. We were told that an entertainer was buying the house. A musician who was with the Felix Mendelssohn Hawaiian band. It was a great relief when we were told we by the new landlord, that we could stay on.

There was a change in our situation though. We lost one large bedroom but were given the box room as kitchenette instead. As a matter of fact this proved to be an improvement and we had our own cooker as well.

To enable the house to be sold with vacant possession we had to move out for a couple of days. When we moved back it was rather strange to see different furniture and fittings. But we were pleased to stay. Accommodation was still very difficult and sparse.

At this time, still being a member of the Woodworkers Society, I did a stint of branch work. First I held the post of the branch president and afterwards sickness visitor. Our new landlord's dad was a member of the same union and I found myself taking his benefits to him when he was ill once.

Harry Brooker, our new landlord, was musical director and piano accordionist for 'Felix Mendelsshon and his Hawaiian Band'. Their first child was called Gary, and once when Enid acted as a baby sitter something very exciting happened. She saw television for the very first time, probably because the Hawaiian Band would have been 'on the box' that evening.

We have always understood that little Gary grew up to be a talented musician, gaining fame as a member of the band 'Procul Harem' and well known for the recording of 'A Whiter Shade Of Pale'.

We always wanted our family whilst we were young. So when Jimmy was expected we were delighted. It put the owners of house in an invidious position. They had been doing us a favour by letting us stay and their family was growing and would soon need the whole house to themselves. But it was a bitter blow when they asked us to move before our baby came.

We had always tried not to ask the family to put us up, but we did ask them to look out for us this time. My sister Rene came to the rescue. She still lived in North Kensington and asked her landlord if there was anything vacant on their books to help us. Again we were lucky. Well partly so, we had at least somewhere to go.

It was two rooms in number 400, Portobello Road, North Kensington, and so back to my old stamping grounds. A back room on the top floor, and an ante room on the first floor. The basement of the house was condemned and contained only a bath and gas boiler. A young family lived on the ground floor and a man, wife and son, on the first floor. A widow lived alone in the top front room.

The rent, including rates, was seven shillings and five pence a week. It was an indication of the value of the accommodation but the amount was reasonable and with the added expenses of starting a family, it helped in a real way.

My wages were six to seven pounds a week. It was like coming home to me. I was born only a few streets away and I went to school in Warnington Road, which runs behind Portobello Road.

When we saw the rooms we were back to reality. Dark green paint halfway up the walls, plenty of mouse holes in the floor and skirting boards, and rather hard on the young mum-t- be. It didn't affect me so much. I knew we could soon do it up snug and comfy, which we did do.

Cream walls, new lino and curtains, and treasure of treasures, we had our own sink in the corner by the window. It only had a cold tap and was minute in size, but after washing up in a toilet basin for years it was a pleasure to have room in the sink for a small bowl.

We got a second-hand gas cooker, of vast dimensions, and we painted a Walt Disney character and stuck it on the oven door, to make it more friendly. The ante room, our downstairs bedroom on the landing, had a great chunk taken out of it to house the one WC in the house. The cistern proudly announced that it was an original Burlington, a minor masterpiece of Victorian cast-iron sanitary ware. The WC pan was raised on a little platform, so you really did mount the throne.

The walls never hid any of its noises from us in the bedroom, but after we'd decorated the room, blue, we settled in. Our co-inhabitants of the house were very friendly and so we got on with the business of preparing for our baby's arrival.

I got work in posh South Kensington. It was a conversion job. Splitting each floor of these large mansion-type houses into two self-contained flats. It was good class work and I enjoyed using my skills.

What I didn't enjoy seeing though, was my carefully cut twelve inch skirting boards fixed by somebody else. We were working in pairs on this job and it was nice to have someone to chat with. But partners need not get on well with each other's work.

After I'd carefully bisected the angles of the walls concerned, and cut joints to suit, my mate would come along with his two pound claw hammer and belt the living daylights out of my nice sharp edges, whilst nailing them to the walls. And these queer shaped rooms had lots of acute angles to be bisected.

This was disheartening enough in itself, but what really infuriated me was the way he precisely measured out eight inch lengths of knot free, floor boarding, marked them carefully with his set square, before sawing them up for firewood. These he took home in his lunchbox. Needless to say the attaché case measured sixteen by eight inches!

Happily I was then given a job to my liking. It was to repair all the damaged and missing mouldings on the site and make new lengths to match in with the old if these patterns were now out of date.

In a front room I rigged up a bench out of an old door and with the foreman's consent, worked through the flats one by one. Dad always had a beautiful selection of moulding planes under the stairs and I'd grown up using them. It appears nowadays that a young carpenter may never get a call for anything like this. The old skills are dying out.

It was the same for the plasterers. It was a joy to see them making up the jelly moulds and cutting zinc profiles to match up with the elaborate cornices of the past. What workmanship and skill.

Cost-cutting and new methods mean nowadays nobody it seems is allowed the time to do this labour intensive work. Get a job on a new Parliament building and you might still see it being done. Like my dad must have seen when he worked on the Selfridges building in Oxford Street.

A little while afterwards this firm was taken over by another builder. This new lot had built up their business doing bomb damage repairs. What a difference here. Costs cut down to the minimum, and piece work rampant, no finesse here. Most of the work needed repairing long before the war. Then to be told it was only the replacement of a top rail in a box window frame that had been allowed for in the price, made one's heart sink.

My concern to do a good job had no place with these young, thrusting employers. Get in and get out, sort of thing. I was sheered off like the rotten wood I was expected to resuscitate.

I thought I'd have a go at joinery. Being trained by dad in an engineering situation which was mainly to repair and replace things, I mostly had the damaged or worn out one to copy. Going inside on the bench had a different meaning. Given the task of making a new door for E.N.V. was to cut the wood, mark it out, do the crafty bits, glue up and go out and hang it.

Here I got out a cutting list, and the sawyer cut all the items for me. After marking out the various bits another machinist took over, and so on. After all the work was carried out by other various operators all the pieces came back to me for final assembly and glueing up. Until then I had always seen a job personally through every stage. A slight difference here, what!

If my first job had been to make a door it would have not caused me any sleepless nights, but I had to make a two sash, up and down box window frame. The one that has a weight hanging on cords to assist opening and shutting of same. It was only the help of the other employees that stopped me from being out of work again.

After we made things in the joinery shop an outside worker would normally do the fixing. Occasionally a big job would come in and we would also be involved with fixing. One such job was a café to be fitted out in Notting Hill gate. The owner had got a short-term lease to open before redevelopment of the Underground station got underway.

Two products new to me came on the market about now. One was a plastic sheeting called Formica, the other was a new contact adhesive called Evostick. I had a shop counter to make, about fifteen feet long, which was to be covered with this new hard plastic, using both products.

From a large sheet of Formica I cut strips to cover the counter surface. I left a bit to be trimmed off afterwards. You spread this rubber solution on both surfaces and then in fifteen minutes or so you bond one to the other.

This glue grabs immediately on contact. I'd gone about a foot when I realised I was out of line. It was no use. There was no turning back with this stuff. In the end, I had to trim the counter to suit the plastic instead of the other way round. How I got away with it, I shall never know.

The owner's name was Harvey, and you've guessed it, he was calling the café, Harveys. He came on to me one day to discuss the fascia he wanted. He drove me to Oxford Street and pointed out a beautiful elliptical shaped fascia he wanted copied. Around its oval design it had leaves folding back, emphasising the shop name enclosed, rather like a flower blooming.

The original was cast bronze and must have cost a small fortune to make. I was to use zinc and plywood. He was very pleased with my copy. This was before the counter incident. I wonder if it had any bearing on his leniency towards me!

A while after this job, I was laid off. Probably the firm got short of work and last in first out sort of thing. But it was a week before Christmas and I didn't like it a bit.

Chapter 8

Building the House

The fact that people were being sacked every day was no consolation. It made me realise that the vast majority of people have to rely on someone else to employ them before they can earn money. The one thing that can no longer be hunted for, gathered or grown for one's own consumption, money.

Since buying the plot and during the waiting months, Les and I were doing what we could on site. It wasn't easy getting over there. But we cleared the grass and thought up plans. We hired someone to draw them up properly and submitted them to the council. They were passed and we were issued with a licence to build. There were conditions of sale, should we sell later.

The maximum price for mine was £1400 and as Les was installing radiators in his house, his was £1600. We marked out the trenches for the foundations and commenced digging. Heady days!

Meanwhile, a new law came into force. The 'Land Development Charge'. This decreed the plot of land that had cost us £250 each was now only reckoned to have an agricultural value. This was about £14. We would be eligible for compensation for this loss out of a pool of money set aside for this purpose. When that would be was not stated.

So when we approached the bank manager for a loan it was useless. He pointed out these facts and we withdrew to lick our wounds. It sort of backfired on the banks and building societies though for it not only affected us, but many builders and developers. In the end they couldn't find anybody to lend money to, although it wasn't admitted at the time.

The usual practice for borrowing money to build was that you build up to ceiling height, then they, 'the mortgage lenders' would lend you enough to go up a little higher. By law they could not lend money on real estate, (ground). But we had a licence. A valuable property in itself at that moment. We didn't have any money to get up to ceiling height. I felt sure our licence might allow them to stretch the rules a bit to suit them so that we could make a start? So it proved and we were able to continue with a loan.

Things were hotting up in London. Our family assets were expanding minute by minute, as per normal. I was able to push them both up the three flights as Enid got bigger. Her favourite trick was to rest a cup of tea on the plateau baby's contribution made to her waist, whilst sitting down in a chair.

It was a very warm year 1948. If we went out special anywhere I used to sew her into her one dress that was large enough. It was a very nice pink colour with a lace trim that we were assured by the market trader was American in origin. The maternity corset offered by the clinic was enormous. Always looking young and fair skinned Enid looked in the pink too. Radiant, I thought.

She was attending the clinic regularly for check-ups and orange juice, and was booked into Paddington Hospital for the birth. Goodness knows how many places in the house we had its telephone number placed, just in case! Sister Rene, Reg and Ruth, and some cousins of the Grove family all visited us in Portobello Road. We saw more visitors then than we had seen since we got married.

Anyway, when the moment arrived, it was dark and late. I 'phoned the ambulance which came promptly and off we went. I saw her settled then came back and went to bed. (In the ensuing years I've not been allowed to forget this). Early next morning I 'phoned for news and was told what I thought to be a girl had been born, but it was soon made clear to me we had a son, one of the first to be born into our new National Health Service.

I walked out of the telephone box with a new spring in my step. Mother and son were well and I could visit them that afternoon. I let everybody know, wrote letters saying our son Jim, nearly 10lbs of him, had arrived. It was August 24, 1948. When I first saw Jim he had a full head of auburn hair, just like my own. It went soon afterwards and he become quite bald.

Mum came to see them one evening. A nurse was just going to explain that only the husband could see the baby at that time, but she was too late. Mum had gone through already and pronounced her new grandson a winner.

One proud and happy mum in bed, and a very happy dad visiting. We felt very lucky indeed. I went out and bought a pram. It was a large cream affair with big chrome wheels and a blue hood. It was very smart and also served as Jim's first cot.

I didn't get many brownie points for doing it without first consulting the person who was going to be its number one pusher. I didn't seem to be a very thinking parent at that time. It didn't occur to me either that we should have had a taxi home from the hospital, or, when choosing the pram, should had given a thought to the sixteen stairs we would have to hump it up and down each day. A smaller version would have been more sensible I suppose.

Jim was a good baby and slept soundly like his dad. Not so his mum. Every so often she'd be up listening to hear that he was breathing alright, and seeing about feeding him. Dads get off lightly here, I think.

I made a cot the size to take a No. 1 mattress. The only timber I had to hand was two inches by half an inch, and one inch by one. My effort was a unique structure. Light and airy, could be curtained off, and be easily handled to get up and down the stairs. This cot went all round the family over the years. It was painted like a Victor Sylvester dance step. Blue–blue, pink–pink, blue. A family dance coloured according to the sex of its occupant.

Les and I worried we were not in a position to get on with the work. We were too far away to use the many odd hours that come in so useful if you were on the spot. We decided to move nearer Potters Bar and jointly bought a house in East Barnet, in Churchill Road. Les and Rose were downstairs. Me, Enid and Jim were upstairs. We were then able to work full-time on the project.

This was 1949. We had dug out the footings early in the year and the hot summer sun had baked the walls of the trenches as hard as iron. It was whilst doing this we must have disturbed a wasps' nest. We were both chased off the site by these angry buzzers!

The trenches were about four feet deep in some places. They looked like a World War One battle situation in France. We hired a concrete mixer and prepared to place the foundations. It started to rain, and rain. The hard baked clay would not absorb any moisture so the trenches started to fill up.

By the time we managed to get it drained the water had undermined the trench walls. We had got about halfway through filling in with concrete when the walls started collapsing.

Poor old Les. I was mixing and wheeling the stuff to him and he was shovelling it into place. We had levelled out the trench bottom all round to ensure that the houses would be built level. Pegs sticking out of the ground to the depth of the concrete required were then banged in

Les was shovelling the concrete mix to reach the tops of the pegs. We got half the concrete in when the trench walls started to cave in. This meant Les had to shovel out the fallen clay and earth before I could tip concrete in.

The trenches got wider. We ended up exhausted, having to place far more concrete than was necessary to support the houses. At one point the concrete was over five feet wide. If No. 1 and 1A Allandale Crescent ever sink it will only be the weight of the footings pulling them down.

Les started laying bricks. In all we used 35,000 bricks and I carried every one of them under my arms. I couldn't get on with carrying a hod. We didn't mind the laying of them, it was the unloading of them that upset us.

Nowadays bricks are delivered in packs, with mechanical handling gear on lorries doing all the work. We had to unload by hand. We tried using rubber covers on our hands to keep the skin on them, but if a double load came one day it was a fair bet I was red raw and sore at the finish.

Not being builders with backup equipment to use, we had trouble storing cement, covering frames, and securing bits and pieces about the site. It wasn't very comfortable, especially during wet weather.

We battled on. Whenever we ran out of money we worked together doing jobbing work for other people. We had plenty of enquiries about work because at this time Les was a fully self-employed person. We kept tally of all the hours I put in on the private work, and settled up at the end of the whole project.

It amounted to about £1000 that Les owed me. All this whilst building our own houses. Les and I made a good team. If we had carried on being partners afterwards, who knows?

Not much money about, Les keeping me in cigarettes, we were really struggling. No money for the barber so Enid began cutting my hair herself. She has done it ever since, and incidentally blossomed into the nicest looking hairdresser North of Piccadilly.

We were doing a good job on the houses. Galvanised window frames set in wood surrounds. A good pitch on the roof. We saw to all the work that could not be got at afterwards. Nice easy-going stairs with half landings.

I remember Jim doing a little job on the stairs once. He'd got a hammer and some four inch nails and banged one in each tread. Talk about every little helps. By now a brother was on the way for him too.

Enid was very definitely expecting and whilst out shopping one day she was shoving Jim in the pram up Southgate Hill. An elderly lady leaned over and looking into the pram that held Jim, a real big bouncing boy now, murmured

'Oh, you poor girl!' She still only looked about sixteen. We had many a laugh about this.

Once whilst living in Tottenham we were politely asked by a publican whether she was of age before finally letting me buy us drinks. Not as though she has ever taken anything stronger than lemonade.

Michael's confinement was difficult. We had planned to have him at home, but the doctor thought otherwise. After all the work I'd done in preparation for the event, raising the bed etc. Enid was advised to go into Barnet General Hospital at eight months pregnant.

After Jim's birth I had stayed home to look after our first born while she went back to teaching. It was only after doing this she then decided the baby was a full-time job and quit work altogether.

Another time I took charge was just before Christmas. Enid wasn't well so I saw to the cooking of the Christmas dinner, a chicken. Afterwards I made a stew from the giblets. It was all right except that when I cut into the meat prior to putting it in my mouth, my plate was suddenly full of grit and half digested corn. I'd forgotten to take out the gizzards. It was hardly a success. It hurt the young mum to laugh at that time too.

In Barnet General they were really putting her through it. Finally Michael was forced to face up to the outside world a month early. She had pre-eclampsia which was much more dangerous then than we knew. A while later, when I saw her again, she was fast regaining her old self. In the corner of the room was our second son. He was covered in very fine hair and resembled a peach. An eight pound peach at that. If he had gone full term he would have been like Jim, a big baby.

I took Jim when I went to collect them both. He hadn't seen his mother for twelve days. From the dozen steps leading down to the pavement she called his name. The look on his face was a picture. He knew there was something that attracted him about that sound, but what? We managed to solve his complexities by the time he went to bed that night.

So now we were four. To complicate things a short time after, Jim caught German measles. There was eighteen months between him and Michael and the difference between seeing to one and then two was quite staggering.

Later, to visit my mum in Greenford meant a bus ride round the North Circular Road. It took two or three hours to get them both ready, load up the different shopping bags and finally get out. Mum understood why we didn't do this every week.

The ease at which these things can be done nowadays belongs to another world. Pack everything in and drive off. We didn't know about the lucky people who could afford it then, so we never missed it.

Our young family was a fortune in itself. Being young with them was the wisest of decisions. Youthful stamina was a big help too. So our second son born on 2nd March 1950, was also coped with.

Back at the building site I was wondering how I could get over my fear of heights once our project rose above ground floor level. But going up slowly with the scaffold in stages, it was no problem. In fact I got quite cheeky and revelled in this non-scared feeling. But once the scaffold was down and ladders became the vogue it all came crowding back.

My brother Fred and sister Rose's husband, Ron Haubner, came over whenever they could to give us a hand. Ron paid a heavy price in doing so. Whilst placing the site concrete his back gave way. It meant weeks of pain for him.

We all suffered to some degree. It was a difficult year. If I were ever to build another house, first I would find an architect. Not an easy thing in itself then.

We did go into an architect's office before we started the house but the plans displayed encouraged us to think we could save money by seeing to it ourselves. But we ended up with the same sameness. Because Les and I thought we knew how to do it all, we did too, the work bit, but at the end of all our labours we both ended up with a semi-detached house like millions of others.

Now with hindsight, a lot more thought would go into the project before a brick was laid. Also in full knowledge now of what I was going to get up to in the years ahead I would probably have built a first class multipurpose work place, with a living area attached, since I have spent the best part of my life at the bench.

But there, hindsight is one thing we can all do with a lot more of. Even the office boy in the architect's office would have pointed out to me that Les was only paying a little more for a real wood block floor than I was paying for my plastic one.

I had also opted to have a heating system in the shape of an ideal boiler that only supplied hot water. With a slightly larger boiler I also could have run radiators from it and heated the whole house as well. Fearful of being in debt was a contributing factor. From a working-class background these things had been dinned into me from an early age. This ingrained habit was working against me in this instance.

We finally got the roof tiled, and the walls plastered out. Les had completed his work and now it was my turn to complete the woodwork. In his turn Les then became my labourer. It had been a good arrangement. A pity the money problem could not be solved in a similarly stress-free way.

Came the day when the building society suggested that we should get one house finished and move in, both of us, then sell the Churchill Road house. Well, it was more than a suggestion. They would not advance any more money until we did.

So once again the two families moved into one house. Les and Rose had the front of our house, En', me, and the boys in the back. Eventually, Les and Rose moved into their house, No.1. Not as though anything was really finished. Upstairs we had all the bits of materials left to finish with and we had not even begun decorating.

Our dining room was connected by a serving hatch to the kitchen. En' was in the kitchen and I was in the dining room. Why? My bench was there. It was there for a long time while I finished all the odds and ends.

This structure of our family history is still with me. The bench could recite everything that has happened in our family since the day I made it during the early days of our building. Two heavy timbers and some smaller sizes, six foot long, which I had dropped the driver of the timber lorry a pound for. It comes in the obscure region of what is known as the paper clip zone. The boss won't miss a small item such as a paper clip, only bigger! The bench was then fitted with a nine inch quick release vice to complete the project.

Since its conception in a Potters Bar building plot, it has graced my workshop in four other localities during my working life. All of which will be revealed as long as paper and pens can be afforded, and my grip stays firm on the pen.

When we finally moved from Barnet into our newly built house we were all delighted to have our own garden. Or to put it less kindly, a builders' tip. It was long and tapered. I was made chief wheelbarrow runner for two small boys, who loved being pushed around.

En' soon had the inside shipshape. You would have thought that everything would be all right now. But it was Potters Bar. At that time it consisted of mostly streets of houses. A house can become a confining area. We were away from friends and family, and we felt isolated.

Our neighbours were elderly and kindly folk who were always on hand when we had to go out to vote and give blood. It wasn't so difficult for me being out working all day. But Enid felt trapped. She had been part of a full social life in her own town of Tredegar, in the South Wales valleys before college, and she missed it all dreadfully.

I was also strangely not really comfortable in our new surroundings. There were some bits of my work that could have been done better, and I would have preferred to forget. The time was when I laid out the flooring boards to dry, instead of nailing them in position first. As they dried so they curled up never to be made flat again, however many nails were put in. Sheer inexperience. After all, take out the war years, and the time it took for me to learn the tools, I was a relatively young practitioner of the art. (It seems Tommy Blackwell might well have been right!)

So it wasn't all puffed out chest and look what a clever boy am I, sort of thing. And so now we had borrowed all the money, young 'Arry' had better start earning some to pay it all back.

It is here good fortune intervenes in a strange way. Sister Lily had a friend who was a production engineer for an adhesive tapes manufacturer. When he learned I was looking for a job he offered me one as a maintenance carpenter on a new factory not long been opened. I was very pleased to accept.

A full circle indeed, back to maintenance work. This time new premises, not many repairs, more development jobs. The factory manager was an architect, which wasn't surprising really because the whole building was a sort of machine itself.

I learned that it was his building, or at least designed by him. Materials were directed to the top floor and as these products progressed they made their way downwards through the floors until the final product, adhesive tapes, came out at the bottom. Much simplified explanation, but basically a correct one.

These were finicky items though. All sorts of expensive materials and liquids went into the product. Petrol, resin, cellophane, ammonia etc. Most of them had critical temperatures to be reckoned with. Especially when the sticky gum had been spread on the cellophane.

The factory was double-glazed and we had problems making and trying out double doors and air locks to keep temperatures and humidity in check. Interesting job, interesting people and techniques. Lots of it experimental work.

I was there when we finally managed to evolve a continuous process. The machine was very long. It spread the gum onto the enormous reels of cellophane, after they had been treated to accept it. This was called the key coating. Similar to rubbing down woodwork to allow the paint to grip.

The team working on the project had a week to prove its capabilities. To me it seemed as though I was a part of industrial history. The firm was a generous payer. There was also a bonus at half yearly intervals. I worked overtime every other weekend and it was only a bike ride away in Borehamwood.

The timber shortages post war unveiled lots of Far Eastern wood, whitish in colour and very dry. When cut by circular saw it smelt like strong pepper. It got in your eyes, up your nose, and had to be treated with care.

Another species, a dark orange colour, was full of grit and as hard as nails. I came a cropper using this one day. Most of the time I'd pre-drilled this timber prior to nailing. This day I didn't. A large nail, after being hit by my hammer, sprang back and struck my specs. The lens shattered in my eyes.

I had the presence of mind to keep my eyes closed, attracted help and didn't open them until asked to do so by a casualty doctor. I was very fortunate that time.

The fact that the adhesive tapes we made were so useful in the house led to a curious situation locally. A joke going the rounds was that there was more of the stuff, seconds mainly, in the town than there was in the works, brought in security. After that there was an official in charge of a series of oil drums full of water, in which these not quite perfect reels were dumped. The water rendered these seconds to a really sticky mess.

The chief engineer, a good friend now, told me that amongst all the other things he'd made himself was a washing machine. I was tickled pink when I saw it. The inside was like a miniature collander, similar in design to the whopping great things used in the laundry business. A horizontal perforated drum was revolving amongst the suds with washing inside. So different from the vertical spinning action I'd expected. I think this was my first experience at lateral thinking. Finding solutions out of the norm. I have always pondered on such things.

As we had now got a garden, it was time to garden. I planted beetroots and spuds, En' saw to the tomato plants. She did get a result worth working for. My efforts resulted in tubers riddled with burrowing pests called eel worm.

My beetroots were about the size of a small cricket ball. When offered to a local cricket club they were politely refused on the grounds of bat damage limitation. They were not a success. The best use for the plot at that time was the regular wheelbarrow runs. Me pushing. The only thing I could reliably plant then was concrete paths.

Being fond of runner beans I sought advice on growing them. Dig a trench, fill with newspapers, put earth back, plant seeds. These plants were very thirsty so the newsprint would retain moisture for them to thrive. We ended up with the best informed moles in Middlesex who were always complaining of the damp!

One of the things I liked working at the tapes factory for was their science laboratory. A group of people there, apart from carrying out routine testing of goods coming in and going out, was also developing new products.

One such idea was to produce a tape that could be used in the packing case industry. At the time metal strapping was being used to ensure lids of packing cases didn't come adrift even though they were nailed on. Using nylon strands, a three-ply sort of tape was being investigated.

This product took a long time coming to fruition, but it's about now, and it's nice to think that this works chippie may have helped in a small supporting way. There are not many areas in any works that there is not somebody looking after the woody bits.

One weekend the family embarked on a coach trip to Southend-on-Sea. One of the attractions that caught our eye was a machine for recording one's voice.

Into the booth we went, but that action immediately struck our normally talkative boys dumb. Coaxing, promises, even veiled threats were tried but it was only on the last couple of turns of the small wax disc that a word or so was volunteered by our uncooperative twosome. Then the ten bobs' worth was up.

The discs only used a special sloping needle. We managed to keep a supply long enough to enable us to bore any visitor and relatives that came within striking distance of the gramophone. Southend was a lovely change and the weather was kind too. The coach fares were three shillings and six pence, (42p in new money).

If we managed to get away for a holiday it was of course Mumbles. We had lovely times on the sands in the surrounding bays. It livened up our thoughts of what the Dickens are we doing living in Potters bar? It came to a head when Herself realised there was nothing to stop us selling up and moving. We had no need to be spending one week by the sea and fifty-one weeks in Potters Bar. What about reversing that somewhat? How about the other way round?

We would be leaving a new house and a good job, but there's more to life than just creature comforts, and at that moment, sticky tapes. My wife had never let these supposed advantages blind us to the fact that it didn't add up to happiness for us any way. And we knew the boys would love the seaside.

When her parents died, within five months of each other in Tredegar, Enid was 18 months old. Her sisters Betty and Coral went with relatives and she was brought up in a family steeped in music, acting, and singing. The Stockton family.

Mrs. Morgan, Mam, the one Enid grew up to know as her mum, took her in. Eunice and Muriel, Mam's two daughters had all known her parents.

Enid's real mother came from Abertillery, and her dad, Dick Leach, was from Liverpool. He was a member of a theatrical family whose stage name was 'The Leas'. It consisted of father, son Dick, and daughter Clara. Once when they were appearing in Tredegar and seeking digs, Ada, Enid's mum, opened the door to her future husband, Dick, and behold the die was cast.

They were a variety act touring the country. The father was a scenic artist as well as being a performer. Clara played the mandolin and violin, and did floral paintings. Dick drew topical drawings for their stage show. Three artists, three easels, with their own electrical stage lighting, working as a trio, topped the bill in Tredegar's Working Men's Hall. We have posters that advertised the fact. All three had excellent singing voices and used them to good effect.

Dick Leach met his future wife whilst in theatrical digs in Tredegar. After their marriage he became an insurance agent and had settled there. David Stockton, a bricklayer, was an amateur singer and brother Bryn, a carpenter, was also a violinist. They also both played the saxophone in a local dance band.

Both had good voices, David a tenor, Bryn a baritone. Dave's wife Eunice was the dance mistress and all were involved in all the popular musical comedies put on by the Tredegar Operatic Society. Enid was always one of the dancers in the show. Even now she remembers lots of the words of those popular shows even to this day.

Dave was also an excellent comedian and made a perfect dame for their pantomimes. This was what Enid was missing in Potters Bar. Not being in the current production. Even when the Stockton families moved to the Mumbles, near Swansea, they were soon using the old British Legion Hall to put on their own shows.

I had seen their productions during holiday visits and was very impressed by all their talents. Another thing was that I was no stranger to the Gower coast and Oystermouth, the actual name of their village in Mumbles, with the lighthouse.

Since joining the first fatigue party en route to the island whilst in the army, I have very fond memories of the place. No doubt there must have been people who also had similar interests in Potters Bar, but we didn't look. I agreed we should move to Wales. What a marvellous decision. What a wife I've got. We've lived by the sea ever since.

Our friends and my family were surprised to say the least. I put feelers out for a buyer. The housing situation was such that I didn't think of consulting an estate agent. As a matter of fact the person who bought it was an insurance agent. He promised me a bit more than the £1400 I was supposed to have sold for, according to the building licence.

But I've never been any good at dodgy dealings and as soon as the contract was signed he conveniently forgot his promise. Just two months after we'd sold the government price controls were lifted, and a similar-sized house a few doors away went for nearly six thousand pounds. Prices had begun to rise all round. The removal firm charged us forty pounds to take us to Wales.

Now, how about the job at the tapes? I didn't want to leave them in the lurch, they had been a life saver for me. But I had a solution. I got in touch with my mate, Reg Clowes. He jumped at the chance and the firm took my word for it that they could do no better than employ Reg. So that was solved.

It all sounds very easy written here from a half a century away. But we were extremely fortunate in the way things worked out. The occupants of the top flat in Mumbles were Rhyce Morgan and his wife Doreen, a nursing sister. She was at that time seeing to an elderly lady in Langland Bay, a short distance away, and she had to live in. They very kindly let us move into their flat as a halfway home. This gave us a breathing space to find a house of our own.

The big house where all the family lived was four storeys high, in an elevated position half way up a hill,. From our top flat we had a lovely view of Mumbles Bay. Our belongings were unloaded and carried up the five flights of stairs to our new home without incident. When it came to the piano though, the two removal men got it up most expertly, but only after giving us an old-fashioned look on being told where we wanted it. There were also about twenty steps up from the road to the front door. But there, every man to his job. I didn't envy theirs at that moment!

This was wonderful. Back with the family in a nice spacious flat with a spectacular view. This knocked spots off Potters Bar. As a matter of fact all the spots, seemingly red in colour, landed on our boys. Both of them went down with measles. It was a worrying time for us all. It was a severe attack and they were very poorly indeed.

Both recovered very happily and life went on. Not so for Queen Mary though. I recall she died shortly after we arrived in Wales. A whole age died with her going.

I knew a 'Queen Mary'. Well, she was only Royal to the people she befriended. It was a Mrs. Store. I've written previously how she and her husband visited the lonely and helped out others with a few bob from time to time. A silhouette of both the late Queen and Mrs. Store would match perfectly. They were of that same passing age.

We had moved from a new house to a new country, so it was inevitable that other things would change too. I was forbidden to go out and work for anyone else. Enid insisted I became self-employed. So I had a letter heading and handbills printed and placed an advert in the local paper.

H. D. Brooks, Carpenter and Builder, Estimates Free. I waited for the work to flood in. The family were very helpful. They allowed me to install my bench in the large basement of the house and operate from there. I was lucky in that the men of the family were also in the building trade, so if I got a big job, I had extra hands to call on.

A week or so went by, nothing. Then Marks & Spencer's new building in Swansea, due to open shortly, caught fire. I wanted to go and work there for a bit of cash. I wasn't allowed to. My beloved's instructions. She was determined I was to be my own boss.

In five weeks I had one job, renewing sash cords in a top sash window. The whole job came to ten shillings. Even then I was out of pocket because I had to buy a knot of sash cord to do the job. But there was to be a bitter blow when I presented the bill.

The client, a lady, said it was too much. Finally I dropped to seven shillings and sixpence. But she did me a good turn. By behaving as she did, far from discouraging me, it put my back up and was enough to make me dig my heels in.

I knew I had nothing to reproach myself for. The job had been a nasty one. Ancient box frame window with coats and coats of old oil paint to contend with before you could get at bare wood. It was like being back on war damage repairs.

Then our grocer asked me to quote for papering a ceiling with patterned paper. We agreed the price for doing it. What joy, a job! How do you paper a ceiling? I'd never done one in my life. I had watched dad of course.

Fortunately, in the basement where my bench was, there were two rooms where the families stored their coal. I bought six rolls of lining paper and papered the ceilings for practice. They are still papered to this day', nearly sixty years on.

Another item sticks in my mind about becoming self-employed. A job in Swansea required removing a grate, fire surround and making good to woodwork. It came to twenty-one pounds ten shillings. An enormous amount to me then.

So when I was paid, I took the men down to the Marine that evening for a drink and celebration. It wasn't 'til the end of the month when the builders merchant account came in, that I realised bills aren't shared. So a lesson was learned.

We so enjoyed being near the sea. Growing up in Mumbles. One of the best things we did for our boys. The Gower coast from Swansea to Rhossili, what a place! Every sort of beach facility you could wish for. Cliffs at Three Cliffs Bay, sand dunes at Oxwich, steep hill at Port Eynon with its old church. These wonders were quite apart from all the other lovely bays with golden sands.

Every Sunday morning I would get out of the way with the boys whilst dinner was being prepared. We would go hunting amongst the rocks. Our pockets would bulge with polished pebbles, strange shells, old glass, starfish and crabs. We have a snapshot of Enid and the boys on Oystermouth beach the very first day we got there. Realising of course we didn't have to leave it any more to return to London. I enjoyed taking the picture on our Brownie camera.

I showed them the island with the lighthouse on it. The causeway had been removed by then. The boys showed me a cave that I had not been aware of. There's something to be learned from every looking.

That year the pantomime was to be Jack and the Beanstalk, to run in the British Legion Hall for a week. They had not done it before it as nobody wanted to be the giant. This was my chance to join in. I volunteered, me, a five-foot eight builder and decorator, expected to become a twenty-foot giant. En' meanwhile valiantly joined the chorus line and led the dancers. Dave, as usual, was the producer.

I made the giant's boots in a way that put me up about fifteen inches, and with a big papier-mâché head I was about nine feet tall. I saw what I was about through eye-holes in the giants neck. En' made the cloak and allied clothing and we were in. Dave was Dame. I painted the scenery too. I've been making props ever since.

So started my interest in show business. I was about 32 years of age and just interested in joining in the activities about me. But from that moment on I thought more about becoming an entertainer than of building.

I was thoroughly at home on the stage. There were no fears about starting a job as on the bench. I must admit to having far more confidence in this new world than in the old.

The show went well. We had two delightful young ladies in the cast. One, Fleurette, was playing Jack. The other, Pam, a niece of Harry Secombe, and a lovely foil to bold Jack. Jack by the way, returned to being her normal sex, and years later became Lady Rhodes-Boyson, wife of the cabinet minister for education at the time.

Fleurette's mother owned a small television set, one of the first in 1953. On Coronation Day our newly-crowned Elizabeth II would have been tickled pink to learn exactly how many of her humble subjects crammed into a small living room that day to watch the ceremony on an eight inch screen, in black and white!

The Legion Hall was not a vast place and years later an artist friend rented it for his studio. As the giant, there was only about a square yard of the stage where I could stand upright. The large head ruled me out of talking, so Dave spoke my lines through a microphone off-stage. I was duly put down by Jack towards the conclusion of the panto but Dave was unaware of this vital climax of my terrorising role. He was trying to make out the words of the script in the gloom of backstage.

So there was I feigning death in the grand manner, while my 'voice' was still pronouncing a very larger than life 'fi fi fo fum'. Before Dave caught up I sustained more cuts than an old pack of cards. But good triumphed in the end. I got no money for all my work but was allowed two adverts in the double page programme, priced thruppence. Heady days those.

On one page, H.D.Brooks, Builder etc, was jostling for attention with my other entry on the facing page stating 'Carnival heads made to order'. Not a titter of work from either of them. Not really expecting to make a fortune, or anything at all from my first encounter with the stage, I wasn't really bothered. We still ate well, and we loved every minute of it.

The three teachers who had so much influence on me came into prominence then. Mr Tyler, who urged me to vary my left hand and not to stomp on the piano, and keep my foot off the loud pedal.

Mr. Huggett, who encouraged my painting skills and Mr Keats who showed me the drawing one of his friends had made from his name.

This name thing had stayed with me over the years and I'd tried my hand at it from time to time, with limited success. Now I determined to make use of it. I made myself an easel to use on the stage.

It was a tripod affair that enabled me to draw at a convenient height. A number of pieces of newsprint, about thirty inches by twenty, were held on to the drawing board with four large bulldog clips. A chalk tray stretched across the two front legs and secured the whole structure.

The drawing board had a central spindle on its back that as well as supporting its weight allowed me to spin the whole paper-loaded surface to turn an upside-down drawing the right way up. A bit of trickery that adds drama to some drawings.

Prior to making it I'd been to the library to see if any books on doing lightning sketches were available. Only a small pamphlet book was there. It was written by an American, named Jerry Spindler. His easel was similar to mine but his paper was held by four pointed nails, with a cork at the sharp end pressing against the papers.

Apparently this subject was called 'chalk talking' in his country. He explained about working out ideas, fitting dialogue and patter, to produce a performance. Giving a few ideas of his own to illustrate the points he made. I only ever used one of his drawings to start with, afterwards I never copied anybody and made up my own material. I thought of two or three drawings to include in my proposed act, and inserted a couple of people's names taken live from the audience, in the middle.

The problem was thinking of a drawing to end with. Performers who have any sort of pleasing voice and can end with a song don't know how lucky they are. There is a clear finish and the audience knows just when to clap. Whether they are sufficiently moved to do so is entirely up to you and what sort of impression you've made on them. There lies the rub.

In the fifties there was no problem buying chalks for this type of quick, and large, drawings. My newsprint came from what is called a reel end, that I had begged from the printers of the South Wales Post. A reel end always held enough paper for my needs then. The paper when it arrived was delivered in huge rolls. After they had used all of the paper a small amount was always left on a thick cardboard core. This is a reel end.

Later, I ordered sheets cut and trimmed to size. This allowed me to avoid the hard work of unwinding and cutting the sheets myself. Previously I had to use a broom handle to support the heavy cardboard tube of newsprint between two chairs, while I unrolled it onto a table for cutting.

Variety theatres had not really been affected by TV then and so there was a demand from stage performers for cartoon chalks. These were a large soft variety, about four inches long by an inch in diameter. Years later, as demand dried up and Variety and supplies dwindled, I had to learn how to make my own.

Whilst I was being the giant I'd also cadged a small part in the palace scene that ends every good pantomime, with me doing a drawing spot. So with the giant dispatched and me being back down to a normal height and wearing a loud check shirt, I made my debut appearance as a lightning sketch artist.

Enthusiastic members of my family and friends were very kind with their comments, and I was delighted to have carried it off. I was amazed how relaxed I felt in front of an audience. Not so a younger member of our family. A friend was looking after the boys whilst we were on stage. One night during the second act we heard a half-strangled wail coming out from the audience.

We both recognised it to be our Michael's voice. He was in an elevated position, standing on a stool, near the hall stove. Leaning against the wall he shifted his stance and in doing so dislodged the stove-pipe.

The first yell came when the pipe gave way. The following wail was all that escaped from his lips before he was deluged with soot from the pipe. Fortunately, the stove was not in use. For not being around during his discomfiture, we both got black looks from his sooty eyes. After this we were regular contributors to the annual panto.

We did Riding Hood and Dick Whittington. I was a robber in the first and Alderman Fitzwarren in the second. The photographs at that time didn't show us in a very good light. Mostly taken after the show, the girls all still looked clean and crisp. We men, however, with make-up askew and mostly dishevelled, looked rather less than glamorous.

Once Dave was in need of a few words to add to the pantomime scripts he'd bought, and let me do a bit to help. It involved a bit of argy bargy between the robbers in the forest somewhere. My contribution got laughs from the audience and I was well satisfied.

It was during this period that at a summer event in the Mumbles castle grounds, I did a drawing spot on the back of a lorry. For this I got two guineas. The total fee was four guineas but I was using Bernard, Dave's son, as a cross talk partner on this temporary stage.

It was my first paid engagement, and Bernard's! I mentioned his wages because in a few years time, when he'd finished his national service, he became a pupil at RADA. He was following Dave's interests in wanting to become an actor. Like father, like son. He also had a fine voice.

I was also more daring now. I drew a cow on the board, and Bernard was able to 'work the udders' and produce a pint bottle of milk, cardboard type, from 'neath the old lady. Highly technical stuff this, and we were well received. And two guineas each wasn't a bad fee then.

The subject I was drawing on the board was inspired by a birthday card from his girl who worked on a farm. It was in four parts. The first page showed the rear of a cow. Second page showed the beast looking round to his rear. The last page showed me finishing off the drawing with a swishing tail and undercarriage. The punch line being, 'I love no udder but you'. All my own work, and, of course seeing it being drawn in front of them, helped to increase its appeal.

Meanwhile back to the day job. With the cheque for the house in London, I established contact with the local Midland bank manager. He was of the old type. A nice person, fair in his dealings, but he knew how to look after his employer's money. If I had to overdraw at any time I had to get his permission. His final words after every encounter of this nature were 'please remember Mr Brooks, the bank must have first call on any monies earned on this job'. Looking back on early account books, most of the time we were only talking of four or five pounds credit.

A good friend of mine, Billy Davis, owned a newsagent's shop at the bottom of our road. Every time we had a chat about the ups and downs of our businesses, the bank manager's name always cropped up somewhere along the line. Whether the poor man's ears ever got over the scorched earth policy Billy and I dished out during these talks, I know not. You can gather where Billy also banked!

Business was steadily growing as more and more people heard from satisfied friends who were also my clients. I made a small builders trolley from a stout pair of pram wheels. I could then push my own boards and ladders to jobs.

A house came up for sale a few hundred yards away from where the folks lived, in Overland Road. Oakland Road was a hilly road that led up to this same road. It runs from Thistleboon to Langland Bay. It was an unmade up road that passed No.2 Oakland Road on its way. This was the house for sale.

We viewed it and liked what we saw. It was one of a string of houses that seemed to lean on the hill on the way up, or seemed to slip down it if you took a more pessimistic view. It was just above our price range, which was a great shame.

We made an offer of the maximum amount we thought we could go to, and left. It was weeks later we learned that our price had been accepted. The sellers, retired folks, we're very keen to join their married children up north in Bridlington. Anyway, we were very pleased they sold to us.

Having a mortgage on the Potters Bar house we were acceptable as borrowers to the same company. There was a snag, however, we were asking for more than the amount of money we had previously got and I was also now self-employed.

Fortunately I had no trading accounts to show I was a newcomer to the business. They accepted my estimates of further income and we were granted the money. Phew!

We were very sorry to move from Rhyce and Doreen's flat. From their windows we could see the whole of Swansea Bay laid out in front of us. Of the night-time, the amber coloured street lamps looked like a string of pearls circling the shores.

The Mumbles train was also a feature then. It ran from Swansea to Mumbles head. From their flat's elevated position our boys had no difficulty whatever in thinking of it as a giant train set. Its single track, with passing places for when each double-decker tram passed each other going in opposite directions, was little short of magical.

There was a great commotion when it was decided to close it down. We were promised a far better bus service in its stead. The whole family went down to see the last train go. Needless to say once the tracks had come out the promises also disappeared with them.

Chapter 9

A New Country

So now we were proud owners of a house in Wales. Moving into No. 2 we were had plenty of help from the menfolk, and we needed it. The piano had to come down again! More friendly news, the folks said that we could hold on to the basement workshop whilst I got myself sorted.

The new house had a very small front garden and a not much bigger back one either. It might have been a contributory factor in the difficulty of selling the place. But it suited us, so we got onto making it user-friendly.

My first priority was a workplace. We had a stone wall to mark our boundaries and so I built a shed right across the back garden space to a depth of about fifteen feet.

Overland Road was still climbing outside No. 2 so we were well below road level. My shed roof was just below the top of the stones, so was unseen by passers-by. This was fortunate because some neighbours could, and one did, object to any sort of business being established in a residential area.

Our objector lived just two doors away. I was very careful not to display any signs of business activity or make noises to upset her. In the end I brought an old grand piano from her and sold my own. I was really doing her a good turn taking it off her hands at the time.

It was full size and in its time had been a magnificent instrument. Its walnut casing looked a treat after a polish. It solved the problem of furnishing the downstairs middle room. Enid put a slender silver vase holding a posy of seasonal flowers, on a lace cloth, on top of it. With the piano stool, and lid up and me playing, the room was full of piano and music. We loved it.

Once we had a large old-fashioned mirror on the mantel shelf. Very elaborately carved and gold leafed. Anyone peeping in could easily have thought they'd stepped back into a Jane Austen novel.

This neighbour had an epileptic son. Once he became trapped in their bathroom after not being well. I managed to gain entrance through the window to open the door. Afterwards we became friends, and worries about my workshop lessened considerably.

Our kitchen door opened up about eight feet away from the new workshop. I don't seem to have ever been more than a few feet away from our family wherever I'd had the bench.

A common sight for me and a great joy during those days was when the boys, before school, were assisting mum in the kitchen. Both had their pinafores on, standing on a chair, each one rolling out pastry, helping as hard as they could. With the back door open I only saw their backs from my bench, but I could imagine the intensity of their concentration on the job in hand.

I tasted many of their products during this period. They went into the oven the same as their mum's cakes did. But why their pastry seemed a different colour after baking than their mum's, I don't know. It was the grey colour of it that was not drawn attention to whilst we were popping them in our mouths. It could of course have been their treatment of the same dough with the rolling pins that caused a bruising?

The jobbing work locally had problems that previous workmen had left for someone else to sort out. The main one was the buildings contained a lot of flints in their walls. These big uneven chunks of very hard stone seemed always to be where you needed a good strong fixing, say for a wash basin or shelving.

Most of the mortar was a lime mix, soft and powdery. Rawlplugs were no solution here. What used to get my goat, especially if I was the second person engaged to solve a problem, was the client sometimes gave the impression I was to blame for the initial failure. They thought they were paying twice for the same job, and picked on me, in a nice sort of way of course, to vent their dissatisfaction on.

Working on my own it soon became clear that there are two kinds of builders. Persons like myself interested in establishing a clientele, hoping to work again for satisfied customers, and the cowboys.

These people were not a bit interested in repeat work. They sought only the cream. They made sure they made money whether the job suffered or not. If the client paid up front there was every likelihood that they would have gone at the first opportunity. And what is more galling is that even when they've finished, we are usually left to clear up the mess of third class work.

What tickled me was one of my best customers was a local builder. He had perfectly good chippies working for him already. I was flattered of course.

Perhaps he just wanted someone other than his own gang for private reasons.

I also worked for other folk who had their own businesses. A spin-off from these clients was I often got work to do for their wives, in their homes.

One client in Swansea had a Welsh produce shop. A lot of this work had to be done at night. I learned a lot about baking bread, making sausage rolls, cooking hams etc. and, as soon as I finished working in the shop his wife would collar me for her jobs indoors.

It was time I made an effort to be more business-like. The next tool I needed was a vehicle. Looking through the newspapers I came across the following small ad which read '1938 Ford 8hp van, plum colour, £38 o.n.o.'.

I had to go to Gorseinon to view it, a few miles away. It was the price of course that was the attraction. I could manage it, without borrowing. It never occurred to me that at £38 the seller expected to bargain the price and would probably accept £35.

It was a small Ford van that had been converted into an estate-like model. Two small windows had been cut in the sides, how and with what means I don't know. It was definitely a do-it-yourself job.

Ordinary window glass was used in the process. The lock on the driver's door was interesting. A short leather strap, looped around the steering column, had a dog lead clip on its end. This engaged with a screw eye on the van door. It certainly prevented the door swinging open.

The van was taxed and the same insurance agent took me on, issued a cover note certificate and the deal was done. The van started easily on the handle, and I drove back home.

It hadn't occurred to me whether my new acquisition could make it up Oakland Road. It gallantly proved it could and so became an acceptable resident against the kerb, outside our house. There were no garages in the whole road. It bore the number plate BNY 13.

I remember making sure that the front wheels were firmly turned in against the kerb. Some days in nervous moments I also discreetly shoved a brick under the rear wheel.

Whilst in the process of getting established as a builder I still had my mind firmly fixed on my new love. To this end I had fortified my act with a half a dozen new, original prepared drawings, and I had practised the name business in great detail. Drawing up lists of names as long as your arm I worked right through them, taking each one as far as I could go.

Some were easy and it was possible to get more than one face from. Others needed a lot of work on. A few I found impossible. I had a strategy for these. It meant do your best and be prepared to make up with a little better patter. Then get it off your easel as quick as possible. I've never had to give in entirely yet!

As a speciality act I had two chances. It could be funny, but more often people think I'm clever. Anyway, I generally got away with it. So, feeling confident, I placed an ad in the local press, the South Wales post. 'Cartoonist available'. I soon got a reply.

A man named Billy Rowe rang me up, 'Harry, we've got an opening for a speciality act in our party, when can we see you'? Billy was a well-known Swansea comedian. They had a booking in the ICI social club that Sunday, could I come? I could!

I arrived there with my set up all now self-contained in a travelling case. Easel board, long legs that now unscrewed in half, chalk tray with a sliding lid, all complete with a gold fringe and paper.

The concert party consisted of Billy Rowe, comedian; Marian Longman, singer; husband Billy Longman, pianist; and tenor Ned Edwards. It was one of the most successful concert parties in South Wales. I did not know this then.

We agreed for me to appear in the first part of the show. I followed Marian, who opened with her songs. I did about 10 minutes and went down well. I was paid half fee, 10 shillings, and I left. Next day Billy was on the 'phone again and he invited me to join the party. So I was in.

During this period a good concert party could earn its members about 25 shillings each, for two performances, one either side of a short interval. Our venues were mostly working mens' clubs and social welfare concerts.

The fees, about twelve to fourteen pounds, were reduced by the cost of transport. Usually a van of sorts, sometimes a taxi or hired car. Once we were run around in a Jaguar car. Its owner was stage-struck and enjoyed being in with the action. Our only problem with him was stopping him drinking too much.

On these jaunts I could be picked up at five on a Sunday evening, and may not return home until two-o'clock the next morning. Nine hours to earn our fee. I was performing for less than an hour but it took all day, and night sometimes, to do it. This highlights one fatal flaw in being a performer. Once you have done your bit, you have to move on and find another audience.

Travelling. It was what left one half of a married couple having to get on with it while you do it. Later on it was the one thing that marred a perfect way of earning a living. Being away from home and family. Yet umpteen folk would give their all to be up there in the limelight. Strange old world.

The money it brought it in settled all these personal reservations. In the fifties, an extra twenty-five shillings in the family kitty was a great help. From Mumbles to Usk or Cardiff, or to any of the South Wales valleys long journeys, it was mostly money driven. But also all of us had greater goals really. We all wanted to 'make it' professionally. Sitting on the floor of an old van for hours sorted out the less keen ones.

The party prospered. Our success produced its own problems for me. Marion and Ned could sing their songs, over and over. Indeed they got requests to do so. The Donkey Serenade was very popular tune then. Ned was noted for the way he could belt it out, in fact he sang so much about it we used to joke, during the wearying return journeys, that he must have had a donkey, and he kept his 'moke' in an 'adobe hacienda'. A mud hut!

Billy and I always had to do something a little different from the last appearance at the club. The audiences were the same. Return bookings meant new drawings from me and another act from Billy. We relied heavily on being novel. I would have been most disappointed if my work hadn't impinged at least a little on their memories.

The names always held me in good stead though. Once or twice I was asked by the club secretary, the one who booked us, to do a drawing of 'old Charlie', a club favourite. If I had been asked to paint his portrait, there would have been no problem. But I only had a couple of minutes up there, with everybody's eyes on me, to produce something that kept everybody happy. So I'd put it off 'til the second spot.

In the meantime after old Charlie had been pointed out to me I would secretly be eyeing him up and doing little sketches of him out of sight. In effect I was making a prepared drawing of him. One that I could trust to bare fruit.

The times I had to do it I was very successful. It normally brought the house down. There was another element to this apparent success. Everybody was half canned by then. That also was a help. I called myself 'Harry Brooks, the Wizard with the chalks'! And so I grew up in concert. It was the mid-fifties.

As well as our own dates, other parties would ring up to find out if I was free for a booking. It seems that speciality acts were thin on the ground. Once when we booked to play Tylorstown, with Billy Rowe working elsewhere, another comic we got to stand in for him cracked jokes that were political, and not to the liking of the audience. Anyway the whole audience got up and went into another room where bingo was being played.

Trying to placate the few members still wanting to see the show, Marian sang her heart out and I did over twenty drawings, hoping to keep things from falling apart when the secretary came over and said 'I'm very sorry, but you can go now'. He paid us off, and we went. It only happened once to me but it was a moment never to be forgotten.

It wasn't a reflection on them or us really. We never used the man again. There was one small compensation to be drawn from it. We got home early that night.

The clubs could be very hard sometimes. One hall was long with a raised bit at one end. The chairman would introduce you to the members who were sat at a long line of tables facing each other. Once you were announced they all turned to look at the stage. If you didn't hold them, they simply turned back and spoke amongst themselves.

In Mumbles I had a couple of offers to become a partner on the building side. One came from a friend, 'Ginger' Clements. Painter and decorator, he was also a member of the Mumbles lifeboat crew. It was he, an expert craftsmen, who taught me the proper way to paint a panelled door. We were still the best of friends when I declined.

The other offer came from Brian Hope, an amazing person who had done all sorts of jobs. His wife Peggy and mine were great friends. We all enjoyed some grand times together.

Brian was a sometime builder. He did a lot of work for an estate agent in Swansea that had a lot of slum properties on its books. He offered me some work. I went with him once to see a job. 'Repair WC door'. Two tee hinges swung loosely with nothing on them. A bit of canvas hung in the wind for privacy.

Another job he had was installing outside lavatories to a line of six houses. They were a little way away from the dwellings and quite separate in their back gardens. When I saw them they were most distinctive. Each one about four foot square and seven feet high with a sloping roof. Common bricks and wooden braced door, there couldn't have been a more public demonstration of what happened inside them if they'd been in Piccadilly Circus.

But Brian was a trier. Once, while I was out on a job of my own, he turned up to install an Aga cooker. Driving a taxi by night was another way of his to earn a crust. There was some sort of 'redistribution' of earnings going on when he was working. I used to listen to him with my mouth wide open. It was a convoluted method of turning petrol into wages. It was far above me, but it seemed to work for Brian.

They had one child at this time, Wendy. He had a small three-wheeler van. Often I'd been with him buying half a gallon of petrol down at the garage. We had a common interest in show business. He had been a stuntman in films and had worked with Stewart Grainger, in Captain Boycott. He was also a marvellous raconteur.

We used to listen to him enthralled about the film work he'd done and the people he'd met. He wanted to be a stand-up comedian and he was well equipped to be so. A tall, good looking person, with an amiable nature that came across when he was in full flight. His weakness was in moments of pressure. He panicked.

To help out with the family income both wives took in summer visitors whenever possible. We also took in students from Swansea University during the winter. Brian also had Peg's dad Les living with them. Les was also very handy, and very good with heights. He did a lot of my roof work for me. He used to frighten the life out of me the way he walked over the rooves. If he'd worn suitable footwear, according to my way of thinking, it might have eased my anxiety. But no, he wore hobnailed boots.

Only small in stature, Les seemed all boots. It was only after a bonnet tile he had installed had become dislodged from a chimney one winter, and crashed down during a storm, that I dispensed with his services. No damage was done fortunately, except to our working relationship. After that if I couldn't get up to examine what had been done, I refused roof work.

Earlier, there had been an occasion when a man from the BBC held some auditions in the Pattie Pavilion in Sketty, Swansea. I went along and did my act. Afterwards a floor manager representing Brian Michie, a BBC producer, asked could I do the sort of drawings that Tony Hart was doing in his very successful children's programmes at that time.

'Well, no, not quite', was my answer. I knew then I was not the sort of person that they were looking for. I did not hear from them again.

My confidence as an entertainer grew to the point where I suggested to Enid that I do some children's parties, well, not alone. If she could go out and get order for me to perform, we could become children's entertainers.

So began a partnership that I enjoyed absolutely. I made games and props for bits of business and she worked out dance routines for which I played the piano. It was plain to me that this was something we could do really well. She with her teacher training had a marvellous approach to the children. Wonderful control.

I went about getting bookings by having a letter heading printed, 'Harry Brooks and Deena…South Wales Foremost Children's Entertainers'. When she was very young she could not quite get her name out properly and a close approximation of it was Deena. She now chose to be known as Deena. I wrote to all the clubs listed in the Yellow Pages including larger firms that I thought might have a party at Christmas for their workers' children and there were many, and it paid off.

There was a problem describing our mode of working over the telephone. 'Are you a conjuror? No. Do you do punch? No. Are you a ventriloquist? No'. We didn't seem to fit into any normal party criteria.

When I explained I was a lightning sketch artist and my wife was a dancer and we do games, they generally gave us a try. After that there was no problem. We got booked again for the following year in many cases, before we left after a show.

Our first booking was for a cables firm. Fee six guineas. It was pre-BNY 13, before I got the van. The show was very successful, but we had to go by taxi which cost six guineas. It wasn't an entire loss though. I explained to the work's secretary how much it cost for us to get there and he paid for the taxi separately. I learned another lesson then.

Anyway, we got a fair share of the work going and prospered. Not so much in a financial sense, but in confidence and ability. Soon we were able to add a whole list of satisfied clients down one side of our letter heading. It looked good. Later a secretary divulged that he nearly didn't book us because we had worked for a rival firm. Sometimes you can't win!

Deena now had a soldier's dance number, Dutch girl, and the one I think was most successful, the gollywog dance. She made a really lovely getup and looked very pretty. On her belt at the back she had a big clockwork key. I used to wind her up before dashing back to the piano to play for her dance.

As I played for her she would gradually run down. It's funny how I never noticed this until children were reminding me in no uncertain manner, by shouting their heads off. Up I would get to wind again, and off she would go. This participation was always a feature of our treatment of children. They love to join in. Providing good control is maintained, it's most rewarding for all concerned.

We could handle all ages with a little forethought. And, as I have learned over the years, a good game is usable in all sorts of situations. It's how it is presented that is the key.

Meanwhile the baby of the family was bringing great joy. It might have been nearly twenty years old but the van was a treasure the whole family had not experienced before. Transport.

Its gallant engine proved it could manage the hills even when it was groaning under the weight of several bodies crammed into its innards. For the local bays we mostly walked as they were closer to hand, but for Oxwich, Port Eynon, Three Cliffs and Rhossili, our van was vital.

So whenever the weather was right, out would come the tools, and cushion replacements would be the order of the day. There was always plenty of driftwood about so our beach bonfires were something to behold. Our barbecues (except I don't think that term had come into use then), were not at all like the modern sedate glow of charcoal you see now.

Whoever was chef that day could have easily been burnt to a cinder, like some of our chickens were. Everything was very basic, but the adults and children all had a whale of a time.

In Rhossili Bay there were the signs of an early wreck with a couple of rusty spars exposed above the beach sands. One day we all went armed with shovels and the like. From the cliff top it all seemed a feasible idea, whilst viewed from beach level it appeared we were being slightly optimistic.

This, Dear Reader, will be amply confirmed by a trip to the said bay. It's slightly less than the size of the Sahara, with nearly as much sand. I don't think we dug for long. But the decision to vacate Potters Bar for the Gower coast was shown to be right for us all. And the boys had a Welsh education.

The schools were revered then. It could be summed up by an incident that our Michael, aged five, was a party to. It was a day away from St David's Day when he explained he was involved in his class's play. He was to play a daffodil. Could mum make his costume? No wardrobe mistress ever worked faster. This treasured memory is captured in a snap the teacher took of her class at the time.

Having a van also meant having a mechanic to look after it. I decided it was a job for someone who knew what it was all about. I was learning to be a builder and entertainer so I handed the job to someone else. Eric Owen, garage owner, and I became friends. His garage was in the High Street in the village.

From his place to my house the road steadily climbed up all the way. If I took my brake off outside our place I could run to his place without bothering the engine. Indeed, on many a wet and windy day, with sparks flying everywhere except where they were supposed to go, to the plugs, that was my strategy.

Engaging third gear to get a kick-start I'd try this for about two thirds of the way down, then I'd freewheel the rest of the way if I could. As long as the bottom road was empty, and often I prayed that it would be, I ran straight into the garage and saviour Eric. Fords, or my one, was not compatible with damp. If the bonnet fitted properly it could have helped.

Eric looked after our gallant thirty-eight pounds worth until even his even-tempered nature gave in, and he advised a change. Also another tool was necessary if we were to be away from the boys doing shows.

Muriel and Bryn Stockton were quite willing to babysit for us. To ease the situation we got a television for them to look forward to when they came over. It was a good move and solved the problem.

Bryn was also a carpenter and very talented in other directions. Apart from playing the violin beautifully (he taught Jimmy to play), he was very good at photography. He had made some lovely cameras in his time. He put his talent to good use and when a job came up at the University for a library technician he applied and got it. It involved all sorts of photographic work for all departments on the campus.

He put my name forward for some maintenance work, and I was accepted. I was seen at work in various departments and I got many private jobs from this. These very clever people doing their own thing at work were sometimes profoundly unhappy whenever tools of my sort were mentioned. One professor, for whom I did a lot of work for, would seem most unhappy to see a hammer, let alone use one. These were mainly academics.

The heads of engineering and other heavy departments were quite the opposite. One lecturer I worked for lived in Mumbles. He could be absent-minded sometimes. Indeed, once riding on the Mumbles train with his two children he got off at his stop and left the children on. His mind was full of other things I expect.

One thing they all had in common was they were very nice folk. They appreciated being looked after and paid promptly. Not so their employers. The University paid accounts monthly so it could be up to two months before you got your money. But of course it was as safe as houses, and you knew the rules before you accepted work.

I had a big job on once for a professor and the family was giving me a hand. Bryn, Dave and Rhyce were on the payroll. One day, on finishing, we all piled into the van when a big man in blue came up. A fully blown Welsh copper, a suspicious type it turned out. ' See your licence please', were his words.

Shortly before a new traffic law had come into force. To carry tools and stuff you needed to possess a 'C' licence. The commercial lorry drivers plying for hire were being undercut by anybody who could use their car or van for a quick cash job. They did not have to pay for the expensive licences normally required to carry for profit.

So the government sought to right this. For people like me, carrying tools and materials for my own use, and exempt from the new law, the 'C' licence came into being. And I didn't have one.

The policeman walked to the rear of the van, put his shoulders to it, pushed, and we moved. Not a lot, but enough for him. He called in a mobile traffic unit to check the van over. We vacated the van and off it went with the traffic policeman driving.

It was an agonising time before they returned. I had been counting up in my mind all the wrongs that could have been flung at us. No C licence, the dog lead door closing system, windows that seemed to have been born via a tin opener, and so on.

But when the van returned the officers got out and said simply , 'get your handbrake adjusted', or words to that effect. I think the two mobile lads weren't best pleased with being called out. It was a good job too, otherwise I might still be in jail!

My application for the relevant piece of paper was in the post next day. I didn't get off scot-free though. I was duly charged and fined two pounds.

Since becoming self-employed I soon realised I suffered two serious faults as a builder. I didn't like heights and I was not very confident at estimating. The fear of not getting work or losing it by overpricing it made me happier at doing day work. Or being paid by the hour.

In a popular builders' magazine at that time, one subscriber, a Jeffrey Pett, was always saying you couldn't run the business properly like that. You must make a profit. If you only get paid for hours worked on the job, who is going to pay for the in between times?

Estimate the job thirty hours work plus materials, work hard, do it in twenty hours. That's the bit that is then yours to keep you in with a chance. That is your profit. A professional type will present his bill by the hour, like an accountant. It works if you can get fifty pounds an hour or more, plus costs.

I used to get rattled with all the adverts that presented things like garages at a bargain price. Prefabricated sections that could be assembled speedily, plus a nice photograph of showing one erected in a pleasant setting next to the house. There was no mention there about the concrete raft generally necessary to stand the thing on. People are shocked that sometimes these costs are greater than the bargain they bought to house their precious car.

Another of my horrors was dealing with rot, dry or wet. I always liked the client to be present when stripping out infected timber. A small mark on the skirting board can indicate plenty of trouble underneath and out of sight. And even when the job is done, they are only back to where they were in the first place. Heart breaking work.

Then there is the occasion when your hourly rate is questioned. 'I can assure you my hard-working husband or wife only gets so-and-so per hour'. Strange why I keep doing it was a thought that sometimes would run through my mind!

On another problem my garage owner friend Eric was a font of information. Earlier I'd asked him if he knew of an accountant for me. He told me of a person in Swansea. This man owned property as well. So an arrangement was made for him to see to my needs. In the meantime I was asked to do a bit of work on his houses. I sent him a bill and he ignored it. He then did my books for the year and sent me his bill. I ignored it. We got on very well for years with this unique accounting system.

But then my accountant retired and sold his business. The new owners, it seemed, didn't own property! I had to learn proper arrangements. However, things soon settled and I have been well served by my professional colleagues, only ever having two accountants to deal with in all those years.

I couldn't seem to let the old van go yet. Deena had to play a leading part at getting anywhere like the valleys, in the dark. Our headlamps were very poor for some of the weather conditions we encountered on these journeys. At road junctions it was she who would nip out with a torch to illuminate the signposts. The lights from the van were lucky to reach the ground, let alone shine six feet in the air. And then signs were in Welsh. But, I thought, as we were no longer in Middlesex I suppose we couldn't really grumble.

At last we outgrew the van. I tried to sell it but nobody was interested. Eric said he would take it off our hands. So a plum coloured small vehicle became a black, larger Fordson van. Our new transport was a lot roomier and in quite good condition. Whatever our tin opener friend had managed to do before, we sadly missed the ventilation it had afforded us. In the summer this black van was murderously hot. Black isn't the best colour to reflect the heat of the sun.

When I said our circumstances had improved with the van there were other things we'd acquired as well. The most important item was a telephone. This brought the whole world into our living room. An answer could be given whether we were already booked or not on a certain day. Most people interested in our services were already using their 'phone to contact us.

The follow-up letter was important too. I had the best letter writer in Mumbles, Deena. She used to write letters for the whole family. Having a good turn of phrase and being able grammatically to express herself well, she was worth her weight in gold. She is still at it now. I used to rough out what I would like to say and she would put it into an acceptable form for reading.

Mind you, the telephone will always be a mixed blessing happy and sad news speeds along its wires. We had some relatives staying with us for a few days, Fred Williams and his wife Rene, were having a short holiday.

Fred belonged to the family that had taken in Deena's sisters, Coral and Betty. He was also a talented artist. We both sat for each other that weekend. The two pencil portraits are very good. I got a fair likeness of Fred, and he drew a cartoon-style picture of me wielding a hand saw. He was a trouble-shooter for a big sheet metal manufacturer. He sadly also died young.

When the phone rang that afternoon, it was my brother Fred. 'Lily is dead'. How terrible that looks written down there. She was only three years older than me and to my knowledge had not even been ill. It was afterwards I learned that she had been very depressed of late and her husband Frank came into the house and found her dead. She'd taken her own life.

The bomb that fell in front of her bus and killed Albert, her driver, and other passengers, had left a lingering mark on her. I went to London for the funeral. I saw Lily as well. She looked as though she was just having a nap. It was so unreal to think she was not to wake again.

I was very sad, and when Rene came in with a small bunch of lilies of the valley, my heart nearly broke.

My mum had gone too. Not then, but earlier. She was ill for a while and the doctors somehow gave her the impression she was malingering. This distressed her terribly. Bringing up a large family, then starting again when John came along, working hard all her life, it was a monstrous impression on their part to make. If indeed that was so.

She was allowed out of the hospital to come home for a day. I saw her then. It was incredible and I just couldn't accept it, but she didn't know me, her youngest. She died shortly afterwards.

Dad had her brought home, to the front room. He wouldn't leave her. She wouldn't be left alone as long as he was in control. When I saw mum lying there she looked very tiny. She had wasted a lot. The hospital had taken out her false teeth. Her cheeks were sunken in hollows. She looked worn out. She was too. Worn out on us. She wouldn't have had it any other way.

After my success in panto as Alderman Fitzwarren, (loud laughter) I was raring to go. My drawings had improved and I wanted to see how I matched up with 'real' entertainers. Deena and I decided I should have a go at London.

Brian Hope was always talking about the fact that he knew Hyamy Zahl. Mr Zahl was a very important agent connected in fact to the Foster's Agency. Brian said for me to go and introduce myself and say he had sent me. Thinking back now, alarm bells should have been deafening by now, knowing Brian.

There had been a time when Carol Levis was auditioning for his discovery show in Swansea. We had been having a go at writing scripts previously and were pleased with the outcome. So, we both decided to have a go.

We prepared a brand new script for a stand-up spot for Brian, and he rehearsed hard. In the past he had suffered from panic attacks, should a difficulty arise, whilst delivering. It was on these occasions when all his carefully rehearsed new material would go out of the window, and he would drop back to the old stuff he was comfortable with. Anyway, that was in the past. We now had a brand new set of words.

We set off to the Swansea hotel where the auditions were to be held. I went in and did my spot first and was asked to appear in the stage show later. Brian went on and made a good start. But auditioning in a cold informal hotel foyer, littered with disinterested folks all getting ready to do their own acts, is no place to rely on for audience reaction. He didn't get a response and lost his nerve again. Back to the old jokes. It was hard. He didn't get through.

We were both wondering what ' through' meant. It turned out I was invited to be one of Carol Levis's discoveries on stage, one Tuesday evening, in the Swansea Empire, now sadly gone.

The evening went well, and Carol in his most expansive way was most complimentary. Referring to my names spot, he would arrange for me to do his name on his television show, later on in the year. We would get together on this. Also, would I care to do another spot on his Thursday evening show. I did so. No payment for either show.

From my point of view, since I never heard any more from Carol regarding his promises for the future, I learnt three important things. First, the male singer who did all the auditioning for him, and sang a number of songs to open each evening's performance, had a voice that was playing up and needed all sorts of lubricants to settle it down. How vulnerable a voice is. No sing, no money. If my chalks break I can still manage, with a stub.

Second, I got to know Lan Clifford, the Swansea Orchestra conductor. He also helped me sort out my music.

Third, I managed to work on a large stage with all the trimmings. I saw the blackness that is the audience when the stage lights are on, and the house lights go out. Also the danger of spotlights when they throw your chalk tray in shadow and you can't see the colour of your chalks.

All in all, I was quite happy with what the experience taught me. Oh, and I rather think the proposed TV spot on Carol's show must have slipped his mind!

After we'd decided that I should try my luck up in the Smoke, I phoned the local paper and a reporter came and took the story, plus a picture. The world, or rather the Swansea bit of it, then knew Harry Brooks was going to seek fame and fortune up in London. I was shown standing by my easel, chalk poised at the ready, with Deena and the two boys, smiling encouragement, alongside.

I had made a larger easel for this venture. The case holding it all was quite heavy, but manageable. Dad said I could stay with him in Greenford, so with the wishes of my family and friends ringing in my ears, I took the train up. From Paddington I took the tube to Picadilly to the Foster's Agency office. I struggled into the very upmarket premises and enquired about Mr Zahl.

On looking back I just can't help bursting out laughing at my position at that moment. I don't know what I expected to happen. Probably, Hyamy would say, 'Oh Brian, a lovely boy, come in lad, how is Brian, er! what's his name'?

I never got past the secretary. The foyer to his office was bigger than our whole upper floor. And I rather think you couldn't see if anyone had leather or plastic soles on their shoes, because of the carpet pile. I could feel Eros outside in the traffic, enjoying the encounter.

Anyway, I got the feeling it was unlikely that I would be able to whip out my easel, do a couple of quick drawings, and land a contract, on that afternoon.

I was kindly referred to a lesser agent, who would come up and see me if I could get a show. He suggested he might get me a week at Collins Music Hall, Islington. Off I went to Greenford. At least dad was pleased to see his boy.

It had also been suggested I could try the Nuffield Centre too. So I tried. A very charming lady was very pleased to give me a showing in the centre and I told the agent about this.

The Nuffield Centre was a kind of stage door canteen. Troops of all kinds and nationalities formed the audience and regular shows were put on there. I did a spot. It was quite successful (so I thought) and was given an open invitation by the organiser to come and perform any time I could manage.

The agent had not been able to see it for himself but a friend had looked in instead. He was sorry. ' I must learn how to 'sell myself '. (I didn't quite know what he meant by this). I enquired about Collins? Sorry!

I could understand that I was extremely raw material to these already practising, entertainer employers. I didn't understand the terminology, but I knew I was an entertainer. So I went to Islington to see Mr Lake. He owned Collins. I told him what had happened and bless the man he said ' bring your stuff up and I'll have a look at you'. So it was that I came out onto the stage at Collins, with a single bulb on centre stage and with Lew and a few stagehands seated about midway back in an empty theatre, I did my stuff.

Lew Lake gave me a week's work commencing in three weeks time. Twelve pounds for the week. One pound per show. It didn't occur to me that we wouldn't grow fat on that sort of money. I was more excited to ring Deena to say I'd got the job. Dad was pleased as well. Mum had never seen me draw and work on a stage. What a pity. I'm sure she would have felt very proud of her son.

I returned to Mumbles to prepare for the great day. Lan Clifford helped me with my music. It wasn't easy, I needed to talk whilst drawing sometimes, and to fit it all in was difficult. I should have rehearsed a lot more. Looking back I realise I needed producing. This didn't come easy. I was a natural performer. What didn't roll off the cuff naturally I found very difficult. What I couldn't do I didn't do.

To solve this I had to learn. I also had a lot of other things to do. Front of house pictures for a start. Bryn's son Carl, also a good photographer, presented me as a suave lad quietly holding a cigarette with a drawing on my easel forming a background. I was very pleased with it. (Very nearly film star material)!

Anyway, it duly appeared in Collins foyer showing a close-up of the 'Lad with the chalks'. I couldn't be the wizard this time, there was another one on the same bill a little higher up than me. He was from Australia. Dalton was his name, a magician. Billed as 'Dalton, the Wizard of Aussie'.

During my week there I dressed with him in the bowels of the earth under the theatre. The dressing room was just like a dungeon. Painted cream, but still out of this world. He'd come to England to try and be seen by Cissie Williams, who was the booking manager for Moss empires.

If he was unsuccessful he was going back 'down under', to plenty of well-paid work. I liked him, we got on well. He offered me good advice, born of experience. He did a silent magic routine. His makeup was a cross between Chester Conklin and Charlie Chaplin. As far as I can remember, Cissie Williams, (only a name to me), did come in one evening, but she never stayed to see him.

I attended the band call. This is a rehearsal of the artists' music. (The term used in the profession was, ' have you got your dots?)' The conductor Tommy, soon put me out of my misery. Going through my music, 'No, you don't want that. No, that's all right for the London Philharmonic, we've only got Alf on the trumpet'.

'We'll put that little gallop in there, you know it boys? Tum, tum, tum, ti tum. Yes, that's all right, you just keep going, we'll keep up'. In the end he took half a dozen sheets of music from me for the band, whilst I took the great bulk of it back to the dressing room, unwanted. This was no way a criticism of friend Lan, I just hadn't given him the best instructions.

In the Welsh clubs, Billy Longman used to play round me. Protect me sort of thing, and fade out when I spoke. I still don't know whether the orchestra got used to me at Collins. They were kind and their professionalism bore me along effortlessly. I had no complaints and enjoyed it all.

The great day came. I presented myself on the Monday morning, getting settled in, I prepared for the show. I was first on after the opening dancers. So on first house on a Monday evening, about six thirty, I was out there. A working class lad from North Kensington 'having a go'.

I don't remember much about the actual mechanics of it, but I was aware there weren't many out front. It seemed very sparse indeed and how I managed to get names from these few I'll never know.

I don't think I did badly for applause, and the orchestra did extremely well, so if it wasn't there, I never missed it. I was then told 'it will improve later on'. This was due to the fact that it was a continuous programme. Not two separate houses.

The few gentlemen out front whom I played to first were probably there early to ensue they were able to see the nudes twice on one night. Yes. Nudes. I'm sure they didn't rush to see me.

There was one hitch. As I took the sheets of paper of the easel I was placing them on the floor of the stage. Afterwards, a shadowy figure emerged from the wings saying this was not to be. He was the fireman. It was against stage regulations to have loose papers on the stage during a performance. For the second show that evening I had to take off the drawings, roll them in a ball and throw them off stage to the waiting fireman.

Next day I was furiously at work making a triangular net arrangement that hung suspended between the legs of the easel, and was
partially hidden by the fringe of my chalks tray. He passed this as OK, so I continued popping the finished sketches into the net.
When the running order for the Tuesday shows came out I had
been promoted. The two lads who were doing a double stand-up comedy routine and had followed me the day before, were now first on after the dancing girls. I'd heard comments about the show going down with a bump after the boys' efforts, so they were put on earlier to enable the show to pick up again after they had done their act. It's an ill wind!

I had two agent's cards sent down asking me to get in touch. Also on the Wednesday the family brought dad in to see me. I had another visitor towards the end of the week. He was a friend of my sister Rose. Also an entertainer, Phil Darben had a cabaret and stage act that he performed with his wife Wendy. I had asked him to come in to see me work and comment. He performed a rope spinning and boomerang throwing act that was very successful.

So Phil came and helped me with suggestions and ideas that might be useful for my future. He also brought copies of The Stage and Variety, showbiz papers. We went through all the venues and agents that may or may not be able to place an act like mine. He also mentioned in passing all the venues that had closed down, or had been turned into supermarkets or bingo halls.

This information with the amount of money I was then getting for a week's work at Collins, seemed to shout out it was a very slim foundation to run two homes on. My prospects seemed almost impossible viewed in such a down to earth way. All the small variety theatres had gone long ago. Bingo halls were also moving into cinemas. TV was making an impact. People stayed at home to be entertained. Anyway, I didn't make a very determined effort to use the agent's cards or get in touch afterwards.

Although I was not disillusioned with show business by any means, I thought that this part of it was not for me. So I returned to Mumbles, a lot wiser, but undaunted. I can't remember whether Brian ever mentioned his friend Hyamy Zahl again!

Chapter 10

On the Big Stage

It was about this time that we went on holiday for a week to Butlin's in Pwllheli, North Wales. It cost forty to fifty pounds all told for the four of us, and I never got over paying for it. All that money for one week, but it was a real eye opener for us.

The programme of activities was staggering. You could not possibly do it all but the effort of trying ensured the day sped by like lightning. We made friends with a young family similar to our own. The two wives would even enjoy themselves going to do the laundry. I would race around fixing up the boys in their events whilst also trying to work a game of table tennis in for myself. As our boys were always used to early evening bedtime, we managed to get the chance to see how the other half lived. The half with money! I have three particular memories.

One night we saw a fancy dress competition was due to start. A quick decision and we bounded back to our chalet. Shortly I emerged as the 'Butlin ballerina'. Deena rigged me up in an outfit made mainly of newspaper. Even the tu-tu. I'd made a fairy's wand out of the Evening Echo. We dashed back to the ballroom to learn that the judging was over. I walked out front. The bandleader saw me and gave me a lead-in with some ballet musical number, and I responded with an impromptu dance. It was well received I was awarded a special prize.

The second thing was the Sunday People newspaper, which was sponsoring an adult talent contest, to be held on camp. We auditioned for a bit of fun. I went to the camp carpenter for a couple of battens, borrowed a blackboard, and with a four inch nail through the centre made a make-shift easel. No colour, just white chalk, and a wet rag to rub out with. My holder of the rubber-outer was of course Deena, who else?

We got through to the camp finals, but no further. I enjoyed it, and had held my own.

My eyes were opened by the fact that one entrant just happened to have a ventriloquist's dummy in his suitcase. It must have cost him a fortune. I then realised these shows were for real. A lot of people try very hard to get to greater things by winning a contest such as this. We had only gone in for a laugh. The fact that we had got into the camp show satisfied us. I also remember the camp officials that were running it. We met them a year or so later but I will relate that further on.

The third thing was as we were leaving the camp at the end of the week, in the coach. Deena said to me it was a shame there were no jobs like redcoats when she was younger and a free agent. These proved to be prophetic words on her part, because two years later we were to arrive at Pwllheli again, but as redcoats this time.

On our return to Mumbles we realised how lovely it was where we were living. Overland Road bounded our house on its way to the bays. The other side of the road was grassy, hilly and unspoilt. It was known as the woods. At the top of the woods was a meadow. Ferns flourished in abundance. On a sunny day it was quite magical. A perfect playground for all the youngsters. I lost no end of tools that went mysteriously missing up there.

Michael had a gang, as did Jim. They would move around like an amoeba. A single-cell life entity. Getting up to their various stunts, one quite separate from the other. About a two-year age difference separated them all. Michael's gang was most noticeable for climbing and such. He fell out of a tree, breaking his arm. Once when he slipped on the stairs, managed to keep his balance, and sped past me through the open front door saying he was 'all right' on the way.

It was Michael who caught scarlet fever. Isolated upstairs he used to confer through a sheet hung over the doorway, to friends and family in a well-conducted manner. In the Dick Whittington panto he was an eastern potentate. The way he delivered from his exotic throne, the words 'down vile dogs', hardly matched his cherubic features. He used this costume to attend a fancy dress party in the Brangwyn Hall, Swansea.

Deena delivered him in a pristine condition, as did some couple of hundred other parents who were carrying out their duties. When we went to collect our little angels a couple of hours later, we all wondered what the Dickens had befallen our fancy-dressers!

Michael's turban was un-wravelled somewhat, and flapping about. His small make-up moustache was untidily littered across his face, and his eastern shoes were demolished. He was flushed as though he'd been hard at something or other and seemed as though he'd enjoyed himself. It was a far, far cry from when he was a daffodil.

Jim's lot seemed a little more studious. He was being taught the violin by Bryn. It was quite something to see him with a small violin tucked under his chin, playing a duet with his teacher. What a shame videos were not available then! We could also have captured another side of Bryn. A multi-talented man, self taught photographer, and like me a carpenter. He had a rare wit. Once during a celebration at Christmas time, he came into the room carrying a plateful of toast. Each piece of toast was an inch square with one baked bean on each.

Another time, after a knock on the door, we opened it to see his perception of Toulouse Lautrec busking on the fiddle. He was kneeling on a pair of shoes, to foreshorten his torso, with his cap on the floor in front of him for any donations. He and his brother Dave could liven up any party.

Jim, always a trier, spotted an ad in Exchange & Mart for a magical trick that consisted of what appeared to be a tiny washing mangle. The trick was you rolled in a blank paper and out came a real pound note. He thought he could use it to make money for his gang.

He saved the two shillings and sixpence and sent a letter with a 'post lorder' which finished with 'if you don't know what I want, look back in the letter and see.'

Both Michael and Jim were fascinated by the amusement machines on Mumbles Pier, and some time later Jim successfully made a one-armed-bandit using second-hand telephone parts. I must have made the cabinet. He was later to start his own amusement machine business based in Bognor Regis.

The great joy was when both gangs could play with their pennies and when all money was lost, inventor Jim could open up the back and re-distribute the money. Not a bit like real life this. But to both gangs a bit of heaven!

They were all bright lads and most of them passed their exams later. One day when I came in from wrestling with the building side, Deena said there was a letter for me to look at. Before I read it through, she would tell me the background for it. On seeing an advertisement regarding children's entertainers for Butlin's camps, she'd idly written away asking for details.

Quite unexpectedly she'd had a letter back, by return of post no less, from Wally Goodman, Assistant Entertainments Manager, Butlin's Ltd. Enclosed were two return train tickets and an invitation to come up to Oxford Street for a chat. Well we were very excited about this, but in no way did we ever think that with two boys aged eight and ten, that we'd be able to arrange our affairs to enable both us to become professional entertainers. Even if it was only for a Season.

This is where we underestimated the family response. When they learned about the tickets, they soon decided to make us go up to London for a start. When we arrived in Wally Goodman's office, I had not gone empty-handed. We had taken a load of props down to the local photographer's studio, and he'd done a rush job of a set of prints showing our different ideas, costumes and props. These I duly showed at the interview.

He was impressed, or said so anyway. He also said the chairs we were sitting on had seated Harry Corbett, Sooty and Sweep's mentor, at an earlier date, and he never got what he was offering us then. Twenty-five pounds per week, all found. For the Season just starting too.

This was 1958. We said we'd let him know, and walked out dazed, but delighted. It still couldn't happen but wasn't it nice to be asked?

The family was very firm though. We had got this far so they would look after the boys between them. At the time it all seemed like a dream. I got to work furiously on more props, thought out new schemes, and Deena got on with our wardrobes.

So it came to pass on that lovely sunny day in May of fifty-eight we packed everything into the Ford van and pointed its bonnet towards Pwllheli camp. One hundred and seventy six miles from Mumbles. The ride was magnificent. The Welsh countryside and the mountains looked superb, the only sadness, leaving the boys. But we had already booked them in for a holiday later in the season.

We arrived on schedule, three days before the campers arrived on the Saturday morning. The rest of the staff were seemingly very friendly. We found out who were on the entertainments side, the Redcoats, and who were on the supervisory staff of other departments, the Bluecoats.

There was a similarity with my army days with the kitting us all out. Blazers two, white trousers two, tie one, transparent mackintosh one, shirts, nylon, three. Yes, very much the quartermaster's stores. It wasn't surprising really, the boss of entertainments was a Colonel Basil Brown. Wally Goodman must also have been an officer, according to his moustache. And the man in charge of us there in Pwllheli, Entertainments Manager, Johnny Johnson, also had a service air about him.

On reflection the Q.M. bit was suitable for the occasion and worked quite well. After all, the camp itself had only recently been vacated by the Navy. Something else also reminded me of my first days in the services. Deena and I never stopped running for nearly sixteen weeks! Next day, Thursday, we all set too with brushes and brooms and did the cleaning chores of our respective areas of work and influence.

When we'd finally accepted the job of children's entertainers for the coming season a meeting was arranged, prior to the camp opening, between me, Deena, and Mr Johnson.

This was in a hotel in Swansea. He showed us previous camp programmes and then we got down to our own junior programme. The set pieces of fancy dress competitions, swimming gala, Junior sports, young Tarzan competition etc., were all pencilled in to fit in with the complete camp programme. Apportioning halls, dance floors, stages, and other venues for all our events, so inter-linking with everybody else.

Deena and I were to be the camp Auntie and Uncle and have two or three redcoats to help us run our part. We learned also there would another full-time children's entertainer on camp. Harold Manley. A first class Punch man and ventriloquist. This was a jolt to me. I thought I had that job. I could see the sense later on with this arrangement.

It was a full time job running the whole programme plus any administrative work that's necessary when your weekly input of children on camp, in peak periods, numbered two and a half thousand. We had another jolt too. We had already started to use Enid's childhood name of Deena on our headings, thus, Harry Brooks and Deena. With the year's programmes already printed, there was a mix up. Instead of Harold Manley becoming Uncle Harold, he'd been billed as Uncle Harry.

So I couldn't be Uncle Harry then. It was suggested by Johnny Johnson that I'd become Uncle Hal. So we became Hal and Deena Brooks. And we liked it. From then on Equity was informed that henceforth I was to be called Hal Brooks. It's strange how things come about. It also helped in another way. Being addressed as Hal, I thought Ah! Entertainments. If it was Harry, building, early days and family.

The outcome of our chat in Swansea was that we included many ideas of our own to augment those of Mr Johnson's. Deena put in a poetry competition and we were amazed, throughout the season, at the standards reached by the children's efforts. The Chase of the Week, (there was always a chase in camp), was changed from Captain Blood to a fearsome monster from another planet. A well-known stage personality also working the season, Al Paige, volunteered to be my monster.

With a stocking over his face and big clogs on, he really looked fearsome. Before ending up caught, and thrown in the swimming pool, he got some very rough treatment from 'the mob'. He was up to it though. Any chaser not playing fairly soon found the Al's clogs very heavy on their tootsies. Deena and I never claimed all our ideas were original but we always tried to be a bit different. All credit to the management, they always encouraged us to be just that.

It wasn't surprising how many people broke into show business via Butlin's. Opportunity is a great thing. The many times we had to try out new things during the season was to be our greatest strength in the coming years. One of our main tools to do this job was the original camp theatre. This had now become the Junior Theatre and seated six hundred. It was well-equipped and appointed, and quite secluded.

You had to go through an arcade to get in and it was a haven of peace when not in use. In fact we used to let the camp pop group rehearse in there occasionally. That season it was Rory Storm and the Hurricanes.

Rory's drummer at the time was Ringo Star who was destined later to become very famous as the drummer in the Beatles. They could rehearse in comfort in there. They didn't get much peace in their own dance hall over on the other side of the camp. Their enthusiastic followers and fans couldn't follow them into our theatre, and they were very grateful for it.

At peak in August the camp had a capacity for ten thousand campers. On one side of the camp were congregated all unmarrieds and young couples. The other, the South side, was for families and our patrons, the children. A bridge separated the complex loosely. Mainly we were over on the South side but occasionally we had to go to the other side, and if you walked it you knew you'd done it. Fortunately there was a free bus service.

But the bit about running for sixteen weeks was a fact. There was plenty of space to run in. So it was that on the Saturday of the camp opening we were both on railway station duty. Welcoming the campers. Giving out smiles and welcomes as only redcoats can, when it started to rain. A bald announcement came over the loudspeakers saying that Auntie Deena and Uncle Hal would shortly be in the Mongomery Ballroom providing fun and games for all and sundry. That's when we commenced running.

Poor Deena. She always runs anyway. So we were thrown in at the deep end. We met in the ballroom wearing dazed expressions carefully disguised as smiles. Fortunately it wasn't as frantic as we had expected. For one thing we'd had three days on camp before opening, and knew where the ballroom was. The campers had to find it first. So we got our hand in during the first few hours of opening, and we both went to sleep that night very tired but peaceful. We'd overcome the first hurdle and the rest now seemed easy. We had managed successfully with a piano and Deena organising floor games. Anyway, when we are together, there's not much to daunt us.

Next day we picked up all the interested children and parents during the morning and they were usually still with us at the end of the week, Friday. Some children never found us. They were quite content with indoor games, following dads and mums with their interests, and generally being quite independent. This wasn't an accident. The whole programme was carefully put together to spread people about comfortably.

If the whole of the two thousand children had come with us we'd have been swamped. Similarly, if there was a popular item imminent in the theatre, and the theatre capacity wasn't enough to hold everybody, I would put on a special programme in the Junior theatre to draw off the children and parents about five minutes before the other show started. Other redcoats would similarly use other ploys to spread people out. An extra whist drive, a longer session of Tombola, later to become known as Bingo.

Critics of Billy Butlin used to say we regimented the crowds, but this sort of persuasion left plenty of choice on the part of the camper. Nobody was forced to do anything.

I had a meeting with Johnny Johnson, or his deputy, Knocker White, every morning to sort out any foreseeable difficulties. We were kept informed about the weather that could throw spanners into any well planned programme. These two were always available. Inconspicuous to the campers in their smart navy blue blazers, but every redcoat knew they were there. There was not much that went on in camp that they did not know about. They knew all the answers, but they were both charming and tough characters.

My impression of Billy B was that he was a shrewd no-nonsense hard worker himself and gathered similar folk around him. I was also impressed by the loyalty shown to him. It was all about work.

The one thing common on camp to all who were there was there wasn't a lot of pay about, but there were a lot of opportunities to display our wares. To meet similar people, working in a holiday atmosphere. To get away for a few weeks. Some folk of course misinterpreted Billy's advertised job descriptions that stated that after you had finished your work all the facilities of the camp were yours to savour of an evening, and on your day off.

He never let on to say how much you had to do before the word 'finished' appeared. I'm definitely not saying it was all grim and hard work. No, the change itself was a big draw. Many a lonely person found a haven from living on their own for a season. Pwllheli holiday camp was a lovely camp in a beautiful part of Wales.

Only one sad occasion I remember was a lady of about fifty-five, a cleaner, tallying up what was left in her pay packet after stoppages. She was in tears. Fringe benefits are no real substitute for money in your purse.

With the redcoats the amount of pay was a considered risk. Consider it as a show date and there were lots of advantages. You could let agents know where you would be for sixteen weeks. Also you might get into one of the many shows that were ongoing. The Redcoats Show, late night cabarets, all could be aimed for, and used. A bit different from my one performance show in the Nuffield Centre! Similarly it was a good place for agents to place their artistes. You had to pay the agent for doing it but he could earn his commission by directing any booker to go and see his boy or girl working for a season at Butlin's.

If the agent did his job properly he could get a better pay deal for his artists. I know a group that left Butlin's because they wouldn't up their money for a season. The following summer they were back. They had been booked in by Reeves and Landport, at much better money. It's a strange world.

Another time an orchestral conductor working for Billy gave me a wry smile when I voiced my opinion about the lack of money. He knew I was a babe in arms concerning these matters. It was obvious he knew not all were underpaid while working for Billy B.

Uncle Harry was a very good children's entertainer. Harold Manley was in his sixties, He had two children and I also met his wife during the season. He was cast in the old mould. He'd performed his Punch and Judy show nearly everywhere. He'd told me that it had been very hard doing the beaches, relying solely on what was put in the hat to see you through to the next date. He would work all day, weather permitting. His hands would be above his head for so long he felt that the blood was coming out of his shoulders.

We had decided to split the evening show into two halves, he first and Deena and I finishing. To fill up his parts on the programme he divided his Mister Punch into parts one and two. His other puppets also delighted me. His Chinese conjurors and jugglers act also performed in the Punch set-up, and these oriental characters were charming. They used to spin plates on sticks and do other balancing tricks. I've not seen it done since.

With their pigtails flying, and low bows to the waist, they were a perfect change to the violence of Punch. His fourth act was a boxing match, and as with all his work, it was very exciting and funny. Finally, his ventriloquist's doll was named Jimmy. A red-haired dummy that reflected some of Harold's own hidden aggressive personality. He was not a violent or unkindly man, and made friends with the children easily, but he knew how to discipline unruly behaviour on the part of his young audience.

He would use Jimmy to pour scorn on them from his knee. His opening greeting from his doll was 'Ladles and Gillpots'. It never failed to make an impact on the children. He was not one to try and cover up his mouth movements too much. The fact was that the doll had such a strong personality, he'd never had to. Once Jimmy spoke nobody looked at Harold.

Apart from sharing the evening show he would do an occasional show in the morning. He also did a show in the nursery. It all worked quite well. Deena and I were very keen, and Harold, an old hand, never stopped anybody from working. It helped eke out his own material and we were all happy with the arrangements.

One very important and very interesting job each week was running the Junior talent contest. For this Deena was admirably talented in her own right, with bags of patience, tact and ability to put people at ease. Johnny Johnson saw this quality too. He once gave her the job of running the Bonny Babies competition. All babies are lovely. All mums think theirs is best. The tact required to compere this show was enormous. Deena did it admirably.

The talent show was a longer drawn out affair. Each week she would have to audition between sixty and seventy children. These would range from a hurried Ba Ba Black Sheep, to a very precocious and sometimes very talented youngster who was there solely to get through to the finals. Their talents were very far ranging, and we met many charming and friendly nice young folk and their parents, doing this job.

We also had our fair share of 'stage mums'. Deena was up to the task though, she wouldn't be bullied. So by the Thursday she had sorted out about fifteen finalists, and with me compering we moved over to the Gaiety Theatre for the show. Our pianist, Elisse Relnah, became a great friend of ours, her accompaniment on the show was first class. She and Deena worked very well together and between them I always had a first class show to present.

The contest was in two sections. Up to six years and then to twelve years. We would get a finalist in each group, each week, who would win a place in the camp finals at the season's end. A free week's holiday to come back for the contest. There was then a cup and cash prizes for the winners.

Two young people I remember from that first year. A young trumpeter Nigel Hopkins, and a dancer, Lamona Snow. Deena and I enjoyed seeing them on TV occasions afterwards and always got a kick out of being present at the very beginning of their careers. We did our best at the job and thoroughly enjoyed it.

We sometimes learned from campers that they had rung up head office enquiring which camp we would be working that season, then booked accordingly. There was another bonus with the talent competitions. If we had any well-known entertainers on camp that week, Mr Johnson would invite them to judge our show. Artistes who were always willing to help us were the Springfield Trio.

Two members of it, Tom and sister Dusty Springfield, did this many times for us throughout the season. I also noted when Tom was doing his act, playing guitar, he rested his foot on a stand similar in shape to one I had made to become a drum for our children's band. We had both used an empty cement drum to do the job. We had both recognised its other possibilities, suitably disguised of course.

Another memory from this first season. Elisse, our pianist, remembered playing for me as a camper in 1956, with my mock-up easel and favourite person wiping the board for me.

Running a weekly programme for sixteen weeks had in a strange way given me the power to remember how many wet Wednesdays we'd had in that time. It's difficult running a sports day when it's wet, and on that day we were supposed to be out in the field, except of course! That's how I remembered all sorts of days that Summer.

We also had a swimming gala, regatta, and sports event. The winners would get medals for their prowess. Gold, silver and bronze. These were always highly coveted and preferred in most instances to prizes. As were our certificates for poetry and talent contests.

I don't know how much they actually cost, but to the recipients they were priceless. The chief hostess of the camp was Pat Johnson, Johnny's wife. She was responsible for all prizes, and always did us proud. Sometimes with mix ups, mistakes, and extra items not in the programme, we always seemed to need more, and she always co-operated generously. A popular adult event, the Lucky Dip, I copied for our own juniors. It was a game show run on the stage for all different ages. We always had a lovely selection of prizes to display on the stage for the children to compete for.

This first year, 1958, opened for us with a fantastic showing of roses between lines of wooden chalets. Butlin's gardeners always gave strict instructions to the flowers and bushes to flower on opening day. They always seemed to. It was an in joke.

We had jokes amongst the redcoats too. One of these was 'where are the nearest toilets? Answer, In 'P' line'. It was as a matter of fact. The chalet lines were marked alphabetically. That year we could still trace Butlin's efforts to get away from earlier holiday camp amenities. Most of the gents' toilets were modern in construction. But in one part of the camp, built in the early days, there were a couple of urinals, reminding us of the tarred walls that had to suffice then. BB had come a long way since then. In another part of the camp was a glimpse of the future. These were in the form of double-decker chalets. A retrograde step I thought, but very necessary for financial reasons I suppose.

One big bonus came from working so hard. Deena and I could eat anything and everything, without spoiling our figures. There's nothing like being able to being able to eat like a horse, especially if you think you're working like one. And we enjoyed our food. We sat with the campers and ate the same fare. I thought it was excellent value. It was also adequate. One thing for which I will always defend Billy Butlin, he always gave value for money.

It was really true that after you'd paid your tariff you only needed half a crown (twelve and a half new pence) to pay for your chalet key. With this key you could then draw your tennis racket, leaving the key as your deposit. It was the same with other sports equipment on the camp. Then when you left camp after your holiday the half crown was returned to you on handing in your key.

We all know you do spend more when you are there, but you don't have to. And with all the shows, all the facilities, and all the services included in your tariff I always thought BB gave good value. This was very true if you had children with you.

There were many interesting people working on camp that year. One of these, a singer, used to be seen by us every night as we passed the Continental Bar, on our way back to our chalet. Wearing a green blazer, (the colour used to denote an entertainer on camp), and suede shoes, with guitar at the ready by a piano loaded with pints from grateful campers, was our friend Clinton Ford. He always gave us a wave. He was a very popular one-off entertainer. (Deena and I were always being offered drinks for looking after their children so well, but actually, as children's entertainers, we were happier enough not to be seen in the bars.)

Our expert snooker player and coach that year was champion John Pullman. A very modest, nice-mannered person I remember. We also met Johnny Leach, the best that table tennis had to offer, also Harry Venner, another expert player of the game. We also had plenty of talent among the redcoats. The Redcoats Show was a great event each week. It wasn't easy to get a place in it. The standards of performance were very high.

Every Sunday evening we met the stars that came for the Variety show that started the week of with a bang. Before the show got underway the management put on a five-minute item that introduced all the camp staff representatives. These ranged from cooks to chalet maids, security men to the Padre. Deena and I had our own spot as the camp's Auntie and Uncle. You can imagine being on stage was a bit frightening for some of these very important people, so sometimes it was a redcoat dressed up in their place. This led to a weekly 'in' quiz. Who was who this week? It was all light-hearted and great fun.

There was a moment when the musical play Oliver was having a great success in London. BB decided we should all vacate the stage singing 'Consider Yourself'. It was a great success and such a lovely tune to march off to. We left the stage in two lines marching down the side aisles, singing at the tops of our voices. Full marks to the composer, Lionel Bart, possibly a friend of his.

When it was over we went straight to our theatre to see to our own audience. Deena would have a little chore to do before joining me. Throughout the season she would ask the variety performers on that evening to autograph her tablecloth. Later she would embroider the signatures as decorations. Most of them did so most kindly. Many had a special drawing worked into their name. It was a grand idea and we got a lot of fun out of these items when shown to the family later.

The subject of autographs brings back memories of the enthusiasm the children showed throughout their stay. Over the season we must have obliged thousands of pleading children, and adults, who wanted to get your signatures in their book. (Someone in the camp had a good thing going selling these).

At first it was common for some of us to add a little message as well. You soon realised that a simple signature, easy to execute, had to suffice, otherwise you wouldn't get much work done. One type of person could become a real hindrance to you. This was 'the regular camper'. They were always recognised by the mass of season's badges on their lapels, indeed all over their clothes if they had enough. This oddity came about because as the law stood then the complexity of drinking regulations demanded that we and each camper were required to become a member of the camp club, before entering the bars.

So each year a different club badge was issued. Very well designed, these metal and enamel pin badges were coveted by the regular camper. There were always anecdotes of various years to relate to you. Quite OK in the rare moments of having the time to listen. Rare is the operative word here. Hence, see loud display of circular ornaments, take evasive action.

The insistence on Butlin's publicity at this time was that we, the redcoats, were there for your comfort and holiday enjoyment. This was aimed at the lonely and the shy. But as always in these broad generalities some wrong interpretations were placed on them by our patrons. If you divide ten thousand campers by about forty redcoats you can imagine if we were shared out equally many campers wouldn't even get a button.

Deena and I chose to be redcoats. Later on, the management asked us to choose a different coloured material we liked, to denote the special position we had with the children. We very rarely used this other costume because as 'reds' we benefited by the great mass of good will that had been generated by other redcoats of previous years. We were instructed to be host and hostess in the nicest possible way. A cheery smile, a hello and a good morning here and there worked wonders at relaxing people. And we were holiday-makers in reality.

Before the camp opened all we had about the place were great, plainly constructed factory-like buildings of little appeal to eye or heart. Sprinkle campers about the place with a redcoat here and there and

the place became alive, solely due to the skill and friendliness of our team. Even if it was pouring with rain here was someone ready to joke about it with you. It was a lovely job. We enjoyed doing it.

The reverse of the coin were those campers who took advantage of us for their own ends. Once, being in our theatre one morning, I saw the door open and in came a toddler about two years old, being guided through the opening by the arms of her mother. What I took to be the elder sister followed and took the hand of the younger child. In whispers they were being told to go to Uncle Hal.

The older sister was about four years old. I soon moved quickly to catch the mother and firmly handed back her charges. She mumbled something about she thought we were there to do this sort of thing. All our girls, Helen, Marilyn, and Deena had many times to be wary about having young children unloaded onto them whilst their parents 'popped off' for the day. We weren't caught out many times though.

The vast majority of parents were only too pleased to allow their child to accompany us on our walks and treasure trails. Keeping a discrete distance behind, in case they were missed. Children come in all shapes and sizes. I am never surprised at the many varieties and types of child that abound.

One boy, about six years old, had a peculiar way of showing his liking for me. Whenever he saw me in the morning he would tear up to me and punch me in the stomach. At least he did this the first time. For the rest of the week I kept a careful watch out for his affections. Just why he reacted in this way I just couldn't say. It had never occurred to me before this that I even faintly resembled any sort of punchball!

During our evening shows we would have children up on the stage to take part in games etc. Peculiar to Butlin's we never seemed to have toilets in the right places. We never had one in the Junior Theatre. Consequently there was lots of waiting for the shows to finish before dashing out to the loo.

One lad up for a game sought to find a spot backstage to save a journey. Nobody would have known except for the slope of the stage. A thin trickle of moisture wended its way downstage towards the footlights, precisely indicating where he was relieving himself. We all had a good laugh, audience included!

I was always surprised who made up our audiences. The bulk of it was children, some accompanied by their parents. We also got a lot of older folk. Grans and grandads. Many of them said how much they enjoyed watching the children enjoying themselves. They would be regular visitors to our shows.

Deena had marvellous control over our audiences. She could get hush very quickly. And in a place like a holiday camp, with the children mostly strangers to themselves, it makes for a reserve amongst them. To relax them takes great skill. A lesson very early reinforced how important control is. A camper came up to me and said he'd been a conjuror for many years, and as he had a couple of props with him could he do a bit one night? I didn't mind, it would be a change. Neither Harold nor I did magic, so I said yes to ten minutes the following night.

Well, it soon became apparent that we had different ideas of order. He'd hardly started before he'd got them all doing Charlie Carolli's answering game routine. 'Oh no you won't,' Oh yes we will'. It was bedlam in a few minutes. The place was packed out too. We hustled him off as soon as we could without hurting his feelings. This sort of behaviour is very easy to start, hard to control, and always works against the well-behaved child and younger element. They get lost in the rumpus.

I learned from Deena very early on that if you can talk quietly to a child, and indeed a whole audience, you can get rapt attention. If you start shouting, they shout back, and nobody is heard in the end.

You cannot be part of a temporary town the size of Pwllheli camp without marvelling at its complexity. About ten thousand people gathered together, however temporary, life goes on. Life also ends in some cases too. An elderly camper may die naturally whilst on camp. A younger person may suffer a heart attack, but the campers hardly ever knew. An accident might make a more public spectacle but mostly the traumas were coped with efficiently, quietly and with a minimum of fuss.

On Saturdays a quite astonishing metamorphosis happened. The camp's population changed dramatically. It was on this day Deena and all the children's staff had their day off. It's so hard to describe the difference between Fridays and Saturdays during the season. From being in the limelight on one day and the next to being unknown, was quite dramatic until you got used to it.

We invariably tried to get out of camp, and away from it all. (There's space here for a loud laugh) Ha Ha. On visiting Caernavon Castle on one of these days, a good few miles away. We were high up on the battlements, wallowing in another age, when from the courtyard down below a small child's voice piped out 'Auntie Deena'.

It was on Saturdays we missed our boys. During the week the hectic activities pushed it to the back of your mind. On Saturdays we were very conscious of the fact that Swansea was over a hundred and seventy miles from Pwllheli. Too far for sensible trips to see the boys. Once we had to go home to sort out accommodation difficulties and it was a nightmare. We started early and got off to Mumbles in good time but on the return journey I can distinctly remember the awful fatigue.

Deena was stuffing sweets into me to keep me from dropping off to sleep at the wheel. I was at my wits end trying painfully to hold the wheel of the van steady, to keep it on the road. After a week's hard work and a journey that length, no motorways then, and getting back in twenty-four hours.

We arrived back about 3am Sunday morning, exhausted. We must have been very fit and strong to have done it. This all had to be added up and taken into account for when calculating the true figure of what it cost us to gain our first experience of doing a job of this nature.

The end of season parties were soon upon us. We were amazed at the versatility of our redcoats team. The entertainments party was held in one of the theatres. All the girls worked hard preparing the food, and the men arranged stunts for our own amusement. There was plenty to drink. Knowing the habits of my stomach I stuck to one kind of it. Dubonnet. I made a pig of myself. Deena took me back to our chalet, very sick. We are neither of us drinkers and we didn't stay 'til the end. I was fagged out after doing our normal day's work, and it showed, but it was a great party.

We all said our goodbyes and Deena and I headed for home. Not everybody went home though. Lots of plans had been laid throughout the past weeks between interested parties. A few of the lads went to London to see what they could find in the way of work. Pooling their resources they rented a flat and tried to carry on in the entertainments game.

For the past sixteen weeks their world had poured out pure gold from all its seams. All found, smart rigout and an assured place to do just what they wanted for the best months of the year. Happy campers just waiting to be made happier by your work, it couldn't end? It could, and it did. You have no work to go back to? Well, not quite that. No work that you wanted to do. Back to the grind. Marking the calendar for the next season. Of course I'm relating to the dreamers. The practically-minded had worked hard preparing for the off season.

Their diaries were full of happy camper friends with addresses for them to visit in the ensuing months. Some had managed not to spend any of their wages. There were always generous campers throughout the season who paid their way for them. These were the survivors. I always thought that the lads had given good value and who am I to be cynical about it. I had taken the soft option, back to being a builder again until Christmas brought the works parties to our attention. Back to our boys.

On our return we summed up. We were older and wiser. We were pros. We'd held our own and had been asked to do the same in 1959. And we loved doing it. I have always tried to imagine a world where people are engaged doing work that they are completely happy with. Would the world's ills be reduced if we could work towards that sort of end? Who is the dreamer now?

Back at the bench I was always making props. Working out games. Some good, some quietly put aside and forgotten. I had no trouble thinking up new ideas. After doing a couple of board and counter games I submitted one called 'Beaver Leap' to Butlin's. Their children's club was named 'The Beavers'. The game had plenty of pace but Butlin's seemed only interested in buying the name. I got twenty pounds for it, hoping the game would be used later. But it wasn't.

Deena's speciality was sorting out the rules for these efforts of mine. Expressing them clearly, precisely and with not too many words, she was a gem.

Back to the charm of our village and our boys. It was on a shopping expedition around Christmas time with the two of them. With their spending money clutched tightly we surveyed the shops most thoroughly. It was a jeweller's shop that got their vote. Not one that dealt in the real stuff, but one for the lesser classes. It was a clasp type brooch that read 'Mother'. It was a unanimous decision on their part. The bearing it home. Keeping it hidden and wrapping it for the great day occupied quite a lot of their time, I remember.

We all loved to ride on the Mumbles train to Swansea. By the University was Singleton Park. A favourite location for a Sunday morning trip, when not scavenging for titbits on the beach. Swansea was really blooming again after the terrible bombing raids of the war, so different from when I first saw the city whilst in khaki.

Chapter 11

Inventing Games

We couldn't manage to get away to camp in 1959 but television quiz shows were all the rage and I had an idea for one such game. At the time I really didn't know how much work I would have to do to bring it to fruition. But during the long Winter days I 'worked up' the idea.

We decided to call it 'Your Number's Up'. Two persons were to play against each other in front of a live audience, with a question master in charge. Each player had a board to play, but a dividing screen prevented each player from seeing their opponent's board. The audience could see both.

Each board had two horizontal lines of numbers from one to ten.

Each number could be moved upwards to reveal a blank space or a letter. Under these two lines of ten positions, a famous person, a well-known place, or an object could be concealed. A correctly answered question allowed you to have a letter or blank revealed to you, by putting the 'Number Up'. Hence the game's name. The first to guess correctly who or what was being concealed, was the winner. There were extra shutters hiding clues etc, which could help you make an intelligent guess.

Deena and I developed the game by playing it on paper. We were excited about getting the game accepted. I thought this idea was worth protecting and sought professional advice from a patents attorney. Snags began to be revealed. Most important being cash. It's an expensive job proving the idea is yours.

For the patents people you had to prove your idea was different from, in advance of, or better than previous patents granted. Anyway I applied for a patents pending, and had to substantiate my claims to have thought of a new way of playing a game of sorts.

I made a model of the apparatus and it was one on which the game could be demonstrated. I took this to show a Woolworth's executive buyer in London. I had been told, incorrectly it seemed, that if Woolworth's were interested in getting the game produced they would ask 'one of their suppliers' to take an interest.

The man who I saw who examined my mock-up assured me that if I were to re-design it to enable it to be packed economically in an attractive package, at an economic price, he would ' have another look at it'!

My next move was to send it to Waddingtons, the well-known games manufacturer, for examination. I tried Spears too. No luck. Then I thought to try Chad Toys in Birmingham. I wrote for an appointment and went hot-foot. This was more encouraging. At least I got some advice that sobered me up considerably.

This kind examiner told me categorically that the contents of the box were not so important as the face of the TV personality on its lid. The game didn't get a look-in. It was the personality that did the selling, and would probably require the bulk of the profit made to allow you to use their name. In any case no game calling itself a television quiz would have a chance if it had not been seen on the box.

So he thought as my idea was sufficiently interesting to him, as a producer of games, to deserve a leg-up, he would give me an introduction to a television producer from Granada TV. This was very exciting. More letters, another interview. This time in Oxford Street, London.

I took my model of the game there and played the quiz to one or two people from the world of television. I was told my idea would be considered and a letter would be sent within three weeks. It was sent after a week. Thank you very much, but! It was worth a try though. From here we have to jump about six months on.

A new quiz appeared on Granada TV using a single batch of twenty numbers under which was concealed a saying or motto. No questions were asked to the contestants in this show, but there were obvious similarities to my own game.

These things take a long time to develop so it seems when I showed my game their similar idea was also nearly ready. I was very keen to know whose idea it was, but the credits of the show didn't say who was the originator.

We changed tack after this. We still had a good game so I built a stage set-up and used it at our next season at Butlin's in 1960. A very good friend of ours, Duncan, a redcoat and first class entertainer, was question master and front man, whilst I operated the boards from behind.

We put it into the camp programme with great success. Colonel Brown, head of entertainments, came and saw the quiz show, bought the apparatus and ordered two more set-ups from me. I made them after the season finished and left my one for use at Pwllheli camp.

Deena and I delivered the others to the Margate and Brighton hotels. We were more than delighted that the faith we had in the game had been justified. It's still a good game. I have a half-sized set up that could be used even now in pubs and clubs. The quiz is a perennial exercise of the mind and will always be so. With an element of comedy, it will always be especially so.

About quizzes, past, present and future. I remember one member of redcoat team in Pwllheli, a handsome man with a mop of dark wavy hair. Bill Stuart. He's been seen quite recently on television conducting the Fifteen to One quiz.

Since the last time I met Bill, things have changed somewhat. The colour of our hair for a start. I was really ginger in those days, now we are both a similar shade of white. But at least we still have some, whatever the colour.

There was an awful lot of work also in making up lists of questions. It never occurred to me we could obtain ready-made lists of questions. I always preferred making these up ourselves. I could keep a tighter control over the game that way. After all it is not only the two competitors that are being entertained, but the audience as well. The main thrust of the quiz is to make it enjoyable to all. We wanted the game to flow easily and at a decent pace.

Here we must rely on the skill of the question master. Whenever I was doing the job I always erred on the side of 'easiness'. Long pauses without laughter being involved slowed the game down. I always kept a few 'light relief' questions handy.

One of these sticks in my mind. It is one I used to settle an audience in with. ' Is a paliasse a bed of straw, or a friendly donkey'? With children I would help them by putting the answer in the question. ' Do you know red is the colour of a tomato'? I'm there to entertain, not to get them through their O-levels.

I have several games even now on my shelves, but unless someone expresses an interest in them they will remain firmly on the shelf. Having got an enormous satisfaction dreaming them up, I no longer fancy the task of trying to get them commercially accepted.

Johnny Johnson tried very hard to get us for the 1959 season, but something came up to stop us going. The welfare of our boys. But we did manage to arrange to do the 1960 season. I also asked Dave Stockton if he would care to come as our children's entertainer. He'd be away sixteen weeks. He was delighted. A tradesman, a bricklayer, but like me he'd always wanted to do more with his abiding love, entertainment. Eunice, his wife, had decided to let him have his chance at last.

We rehearsed a lot of pantomime stuff to do in the evening shows. This included school scenes from Babes in the Wood and various pieces lifted from other shows. As the official children's entertainer he was also going to be asked to judge various contests on camp and he enjoyed the prospects immensely.

In a way I was paying him back for all he had taught me since joining the family on getting married to Deena. We worked well together, as I did with his son Bernard, later.

The second season for Billy Butlin showed us more relaxed and able to enter more into the evening shows. In 1958, after we'd seen our young clients out of the theatre of an evening we were expected to join in with all the other reds in the ballroom for what was called 'swanning'. A kind of mix and mingle with the campers. We did this until Goodnight Campers was sung to the tune of Goodnight Sweetheart by all and sundry, to close the dancing, and the evening. In 1960 we were excused this duty.

Instead I did an evening cabaret spot in the Gaiety Theatre. I did a drawings act to keep my hand in and also ran the Numbers Up game with Duncan. This afforded us adult company and was a very welcome change.

We had two Australian girl redcoats that year. Mel and Shirley. Both were teachers. They each had a moped bike. My first sight of them was with their crash helmets on. Neither was a slight person and the smallness of their transport emphasised this. My first thought was we actually have got two martians on site this year! They were very good reds though.

The Butlin's children's Beaver Club was all the rage. All sorts of Beaver bits could be bought as mementos. The Beaver badge could be sold by us and to help sales along a part of the price collected could be kept. A commission. I let the girls have this concession. We even had romance in our gang. A lad from Mumbles was working as a security guard in the camp and he eventually met up with 'our' Mel. So an Aussie girl and a Welsh boy became a very happy couple.

Not having been involved in the selling of badges before, I didn't know how lucrative it could be. I'm told they did very well out of it. This was the year when little elephant money-boxes were being given to the children. Dave turned one into a bubble-blowing Dumbo for his infants' show.

Throughout the week a movie camera team ranged the camp recording the campers' activities on film for a Friday showing. It was well watched. Now and again bits of our programme would be captured. Our walks down to the beach. Sports day. Fancy dress competitions. It was all very exciting.

The camp photographic department were well at it then. One photographer became a good friend. It was years later when I was doing an evening show for a Butlin's gig that we met again. He explained he also tried to get in to the Entertainments Department that year. Not able to do so, he took the job as a photographer. He was currently appearing in the ITV television programme ' the Comedians'.

I only knew him by his nickname, which was Tonk. His job then was to snap everything and everybody on camp. The photographs were then displayed and sold. After being on view for two weeks, our reds got hold of those unsold, and distributed them to whosoever featured. Deena and I have a good few of these photographs to remind us of these happy times.

When the season ended we were determined not to leave the boys again. A new camp in Bognor Regis was being built. I wrote to Wally Goodman, asking if we could work there. I still have the letter from him saying we could work on any of their sites, we only had to ask.

So we chose to leave Mumbles and move to Bognor Regis. We would buy a house there and live out of camp. The season opened in May and we got down there a few weeks beforehand. Duncan and his sister Maimie were running the Butlin's Winter Social Club and they let us stay in the house they rented, to enable us to search around for a property.

We looked for a week but still couldn't solve our problem. It was the same old reason why not. Cash. There were plenty of places for sale but above our price range. So we returned to Mumbles.

After a while Deena came looking on her own. She found a house within an hour or so of leaving the station, bought it, and telephoned me excitedly to say what she'd done.

Apparently she'd seen decorators working in this house and went in to find it had not been put on the market yet. A grand piece of luck and her boldness resulted in the Brooks's family now owning No.1 Argyle Road, and its name, Lyric.

It was very central and from upstairs we could see the sea. The house had been converted into two flats and was being changed back again. At the back of my mind I thought if we could not make a go of it, we could let part of it until we could. Keeping it to myself, I also thought should anything happen to me Deena could use it to earn an income for the family. Also, we were nearer London. Only two hours away, should we ever need to go up there to work.

The builders decorating the house, that had previously been let furnished, soon made it empty for vacant possession by piling all the household furniture and what have you in the back yard. I reported this to the council and they sent a lorry around and relieved us of it.

When cleared, the yard come garden also revealed a building, a sort of shed. It seems in earlier days the other side of road was all fields full of cows and my find was part of a dairy. In my mind's eye it was already being converted into a workshop for my bench.

Things were falling into place. Something else was becoming clear too. Bognor seemed just right for us. The right size and seemingly a really nice seaside town. I felt very comfortable here.

Leaving Mumbles after nearly 10 years was not easy. Jim had passed his O-levels and now we were awaiting Michael's results. So there was an opportunity to move. We had expanded ourselves so much during this period that we were really quite different people.

Unlike our previous move from Potters Bar to Wales, our move to Bognor Regis was heralded by the local newspaper, complete with picture, citing us as Butlin's children's entertainers. What a difference, we'd arrived.

One memory from Oakland Road will always be with me. A little while after mum died, dad came to stay with us for a few weeks. One of the ways we used to entertain our visitors then was by hiring a Grundig tape recording machine from a local shop. We could all make an input, and most of us had not even heard our own voices. It was all very new and sometimes quite hilarious.

With the games we played with the machine it soon became clear that dad was a deeper personality than we'd thought. He was not a bit pushy, so not until joining in with us did he impress us with witty and well-informed comments, which we were hardly expecting.

We loved having him with us. He'd always said that if he ever won the pools he would buy 'Deeny', (he always called her that), a washing machine!

Since I had become self-employed, finding my own work and establishing a new business was not easy. Although the camp had opened for a short period the previous year it was by no means finished. So although I had a season to do in May, I had to earn a living in the meantime.

I tried a week's piece work on a local development site but I didn't like it. I hate piecework. I looked around the local builders for a chippy's job. I remembered the enormous change that took place in the local builders face when he heard I had worked for Butlin's.

I was dropped like a hot potato. Apparently Billy Butlin was not a popular person at that time. It was always the same when he tried to set up in an area. The district would split down the middle either for or against. Those who wanted him for the employment and money he'd bring with him and those who just didn't want him at any price.

So I went and got a job finishing off the camp. I was employed in building the toilet block near the nursery centre. Then at a certain date I took off my carpenter's apron and donned my red coat. There's continuity for you!

We were helped considerably by Deena's sister Coral who came down and lived in our new home with her family, and also looked after our boys. Deena and I lived on camp, but the boys were always popping in to see us and so we could genuinely begin to enjoy our work for a change, no longer feeling guilty about leaving them. Thank goodness for Coral. She's an absolute gem and we couldn't have done it without her.

The days before the camp opened I remember were very hectic. Billy himself came down to see the progress. Of course the place looked like a building site but he soon changed all that. Everything not required was put to the flame. Large bonfires devoured sheets of this and that boarding. Anything that would burn, did burn. To me it was a tremendous waste. Thinking of what I could make of all that material! But very soon the place was really ready and was opened on time.

In Bognor Regis we had more redcoats to help us run the programme. The weather was lovely too. Far too good really. On opening day the camp was all green and freshly turfed.

Then the sun came out and shone, and shone, and shone. The grass curled up and withered away. Our sports field was burnt like cast-iron. It was very difficult to find a safe patch for the children to run their races without the fear of cuts and grazes should they trip and fall.

The grass between the chalets also lasted only a couple of weeks. They looked like lines of slums after a while. In fact the nicest lines of chalets were the redcoat lines. We were away busy all day so our grass never got trampled on like in the other lines.

The redcoat chalets were smaller than the rest of the camp but were adequate. They also had another distinction, they were decorated somewhat. All prettied up with whatever we could 'find' about camp. Quite a few seagulls hung from the ceilings of the plaster variety, having been ' won ' from the Pig and Whistle Bar, along with other knick-knacks.

Our own chalet walls were adorned with some spare props. A giant size revolver in particular. About two feet six in length, and looking very impressive.

It was a very good season and we had a very good team. All new to Deena and me, fresh from Pwllheli. Our junior theatre was not a patch on the one we were used to. After all, the Pwllheli one was a proper theatre with all the trimmings. Our new one was just a stage to put on children's shows.

Still we managed quite well. We were able to use the adult theatres for the talent show. The Gaiety Theatre in Bognor was very big, seating over two thousand campers. There was a bit of a hiccup though over this talent show. The dance band leader that season was Eric Winstone. He was contracted to put an hour's stage show on each week, a kind of band show.

Eric had taken over what we considered as 'our junior talent final' to fill his hour. I protested to new entertainments manager now, Mr Markwell, but to no avail. Eric had got away with it before and intended to do so again. We had no Elisse here and Deena had to use Winstone's pianist, Billy Penrose, for auditioning and accompanying the children to do their bit.

A brilliant musician but a strange fellow in some ways. Anyway, suffice it to say she had a very different season doing the talent in Bognor than before. And I was not needed to compere the show either.

Mentioning Elisse again reminded me of the important part her husband, Walter Swash, played in our seasons in Wales. He was the theatre manager and saw to all my bits and pieces. He soon realised how green I was to the business and was a great help.

The ageing footlights were causing trouble because of weak springs in the lamp holders. Walter, with a spot of solder on the bulbs' contacts, soon had them working again. I was also amazed by a new tool he had which he used to replace torn material from the back of the piano with a fresh piece. It was the first time I'd seen a staple gun. I determined to buy myself one at the first opportunity.

There was another world shattering event also in that first season in

Bognor. The first proof from the medical world of a connection to lung cancer from the habit of smoking. It caused a great stir, this report. I was smoking up to twenty Players Weights a day then, and I tried to give it up. I managed to cut it out for a couple of weeks.

During daylight hours over the camp radio system, we were very used to the slogans and advertising jingles of various products of well-known manufacturers. One of these was for Tom Thumb cigars. The jingle would go, Tom Thumb, Tom Thumb, te tumpty tum de tum. I resolved to try the small cigars instead of cigarettes.

I did this, and found them very strong to the taste. In fact after a few puffs I felt quite satisfied and had no desire to inhale. So I managed to wean myself from inhaling the smoke. After this I could accept a cigarette without inhaling.

I reasoned that as inhalation must surely be the dangerous bit, I'd effectively kicked the habit. This proved to be so finally. It wasn't long before I managed to stop altogether. After a cold I was always very chesty, accompanied by searing pains when the cold was a severe one.

Jumping forward to the present I realise how timely that warning was when it came out. Nearly 50 years on, with a new heart valve and two bypasses intact, without any illness to speak of. And now with two cataract ops also to my credit, I consider myself a very lucky person, and very nearly bionic!

Michael had passed his eleven plus exam, and he and Jim were now attending Bognor Grammar School. Before this Michael was at Lyon Street Juniors. He commented that he was well able to cope.

The Welsh curriculum put him slightly ahead of the lessons being taught when he arrived. A trait in the Welsh character was to go to school to learn. My own experience bore that out by the large numbers of school teachers then that were from that country. One thing also changed, but more slowly, the boys' Welsh accents!

This move was all about our lads and family life. Another change for them was they were to be out numbered by the opposite sex. Coral, and her husband Vernon, had three girls. Angela, the eldest, Jennifer and Bronwen. For the sixteen weeks our boys were to be in the minority. Fortunately the cousins had always been the best of friends.

About the same age, they were very supportive of each other. With two of the family inside the camp it was only to be expected they would all be in and out of camp like yo-yo's.

Now on my one day off I found that I was required to take our two into camp at six in the morning. All camps are pretty large and luggage is mainly heavy. There is also a finite number of luggage trolleys. The local boys could earn a few bob by getting a trolley and helping the campers to their chalets.

They were not allowed to charge, but relied on tips. Jim was saving up for a drum kit so was very keen to be there early. Most of the time it worked and both visitor and lad would benefit. Not always. After struggling across camp we heard of many lads having to be satisfied with hardly a thank you.

Neither of them were afraid of a bit of work and there was another little job they liked. The law had been changed to allow money bingo. Up until then winning cards got vouchers to be used in the camp shops. Now it was cash. Knowing our reds, our enterprising two lads found themselves work on the Tombola, or cash bingo, as it is now.

Before the process was automated, the lucky number balls were drawn from a revolving cage, read out by the caller, then placed on a board for checking. Speed was of the essence to get in the most games each session so BB could have his 'cut'.

With great speed and not a little skill, Jim used to remove the balls from the cage and Michael placed them on the board. When the winning vouchers were being handed out the caller reminded the lucky winners how their good fortune came about, and the boys got handsome tips.

New to the junior programme that year was a clown act. They were called the 'The Lesters'. These outside specialist acts were always being brought in to supplement the camp's weekly programme, and this year they did one of their acts for us in our theatre.

The Lesters were a Danish family. Dad, son and daughter. The father's entrance, in a tiny car, was excellent. I never saw him get in and often wondered how he got out of it, even though I watched that bit.

They were doing their two acts in both Bognor and Minehead camps that year. A comedy horse routine and trampoline speciality was the other act. They doubled up with the Gaiety Theatre and us. It was the one and only inclusion we ever had working in our own children's show whilst we were with Billy Butlin.

In the redcoat show this year was also a clown act. Peter Picton, 'Pierre the Clown' and his partner Derek, were breaking in a skating act. Derek also played the accordion. It was a while before I realised it was the skating act clown, out of makeup, we passed him each morning handing out skates to the campers.

A tall good looking bloke waved a greeting to Deena and myself, as he sorted out wheels for the campers feet. We became friends. He was very taken by my props. He also had his own transport, a Land Rover. A rare possession amongst the redcoats then.

Weeks into the season I was still having to battle with the lack of grass for the sports event each week. Before the turf had been laid prior to opening, most of the builder's rubble was very much strewn about the place. As the sun burned at the turf ugly edges of bits of brick broke the surface. A nightmare every week curbing the enthusiasm of the young athletes.

This year I chose it would be the year of the Martian. Our chase would be for a figure from another world, conveniently spotted just after breakfast every Wednesday morning, I remember. I really enjoyed these hours chasing a redcoat dressed appropriately for the part, who, when caught was thrown into the swimming pool in time to get to first sitting lunch. Such precise timing!

I always used the time-honoured ritual that preceded all these ventures. I don't claim to have invented this, but I thought it well worth copying. I get everybody down on their knees, and with heads near the ground, they repeat after me the ritual initiation incantation. 'I know in my heart, I know in my mind, that I have got, a popped up behind'. After a laugh all round the Martian is sighted and the chase is underway.

I was always amazed at the fancy dress competitions. Deena or I compered our shows. We had two classes, boys and girls. Lots of costumes were thought of on the spot, others brought their costumes with them. The most beautiful things on earth are the children, and some took one's breath away. It was a constant joy to be involved.

Young Tarzans in their macho competition, could strut and the march about as they thought fit. Flexing their muscles as well as anybody they had seen on television.

The Bognor camp had a decent pond to run the regatta on. The pond's normal inhabitants, the ducks, got short shrift when our determined rowers lashed out with their oars. I know our local birds kept a very sharp eye out for them on our regatta day.

The Bognor beach was not a place to conduct a trail of children on. Unlike this new location, Pwllheli shores were largely deserted and you could watch everyone in your charge. There was not much sand there, but the children loved poking around. I missed these walks very much.

Quite a few redcoats lived in Bognor so after the season ended, we sometimes would meet them doing all the ordinary stuff of living out of uniform.

The finals of all the other camp's contests took place in Bognor a week before we closed. It was an exciting, and sometimes a heartbreaking time for the weekly winners. Resolving the table tennis, snooker, talent and other contests made for a hectic week.

A few of these top finalists ended up competing in a national show. The senior talent show was one such event. As I've written before, Butlin's to most people meant just summer holidays. For others it was a chance to get a toe into show business.

For the entertainment agency that wanted to advance the career of one of 'their boys or girls', it presented an important opportunity. The real prize of being seen on a 'wider' stage was far more rewarding than this free week's holiday.

Almost, it seemed, before it began the 1960 camp season at Bognor had drawn to a close. We decided to have a few days off, before donning my carpenter's apron again.

But, dear oh dear, something was happening to us both. We were still eating as much as we liked but we were no longer in that mad racing about environment that was camp life any more. Both our waists were pushing at trouser and skirt bands alarmingly. It was then we both gave up sugar in tea and coffee. A small measure that helped us settle into a less hectic routine.

It was quite a surprise when 'Pierre the Clown' called on me a short while after. He was booked in for a Christmas season in Paris, for The Circus Bougloine. Would I make him some props? It seemed a simple request. He had seen us work and some of the props Deena and I were using. He knew I had made them.

After some thought I devised a new camera gag for him. It had a flexible viewfinder, like an elephant's trunk, and the whole thing could be collapsed when requested.

The finished camera gag promoted another visit from Pierre when he returned 'from the continent'. On looking back that phrase 'from the continent' used to amuse Deena and me. We soon learned that whenever Pierre was asked where he was working in or out of work, his reply would invariably be 'I've just returned from the continent'. This was the beginning of our relationship, post Butlin's.

Chapter 12

Becoming a Clown

When Pierre arrived back after his French engagement, he asked if we would be interested in doing a cabaret act together. I sensed that another turning point was about to occupy the scene. From woodworker to builder and then entertainer, what about this performer wearing a red nose?

For a long time now, making people laugh was increasingly becoming attractive to me. So wearing an overlarge suit and big boots might just be what was in store for me, I was only forty after all! Throwing in our lot with Pierre needed a great deal of thinking about. However, here was a challenge, cabaret is a completely different kettle of fish. We were intrigued, and we said yes.

Pierre had the notion that we'd build a magic cabinet for our first venture. He was far more knowledgeable about acts and matters of the circus and theatre. One thing going for us though, on my eighth birthday I was given a pair of roller skates. I was good at skating on ice too, so the fact that the magic cabinet involved doing the act on skates held no fears for me.

The cabinet, magic or otherwise, was about four feet square by seven feet high. It was raised off the floor with an arrangement of tubes supporting all round drapes. There was a ramp of four feet long running down from the front to about a foot from the floor. It had two grooves in its length about eighteen inches apart. A mannequin butler, on wheels, could run up and down the ramp when commanded.

It needed four people to run the act, Pierre, myself, Deena and Gill, Pierre's girlfriend at the time, later to be his wife. Deena, the 'inventor' of the cabinet, would come out and announce to Pierre (clown) and me (straight man) that her cabinet could produce anything they wished for.

Pierre immediately ordered two double scotches. Deena then pulled out a pistol, fired a shot in the air, and down the slope came the dummy butler holding a tray of drinks, which we imbibed. A telephone is sounded off-stage. Deena goes off to answer and leaves her pistol. Back up the ramp goes the butler. Exciting possibilities with the inventor out of the way. Pierre is soon firing his first shot. More and more drinks. Both get tipsy. In their haste to get drinks from the tray dummy's head is knocked off. Panic. Inventor will soon return.

Pierre puts his skates on and hides behind the cabinet curtains. Deena comes back, orders a custard tart, and fires the gun. Down clops tipsy Pierre, aims for me, I duck and inventor gets the tart. Thus the act.

The preamble to this was the making of the prop. It wasn't long before Pierre 'phoned me saying he'd got a booking. It was an unpaid job for the Mayor of Westminster's Charity at The Savoy. One thing about Pierre, he could get work. Not an easy thing by any means, in show business, paid or not.

We had to set up early, being in the middle of the ballroom. Gill took her place in the cabinet behind a second curtain, concealed early on. We should have been on at a reasonable time but as happens at these functions most performers are using it as a show date and they take their time. And others' time as well.

It was past midnight when it was our turn. Gill had been hidden in the cabinet all this time, over six hours without 'relief'. How the poor girl managed I don't know. There were a few pithy comments made later I remember, whilst returning to the coast in the early hours. Pierre was living in Worthing then, we were all in high spirits. The act went well and for the first time out it wasn't bad. It needed a lot of working on though. We came back quietly triumphant but secretly pleased there were no further bookings in sight.

We lashed out left right and centre about this time. Looking for ideas, making new props, trying out this and that. Pierre was able to find money enough to do all these things. Deena and I contributed our ideas and skills in the making of them, including costumes. It was a fair compromise. We pushed Pierre at the expense of our own names and reputations. It's hard enough pushing one name in this business, let alone three.

We got on the Easter Parade at Battersea Park. We did that show three times. We made carnival heads for our sons and one or two of their friends and together they made up our group in these ventures. It was a marvellous experience. It taught me what a big comb and feather duster can turn one into. I revelled in the seeming simplicity of comedy. An engaging smile, red nose, large boots and heaps of tact and friendliness. I warmed to the job of being a clown. Gradually a character was emerging. It was the real me coming out at last.

One year, instead of walking the three mile route, I donned the giant costume and got driven round in a lorry. I'd made this previously when we put on the panto 'Jack and the Beanstalk' in Mumbles. When the parade finished, the lorry drew into a car park and I was forgotten. I was strapped into the carnival head and still being nine feet tall just awaited the arrival of one of our party to untie me. The road was bumpy and to make me safe I had been lashed to the lorry. I was stuck. After shouting myself hoarse through the eye holes in the giant's neck, somebody finally realised my plight, and cut me loose.

Shortly afterwards we had a stroke of luck. An agent let it be known that he was casting for a circus film starring Pat Boone and Nancy Kwan. Pierre and I went over to Shepperton Studios and saw the producer, name of Dan Petrie. He was from Hollywood, heading the team to make 'The Main Attraction', a film to introduce Pat Boone to the adult world. He was a great star to the teenyboppers but it was time to move on.

The list of co-stars was formidable. Leading lady Nancy Kwan, Kieran Moore, Mae Zetterling, Yvonne Mitchell in supporting roles. The dialogue with Mr. Petrie went something along these lines. Pierre, 'Yes we could do it. Yes we had plenty of experience. Yes, we could bring our eight clowns along'! (eight clowns?) I have told you Pierre could get work, but this was ridiculous. But we got the job. Three days filming all told.

When we came out of the producer's office we smiled at Yvonne Mitchell, waiting in the corridor for her turn to go in. She smiled pleasantly at us. We went out into the open air and out of earshot from everybody we literally exploded with laughter, cheek and excitement.

The film director told us we would be doing clown run-ins and be involved in a comedy band. Pierre mustered up three or four other clowns. Duke Dupree was one. Derek Fitton, a tumbler friend of ours who used to do film stunt work, another. Bill English, Clown Smiley, was another. Bill was a great friend and a first class piano-accordionist. He had a fine tenor voice also.

I think I took nearly every prop along that I'd made up to that time. It was an interesting assortment to say the least, including a camel. I was fascinated watching the goings-on whilst waiting to do our bit. A powerful memory was of Mai Zetterling doing a spot with a fantastic ventriloquist's doll. It was beautifully dressed, blonde hair, long lashes, full of oomph – and it smoked a cigarette. It was a joy sitting there.

Bill McGuffy was the pianist for rehearsals. (The actual sound track was already pre-recorded with Pat Boone's singing voice on). Kieron Moore was second lead. We watched Nancy Kwan riding bare back for her part in the film. One time she fell off. It was then I realised what the film people call an 'important property' was, and how it is cosseted in these fraught moments. In an instant she was surrounded and fussed over. An 'in' person was saying they'd already phoned for doctor so and so, and the whole company attended their asset. A valuable property whilst the film was in production, was being protected.

Pat Boone was a very nice person from what I saw of him. His family was in England with him and I have very some very nice photographs taken of us clowns with him and his children. There were some international circus acts booked for the film. It was a great cast. We thought this was it, for us too. There were other clowns on the film as well. We met them in our dressing room. It wasn't exactly a friendly encounter. I suppose they thought of us as upstarts in a way. We may well have looked a bit green as well.

I wasn't exactly impressed by them either so the feeling was mutual. One 'old boy' (if anyone can really know someone's age in clown makeup) was booked for background scenes and atmosphere shots for the whole production. He was on the set full time. All I ever saw him do was walk about pulling a wooden tortoise behind him. It might be unjust to judge him from this momentous bit of business, but it wasn't us who started a feeling that we were not welcome.

All we wanted was for a chance to show what we could do. My ideas were not standard run-ins and sometimes this upsets performers. But what in effect we were there to do was not proper carpet clowning as such, but to provide two entrees into the ring as a troupe. After all the waiting and learning about the pecking order in doing so, it came to our turn.

We were told to do a run-in and get amongst the audience. A chaotic rush into the ring with all of us trying to work in certain areas, whilst the cameras took in the whole scene. On the word 'action Pierre and Company', we rushed in very vocally and working like mad. I chased Pierre into the stalls with my giant revolver and, at the appropriate moment, fired a string of sausages from it. He was carrying an old and battered suitcase and as he clambered over the seats, amongst all the film extras playing the audience, he let it fly open.

All manner of unmentionables were scattered over laps and shoulders. Everybody was shrieking and reacting with great gusto. It was all heady stuff. We thought we were the bee's knees. Then when the director said 'cut', it all stopped. We stood puffing and panting and feeling dazed. It was a sobering thought to realise that the crowd were also under orders to laugh and react. Then the director's voice said, 'That was fine Pierre, can we have it again please?'

Oh dear! What a lark this filming! So we gathered ourselves together, repacked our props and waited the same command . 'Action , Pierre and Company'.

We must have got a good take the second time. All the film crews seemed satisfied, so then we got ready to do the comedy band. We thoroughly enjoyed the making of the film and matured a lot doing it. We were all invited to the film premier at the Plaza cinema in London. Deena, wives and friends of our team were guests whilst we donned makeup again to dress the foyer and provide atmosphere. It was quite a night. Our first big occasion.

The press were there in strength. I asked one of the photographers if his pictures would appear in Bognor Regis. He was very amused. I think he was from Associated Press, (world-wide coverage). I thought it was funny too! And so the place settled down and we all watched the film.

I didn't recognise it as the same film we had been in. The story line had been rearranged somewhat. Pat Boone met Nancy Kwan in the film, they ran away to the Alps and had a love affair amongst the mountains and snow. Oh, the circus bit? Our three days filming was cut to a few seconds showing. We nearly missed it. Our big chance shrunk back to life size. In the film credits we were styled as, 'Bill Picton and his Clowns'. Well, that's show business for you.

After the film we added a skating act to our repertoire. It was built around a see-saw prop that we skated over. Up and down. It looked quite spectacular. I was cast as the straight man showing Pierre how to do it properly. The comedy came when he tried to copy me.

We got a booking to do it for a Butlin's reunion in the Albert Hall. The Hall floor was a perfect venue for a clown act, if a little slippery. Our skates had rubber wheels, but it was still dodgy. There was an added bonus to this job. It was being shown on London Television. I was very thankful that when I skated over the see-saw on that occasion everything went copy-book style.

Looking very confident and taking a deep breath, over I went. The comedy afterwards went very well and we did ourselves no harm by being seen on television either. It was something we could add to our   letter headings. The following year we had a return booking from Butlin's at the Albert Hall again, so we must have pleased them.

We did a table balancing act this time with Pierre's tumbling expertise being shown to the full. His entrance, carrying and banging on a big drum, he rolled down the steps leading to the floor, in great style. We got a terrific reception for this. I had built a table with an unnoticeable trap door in its top. On this was placed a chair with a removable seat. The fun bit was Pierre showing off as usual, climbing first onto the table, then demanding the chair from me. He was by no means a slight person and when he finally mounted the chair, tottering and swaying about, he kicked the chair top away and tumbled through the chair and table onto the floor. Finish. We didn't do this act many times. A good job too. I would have soon be on the lookout for a new partner had we done so.

Only one thing soured the afternoon for us. When we came off, Wally Goodman came across complimenting us on the act. As an afterthought he mentioned that as they were not televising this year, he'd made a mistake with the fee. So he cut it in half. I still haven't forgiven them and Hal and Deena Brooks never worked for them again. All that apart I have ever since been grateful for that opportunity to perform in the Albert Hall. A wonderful setting for our kind of comedy.

We did a lovely job about this time. It was the Jersey Battle of Flowers. We took our sons, Deena, and a couple of friends across and enjoyed the break. We had to leave on the Wednesday by steamer ferry from Weymouth, do the Battle on Thursday and come back on the Friday. Time for an enjoyable sea voyage and a complete change. We were all to dress up and provide comedy on the route of the procession.

This route was actually a stretch of dual carriageway about a mile and a half long. We went up one side and down the other on the return, entertaining the many thousands of holiday-makers who were lining the pavements, watching this massive floral procession complete its journey.

Some of us changed props and business for the return leg of the route. Deena wore her 'wopsey' outfit. Son Michael was dressed as the Sultan of Morocco, and Jim had a giant yo-yo to work. I did my comb and shaving business and Pierre's trousers somehow kept on coming down. My shaving prop was a converted cycle battery horn. It had a length of cable with a plug attached. I adjusted the button switch so that I could use it like an electric shaver. So, after a dust down with a feather duster, a quick comb of their quiff, I gave a short sharp 'shave' to any one who'd placed the plug in their ear.

It was a very warm day. I saw Deena nearly fainting in the heat with her carnival head and costume becoming a torture after this long walk. She had been dancing nearly all of the way. No wonder she was grateful when I spotted her plight and escorted her to a rest tent. Our young Michael was looking very dejected sitting on the kerb, worn out. What seemed a lark when we spoke about them joining in, at home, was rapidly becoming hard work indeed, even torture! His face was a picture of fed-up-ness for an eleven year old. But we all stuck it out like proper troupers.

In the evening Pierre and I did the skating act on an open air dais raised about six feet above the ground. Also on the bill was 'Daisy the Cow', a very popular TV act at that time. As there was no commentator up on the stage they asked me to speak their dialogue for them. June and Jimmy Kidd, 'Daisy', were great friends of ours and I hope I didn't let them down.

I had made an addition to my easel so that when I drew a very belligerent sergeant major standing beside a cannon, I was able, at the finish of the drawing, to fire a shell from behind, seemingly to come from the cannon. Happy days! But I was exposed as a stage act. The people who were behind the easel complained noisily 'we can't see, turn around,' and other coarse sayings peculiar to the Jersey vernacular, I understand!

Came the main skating act. From the ground the stage looked a good size. Up there though it seemed very small. When the final charge over the see saw came to be made Pierre couldn't control his speed in time. He went off the stage, flying into the audience. Talk about a climax. The crowd never knew it was an accident. Pierre was badly grazed and cut, but didn't show it. He wasn't one for fussing though he had cause to wince on this occasion. It must have been very painful. A skate was ripped off his boot.

It was always difficult getting Pierre to rehearse where tumbling was concerned. He always said if he got hurt during the act it was too bad. But to get hurt rehearsing was silly. I couldn't tumble to save my life. We both got on doing what we could each do best.

With the skating act came the opportunity to do more television. We went to the BBC studios in Bristol to appear in Vision-On. Primarily the programme was for deaf children with emphasis on visual promotions. We were included in a programme about skates and clowns.

When we arrived at the studios at about 10am, we ran through the act for everybody to see, and time. Then we did a camera rehearsal for positions. In the afternoon we did a dress rehearsal, then at about 4.30pm we went out live. This was a new experience for us. We were actually produced for this spot. The director made suggestions and we did our best to comply with them. We could have done with a lot more producing and polishing in those days, but this was a good start and we heard that we'd come over well.

About this time we also appeared on another BBC children's show. Crackerjack, compered then by Eamonn Andrews. The show came from the stage of the old variety theatre, the Shepherds Bush Empire, now a BBC TV studio. We did the skating act again but I also built a sort of robot-looking machine rather like a fantastic dentist's chair, with futuristic control panels and flashing lights. We used this prop to instil in Pierre an instant lesson on roller skating. We weren't given much room on stage to do all this. Only a tiny space, amidst all the other props laid out for the rest of the programme.

I was experimenting with making flashes then. I built a flash pot into the chair and between two electric terminals placed a bit of fuse wire. When I threw the switch, a current shorted across the wires, made it red hot, and this ignited the magnesium powder I'd sprinkled over it. The studio lights were so bright my flash was hardly seen. We never saw it at all when it was fired as we had our backs to it at the time. Fortunately for us this programme was recorded. It was broadcast later on a day we were doing a hospital children's Christmas show.

We engineered a short break in our show to enable us to watch the programme. This was a revelation. We were not destined to set the world alight yet, on that showing anyway. Perhaps we were too critical. Still it was nice to see us for ourselves. Normally, trying to get at the truth by questioning others about a show that went out live, could be hard work. (The significance of the flash? When it went off one of us would say 'what's that?' Answer, 'a news flash'). We both laughed when we saw it go off during the programme.

Seeing myself on TV was quite an experience. I just could not tie myself up to the figure that was me on the screen. It was similar to hearing one's own voice for the first time. It was all rather unreal, this real you. One of the thoughts that go through my mind whenever I see myself on television or film is 'isn't he old? Really this ageing process proceeds so stealthily and one is so unaware of all the years flying by, more so when you are thoroughly absorbed and enjoying every moment of what you are doing.

I am never more alive than when I am performing or working an audience. I hope I feel really old when I finally go from this earth. Quite worn out. There are two nice memories of doing Crackerjack, one was to find out how pleasant a person Eamonn Andrews was. We didn't speak much, and I'm sure he would never have remembered me, but he was pleasant and reassuring.

The other memory was that the programme was transmitted when we were busy elsewhere, so I'd asked a photographer friend to try to photograph the TV screen whilst we did our stuff. I'm very pleased I did as now I have a couple of misty snaps, in black and white, as a reminder of those early days on the telly.

During this period I was still very much a builder. I couldn't afford to go on speculative excursions too often. I never had any actual money to spare. What I did have was the time after my daily building stints to make and develop new ideas and props that we could incorporate into our existing acts.

At this time, newly removed from my established business in Wales, money only dribbled in. Two boys, a mortgage, van upkeep. There was no spare cash about. Poor Deena. During this period she never got a regular wage. Like me, she contributed her time. Doing all the sewing, making and laundering our clothes, packing suitcases, checking props and lists of items we had to take.

The slap-up feeds she would have waiting for us at any hour of the day or night on our return from a job had to be seen to be believed. It was a good time, a hard time, but she helped make it an enjoyable time.

Then something turned up from a different quarter entirely. TV commercials. We got a spot in a television film for ITV. It was a pilot film for Handy Andy, an all-purpose household cleaner. A pilot film was a tryout. If when finished the manufacturer liked it, it would be screened to sell Handy Andy on television.

We were playing the part of a dirtying gang that swept into people's houses, messing the place up and generally causing disarray. There were six of us. We were using an old-fashioned, bell-clanging, fire engine for transport. The gang would sweep into a suburban housewife's kitchen, play havoc, and rush out, laughing and jeering. All-in-all very unpleasant characters.

Except at one front doorway. When we rang this doorbell, a young mum, 'who knows all about us', instead of being swept aside like all the others, stood her ground. She did more. She stood erect, one hand outstretched in front of her, brandishing a bottle of Handy Andy at us. A brave gesture indeed. And it worked. We all fell back cringing and moaning that it wasn't fair. Then we all scarpered. I liked it. It was good slapstick with a chance to mime and make up business.

One thing that surprised me was an incident that happened next day when we'd finished all the exterior filming. We were in the studio set of an ultra modern kitchen. Beautifully furnished, lovely elegant curtains and drapes, fine fittings and crockery. When it came for me to have to brush the crockery off the table in a nonchalant way, whilst throwing soot all around, I had pangs about the waste. I had to force myself to misuse all these lovely props.

To throw tomatoes and eggs at lovely wallpaper. Scattering soot around like a Morris-dancing chimney sweep. Deena and I had never owned anything so nice in our lives and to break it all, even for a living, went against the grain.

After all that the pilot film didn't get any further and was never screened. It did me a good turn though, more film work, from the producer. He'd liked the way I did my bits in the film and used me several times afterwards. The producer was Roy Fry. I used to see his name come up in the credits on BBC and ITV films. I would get a call to be up in Chelsea early in the morning (where the studio was), to start at 10am.

One custard commercial I worked on was quite something. The film set was a magnificent dining room with a marble top table, prepared for a tremendous meal. A very lovely girl, beautifully dressed, was seated opposite me. Elegantly eating her afters (sweet), a plate of custard. I played her husband in my tramp outfit. Grubby, with a drooping moustache, with my own bowl of custard. I was to eat my custard with a wooden spoon, noisily slurping it up. All deadpan and straight.

There were two problems. Keeping the custard hot. It had to be filmed steaming in the bowl. The other worry was my moustache. I was acting with such gusto it kept getting soggy and dropping off. It was as if the custard delighted in attacking the gum on my 'tache. A question of two sticky mixtures cancelling themselves out. I didn't let on that I was a novice at makeup at that time in my career. But we won in the end.

What the end was I mostly never knew. Once you'd been paid and the job finished on a film, there was no way of knowing what happened next. Unless, of course, it appeared on the television or cinema afterwards.

These productions were mainly pilots though. After arriving at the studio for an early start it came to lunch time. I was taken to a local pub nearby and from the menu I chose T-bone steak. I did so enjoy it. I was very conscious that I was the only one eating. The film crew looking on, suggested there was not a lot of money to spare on these pilots.

Then, a film promoting throwaway cigarette lighters. The set was a street scene. The producer would say what was needed and I did it. Then, he said , 'Hal, would you go up to the lamp-post and do something funny'! Dear reader, solve that one. Me, still somewhat a novice at this clowning business, I don't remember what I came up with. Probably the shock of the request erased it from my mind. We were still on talking terms afterwards though so he must have been satisfied.

Then one day I had an urgent call from the studio. The producer asked if I was interested in playing a straight role. I assented, and was booked into a London hotel overnight, to enable early shooting next day. I was taken from the studio to be looked at by the promotional company executive who had the advertising folio for the film, a TV commercial.

We arrived in this smart office building and passed through a room containing what seemed to me a dozen or so people awaiting an audition. Whether they were there hoping to get the job I was doing I don't know, probably not. But it did cross my mind how lucky I was.

We met the lady advertising executive and she agreed with the studio that I looked the part. It was agreed to commence shooting at 3pm that afternoon. We all sat down for a cup of coffee. Before I could drink mine, the telephone rang. She answered it and then put it down. It appears they were unable to book transmission time for the commercial to go out, so all was cancelled.

The advert was for Alka-Seltzer. I was to have played a semi-straight part without makeup and it was to have been networked over the Christmas period. I got out of pocket expenses but that was all. In my bid for stardom it had been a near miss.

Chapter 13

A Second Season in Bognor Camp

Deena and I did the season of 1962 in Butlin's, Bognor. Pierre Picton meanwhile made use of the magic cabinet in Battersea Parks children's shows. He was being partnered by Duke Dupree and Duke's father took the inventor's part. Deena and I popped along one Saturday on one of our days off to see them. The act went down well with the audience. The cast were comfy backstage too. Duke had installed a four gallon barrel of beer to prevent any frogs getting into any of their throats.

It was good to see the act being worked by someone else too. You can get a more detached view of a thing like that. During the season Deena and I were not sleeping on camp. We were at home each night with our boys and Coral's girls. Coral, Deena's sister, was still seeing to our boys during the daytime. The camp was larger this year. Lots of staff were living off camp to make room for more campers.

Deena and I were generally off camp by nine-o-clock. No more 'swanning' in the ballroom for us. I didn't mind the job of mixing and talking to campers after our day's work with the children. But now we had proved we could do it to our own satisfaction, we had a home to go to.

When I moved to Bognor I resolved to do more painting and to this end we enrolled in adult evening classes. I also took advantage of the fact we had 'sitters' in the house. They all sat for me in the evenings. I painted Coral and Angela once, and Bronwen and Jennifer twice. Now Coral has a portrait gallery of her own. I've tried in the intervening years to prise back the collection, but no luck. Still, it's very nice to see them whenever we visit her in Tredegar. I note I painted a lot more smoothly then.

Pierre had married Gill and they now lived in Worthing. Only sixteen miles away from us now. A bit different from Beckenham. Then something happened that changed both of our lives considerably. It came in the shape of an old car, a

Model T Ford. Pierre heard it was for sale and we went to see it. It was being used by Jimmy Jewel and Ben Warris in panto in Southampton.

It was made in the twenties. Left hand drive with an excellent conversion job done on it in the engineering sense, by a French engineer. There were more foot pedals and controls on it than a Wurlitzer organ, but its appearance had not been sacrificed in any way. It still looked like an upright piano to me.

After watching Jimmy and Ben work their act with it we were very impressed. The car runs in, and for whatever reason, stops. The driver gets out and explains his presence. He then decides to continue his journey. He cranks the handle, the engine starts, but as soon as he steps on the running board the engine stops. He gets out and winds the handle. The car starts, but before he can get in to drive it off, the engine stops again.

If it was funny to see a man struggling to start the car by winding a starting handle 'til it roared into life, and it would be uproarious if it stopped again as soon as he got into it. Basically that is the car act. The prop had been organised to seem as though the car had a mind of its own, and one generally lost the battle to obtain supremacy over it.

Pierre decided to buy it. Before we took possession, both families went to see the pantomime and the car. I was very pleased to see in the show also Jimmy Jewel's dad's prop, the Haunted Room, being used in the ghost scene. It was a first class routine with a story of its own. With plenty of surprises and ghostly happenings it was a sure fire success. Jimmy and Ben were expert laughter makers.

I also enjoyed their Christmas cake routine. The many coloured two or three tiered cakes they worked up out of soap flakes and colorants had to be seen to be believed. From the audience they looked very impressive. I'd watched backstage while they made their cakes prior to each performance. It was my first sight of this sort of preparation. They used a mechanical whisk to work up and fill a few buckets with different coloured, stiff foam. No ordinary cakes looked as inviting or as glamorous as these pretend goodies!

After the show we loaded the Model T onto a lorry and trailer and brought it back to Bognor. We had already hired a garage to put it in. It was bitterly cold weather with snow around. Then we looked around for a place to rehearse in. On the outskirts of Bognor we had a Territorial Army unit. The CO kindly let us use his gun practice room which was large enough to travel a full circle with the car's lock to rehearse our own routine. In full lock we could turn in a thirty-two foot diameter circle.

Gradually during this period I was trying more comedy business as well as being a straight man to Pierre. Always at the back of my mind this aspect of comedy and humour was for me. Even whilst working with Deena the big boots and red nose side of entertaining continued to be more attractive to me.

During the film I used a makeup that just fitted my face. A little shadow under the eyes, a line down the sides of my mouth, and a very sad expression, fitted my features like a glove. The trouble for me is I am not really a sad character, I'm a sunny sort of bloke.

Through trial and error I gradually evolved my own makeup. I hardly use any these days and therefore I can exert a high degree of facial expression without a lot of clutter. This can also be a disadvantage if your audience is well away from you, such as in a ring or doing gala work. My main work is with children though, and my size thirty-two boots kind of sets me aside from normal folks.

Working with the car was very different. There were so many foot pedals on the floor that to get amongst them I had to wear a pair of football boots minus the studs. These brought my normally size ten feet down to a very slim nine. To enable Pierre to arrive in his great entrance coat, big boots and big hat, I had to do the bulk of the driving.

There was very little leg room in the model T but I could just manage to get behind the steering column to drive. The fact that the steering wheel was loose, and could lift off, had to be watched closely. It was a god gag to be seen to tug on it and for it to come away in one's hands, but only at the right time. It could be a positive embarrassment if the car was moving.

To jump off the moving car when it was going around in circles, waving the steering wheel in the air, was a good laugh. The audience was not to know the car's steering was locked to keep the driverless car in a safe circular path. We used to pretend it was chasing us. A clever arrangement with the car's gearbox cut out top gear. We had two pedals for movement. One for forward, one for reversing. A third pedal was a foot brake.

After all the fun of the chase we could jump back aboard and kick out the locking device, and the car was then under our control again. Simple, but very effective. How often can you point out a good effect and marvel at its simplicity?

Take the case of stopping the engine at will. After all the apparent fuss and bother of us getting the engine started, by the handle, by cajoling it, or by giving it a good kick, as soon as we jumped on the running board, ostensibly to get in, the engine would stop. There was a cut-out button on the running board. Standing on it would stop the engine. So simple, so effective.

Mind you, the starting action was also simple. The car's engine didn't actually start on the handle. There were a number of starter buttons placed around the body of the car that enabled us to start the engine at will. For instance, when bending down to grasp the starting handle, it was natural to steady yourself by holding the mudguard with your other hand. That spot on the mudguard contained a starter button. So simple.

During the act, before moving off, Pierre would slam the near side door and the off side door would mysteriously open. It looked very funny when well done. Round he would go and slam the off side door and the near side door would open. It was the extra foot pedals on the floor of the car that managed this effect. As he slammed one door, I opened the other, out of sight, with my foot.

With another movement I could send both doors crashing to the ground. All very spectacular stuff. The car's best feature was its finale, or getting-off gag. Pierre now sat in the rear seats. As I drove off, with a loud bang the whole of the back of the car appeared to fall away with Pierre in it. It would shoot him head over heels into the arena, with me driving off into the sunset, followed by him chasing after me. At the appropriate moment he had kicked his own pedal that let the whole back drop down, allowing him to tumble out. He had let his own bang off too.

These bangs were quite frightening at first. I'd learned to make flashes but we had to buy bangs. These were theatrical maroons, large firework 'bangers'. The instructions read 'to detonate please place in a dustbin and stand clear'. We didn't use a dustbin but a bang box, hidden under the car. It was made out of quarter inch steel plate welded together with holes drilled into it to let the blast out. It had a sliding lid to allow fresh maroons to be loaded and spent ones removed.

These maroons were electrically detonated so we fire them precisely when required. We were a bit gung-ho about these things and both Pierre and I had narrow escapes when they exploded accidentally. We very soon adopted a safety procedure that protected us from blast and flying bits, but this did not stop the noise. This was frightening, when close up.

This dangerous side of clowning, using bangs, flashes and other special effects was a problem that had to be kept under strict control, and contained by routine. If anything happened to us nobody would want to know. The organisers of the event we worked at did not take any responsibility for our mishaps. Contracts we signed usually made it quite clear we would not be able to blame the agent's office either.

On the bonnet of the car we had a flash pot. I was still using hot wire to ignite the flash powder. We would use the car's batteries to set these effects off. Once whilst putting the bonnet down I shorted out the flash and it fired into my face. My clown's nose and makeup shielded me a bit, but I was badly scorched around the eyebrows and cheeks. It happened immediately before going out to perform.

I had to go out. I remember how cool the breeze was on my burnt parts. When I came off, I went straight to the St. John Ambulance tent for treatment. A few days afterwards the skin of my face peeled of as though I'd been sunburnt. It's not something easily forgotten. Nobody at the Marconi works gala in Chelmsford ever knew about it though. After that, as soon as flash powder was introduced, we put a tin can over it until the act commenced.

We were getting to know the car well, practising the bits in the gun room as we pieced an act together. We had a photographer down to take some publicity shots for us. From these we produced a collage of sorts to enable us to canvas agents for gala work.

Pierre thought the continental style of name would help. So instead of being 'and Co', I became 'et Cie'. Pierre et Cie. Looking back on those early photos trying to simulate working shots, we can admit only that they were a good try, but they had to do until we got work. In fact from our collage photos we seemed to have worked everywhere of importance that mattered. They did the trick though. We were launched as a car act. Since that time I've changed my mind about working shots. A semi-posed shot by a photographer working together with us is far superior to an indifferent action shot.

Once we had mastered and knew all the movements and capabilities of the car we looked at how we could put our stamp on it. I changed the headlamps into large eyes, of a feminine nature, complete with large lashes. A large grin was painted on a large mouth that concealed the car's bumpers. In the corner of the mouth Pierre had found a horn from an old gramophone which I upturned into a large pipe. So the Model T took on board the look of a pipe smoking, toothy grinned, eye fluttering vehicle, transporting two very unlikely lads that had definitely made it their own.

The gearbox of the Model T was bathed in oil. We thought that by tipping the car up on the ramp to the trailer this oil could get into the clutch, and damage it. Because of this we drained the sump of oil every time we loaded the car, and put it back in for the next performance. It was only much later when we obtained a manual from Ford that we discovered the clutch was supposed to be bathed in oil all the time. As car mechanics we were rather lacking in those days!

The great day came when we fulfilled our first engagement using the car. It was in Nottingham at the Ransom and Marles works gala. We were required to do an act lasting twenty to thirty minutes in the arena. We managed to stretch out the time with 'diversions'. One of these extras was Deena in her 'wopsey' outfit. Another, was son Jim dressed up to appear as an assistant to the clown duo. He was the chief door 'picker upper'. It was all very well having a car that fell to bits, but someone had to pick them all up.

The larger the arena we were performing in meant a lot more running to do. Pierre and I were OK, we rode in the car. Anyway, we did a good job and we all, both families, went home satisfied. Gradually we pulled it into a semblance of an act with a beginning, a middle, and an end.

The two main characters were taking shape. Pierre, the great big figure, flamboyant and loud. Me the support and feed. I chose to become a policeman. Rather a straight pinch from my boyhood heroes, The Keystone Cops, I suppose.

Deena made me a uniform and I worked on two gags for myself. Both were to do with my policeman's helmet. One was a standard clown effect, water spurting into the air out of the top when required. This I would activate should I sit down on any surface that bore a relationship to water, such as sitting on the bonnet of the car to rest, preferably on the radiator. It's a good laugh in the right place. To make it work was not so easy.

I had an old Pyrene fire extinguisher strapped to my person, filled with water. This brass cylinder had an opening with a screw-in stopper and a car tyre valve soldered into its body. When filled with water and sealed in with the stopper the valve allowed the water to be pressurised by being pumped up with air from a foot pump. A tap, when opened, then allowed the air pressure to push the water up a rubber tube, leading to the helmet. This procedure carried out by a competent engineer is a dawdle. By me, using second hand gas taps, rubber tubing, and dubious soldering skills, more risky.

The solution was persistence bordering on stubbornness. There were two potential drawbacks. One, an air leak which could render the tap useless, the other, a burst rubber tube that soaked you with water within, so that you just suffered silently in secret.

The second gag was a balloon, also from the helmet. This required a cylinder of air pressurised to blow up the balloon when required. Similar problems to the water gag presented themselves. Keeping the air in its pathway to the helmet and the concealed balloon was one. But the fly in the ointment was air pressure combined with a flimsy balloon. I couldn't slow it down to blow the air in gently. The balloons were blown to bits when I turned the tap.

I could write about the conquering of this idea for a long time, suffice to say I managed it and used it to good effect then, and later in my career. Where the air came out of the cylinder, I filled it with solder. I then drilled a very small hole through the solder that only allowed the air out slowly, just enough to blow up the balloon without damaging it. Success! The only snag was I had to carry these pressurised props with me throughout the act. There was no way to discard them 'til we got off, being firmly strapped to my body.

This business of props used in the arena, which was sometimes the size of premier football ground, separates the gala performer from a stage act. All items used had to be taken in and brought back out. No ring boys or stage hands to help remove used props. Very different from doing a children's party. But I was also aware the extra challenges meant we had less competition 'in the field'. In fact I always think a gala performer is a cut above the rest. More about this view later.

Pierre showed me a target launcher one day. It is a device that uses a point two-two blank cartridge to fire tin cans into the air so they can be shot at, clay pigeon style. A spring mounted plunger strikes the cartridge after being released by hand. He suggested it could be used to fire other things too. With our first effort we mounted two extra headlamps on the car that each encased a can, which then shot the lights upwards about fifteen feet or so. It was a definite plus. So whilst scrambling about beneath the car, trying to 'fix the engine', we had two extra gags to use.

These static gags were most important whilst working with little or no space to drive the car, such as when working on a stage. This lead to an idea of a rising co-drivers seat. Pierre thought it could be managed hydraulically. I wasn't so sure. In the end it was as I thought, too slow using oil. Compressed air was the answer. A pneumatic ram would thrust Pierre up about three feet with him being in complete control. It was a fantastic gag. Going up was spectacular enough, but coming down made my eyes water.

Pierre, being over six feet tall and not at all daintily built, posed risks. Henry Ford's car, the darling of the early American motoring public, looked big, but I can assure you there was no spare space in the driving compartment. When the seat came down, wallop, There was no way to slow it down. We had a long metal rod in the shape of a TV aerial by his side that was the control lever. Its length meant he could grab at it 'whilst in an elevated position', to let himself down.

The yell of terror he let out as he came down never had to be forced, or even rehearsed. The original gags we were adding to the car definitely set us apart from other car acts.

To power the ram a tank of compressed air, filled at one hundred pounds per square inch, was slung under the chassis. It was filled with air from a compressed air cylinder. Nearly a yard long and nine inches in diameter, it weighed a ton. When it required re-charging we had to go to Southampton to a British Oxygen depot to replace it.

By the time we got the seat installed we also had a change of transport. We now had a three ton Albion diesel lorry. The milometer of the vehicle had already gone round once doing its daily round of deliveries of HP sauce. But it was just what we needed and it had a beautiful driving position. With an enormous steering wheel, sitting bolt upright one could drive comfortably for hours, and being diesel, there were no starting problems caused by damp.

To make the lorry user-friendly we visited a scrap metal merchant in Chichester. From the mass of iron and steel in their yard we selected two lengths of four inch iron channel about fifteen feet long. We positioned these as ramps for the car wheels, and with a winch fixed firmly to the lorry floor, we could haul the car up into the lorry. The task of winding it up kept us fit and put us in line to imitate a prime set of 'Charles Atlas' muscles.

Later we organised the job of keeping the Model T's two heavyweight batteries charged up, by using the lorries own alternators as we journeyed to different jobs. Once when this was not done, we got to Sutton Coldfield for a large do, and the batteries were flat. However, this did not deter my ever-resourceful partner. Between us we got round the scout master of a troop, also in the show, and we soon had a line of panting boy scouts pulling us on, and off, whilst we did a very static show.

The Ford's conversion meant there was no facility to charge batteries on the car. I doubt whether we did a dozen miles all told in a season. It was a stage prop that looked exactly the same as before the conversion. We benefited from this fact. Everywhere we went car enthusiasts would flock to look at it. It was a star in its own right. I learned recently it is now enjoying a well-earned retirement in the collection of a very famous pop musician.

In the beginning we were often booked because of our 'star car', for at this point Pierre and I were not exactly household names. We were to do many miles in the lorry getting to work. On long journeys the routine was something like the time we got a booking in Hull. Deena fed us with a huge breakfast at four in the morning. She had stayed awake doing props, to see we didn't oversleep. She relaxed only once we had gone.

A long journey up to the show, and the same back afterwards. Always getting well under way before pulling off to have a meal. These were largely pre-motorway days. The cafes en route were in a world of their own. The one I remember most was the all-nighter at Gloucester. It was before the M4 motorway bridge was built.

It had obviously started out with a white ceiling. Over the years the atmosphere, cigarette smoke laden and moist, trapped behind closed doors in the early hours, had darkened it to a very deep brown. It was always heaving with the life and chatter of lorry drivers, fellow travellers and sometimes even clowns.

Arriving back the following day at four in the morning, Deena would be ready with another meal. On one of these trips my watch went missing. Next day we found it in the grate. When I put in an insurance claim the company queried 'having a fire in mid June?' They accepted our explanation of all night vigils.

One occasion we got a job because of the car was a dinner given to the Minister of Transport, the Rt.Hon.Ernest Marples. The Society of Advanced Motorists was giving him a slap up meal in the London Hilton. We were the cabaret. It was very early days for us then, and we had little experience of handling such a large prop.

First of all we just, and only just, got into the lift. When we reached the function suite the car was too wide for the entrance doors. Pierre was equal to the occasion and out came the screwdriver. Whilst taking off the hinges an engineer from the hotel saw us, and after taking in the shock at these two clowns dismantling his beloved workplace, he started to explain what the button he was pressing on the wall, was for. He had no need to have said anything because the whole section of the wall started going up, including the now 'hinge-less' doorway.

Pierre was putting the screwdriver away when both of us got a shock. The wall began disappearing up into the ceiling, revealing a ballroom of considerable magnitude containing thirty fully laid tables of twenty covers each. We were to do our car act at the other end of the ballroom, and there was no way through.

If grovelling was ever needed it was needed now. As well as having his doors partly dismantled, the head waiter was now faced with the prospect of all his carefully prepared tables having to be moved to get the car in. Having explained this to him, Pierre and I pretended we'd left something in the lift, and scarpered.

It was to be a memorable occasion. My makeup and nose were still in their infancy then. The nose was a table tennis ball painted red, with a cut out bit that only just let my nose in. When we finally started to perform the first unplanned piece of business was that my nose shot off, proving how shiny the floor was, 'cos I never saw where it ended up. I expect there are a few dents in the parquet floor even to this day where the doors were dropped off, and to what a clatter. A full half pint of water from my helmet was recorded by the Met office, and our bangs in that confined space may even have shocked the minister to sign the contract to start building the M1.

After we'd concluded our obligations we somehow managed to vacate the city, and charged back to West Sussex, to have a good think. It was whilst we were doing just that, I realised I had forgotten to get his autograph!

Chapter 14

A Stage the Size of a Field!

It's difficult to imagine today how vibrant the gala scene was in the sixties. I knew of, and dealt with at least four agents who mainly did outdoor and large entertainments. Apart from having a decent act, (we were much improved by then), the model T had an allure of its own.

Britax, the safety belt manufacturer, booked us to demonstrate the worth of using their product in your car, whatever the situation. Pierre suggested putting seat belts in our car. We were sent to a garage that did normal business for the motor racing fraternity. A bucket seat was made to fit our telescopic seat, and Pierre's bottom.

With it safely in position we arrived outside the Earls Court Motor Show, Addison Road entrance, with a gaggle of photographers, pressmen and the staff of Britax abounding. Up in the air went our daredevil motorist, red nose and all, to the sound of clicking cameras. It was a great morning. I was not in clown for this.

Pierre's entrance coat demands a mention here. A new kind of long fibred floor covering was being advertised, in bright colours, and a very luscious pile. Pierre sought out the makers and came back with a sack full of off-cuts. I would have loved to have heard him putting on the style introducing himself in his expansive way. The plastic material sprouting these colourful tufts was very tough.

Poor Deena's hands. She made an entrance coat out of these pieces. Pushing the needle through in the sewing process was testimony to her devotion to the trio. The result was fabulous. Pierre, no shrinking violet, was transformed into the multicoloured shape of a giant tea cosy on legs.

He had a job getting into the car with it on. I'm sure we added to the excitement of that period. A few years on from this I was constantly being approached myself to sell my bright clothes to up and coming teenagers, wanting to set themselves apart and impress the fair sex.

Pierre in plaster, Bernard Stockton pushing

Fire engine prop I made for Model T

Filming with Billy Cotton on Jersey Beach

Made up for the Boone film

Seen on TV in BBC Crackerjack

*Filming with Pat Boone in
Shepparton Studios*

*As footman in Brighton
Theatre Royal*

In stocks with Terry Scott and Hugh Lloyd

Footman paints leading man Craig Douglas

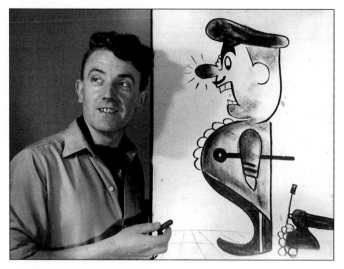

*A front of house
picture for Collins*

*Turning Hal
into Kerby*

*Footman again with Norman
Vaughan and Bill Pertwee*

A junior class in Caterham

My Road Safety Poster game

Tufty at a Playgroup

Road safety words by Hal and Deena Brooks
To be sung to the tune of 'I'd Like to Teach the World to Sing'

If every boy and girl would learn
To use the Green Cross Code
Oh what a difference it would make,
To safety on the road,
Take care of all both big and small
By doing what you should
It's your lookout think what's about
It's all for your own good.

It's the wisest thing.

If every boy and girl would think
Now winter days are here
It's not so easy to be seen
So let's make one thing clear
Wear white at night
Hold something bright
You know it's best by far
Be SEEN remember always
You can't argue with a car

It's the wisest thing

If every Mum and Dad could know
You'll always do your best
To find the SAFEST place to cross
You'll put their minds at rest
Your teacher too is proud of you
To know you'll always find
The very safest place to PLAY
So please keep this in mind

It's the wisest thing –
Now you will all agree – It's the wisest
thing

Press coverage of my Road Safety acts

Touring Salisbury with the Michelin Man

Drawing in a class

ME (JERSEY BATTLE of FLOWERS

Deena as Wopsy in Jersey
Battle of Flowers

TEMPERANCE
HALL
MONDAY MAY

LEAS

SIFFELO

Deena's family THE
LEAS

Road safety in Wimbledon
parks

Working in London's Parks

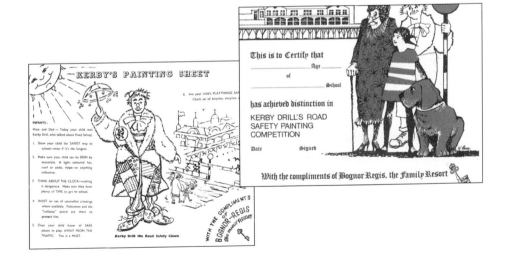

Colouring sheet and certificate

Pancho Pete

Deena's fancy dress costumes

*Our Craft shop
in Aldwick*

Me painting Kerby Drill

Some papier mâché pots

Two of my big carnival heads

Two pottery heads, after pottery classes

Using the bandsaw

*Kerby, Olly and
Capt. Jim*

*First time with my
name in lights*

*Jim's first
'Leaderboard'*

The young tree

Our sausage tree, now fully grown

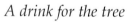

A drink for the tree

Goldie and Kerby divining for water

Kerby in a Tu Tu

The finish of the strip dance

Sammy's got a handful

*The sausage bomb
explodes on Kerby's rump*

Sam holds up a battery

Bamber ready for action

Sam sounding air-raid siren

We got a three day booking on a prime gala date, The Birmingham Tulip Festival. These multi-day bookings were so welcome. Apart from the money, being new to the game, it meant a chance to polish the act. Two performances a day meant a fair amount of experience by the end it. Extra gags could be tried out. The weather was fine too.

Then the lorry played up and things seemed to go against us, but then we had a real stroke of luck. Also on the bill was a high wire act called 'The Derricos'. Dad, Edgar Davies, wife Annie and sons Brian and Derek, a lovely family. Edgar came over and offered to help. It was clutch trouble I think, but by the end of the festival we were roadworthy again. The rig of The Derricos was about thirty feet in the air. Edgar walked the boys across the wire in what seemed to be an aerial wheelbarrow.

All exciting stuff. But what used to put the wind up me was how the boys got up there. A pair of guide wires at either end of the rig, held the main poles upright. A small platform was at the top of each pole with about forty feet of taut wire stretched between them. Dad climbed a ladder to get up, but the boys walked up the sloping guide wires to begin their act, without any aid at all. Arms outstretched for balance they went up and came down, the same way, each performance.

How Annie could bear this ritual I don't know. Most times I would watch as quiet as most of the audience did with me. Brave lads. A wonderful act, lovely friends.

Another three day stint we got was in Jersey for the 'Miss Battle of Flowers' competition. Booked for the car act this time we flew over from Hurn Airport. It was only a small plane and the car was the main cargo. Securely strapped in place we drew out onto the main runway when the pilot did all the things a pilot has to do before flying off.

I thought he was after shaking the plane to pieces. The racket and vibration, plus the apprehension of being in a plane for the first time, I thought they did well strapping us in our seats. It was one way to stop deserters, and make sure the pilot had someone to talk to on the journey. Then we were off. Next, during all the talk of custom free goods, we were in the air. A wondrous moment indeed . The shades of green and blue of the shallows approaching Jersey on a sunny day were quite magical.

We met another ariel act on this occasion. 'The Aeronauts'. Bill Sawyer and partner Doug. At the top of a very tall mast-like rig they had a 'space rocket' revolving around it. High above the ground hanging by their feet and hands in turn they did their routine, whizzing around. Bill's wife was governing their speed from the ground.

On one occasion both Bill and Edgar were on the same bill. A very unusual thing to have two ariel acts on together. In normal circumstances when up aloft, both acts were as nimble as monkeys. One evening they went up each others rigs. What a difference their antics then. I'm sure they acted more carefully than had it been me up there. Mind you, can you imagine me being up there? This epistle would never have been written had I tried. I don't mix well with altitudes above three feet!

When we got back from Jersey we came down to earth with a bump. It seems we were booked by one agent through another. Both demanded their ten per cent. We were not strong enough to resist this request. I have never baulked at paying my dues but this made us very angry and wary of getting into the same situation in future.

At this time Billy Cotton and his band were the biggest Saturday night show on BBC TV. Always on the lookout for new situations, his TV producer, Michael Hurll, booked the car to appear in a kind of Keystone Cops episode in a filmed insert for one of their shows. Pierre and I were booked to drive and act as 'nursemaids' to the car. Having it ready at all times during filming.

As the car was a stage prop and not 'roadworthy' in one sense, we were to shoot the film on army ground at Aldershot. You don't need a licence on private ground. Briefly, the script was Billy Cotton went off to the coast for a day in the car. During the journey a wrong turning is taken and without them knowing they run into an army minefield.

It was great fun watching the pyrotechnic expert let off these big bangs just as the car went past the places where the 'mines' were 'buried'. Pierre was driving at the time. I remember watching the man touch about a dozen connections with a live wire consecutively as the car progressed across the 'minefield'.

We were directed to cross a ford over a fast running stream. The concrete roadway was about six inches beneath the water level. It saved building a bridge. There was to be no driver visible. The car could only run without steering it in its pre-set circle. I was the driver this time, so I crouched down out of view below the dashboard. I could steer that way but I couldn't see. I went off course and demolished a concrete bollard. The shot was abandoned after that.

It was great watching the recording a couple of Saturdays later. It was deemed a great success and we were booked for four more films, to be made in Jersey. The story of one was of an old fashioned 'fireman save my child', sort of thing. The car had to be turned into a fire engine.

The producer asked me to quote for a conversion job, so I made a prop that sat on the car making it seem to be able to douse a fire. A large boiler with a fire stack that could belch smoke, flames and the odd drop of water to squirt where needed. It looked very pretty. About this time I met another BBC producer, Terry Hughes, who was Michael's assistant on this jaunt. It was a happy unit we enjoyed doing bits to help out. I was officially booked as a 'mechanic' to keep the books straight.

The weather was kind and we were on schedule. In one scene we were to tow the band's piano up and down a country lane and it shakes loose, and runs backwards down a hill. It's surprisingly difficult to make a piano go on its own in a certain direction. I thought the crew's efforts to get the piano going should have been used in the film instead of the intended shot. It was far funnier than the scripted business.

We were well into the holiday season so wherever we filmed there were always lots of holiday makers watching us. On the Friday, we were filming on the beach. The story involved Billy and the Boys doing a show on the sands. The car was not in this sequence, the piano was though, and it to was to prove to be the villain of the piece.

Billy was conducting the band with the vocalist, Alan Breeze, playing the piano. They were all acting playing flat out, busking in great style. Plenty of action. No sound was being recorded then, it was to be dubbed on later. Jim, the BBC pyro-technician on this occasion, was to have placed a smoke charge under the piano to be let off at the end of the piece. This moment was to have been when the pianist would end the playing of the tune with a grand gesture, a sweeping movement away from the piano towards the conductor, Billy. When Alan turned, so the smoke would go off.

The audience for the 'show' was made up of the girls who were also working on the film, and me. We were seated in front of the piano on deckchairs, making the appropriate movements as befitting an audience. Comes to the end of the tune, tum-tiddly-tum-tum, BANG! Alan swung away from the piano towards Billy Cotton, promptly covering him with his own body. It was a good job he did too. Instead of a puff of smoke there was a tremendous explosion. I don't know what was put under the piano but it was far more than a smoke charge.

There was no iron frame or strings in the piano to enable it to be manhandled more easily, but the keyboard was still there. Or rather it was before the explosion blew it to bits and towards us in the audience. I felt things tearing into me, not realising what they were. The silence that followed the explosion was thick with shock. The onlookers higher up the beach and the camera crew were mostly out of range of the bits of piano that were propelled in all directions by the force of the blast, but we were not.

I first noticed someone sobbing next to me. It was one of the make-up girls. I moved over to see if I could help. The next thing I remember was she became more distressed at the sight of me. Something was dripping onto her face. It was my blood, from a wound in my forehead. Around me other people were now gradually taking in what had happened. Jim, who let the 'thing' off, was in a bad way. It looked as though his face had been pushed to one side. He was bleeding badly. I remember Pierre and someone else getting a car and loading him into it to get him to hospital.

In the ensuing few hours at the hospital I took stock. The fact that we in the audience had been lying back in an inclined posture in the deckchairs had helped us somewhat. I had been struck in the ankles, knees, chest and forehead. The chest injuries were caused by ignited magnesium. Red hot pieces had burnt themselves into my nylon shirt front. The burn marks were unmistakable. I needed seven stitches in my forehead.

The hospital didn't bandage me. I was smeared with a new transparent gel that formed a skin over the wound. It did not hide the injury though. I was more distressed having my wounds on show like this than if they had been bandaged.

I seemed to have wandered about for ages, and whenever I stopped to sit anywhere, people stared. I rather feel it was the after effects of the explosion that were the most upsetting. I still don't feel the same way about bangs as I used to before this accident.

I hadn't noticed my wrist watch was missing. A Policeman found it some thirty feet away from the deckchairs. It wasn't working. I had aged considerably. Billy Cotton being involved, the news spread rapidly. I phoned Deena to assure her all was well. It seems that the movement of Alan Breeze away from the piano towards Billy at the finale saved them both from the blast.

A local photographer got a picture of the explosion itself. It was a remarkable photograph and appeared in The People and other Sunday newspapers. The aged copy of the one I have still shows a remarkable moment caught on camera. I never heard much of the other folk's injuries as the BBC then cancelled the films. What a shame, they might have done a lot for Pierre and I if they'd been shown. I heard later that Jim, the pyro-technician, lost an eye.

We'd arranged for Deena to fly out for a couple of days holiday together. So instead of her flying out, I phoned to say I was on my way home. I totted up the cost of a new shirt, socks and wrist watch and sent my bill to the BBC. They sent a cheque by return. We were hoping for more work from them so didn't make any more of it. We didn't get any more work.

The sixties were momentous times. A shot fired in Dallas was felt throughout the world. President John F Kennedy was assassinated. Pierre had managed to get us a showing on 'Blue Peter', a top children's show. BBC programmes were falling in disarray all about us, the president was being buried on the day of our transmission. Will we or won't we get on air? In the event we were one of the first shows out after the funeral.

Checking everything in the studio we realised we were very low on compressed air for the seat. We never got round to having a pressure gauge put on our cylinder. There was not enough pressure to hoist a not too sylph-like Pierre up aloft. The old saying 'necessity is the mother of invention', is never truer than in a clown situation. The TV world was waiting for us to be funny and so instead of getting a laugh going up, we played it for one going down.

Having plenty of air to send the seat up empty, Pierre got laughs sitting on it, or trying to get on it, whilst it was a yard up in the air. The studio didn't know the normal business. We got away with it. Mind you I did manage to knock one of the studio scenic flats, flat, on the way out. Since then I have always felt very keenly for performers who, through natural or unnatural causes, such as disputes, have lost an opportunity to be seen on the box after all their preparations and expectations.

We did a show for another ITV children's show, The Five O'Clock Club, after they were pleased with the car act. This time we were booked for the skating act. Then suddenly the TV schedules were re-arranged and our date was cancelled, but we were booked for a TV spot on a Billy Smarts Circus Show.

Smarts rarely put their travelling show on the telly, they booked in extra people for a one-off performance. We were one of these. It was to be recorded in Southsea, Hampshire, and broadcast over the holiday period. This was to be my first taste of the Circus. Although a brief encounter, I was looking forward to it. One can't get to know the circus way of life without being in it, lock, stock and barrel. I was used to working large areas and the stage, I wondered about the circus ring.

The BBC producer used the fact that elephants liked a dip in the sea and got Pierre to go down with them in the car. This was a few days before the recording. Then on the actual filming, this part was run as though they'd all just come down from the beach.

As the car was shown entering the tent we were ready to assume our act, which we did on cue. The intimacy of the audience was a plus. I like being in touch. The ring was larger than I'd imagined but most of the audience could see you. The tiered seating helped. Pierre had been with the circus all week. I came for the day after my work at home, so it was strange taking it all in. Plus we didn't have much practice in the ring before going on. But it went well and we looked very credible when it was shown over the holiday.

Both families were there, including Pierre's dad. The front row seats of the ring were taken up by the Smarts and other circus children. An hour's show on the television unfortunately takes a little longer to get in the can. It took the whole day. The audience responded well to the requests of the deputy directors. The resident carpet clowns had a major job on their hands supplying interval entertainment, run-ins and generally keeping everyone happy. All the stops and starts of a recording session meant the audience earned their right to 'appear on the telly'.

I liked working in the circus ring. My fear that we wouldn't have room to let the car run free proved groundless. We had plenty of room. Benefiting by working in a circus atmosphere, I took it as a challenge. There was not much money in it, we took it as a show date. Also it was it was Pierre's show. He was more circus than me. He'd been with Smarts a few days and coming in later I felt very much like a junior partner. If a partner at all. I was increasingly getting fed up with being '& Company'. Pierre didn't help much here either. Once when I was going to do a job in the West End, I was in a taxi with a Daily Mail photographer. We introduced each other and when I said I was Hal Brooks, Pierre's partner, he said 'Oh! I didn't know Pierre had a partner'.

I couldn't really blame anybody. I didn't have Pierre's ability to remain in town on spec, I still had to earn a living in between jobs. So he had to push on alone on many occasions. One memory that still sticks over all these years. In

Southsea I had walked through the elephants tent, between two lines of them. They were about eight feet away from each other, but the heat they generated between them could be felt as though you walked through two rows of electric fires. Quite incredible.

Funnily enough we didn't have to wait long to be in a circus again. If size was being judged, we were at the other end of the scale. The 'Weight's Family Circus' was just that, a family affair. The annual Magicians Convention was being held in Hastings. We were booked to perform the car act

I got on well with the Weights family. All troupers. I only met them the once but it has left very nice memories. Two friends of mine from Bognor, magicians both, were in the audience, so I was glad it went down well. The drama they were never aware of was of what happened to my tooth. For a long time I've had a single artificial tooth on a small plate which improves my looks somewhat!

During the action, shouting, it shot out of my mouth. As we were working on grass, I kept my eyes open for it. When the whole show was over, and the ring was clear, I went over it on my hands and knees. If the plate had been pink it might have been easier to locate, it was transparent though. But lucky me I found it. The car must have run over it, pushing it down into the soil, so protecting it.

We were attending a gala show in Eltham one Sunday when real tragedy struck. The ground was slippery and we'd made a good entrance. Pierre had just set the car in its free running circle, and jumped out of it, holding the steering wheel above his head. My bit was to grab hold of a back bracket (put there specially for the trick), and then be dragged off my feet and get trailed around a couple of times before letting go. Then after sitting on my bottom, having to scramble out of its path as it comes round again.

All exciting stuff and visual slapstick. Then Pierre did a couple of crossovers in front of the moving car, which was by this time going quite fast. Then he slipped. I saw the car go over his leg. We rather used to get carried away in our antics during this spot, but I realised it was a calamity. I tore over to the car, dragged it out of its locked path and braked it to a halt. I went over to Pierre and he was yelling something or other. The crowd were shrieking. It looked very good from there.

They didn't realise that anything was amiss. When I tried to move him we both realised the leg was broken. I went over to the stewards and commentator and asked for an ambulance. It was all very sad. The crowd were very sympathetic when given the news. When next I saw himself, he was in plaster from toe to hip. It was a compound fracture. He never complained of the pain though it must have been rough. Whatever happened, Pierre would never complain, he just got on with it.

So there we were. Well booked up for galas all over the country, and half of the act in plaster, which weighed a ton! Our saviour came in the way of Deena's brother-in-law, Bernard Stockton. Dave's son. Between us, with Pierre in an invalid chair, joining in from the touch line   you might say, we fulfilled all our engagements. It was tremendously hard work though. Six foot plus Pierre, now thoroughly packed in plaster of Paris, having to be pushed over soft grassy surfaces. We were whacked out at the end of every performance.

Bernard was no slouch at comedy either. He'd been to RADA and was a trained actor. He was modelled, as was I, on his dad, who was a very funny and competent performer in his day. So we still gave good value. I think Pierre felt very frustrated having to watch us sorting out a routine to suit ourselves rather than Bernard simply copying his routine. But there was no alternative, we all had to grin and bear it.

We were also booked for the Jersey Battle of Flowers again. This time the wheelchair was transformed into an asset. I built a prop around it to make it look like a pram. Our plaster-loaded leading man was dressed as a 'bouncing baby', complete with bonnet, and we 'attended' him on our journey over the procession route.

Pram pushing Bernard was dressed as an outrageous nanny with bright red lips and enormous bosoms. In the pram was 'baby' Pierre, every so often shouting for his potty. In fact, all in all, it was one of our most successful comedy routines during those fateful healing months. 'Out of adversity...' sort of thing.

Shortly after Pierre was fully recovered he attended the Brighton Toy Fair. A firm called Bendy Toys came out with a creation from the authoress, Elsie Mills, of a road safety conscious squirrel called Tufty. He and his small animal friends were woven into stories about keeping safe, which young mums could read to their children. This was an effort to prepare children from an early age indeed, to be aware of the dangers of traffic.

Bendy Toys gave us a supply of their Tuftys to spread around the schools as a contribution to road safety, and (of course), publicise their toys. So Pierre suggested we do some road safety in schools ourselves. I made a few props relevant to the subject and we arranged to talk to children from Lyon Street

School in Bognor. The headmistress was the sister of a well-known BBC producer Brian Michie, who used to run TV talent shows. She welcomed us into her school and so began our first road safety venture.

Pierre went in as the clown, I preceded him for introduction sake, and to feed him material. I made up a couple of drawings about belisha beacons and zebra crossings that aided and abetted him in trying to spread the official road safety message called 'Kerb Drill'. This was to 'look right, look left, look right again, if all clear, quick march across the road. Don't run.' Later this was to become the Green Cross Code.

I was dressed ordinarily and was on hand to allay any tears I might detect welling up in any young, concerned eyes. Not every child took kindly to this seemingly giant of a man, who didn't look a bit like his own daddy, towering above him, telling him to look this way and that. Mostly though, the children loved it. We managed to hold the floor for about twenty minutes or so. The teachers were pleased too. It made a bright change to school normality.

I feel sure we were effective. We were careful not to confuse or do any damage. I'm sure the teachers would have remarked if our presentation had been in any way unsuitable. Finding this new audience in schools looked very interesting. It could be a great source of midweek work. A good bread and butter job.

Pierre also found another opening for this kind of work. The Apple Growers Association were, at that time, pushing their product, apples, and linking it with dental care. It was reasonable to suppose that an apple after a meal would help keep your teeth healthy. Anyway, that's what the old saying says. And of course who better to help their campaign prosper than Pierre and Company.

Chapter 15

The Apple Saga

A bonus with the apple pushing was that it had the backing of the Dental Council. So work really started coming in. With tours arranged by the Dental Council and the leaflets to go with it, plus the apple which was provided by the Apple Growers Association, to be left with each child, things gathered pace.

Pierre had worked out a tooth routine and was very successful. I came and watched him work and if jobs came up that clashed with his school tours I used to stand in for him. I thoroughly enjoyed this. I adapted his routine to suit me, and one could do a very good teeth show in 15 to 20 minutes. More importantly, it wasn't necessary to divide the ages. You could do a whole school in one go, hall sizes permitting. I made giant toothbrushes and combs for us both.

I remember the source of bristles I used for this. Two lines of cheap wallpaper brushes glued together comprised the 'bristly' bits. I did a week in Durham and one in Workington. As Pierre had been booked I just pretended to be him, only telling the teachers. It was too complicated to tell the youngsters. Pierre also suggested I became 'Pierre number two'. He would work one area while I worked the another. I firmly declined this offer. Every day now I was feeling more like Hal Brooks.

We had very different ideas about school work. If I went in and made a mistake I didn't mind 'taking the can' for it. Likewise, if I had done a good show, I wanted recognition for me, and hated posing as someone else. The teachers were adults and also didn't care for this deception. Then a moment arrived that had a deep significance for me. Pierre was otherwise engaged and asked me to stand in for him for a three day road safety tour of schools in the London borough of Southwark.

As soon as I had accepted I knew I wasn't going to be content with a shallow look right, then left, sort of thing. I needed more meat in the act. So I seriously began to think about props and ideas for presenting road safety to children.

Deena and I got together on this. Her teacher training and ability proved invaluable to me. We discussed areas of instruction that could usefully be used by me, a carpenter, and clown. Gradually we built up about twenty minutes of instruction and lesson, plus ten minutes of comedy with which to sugar the pill.

Obviously we wouldn't have poked fun at road safety rules and so came up with a method so that when our young audience were hanging onto every word we would slip in a road safety point. The idea was to get the children's full attention with bit of fun first, then on to the serious business of road safety.

Fortunately this booking was made well in advance and I had plenty of time to prepare. Whilst all this was going on, one other thing had to be sorted out. I needed a character myself. It was all very well not being Pierre, but what was Hal Brooks going to look like?

Deena and I discussed costume, colour schemes, and makeup. We decided I should become a bright colourful character, which suitably expressed the 'real' me. The name bit didn't change though. I was once again Uncle Hal, Clown. We both felt relieved and free again. It was all very well agreeing to suppress our own identities as Hal and Deena Brooks to push Pierre the Clown, but we missed being just ourselves, as children's entertainers.

The entertainment business is a very tough profession to succeed in and it was common sense in the beginning to push the front man, Pierre, but I couldn't ever see us surfacing as ourselves again, unless we made the effort. Besides this, Pierre was doing nearly twenty weeks a year in schools, on teeth, at this time. To me, that meant twenty weeks when I had little hope of being employed as one half of a clown duo.

So events were forcing me to take up the motley completely. I wasn't upset at having increasingly to leave behind the supporting role and to be in charge of my own ship. I enjoyed not having to think of anybody but myself whilst performing.

Pierre was always asking Deena to write verse, make up stories, and generally use her talents at writing to feed him ideas that might have a commercial application, or further our fortunes as a trio. She also composed most of our letters too. She wrote a fine verse about not talking to strangers, and it was exactly right for the understanding by children of the dangers of being improperly approached. She also wrote a whole series of verse, in story form, 'Pierre and a visit to the circus'.

Our son Jimmy, then at school, did some drawings about the circus. With some of these drawings, plus the verse, Pierre found a sponsor to put it into print as a booklet. The sponsor was Duckhams Motor Oils Ltd, and the booklet was called 'Pierre the Clown's Road Safety Book'.

There was another contributor to the success of the book, the RSO of Southwark, Vic Golds, MBE. New road signs were about to be introduced and Vic had them hot off the press. So interspersed between the verse and circus pictures were the new traffic signs and explanations of their meaning. The artwork was beautifully done and the booklet well received. It was free at the first printing but there was such a demand that Duckhams had to accept a small charge for a subsequent edition.

When I saw the mock up of the book I noted there was no mention of Deena's contribution at that time . I mentioned this to Pierre and insisted she got a credit. In the end we were allowed a line stating 'additional material by Hal and Deena Brooks'. (I didn't know of Vic Golds contribution at the time). It was omissions like this that used to upset me.

The car was still attracting work in its own right. It was booked for a pantomime in the Theatre Royal, Brighton. Norman Vaughan was Buttons and Bill Pertwee was partnering him. I taught them the car act and rehearsed them until they felt comfortable using the prop. Bill was to do the tumble out of the back whilst Norman drove off. I was with the car during the pantomime run, getting it ready for the scene where Norman and Bill were using it to go to the ball.

It was Cinderella of course. My job was setting the various gags up on the car and have it all ready for them to enter from the prompt side, conking out mid-stage, where they went through the car routine. Norman was doing the seat business. He didn't like it either! He said 'Hal, let's adjust it to go only one notch, instead of two'. I agreed. It was just as good a gag. The laugh came when he went up in the air, not the height it goes.

I arranged this by putting only sixty pounds of pressure into the air tank that pushed the seat up, instead of the full amount of 100 pounds per square inch. I enjoyed the four week run of the panto. It really put me into a steep learning curve about stage work.

I also had some small parts in the show. I was a doorman and footman in the palace scene. In my stage costume, with a couple of lines to speak, I even managed to work in a joke about Green Shield Stamps. Though when I tried to enlarge my part I was quietly put back in my place by the ugly sisters. Barry Howard was one. His props were very eye catching.

There was panic halfway through the run. Norman went down with the 'flu. John Inman arrived to stand in for him. It occurred to me at the time how completely different were the two interpretations of the role of Buttons. I enjoyed both styles. I remember being a little worried at the contortions that went on when getting the replacement 'flu-less performer into the now empty costume Norman used. A very general shoving and pushing by anxious dressers were the order of the day. I'm not sure the shoes fitted either.

Bill Pertwee I already knew. Bill came to live in Bognor when I was still very much in the building game. He moved into a large house there and I did quite a bit of work for him, woodworking and decorating. He was very handy himself but was getting very busy then, and just didn't have the time to do it all himself.

Another pleasant experience for me at Brighton was doing a spot of painting. We had quite a long wait 'til the evening show after a matinee, so I took my paints along with me. As well as sketching the dancers waiting to go on stage, I did some pencil portraits of the stage hands. Three of the staff sat for me, and the male lead singer of the show, Craig Douglas, sat for an oil portrait. It wasn't bad either! It gave the local Argus something to write about. There was a nice photograph of me painting Craig in his dressing room and a write up about me and my road safety work.

A few weeks before this panto we were involved in another Christmas show. This time for the BBC. Coincidentally it was another Cinderella. I was again to be nursemaid to the car and instructor to boot. The stars driving to the ball this time were to be Terry Scott and Hugh Lloyd, with Peter Whitmore producing. We rehearsed in a Territorial Army parade ground in London.

The first day was to be a traumatic experience for me. Our family transport had recently taken a change for the better. In fact we were out of this world. From a ten hundredweight black Fordson Van I changed to a Vauxhall Victor estate car. This was sheer luxury. It was in good nick too. Not new, (I haven't managed a 'new' car even yet), but it had been well looked after and was cream and Capri red.

It takes me a long time to get settled in a different vehicle and I had to go up in the London traffic, not feeling very sure of myself at all. When I met Peter, Terry and Hugh at the rehearsal room, they suggested we all go to see where the car was to be rehearsed. They all opted to go in my car. I was very nervous. I didn't let on, but I don't think they were unaware of my nervousness.

I went over all the gags with them and Terry was quite adamant he didn't want to 'clown it up'. He thought it would be stronger to underplay the action, and this they did. I agreed with his suggestion that gags should flow naturally and not be isolated events happening on their own without rhyme or reason.

To give cause for the seat to go up we put a tube underneath the car and I made it look as though it was the exhaust. Then when Terry and Hugh repeatedly jumped in ready to drive off only to have the car stop, Hugh would say, 'I'll see if there's a blockage'. Whereupon he drew a pole back out of the tube and with a 'one, two, three', he would ram it apparently up the exhaust, whereupon Terry yells and lets himself up in the seat. It was good gag, I made a mental note of its success.

The show was recorded in the Golders Green Empire, in front of a live audience. Earlier on stage someone came up behind me and called 'Uncle Hal and Auntie Deena'. It was the star who was playing Buttons, Jimmy Tarbuck. He said whilst hanging about in Pwllheli Butlin's camp awaiting the result of the talent finals, he often came across to the children's theatre and watched us working with the children. When I told Deena later that evening, she was very pleased.

Strangely enough the following year the Model T was booked for a panto in Wimbledon. Surprise, surprise, who were the stars in it? Terry and Hugh of course. This time it was 'Babes in the Wood'. Terry played the Dame and Hugh was one of the Robbers. So the car act was soon in the swing again, with this same duo still going to some palace or other.

With plenty of time on my hands during these jobs on stage, I tried to think of every eventuality that may arise. I had extra props hanging from the other side of the car in case the engine didn't start. I also had a brown coat handy in case I had to push it on. The car, which used petrol, brought me in touch with the fireman again. I only kept one pint of petrol on stage at a time. This I kept in a dustbin, along with the flash powder and bangs.

There were two petrol tanks on the car. One held a gallon for field work, and the other about a pint for the stage. This small tank was circular and wrapped round with asbestos cord. Two separate taps controlled petrol supplies to the engine. A point 32 blank firing revolver also helped us out with smaller effects.

One couldn't always do the preparation work as quietly as one wanted. There is never enough space backstage for comfort. During one show, I remember 'Robin Hood' coming backstage and blowing his top because I distracted him whilst he was 'Robin Hoodin it' out front.

I apologised of course, but sudden lighting blackouts in the plot often meant that a spanner dropped, is a spanner remembered. Later on 'Robin' became a sailing ship owner in The Onedin Line. I hope he got as much co-operation from his shipmates on the high seas as this humble mechanic tried to give him in Sherwood Forest!

Towards the end of the run, Terry's dresser, a young lad, had to return to school after the holidays. I stood in for him until the show finished its run. A highlight of Terry's Dame was his strip routine, prior to getting in bed. During the playing of 'The Stripper' he saucily shed   about fifteen items of erotica including loud underclothes, blousey bloomers, and some pantaloons with a large eye that winked at the audience. The eye sometimes stuck, and I evolved a way to keep it mobile. I enclosed the cord that operated the eyelid in a plastic tube to stop it kinking.

When he'd finished the strip and all was done, he flung himself on the bed after removing his stays, and with a final crescendo, the bed collapsed under his weight. Blackout! A brilliantly funny act. I very much enjoyed working as his dresser for those few weeks. I'm not one for champagne as a rule but the stuff Terry kept for appropriate occasions, such as visitors, was very appealing. The occasional glass, with its bubbles, tickled my fancy.

One day the visitors included Peter Whitmore, Jean Whitfield and Jimmy Perry. Jimmy knew of my association with Butlin's and Peter from the BBC panto. I mentioned to Peter I was a lightning sketch artist. He was producing the children's show 'Blue Peter' at that time. He kindly gave me an audition for the programme. I pitched my effort for too young an age. You don't get many chances like that, and I muffed it.

On that show, Dickie Henderson played Buttons. Every night he charmed me with his skill and poise and the way he worked an audience. Like the conductor of a very large orchestra. Superbly in control.

I heard a comment from one agent that surprised me. His client, a famous star of the time, had suggested he was 'being passed over'. He was firmly told to 'wait his turn'. Being very much a loner in the lower orders of the profession, I allowed myself a quiet smile.

Terry and Hugh also co-operated with some photographs with me in clown garb. Some were published in the local papers and the RSO of Merton, (Wimbledon's new name), booked me for some work in his schools. Not long after this that Pierre and I got a show date with the car at the Victoria Palace, but it was for a well-known charity. No money for us.

Terry was also on the bill. He did an act as a sort of mediaeval strolling troubadour. I loved his costume, it was like that of an elaborate Jester come Mister Punch mixture. Overlong turn-ups to his pointed shoes, wobbling about as he pranced about the stage. I never saw him do this act on television. It was a joy.

It was a big show and large bill. Pierre and I dressed in with Terry Hall of 'Lenny The Lion' fame. It was always a bonus for me meeting all these talented performers. There was a snag with Terry Scott being on the programme, Pierre and I had already agreed his presentation of the seat routine was better than ours and had already put it into our programme. We hurriedly went back to our own way of doing of it, just for this one night! Both ways were very funny anyway.

I did a birthday party for one of Terry's children. In a spare moment he showed me his 'booking' system for work and other dates. We had one thing in common. We both employed a 'Boots the Chemists Year Diary'. His seemingly in greater disorder than mine. He also let on he had a phone in his loo! Maggie, Terry's wife, invited Deena and I over for lunch a little later. She was an excellent cook and we enjoyed a lovely couple of hours together.

Increasingly now I was drawn to being myself. My first solo road safety show was in Hove, Brighton. I had assembled some items of interest and Deena had given me bits of verse to say to promote a laugh or two. I made what was to turn out to be a lifetime prop and laughter maker. It was a small child's umbrella, with pretty lace edging, that didn't wait for rain to fall. It made its own. A little copper tube squirted water out of the umbrella's top from a rubber, (medical kind), bulb held in the hand. A simple way of producing an instant shower.

Another aid for me was from a drawing I saw in the first Tufty book by Elsie Mills. A playball the size of a football, with the words 'Play with me in safe places' carefully written on it. Remember, I was no stranger to entertaining children, but now I was a proper clown. Makeup, large coat, big boots and gloves, topped out with a red ping-pong ball on my nose. So I set forth.

My first lesson about clowns. Not all children like them for a start, especially under five-year-olds, and sitting in a group they can't do what comes naturally, flee! Or can they? You try to stop them! A lot of children can't get on with Father Christmas either. In summing up, my first solo venture into schools wasn't a raging success. (I never got a return date from there anyway).

Deena and I put it all through a post mortem when we got home. It was all very agonising, but very necessary. She pointed out the teaching defects. I brooded about props and ideas. I was getting the hand of linking items to make a sensible whole. Then I had an idea about Tufty as a glove puppet and a routine about a zebra crossing.

The zebra crossing was one Mr Hore Belisha's ideas for crossing busy roads, hence belisha beacons. He was the transport minister that initiated them. This was before the pedestrian crossings that we know now. I was really excited about this. As with most of the successful props I've made in the past, this one felt right. It's strange this feeling. Anyway I got down to making it. Son Jim helping me with the electrics, Deena making the puppet.

A bit of luck, I already had a case the right size, with a hinged lid, and carrying handle. With the case at table height, I could set the lid at an angle to the audience. By raising it so, I could place a set of black and white stripes, (representing a road crossing), on the lid that was in full view of the audience. There were two sets of markings. It took four black and three white stripes, (painted on hardboard), to go right across the lid. On another piece of hardboard I painted a whole crossing.

My idea soon developed into a good routine.

A school hall, a room in the village hall, church or play centre.

On a table out front, the assembled children see a small zebra crossing, complete with a belisha beacon on either side.

At the appropriate moment I mention we've got a visitor. It's Tufty. I go over to the set-up and look in. I say

'He's asleep'!

I knock on the lid.

'Better say wake up Tufty'.

There's no difficulty getting a response here. Inside the case, I squeeze Tufty's 'voice' a couple of times. The squeek that it makes is from the noisy bit of a child's cycle hooter.

'You've woken him up'.

I have both hands in the case, putting the glove puppet on my right hand.

'Come on Tufty, the boys and girls are waiting to see you'.

By now I have the puppet in on my hand with his 'voice' in my palm. Looking in I say

'He's having his breakfast. What are you eating?' (squeeks),

'Cornflakes'.

From the reaction of the audience they also are no strangers to this delicacy.

'What are you eating with your conflakes? (squeeks),

'Christmas pudding'.

Chortles from out front.

Bringing Tufty out into view, I hold him standing on my left hand, facing my audience.

The little fella closely resembles the Bendy toy from the front. The same colours and stance, wearing feet I'd taken from an actual doll. Deena had fashioned a very good likeness in the face and from his rear flowed a beautiful, squirrel-like tail. (Where she obtained this I never knew.) After a bit of banter saying hello, Tufty asks if they'd like to see his tail. I then swished it over his head in a grand manner.

Down to business.

'Tufty would like to ask you some questions. 'Did you know this is a Zebra crossing? Did you know it's a safe place to cross the road?'

With the puppet squeaking in my ears, plus the waving of his arms over the crossing, I used my method of imparting my gems of knowledge to the children. (For playgroup and infant ages). Telling the answer in the question. I always was conscious I was there to instruct, not to question.

'Tufty says he would like to help you to remember. He's got another crossing in the box'.

Into the case he goes, where I shed him from my hand.

'I know, I'll take these off and see what he's got in there'.

Clearing the lid of the full set of stripes and the belisha beacons, I then instructed Tufty to hand out the pieces to me, now that the inclined lid of case is clear. A rattling is heard from below.

'Oh look, he's found some black and white stripes. I know ,we'll put these right across the road'

As the stripes are handed out I say either

'A black one or white one'

As each are placed next to each other. I encourage the children to repeat it with me. Not wanting to be too slick, the fourth one out is decorated in a blue and white pattern. To Tufty,

'That's not right, it looks like a racing car'.

I then do a couple of 'VROOM VROOMS as though in a car.

Back to the right colour.

'A white one, a black one. Oops. The next one is plain white with red spots on it'

'Oooh, look! This ones got the measles'!

Most of my audience know about measles

'A white one,'

Well not quite, someone had been playing noughts and crosses on this one.

'A white one, and last of all a black one'.

Now all of the stripes are laid across. Tufty hands out a belisha beacon pole. I place this in one of the sockets.

'Now we have to find the right coloured ball to go on top'.

I have a compartment in the case that holds a variety of 'wrong' items. 'We'll try this pink one. No?

How about this red one?

What colour should it be then?

ORANGE is called out. Next I put a plastic orange, complete with leaves, on. Exasperation! Me

'I like this one',

I put a plastic banana on. Lastly I put on a bunch of grapes on.

'Wouldn't it be nice if there were real grapes there?

'Then every time we crossed the road safely we could pick one,' Smacking my lips whilst pretending to eat one.

'I'm not having much luck with this,'

Taking out the beacon pole.

'I'll try this one'.

Inside we have a variety of wrong ones to try. They are all painted like proper belisha beacon poles, each with a small orange globe on top. (I got these from Woolworth). They are small plastic oranges, and look just right. I never had any one order of bringing these out, it relied very much on the way they had been put away after my last show, except for the last two.

The seven beacons came out one by one, with a comment from me, prompted by the reception shown by my audience. One had two separate heads, like a letter T. Another had a ziz-zag pole, like a lightning strike. Another had a flexible pole, which I named as 'Willy Wobble', giving it a push when in the socket. One pole had four oranges spaced out down the pole. An unusual one was a spiral pole. My comment on putting this one in was probably, 'and the wind goes up the chimney just the same', mimicking the nursery rhyme.

We are now coming to the end of this bit of nonsense.

'Look, I've found a straight one'.

It is straight, but with twice the length of pole.

'Hold on, I've got a shorter one'.

And it's far too short. Exasperation sets in and I say,

'I know, we'll use Tufty's.'

When I'd cleared the top I had laid his Beacons carefully to one side. So now with the proper ones installed I say

'There, these are the ones we look for.'

These beacons Jim made for me are really extended light bulbs. The small bulb at the top is connected through the stem of the pole to a contact in its base. The orange globe on its top is transparent with the bulb inside.

From controls inside the case, I now use a push button control to make the lights blink, aided by two six volt batteries also in the case. There are two more switches, one for each light.

I start making the lights blink.

'There, we can also see them at night, telling us we should cross the road here. The lights are saying to the drivers of cars, lorries and buses. Look out. Someone may be crossing the road.' After this I have a word with Tufty. Can we have the lights out now, please?

(Squeaks are heard,)

'Oh dear, Tufty says there's no switch for putting them off'.

Both lights are on now.

'I know, we'll blow them out. I'll say one, two, three and we'll blow this one'. (Pointing to the one on the right).

'One, two, three BLOW'.

I switch the left one off.

'Oh dear, someone blew the wrong one'. (Pointing to the one that is now off).

'I think we should all blow this one now!' We do so, and out goes the other light.

'Well boys and girls I think we should thank Tufty for helping us remember where to cross', and lead them into a round of applause.

The whole routine took about eight minutes, and in my opinion never failed the children. I delighted in performing it too.

I did manage to have it up and running for the three consecutive days in Southwark Schools. These three days were marvellous for me to work out the finer points. As it happened I did twelve performances in all, and I trust I knew more about my box of tricks after the final show, than the first. The teachers were very complimentary and encouraged me to seek elsewhere for schemes to involve children in.

There was another reason why I was hoping for more school work as well. Deena had had enough of being out front. She was very content to be helping out back-stage but felt she should hang up her dancing shoes. I knew how much I would miss her, but it was inevitable. I had to get more solo work and manage on my own, instead of as a duo.

From my point of view, schoolwork was very satisfactory. Hard work and exhausting, but worthwhile. It was emotionally exhausting really. Even after a children's party I wasn't myself until after I'd had a nap.

Now having four shows a day to do, I could have done with a week's sleep. On top of this was the fact that one couldn't reliably get into London at nine-o'clock in the morning. I was commuting each day, seventy miles each way, in the Victor. I left home at six in the morning and got back home at 7pm.

I got to the Elephant and Castle, Southwark about 8am., and put my feet up until we could get in the schools. Such was early morning traffic, one could not make such a fine adjustment when to arrive. Going home in the evening was easier. Schools were finished at four so I was well on my way out before the evening build up. I made for Dorking for my first nap. Sometimes I stopped twice.

One night on a sharp bend I drifted towards the left. Fortunately it was a hedge and the sounds it made woke me up, otherwise I might not have been writing this. This incident precipitated me to get get a motor caravan. Then I could go up to the Smoke on Monday, returning on Friday, having arranged with the RSOs for me to park up in local council yards overnight. Looking back I should have named the van 'Pal', after a well advertised brand of dog food which 'Prolongs Active Life'!

So I continued to build up my acts. I had no difficulty introducing comedy and I developed drawings on road safety that made me 'look clever'. Introducing a Birthday spot for any child whose birthday was on that day, or near, enabled me to play the piano for the singing of Happy Birthday by the children. It's funny that young children always buzzed with excitement when I said I was going to play the piano. 'Clowns can't do that', or so they think.

They are always tickled pink when you do something out of the ordinary. They don't really expect you to be able to draw. I think it was because, at the back of their minds, they thought I was a teacher or policeman dressed up, or you are not a proper man underneath! Eating arranged dinners in schools there were lots of comments by the children. 'Am I like his daddy underneath', the mind boggles. 'Did I grow into a clown?'. Now there's a question for the Brains' Trust!

Since I've been in many schools of very mixed races, colours, and creeds, I often wonder what some of these children must think of someone dressed up as a clown. But in my experience if you do something funny that tickles them, they will laugh. What a relief that is too. Mostly there's a touch of fear in the first laugh but when you settle them down they can become the most rewarding of audiences.

Many's the dubious sweet I've had offered me after a show. The history of the sweets' travels would probably make your hair stand on end. Once I had a confection offered me, (made by mum of course), of the snap crackle and pop variety. It was bound together with a syrupy toffee arrangement, or nearly so. I was not in a position to down this delicacy at once so I placed it down on a table. And lo and behold, before my very eyes, it oozed itself flat in a smooth sort of pancakey action.

In these circumstances I depend on a quality gotten from my army days. Pop it in the mouth quick, and there, all gone! (I hope.) The hardest bit sometimes is the all important smile of enjoyment that is the child's reward. But I'm only kidding. Often the potato crisps offered me are crisp. The shy smile, and the open plastic bag containing these shreds of pomme de terre, are gifts of the heart, from these tiniest of the Queen's subjects. I don't refuse if I can help it. The quality of giving must be matched by the delight of acceptance. It's just that once you accept one you get a hundred little hands thrusting eagerly forward. These may not sound like problems to most people, but they are my problems. Nice problems too.

Increasingly it seemed that Pierre and I were not working together much these days. We did a couple of children's shows on television, including The Five O'clock Club again. June and Jimmy Kidd were on one show, doing their Daisy the Cow act. Shortly afterwards we heard that Jimmy had died. He had relatives in Bognor and I used to see him when he was visiting them. Afterwards, June teamed up with her son Paul. Paul also had a car act. He was known as ' Paddywack the Clown'.

And so it came. A letter from Pierre saying he wanted out. 'He couldn't see the way clear for the car act to support two families.' Although I was half expecting it, it was still was a shock. I was more sad really. We'd had some good times together but now it was ended, just like that. I have mentioned before how I started writing in the seventies. And now over thirty years on I don't intend to say what I wrote about this originally. Suffice to say one never knows of one's potential, but when it comes to the push, you find out.

With hindsight, I should be thankful. We are friends again and the past remains in the past. Deena and I would never have had the sort of shove we got when we first agreed to line up behind this restless charmer with his continental name and his ambitious nature. All three of us will never forget or regret the things we experienced together. The phrase about space comes into mind, 'To go where no man has gone before'.

It has occurred to me that being now at a crossroad in my working life, most of my writing so far has been about Pierre and me. So to express my thanks to the other member of our trio, who tirelessly worked on our behalf with her letter writing, composing verse and generally being a reliable 'dogsbody' in our rush 'to get on', here is my favourite item of Deena's art...

It's true you'll very often meet,
the kindest people in the street,
Who'd really like to be your friend,
but don't take chances, some pretend.
They offer sweets, and stop and talk.
Suggest you take a little walk,
Or in their car to have a ride,
But never, never step inside.
Tell your Mum, she knows the dangers,
It's best you shouldn't talk to strangers.

Deena.

Chapter 16

Getting to Grips with Road Safety

Looking back now at the time Pierre and I parted company, after nine years of working together, I am left in no doubt as to the extent it affected me. He'd always done the business for the Teeth and Apple tours. The car belonged to him so that also put paid to my summer gala earnings. I still had my building work and children's parties, now solo performances, with which to confront wolfie at the door. Fortunately, my interest in school work, road safety, was as strong as ever. Now I turned to put this to full use.

A RoSPA monthly publication, 'Care on the Road', a road safety journal, was at hand to advertise in. I also wrote to Vic Golds in Southwark, asking for an expenses only date in his schools. He managed to get me a week's tour a few weeks hence. I used this time to work out more routines and also to write a letter to each RSO in the London Boroughs saying where I'd be on each day of the tour, which schools, and times of performance. I invited them to come and have a look. A show date. Three came.

One said his budget couldn't stand the expense then, but he'd bear me in mind for the next financial year. Another watched, but nothing came of it. The third was Ted Davenport, an ex-bus driver, and RSO for the London Borough of Lewisham. He'd liked what he'd seen and started using me from then on, giving me for four weeks in his schools over the year. He was also instrumental in getting me work in Lewisham Parks during the holidays. Normal child stuff, that was!

Ted put me in every situation in his borough that he considered I'd be a help in raising road safety standards. Playgroups, where we got to young mums, OAP clubs, special schools and protected work places. I managed to keep pace with all his placings, and so built up a wide repertoire of relevant material. This just suited me. I loved making up props for new ideas. Keeping talk to a minimum, always working for the visual impact.

I used to update ideas from the Royal Society for Prevention of Accidents (RoSPA). They were a gold mine of colourful posters and punchy slogans. At the time there were other acts using the schools for midweek work. Some of them did not do much more than remind the children about their kerb drill before starting their own business of entertaining, I wasn't going down that road.

Another well established school act was Rob and Cath Carpenter. 'Rolo and Shandy'. A musical clown duo. I met them much later when they were working at a craft fair where I was exhibiting. I never saw them working in schools. I never met Coco either. Our paths crossed once. Coco of course was the forerunner of public road safety in schools. He was a very famous clown with Bertram Mills Circus. Wherever they tented he would visit their local schools spreading the message. He would attend schools in full makeup. With his very large boots, and a walking stick fashioned like a belisha beacon, he seemed a giant of a man to his young audiences.

That caused a problem for the RSO of Caterham. She was Mrs Grace, a very nice elegant lady, who like all of the RSOs I met, was always on the lookout for anyone who could be of help to keep her young charges safe. Coco mainly dealt with juniors, so I did the infants. For the younger element I often didn't put makeup on. I also have a routine of dressing up in front of them, where I get the comedy whilst dressing. This meant that by the time 'lessons' come up, they are happy with my appearance, and quite relaxed. This practice stood me in good stead whatever the age I was working to.

I remember one head teacher who wanted me to be 'discovered' in the middle of a hall of children. She had told them to shut their eyes while she intended to shepherd me to the centre. Firmly declining the offer, I used my own solution to approaching mixed ages of children who weren't with their mums.

My aim was to try and show I was funny before I opened my mouth to speak. I'd been expected as a clown so, 'clowns are funny aren't they?' The point I'm making is you need to be in control from the start.

One school I recall, as I came into the hall, the teachers were preparing to leave. There are two points here. It is not up to me to keep discipline whilst I am performing. If you are doing your job properly you should have their attention and the problem of keeping order wouldn't arise, but should one of the children step out of line, then teachers are in a much better place to respond.

The other and far more important point is that, if the lesson is to have any lasting benefit it is the follow up, by the teacher, after I have left, that sorts out the laughs from the bits that save lives. If the teacher isn't present a lot of the impact can be lost, by not knowing what the children were laughing at. I had many teachers come up to me and say, after a show, 'Thank you Mr. Brooks, I'll be able to get another lesson or more for the class out of what you presented today.'

Another thing happened when I was busy promoting myself for work. The Bognor Regis Tourist Office helped me by printing colouring sheets that I had prepared for use in the schools. These had an outline drawing of me, in clown, with six road safety points printed for parents' eyes. My reasoning was that children that age always want to show their parents what they did that day in school. So, here was a sure way of getting the road safety message into the house. Not just a verbal message, but a printed note of what I was saying to their offspring that day.

The painting sheet also showed a very sunny Bognor Regis seafront view with 'Welcome to Bognor Regis' written in large letters. It was a great help to me and I'm sure the outlay by the town was justified. It snowballed in fact. Wherever I went, the RSO who booked me had his own version printed. I have a collection of them as mementos.

I must admit now that later on I quietly dropped the idea. When I first started touring the schools, I did four shows a day. Infant show first, then playtime, and the junior show after play. I had lunch at whichever school that could accommodate me, then I would move on to a second school in the afternoon to repeat the sequence.

I was always accompanied by a member of the RSO's department to help with props, etc. I noted the behaviour before the colouring sheet altered dramatically to my way of thinking. Beforehand I barely had time to set my props up for the junior show when in would come running excited youngsters waving their own drawing of me, with an enthusiasm that belongs to the young.

Their teachers and I then noted the bits that had stuck. Mostly it was the funny bits, but also bits of Belisha beacons, crossings, Tufty and the like, the other bits I was being paid to interest them in. So here was a dilemma. I thought I was cramping the children's natural ability by the strictures of just colouring a picture of me. I did not try to stop other RSOs from producing their own sheets, but I no longer pushed it.

I have developed an ability to accept any name from an audience and make it into a reasonable face. I still do it today. At 88, I only need a pad and pen to entertain in most languages. With Deena as my interpreter, we successfully entertained in Holland and the Azores. Everybody has a name and a face, I show them a kind of 'second' persona. Am I not a lucky man?

This small seed of my ability to do this was planted in me when I was at school. Mr Keates, a headmaster, showed all of us in assembly one morning a drawing one of his friends had made from the name Keates. He'd turned it into a face of a farm worker with a straw sticking out of his mouth. Thirty years on I had developed this idea, seen so long ago, into being used to earn a living as a lightning sketch artist.

I think you can now detect how deep my feelings are about what is said in front of an audience of children. Their minds are like blotting paper, and if you can assist some bits of worthwhile information to stick they could be there for a lifetime.

It wasn't long into doing schoolwork that I had the idea of a name change. It occurred to me all day I was pushing the 'Kerb Drill', why not add a Y and become Kerby Drill. So uncle Hal became what I've been known as ever since. I registered it with Business Names, Equity and my bank. The Press liked it too. I've had my difficulties with it as well. Half the time I get called Kirby drill. A lot of people do not know of my connection with the edge of the road! Then when the Green Cross code was introduced it didn't help. But I'm not going to change now. I prefer to patiently explain its origin to anybody who wants to know.

And so the building up off 'Kerby Drill the Road Safety Clown' went on. Eventually I was working in Southwark, Lewisham, Islington and other boroughs that sought my services. I was lucky to be about when the New Kent Road was being constructed. It's not hard to imagine the difficulties of major road constructions in some of the busiest places in London.

The constant journeying back each night was taking its toll on me. By the Wednesday I was whacked. Such tiredness is dangerous to yourself and other road users. So enter the Brooks' household, a Volkswagen motor caravan. It was not a large vehicle. If you needed to sleep you had to use the table to make up the bed, sort of thing. Dual-purpose innards, you might say. But it enabled me to stay overnight in whatever district I was working in.

I arranged with the RSO to again get permission for me to put up in the council depots overnight. Mostly then was I safely off the road. Before this I vividly remember staying my first overnight in the middle of Catford. The van had a canvas lift up roof, so there was no sound insulation.

Catford is never asleep, traffic-wise anyway. As I had just pulled off onto the grass in the town centre, I didn't think to get permission. The police came and checked me out. Against the by-laws apparently. Anyway, one is so vulnerable at these times.

I recall much later on when we were doing a craft fair in Lewis. Deena and I pulled into a public car park for the night. A quiet Sussex town...? Around midnight a gang of motorcyclists used the park to demonstrate their riding skills. That time we were really buzzed. I think that is the word. They tore towards the van, pulling over at the last minute. Like a pack of Indian braves, they kept this up for a good hour. This time it wasn't so scary as we had a bigger van. They would've come off worse should we'd have touched. This was before the days of mobile 'phones.

I had another shock doing another craft fair much later. I was alone in the van at this time. I was exhibiting my woodwork in the Wembley Conference Centre. The car park was the size of a few football pitches. One night I was visited by two or three cars seemingly intent on seeing how fast they could go before having to brake. This really was frightening. The noise was terrific and it wasn't possible to say in what direction they were travelling in. There were quite a few night watchman on site but they kept a very low profile. One could hardly blame them either. Since writing this of course things have changed somewhat. A new Wembley Stadium has been built.

During my stays in different depots I met some very interesting folk working as night watchmen. One lived for his cats. All were friendly and welcomed my company. One young man, a student, was using the job for wages and the quiet for studying for his degree. He intended going back east to become a politician.

It was amusing to me to see the way I was perceived by all the council staff. Not many had seen a working clown, and sometimes with an early start, I'd have made up and be dressed when I was picked up, ready to start the day's visits to schools. I was always tolerated in a friendly manner though.

Not quite to do with clowning, but of enormous interest to me was that one night, I discovered someone in the offices had discarded an old office type chest of drawers. Seemingly of the times when Dickens was writing. Well over a hundred years old. The wood was pine and the drawers were pre-plywood days, so the bottoms of the drawers were thin pine, with beautifully coloured grain. It was left out to be burned, but I dismantled it carefully and put the wood to good use much later, making wood sculptures for the crafts' side of my life.

I sketched many friends I'd made during these evenings. One occasion showed a darker side to the job. The depot I was staying in also happened to be the dustbin collection vehicle garage. There was a dispute between the workers and the council and a strike was called. It was all very bitter.

Nobody was allowed in or out of the depot. The RSO had quite a job convincing the men that we had no axe to grind. I simply wanted to get out to the schools, and help possibly their own children to get home safely from school. I'm very glad to say the dispute was settled that very day. Phew!

At the same time I was still earning a crust with building and children's parties. Bernard Stockton had elected to come to Bognor from Swansea, and settle with his wife, Betty. We put them up whilst they looked around for somewhere to live. Bernard and I always worked well together and this was borne out when Pierre broke his leg. He was also a first class sales manager. Being a deputy manager at Woolworth, he was a fine salesman too.

During talks about things to do together, a shop was mooted. Deena was very excited about a theatrical shop with fancy dress hire in the background. Bernard was keenly interested in the shop side of the business. Makeup, wigs, party goods, an agency for collecting entertainment work for ourselves, and farming out work we couldn't do. It all seemed very exciting and I encouraged them both. I was not all that keen about a shop as such though, but as long as I didn't have to man it, I was happy to help the project along.

A small lock up shop on the forecourt of Bognor Railway Station became vacant. The landlord was a Mr. Robertson, the owner of the cinema opposite, the Picturedrome. A very kind and gentle person in poor health. We promised not to compete as a sweet shop or to upset other shopkeepers also on the forecourt, and signed a contract for five years. The shop was not large. If one wanted to swing the proverbial cat around in it, it would've had to have been a kitten to do it. But it was magic for Deena. I worked hard at making shelving, counters, and fitting it out. They sorted out stock problems. They were not newcomers in this.

A while before I had made them a set up stall for Chichester's weekly market. Going to auction sales, buying job lots of glass and china, then after cleaning and pricing, they would sell them in the market. The name of their stall was 'Lucky Dip'. So it was a kind of natural progression on their part.

Bernard was also intending to work up a service supplying stage makeup. It was something he and Deena were very good at. They would contract to make up amateur productions and even take demonstrations around to women's organisations and schools. Both had plenty of experience in musical comedy, such as The Desert Song, New Moon, and The Merry Widow etc,. So it was an attractive idea, and all was set to open in two weeks' time.

The shop was to be called Deena's. We had a lovely fascia made that included balloons in the design. It looked good. Fred Jackson, our blacksmith friend, made a decorative grille of wrought iron for the glass shop door. This was to comply with the requirements of the insurance people. They declared that the sort of goods we were going to sell would attract the wrong sort of customers. Like stage costume jewellery, etc., hence the grille across the glass. Nearly ready. I was up to my eyes in shavings and sawdust and paint splattered. Then the bombshell.

Deena came down to the shop and told me that Bernard's wife, Betty, was going back to Wales. So was Bernard, so off they went, that day. She couldn't settle. Hey-ho here we go again!

It was a great pity really. I'm sure that we could have used the shop and agency to have provided a good income for two families. It would have taken time, but we had plenty. I was still building, and they had no rent to pay. They had the upstairs rooms of our house and Bernard and I were already doing a good cabaret spot together that we could have developed very easily. He had a very fine voice and his rendering of 'If I Were a Rich Man', from the Fiddler on the Roof, with me on the piano, plus good comedy, plus my drawings, had promise. I thought it was a shame we didn't give it a go.

So let's take a deep breath. We were left with a lease of the shop to run for five years, two weeks to opening, and half the cast missing. So, we got on with it. Deena gathered together all the clothes and props she had accumulated since becoming an entertainer, plus the results of the hard work she put into her fancy dress clothes.

I put a long hanging rail in the shop, discreetly concealed behind a curtain, for the dresses. There was a glass fronted counter cabinet already there. This we used to display the pretty bits and rings, tiaras, bangles and tat. Tat was the name we gave to all the interesting second hand bits of jewellery that women, (and some men) liked to browse over. Outrageous rings, bold badges. In lots of ways we were leading the field. In fact, some of Deena's ideas were discovered or re-invented by others later on, and then claimed as their own.

We had lots of carnival heads to choose from and she used one or two of these for our window display. When finished it was a picture. This large Spanish lady carnival head peering out from under jet black eyelashes as large as plastic washing up bottles, which indeed is what they were. A joke of our household is that we may have run out of the washing up liquid but we have plenty of empty bottles in the shed. I collect the empties as a source of soft plastic. The printing can be cleaned off with spirit and when ironed flat, is remarkably tough and durable.

Once in the early days, when we were making carnival heads for a job in Jersey, I rang the local television station, Southern. They invited us along to the studios with a selection of heads for inclusion in their evening magazine programme. After the show we had some studio hospitality in a little pub opposite. One of our interviewers was Dickie Davies, a very friendly, amiable person who later on became the well-known presenter of 'World of Sport'.

Bognor isn't a very big place and our shop wasn't more than a flea bite in the size department but we did cause a little stir when we opened. Not having much money in the kitty we couldn't advertise much, but being of the specialist nature word soon got around the amateur theatricals that we stocked 'Leichner'. This was the magic name in stage makeup.

Although tiny in size the shops shelves took a lot of filling. There's nothing so uninviting as a half empty shop. So out came more props. My paintings were also hung up on the wall, discreetly priced! Party hats came out of boxes to create a carnival atmosphere and fill awkward spaces. A copy off The Stage was placed on the counter. I don't know what we thought that it would do for us. It turned out that it obscured the sight of the rings and brooches underneath the glass, so it was moved. We called ourselves a theatrical shop and sadly it didn't exactly ignite Bognor round the edges. But we were friendly and enthusiastic. The motto for all of us Brooks's must surely be 'enthusiasm, the real gold in life!' translated loosely as 'get stuck in and get on with it.

We had a lovely stock book and a lovely cash book, and even a drawer for putting the money in. It was only a small drawer. What a good job that was too. Our cash float up front didn't look so lonely bunched up, huddled in one corner for company, hoping to be joined by other people's money. We had many a laugh about this, but we got by.

I was still hankering after gala work. I had floated an idea with Jim and Bernard about a trio of army types putting up a sausage tree wherever an attack of 'bungy blight' had attacked the sausage crop. This tree would have to be a Mark 2 variety, resistant to the blight, that had recently been developed by the

'Ministry of Agriculture and Sausagery'. An officer in charge of two squaddies, assigned to travel the country to wherever an attack occurred, to demonstrate the tactics and procedures necessary to defeat this new scourge, before it became rampant. Son Jim would be the captain in charge, Bernard main comedy and me supporting.

I had already started to make the tree. It started off looking very spindly and rather like the Osma tubing commonly used by plumbers for rainwater down-pipes, which of course it was. Wrapping it round with hessian pipe lagging gave a kind of autumn look to the grey plastic underneath. With a dab of paint it could look very seasonal indeed. Our title would be 'The Super Sausage Squad'. But now, apart from the shop being understaffed, the trio had been reduced to a duo by a wish to go back to Wales. Ah, well!

Chapter 17

The First Shop

Getting by in the shop meant we were getting a routine going that allowed us to manage. Someone being in the shop when someone should be, and the home being attended when needs be. I had a direct telephone line put into the shop from the house. This helped no end. We could keep in contact in case of an emergency arising.

About this time something sad from the family front intervened. My dad died. He was over 80, and was always interested in our latest projects. A carpenter himself, he had the satisfaction of seeing his three sons all take up the tools under his supervision. He had many talents and his sons absorbed them to the hilt. My first toys were his shavings and wood off-cuts.

Whenever I could, I went over to Greenford to see him. We would be chatting away and he would close his eyes and drop off to sleep. I know now where my capacity for 'dropping off' comes from. I took my paints over one day and started a portrait of him. At this time I was using poster colours. It was a proper stop and go affair. I would concentrate on his other features whenever I saw his eyes close. It didn't get finished, this picture, but I got near enough for a likeness.

When I look at it now it invokes far more memories for me than ever a photograph could do. He always reimbursed me for the fare from Bognor. He and mum never had an easy ride bringing up seven of us. He always marvelled that mum had managed to put a bit aside from his wage packets.

So the shop was open. Deena became manageress, window dresser, buyer, cleaner, and housewife all rolled into one. The excitement and newness of the venture made it all worthwhile. We decided to stock jokes and Deena ordered all sorts of tricks and effects and the local children loved this. We got very good at demonstrating too. Most lines were very good sellers. I was surprised how extensive the business of 'jokery' is.

Our main supplier was a firm from Keighley, Yorkshire. F. Stell. Their range was gathered from all over the world. Many things came from Germany and the rest of the continent. Very elaborate pieces of machinery sometimes.

The directions took some sorting out too, especially if they were in their language of origin. Germanic alphabet and the Japanese language didn't help where a routine was involved. One thing was common to all nationalities though, the 'smellies'.

Deena decided very early on not to sell stink bombs or anything similar, and to impose a restriction on the sale of these items. We felt it unfair to the local supermarkets and cinemas to unleash noxious smells into uncaring hands. The result of a stink bomb on carpeting, for instance, is entirely different from one dropped in the street, and this sort of action appealed to a certain type of practical joker. A strong streak of cruelty sought an outlet sometimes, and we were not going to further it if we could help. Very un-businesslike really. There were very good profits to be made on these items.

Most of the joke items worked using shock tactics. Embarrassment or just plain crudity. The labels were very interesting sometimes, 'Dirty Fido', for instance. Indeed, on reflection, to be engaged in the manufacture of a plastic artefact resembling the 'doings on the carpet' of an untrained canine, seemed a somewhat dubious way of earning a livelihood.

The mind boggles at the production line of such shapes seriously being inspected for 'faults'. The final flourish of the paint sprayer putting on the last coat of pigment, a suitable colour, before stepping back, (mind how you step back). Joke as I may items like this sold by the gross!

Some toys were really funny. I have in mind 'Dracula's money box'. Here was a clockwork mechanism shaped like a coffin, a la Dracula! There was a shallow slot at one end in which you place a penny. As you put the penny in, its weight activated the clockwork mechanism. A whirring noise, and a creepy sound began, then ever so slowly, the lid of the coffin started to lift open. A green ghostly claw-like hand crept out slowly towards the penny. Then suddenly it rushed forward, grabbed at the penny and whipped it quick into the coffin, the lid closing seemingly all in one movement. One really jumped at its speed. I was fascinated by it, so were many buyers. It wasn't cheap either.

One of the best selling lines in this set-up was the 'pretend cigarette'. The children came in and wanted to emulate grown-ups smoking. Probably their dads. A simple tube of card with a red end, loaded up with powdered talc. The children used to puff away and out goes the powder. It looked like smoke too. Their faces were a picture. Intense with the concentration of being grown up. Whatever one thought of this joke, at least they were not potentially so lethal as the real ones, but I'm sure we wouldn't have sold them today.

Masks were a great seller too. Mostly made up of stiff plastic or cardboard, they were gradually being ousted by quite sophisticated latex rubber creations. These could be really horrific. When you heard that the buyer intended to appear otherwise suitably clad, with the mask on, and surprise their friends up a dark alley, well! I wonder if anybody had heart attacks subsequent to this 'joke appearance'.

There were claw hands, hairy hands, hairy feet, hatchets and knives through the head, and all sorts of gruesome things to gratify the wish for the macabre. There were two distinct categories for the practical joker. The child putting on a reddened thumb bandage and pretending to mum he'd been injured. Then the great laugh when he 'showed' mum he wasn't really hurt. All good mums got taken in. They never saw through this great artificial wrapping, a bandage suitably bloodied (with paint) until the offspring chose to let them into the 'secret'. Well this is all wonderful growing up business isn't it?

The second category encompassed the serious side of 'putting one over' grown-up wise. One got to know the customers. You realised the adults were often more childlike than the children, going to great lengths to set up a joke to catch someone else. Sometimes there seemed to be an element of cruelty. The fun a child gets from a joke is shared. No victim. A good laugh. Everyone in on the joke.

We had poems and verse that we had idly ordered out of curiosity, but we couldn't display. As a maker of things myself I was struck by the ingenuity of manufacturers in using materials that lent themselves to the product perfectly. The severed thumb sort of thing. In a box, all clammy and soft with gory edges. Another was a dead mouse. This material felt cold to the touch. I remember using one of these as a party game. We had all the girls coming in one by one and blindfolded them. We were going to test their qualities of recognition.

I had about six articles that I placed on their outstretched palms, one by one, saying what it was. If they agreed with my definition they should say 'agreed'. First I would place a matchbox, 'agreed'. An egg, 'agreed', fork 'agreed', and so on. All very easy and relaxing. Then I'd put on the joke mouse, 'a dead mouse', shrieks. End of game. It was so very real. Cold to the touch and me telling them it was a dead mouse, their imagination did the rest.

A run down on a joke shop must contain a mention of the 'pooh pooh' cushion. What a fitting name. We sold two qualities, light plastic and heavy rubber. Both were Hong Kong made and both made the same rude noise when someone sat on one, probably concealed under a cushion. I am sure more were sold than used. It's all very well having a laugh in the shop about these things over the counter, but I'm sure it wasn't quite so easy to use them, except in secure family circles.

The fancy dress side was blossoming too We always tried to avoid being caught up in over-fussy demands from customers who wanted perfect correctness, as in historical costumes. Deena's dresses were colourful and pretty, easy to wear and comfortable. This was the era of the miniskirt and so it was all the rage in fancy dress too. A pretty short skirt, black fishnet tights, and frilly bits formed the base for many costumes. Add a lace tiara, white apron, and feather duster and lo, an 'upstairs maid'. A Hungarian costume with lovely embroidery was always out working. Deena's copies of more elaborate costumes were also a great success.

I made appropriate props to go with them. Beautiful chunky jewellery made from all sorts of coloured leathers and guilt, made all the difference to setting off a costume. Large Roman type badges and clasps were marvellous on simple blouses or slips. Deena found she had a flair for selecting the right thing for the customer. Often we had a good laugh about this. She would be able to select a particular costume to suit character. And so after viewing all our stock, nine out of ten chose the dress Deena had mentally noted for them on seeing them initially.

We couldn't hold many dresses in the shop, so most were kept in the house. As people normally booked well in advance, it was quite often that five or six of them would arrive to get fixed up together, and being old friends, these fitting and choosing sessions were often hilarious affairs.

Howls of laughter would emanate from the front room whilst costumes were tried on. We were often told by our clients that they had enjoyed these sessions as much as the event itself. But it meant a lot of extra work by Deena working this way.

Most other hire shops never behaved in this happy-go-lucky way. We were not strict about deposits either. But this was indicative of the friendly nature of the business and the way Deena conducted herself that we weren't often taken advantage of. There was always the odd one or two, but we had long memories, so it was remembered who were the baddies.

I used to do my turn in the shop on Saturdays. Shopping and house work still had to be done. When there was no-one in I could always keep gainfully employed somehow, either mask making or painting. During the summer, Butlin's provided staff and campers interested in our wares. One such person was the well-known Welsh actor, Wyn Calvin. I remember him buying a clown picture from me.

Makeup went well at this time too. We had some customers from London too, regular users of our fancy dress. After every wearing our costumes were cleaned and fresh. We soon found out that a hundred costumes in stock didn't necessarily guarantee custom. If you had twenty well-chosen popular dresses in prime condition, they would always be in and out.

Our nearest competitors were over twenty miles either side of Bognor. So, all in all, we could have made a good living there. It had one snag, it took all our time, and time is more important than anything. We be-grudged staying in the shop just to sell things. It was fine when busy but other times it was murder. The waste. A shop is a terrible disclosure of humanity too.

Most people were friendly and civil, not all though. These others took some getting on with. You would think that in so small a shop there would be no problem with shoplifting. You would be wrong. Deena encountered some very determined efforts of 'customers' intent on shopping without paying.

Then there were the people who needed a chat. There was no escaping, without being very rude. You were a captive. We were not unfriendly folk, but some people batter you with talk. It wasn't conversation, there was no two-way exchange of views. You had to resort to ploys to get them out of the shop. Gradually, jokingly, chiding them with comments until you could become quite firm whilst holding the shop door open, smiling all the time. The smile is the key. It saves potential throttling or actual bodily harm. I think Deena used to make the excuse to pop out for a short while. This was the only benefit of not having a toilet in the shop.

We had the shop for a couple of years or so. I didn't regret the experience, but vowed not to become a slave to opening hours again.

While we were doing all this I was still building and doing children's parties, in between expanding my area of working in schools to country wide proportions. Friends would ponder how we got up to so many ways of earning a living. It was very simple. What work came in, from whatever source, we just got on with it. If wages were involved, that pointed out the priority, to get the job done, then ponder about the rest.

My main pondering at this time was centred around my own gala act, 'The Super Sausage Squad'. The plot was now complete, most of the ideas for props were worked out and clothes designed. I was trying to mock up a brochure to send out to the agents. The sausage tree still looked very skeletal but was quietly looking more robust with all the new ideas that were unfolding. Jim and I pondered also about a third member. Whilst in the shop I had noticed a carnival volunteer buying items to dress up his collecting costume. I was also doing a spot of collecting that year.

I made contact with the red-nosed individual and found out he was a Howard Goldsmith. A garage proprietor who had a small holding on the outskirts of Bognor. He was not new to the entertainment game. He and his wife Bess had been puppeteers. We got on well together. I explained the predicament we were in, what we were about, and asked if he would stand in for our first season out. He and Bess invited us round to his house where we met their daughter Lynette. Being of sound mind and independent nature, he said yes. So it was agreed, Jim to be Captain, Howard support, and me to take the lead.

Howard did his war service in the navy. So the basic idea of two squaddies and one bossy boots, railing against the nation, appealed to him. He was also a past chairman of Bognor Town Council and with garaging experience, he was to be a great help in sorting out the props with me and Jim. We made a good trio. Me with wood, him with engineering skills and Jim's electrical know how, gelled very well together. I had made a sausage firing cannon that looked extremely like a tomato sauce bottle. Howard engineered a trolley for it like the ones used in Nelson's days.

We all agreed I was to be sole owner of the act and props. The money would be split three ways after expenses. We would all be consulted on dates. This was very necessary because as we were all self-employed, our businesses came first. I had already spoken of our plans to the main gala agents, who were expecting our brochures for their clients, So it was The Super Sausage Squad, (Kerby Drill and Co, Clowns) was born. The trio was complete for now.

Whilst we were fleshing out the story and business, I was getting very busy with road safety work. Fortunately most galas were held at weekends so school work didn't clash. I was now working in Alton, Petersfield, Essex, Gravesend, Grays and many short dates where I was increasingly being used to spearhead local safety promotions.

It was about this time I met Walter Davies, from Gwent. Walter was a highly-charged council officer fiercely dedicated to his job encouraging road safety sense, whether it be in schools or otherwise. He was also on numerous national committees and a real powerhouse of a man. We hit it off, he liked my ways and began to give me four weeks work each year to tour Gwent schools.

It was he who published our version of 'I'd Like to Teach the World to Sing', the song that was used to publicise Coca-Cola on television. It was very popular with the children. If you are going to use a tune to put over road safety messages, it's hard enough to get the words to stick, let alone trying to teach an unfamiliar tune at the same time. So I made a large song sheet for the words that could easily be read from the back of the hall, and hung it from the top of my easel.

Then I had an idea. Son Jim played the violin and guitar, and had a very pleasant voice. So I got him to record the song with Deena's new road safety words, on a portable tape recorder. So with the song sheet before them, I played back the tape for all the children to listen to. Then I went over to the piano and we all sung with great gusto, the road safety message. It worked a treat. I started to use it for the juniors show. Walter had it published for me so I could leave each school a copy for their own use.

I mentioned to Walter one day that the schools were not too keen to accept performers like me at the beginnings of terms. He then did his best to get me a more continuous programme of work around these times. I often dined with him and wife Pat, when in their district. I painted portraits of them and their two boys Howell and Gareth. These were lovely times. He also had manufactured 'Kerby Drill' badges for me and we always had plenty of handouts to remind children of our visit. With hardly an exception all the RSOs I dealt with had a similar full-time commitment to their young charges.

Walter kindly sang my praises to other department heads, and I was given work during the summer in Gwent. It was about this time that the interest in leisure centres across the country peaked. These new establishments were very keen to 'be the best' sort of thing. After my shows during the day, I parked in the local leisure centre. Not the usual council depot by any means. A competition was in being, choosing the best leisure centre, countrywide.

By this time I was well known locally, and when it was learned of my interest in painting people, the staff requested me to paint portraits of the half dozen or so people who were likely to be duty officers when it was their turn. So instead of just a photograph of who was in charge at any given time, my portraits were used instead. It was a blatant bit of one-upmanship, but well within the rules of the competition. I enjoyed painting them of an evening, and afterwards, the few recipients, I was told, would not relinquish them. That pleased me.

Whenever I was touring in Gwent I always managed to get home on the weekend. Leaving about four o'clock after school, mostly from Cwmbran, the M4 motorway has figured largely in my life. In the fifties it was from Potters Bar to Mumbles. I watched it grow and extend itself to London. By the time I was road safetying it was almost finished, to Swansea at least.

One journey to be remembered. I was halfway back when my VW camper seized up. I was doing fifty or something when a valve dropped down, or out. The AA took me to a safe lay-by and Jim came down and towed me home. Not a nice experience, and very cold I remember.

The agenda very much whilst I was at home was to get the Sausage Tree on the road. My friendly blacksmith, Fred Jackson, was called upon to make a brace to reinforce my woodwork at the bottom of the tree. A bomb box was to be added for the finale bang. The extra weight of this added to the stability of the structure. Being about 15 feet in height it could have easily become a victim to windy conditions, which were a usual feature when working in gala fields and showgrounds.

There was another tricky problem to be solved if the tree didn't appear to satisfactorily collapse when required to after a big bang in the finale. We got over this by the use of a hinge in its middle, plus a very reliable safety catch which Fred devised.

You can imagine that now we were into serious engineering rather than the plastic down-pipe preliminaries that we started off with. Now we used a length of scaffold pole for the trunk, so welding was the norm rather than impact glue. Six large nuts were welded onto the 'trunk' to enable six flowers to be screwed on. All highly technical stuff this, certainly not to be found in garden centres.

The squad had its own flag. A short mast was fixed to the strongest gate-closer spring we could find. This was held captive in the tree's branches until with a flourish on the trumpet, it was released with much solemnity, to reveal a single pink sausage on a brightly coloured background. The flag sprung up above the tree and the squad would now be ready for action. At least that's how far the script had got by then.

Deena was working hard on our clothes. Captain Jim's suit was relatively easy. He had a proper sam browne belt that just did the job. He elected only to wear a small moustache. This hid his youthfulness. Material for the outfit was a light khaki colour, brown shoes and leather holster for his revolver, plus an officer's type hat. Our Jim looked very authentic.

Howard had elected to adapt the name 'Goldie' for his clowning career. A similar sort of material as Jim's was made up into a uniform of the type used in the Boer War. Short trousers, puttees, jacket and helmet. I made a special pair of boots for him. These were quite large army-type footwear with well worn toe caps opened up to reveal large pink toes. To make them comfortable and safe to wear I had fashioned them around a pair of size ten shoes. Keeping all the materials light in weight they were very manageable. A cobbler friend of mine applied a light leather sole. Howard loved them.

To balance the size of the boots I made the soldiers' putties in the shape of a pair of turned down socks using plastic foam. They counterbalanced the boots beautifully. Howard was not a light person and with his height and large ammunition pouches slung around his shoulders, he cut a dashing and formidable figure. He seemed to be barrel-chested too. This was not through any deformity. Two gags, balloon out of the head and water from the helmet, were strapped to him using a leather waistcoat. This made use of the effects I had earlier perfected whilst being policeman to Pierre in the car act. The helmet was also covered in khaki to match the suit. Finally the trousers were made to fly away when required, at the end of the act. Velcro is a favourite fastener for this exercise amongst the clowning fraternity.

Deena had two outfits to make for me. One for our entrance routine and a working outfit to chase about in. I made a comfy pair of boots that were fashioned over slip-on shoes with elasticated sides. My tunic was a cherry red colour complete with an army belt that had a flash box built into its back that I set off when Jim took a pot-shot at my rear. I had a lovely black busby with a built-in crying gag, and a comfortable chin strap to hold it all in place. My trousers were black three-quarter length shorts. We all looked as though we were part of the same army but with individual features that could be recognised from a distance.

My entrance hat I made from an old floppy cap that Pierre had left behind. I re-fashioned it from inside with foam, and painted it with black and white squares. Years later I learned that Popov, the great Russian clown, also had a hat similarly decorated. I wonder if he knew of mine? I certainly didn't know of his.

My entrance coat was large enough to cover my strip routine costumes. It was decorated with large gilt flowers. The strip costumes will be explained later. All we needed now was plenty of practice, and possibly a date to look forward to!

Chapter 18

The Tree Grows to Fruition

Now that the shop was in the past I could really get my mind going on developing the Sausage Squad story. Now with our trio complete, I was pleased that neither Howard or Jim disagreed with my intention of being original if possible. They were of a similar mind that we were not into any copying other presentations. We wanted a novel act, very unusual, with good colourful props. An act with a strong story line, and FUNNY.

My dad's sons, having all followed his profession, I never thought that my two boys would follow me, but both showed talent in that direction. In the annual pantomimes in Mumbles they always played some part or other. Soon after we moved to Bognor I got out an act for Jim, using a quartet of instruments.

In it he played his own violin, a half size violin and a very tiny one-eighth size prop violin I'd made, complete with case. A fourth, larger tall thin violin with an extending neck, made up the number. Michael's job was to provide the sound effects off stage for the two prop violins.

The Young Wives Group that had booked us were very well pleased when we performed for them in the Village Hall in Wick, Sussex. We were graced by a visit from the local press, and Jim in motley had a very charming picture in The Littlehampton Gazette. Also in the photograph was a young lady of about two years, who was having difficulty with her dress, her napkin was showing!

So it wasn't long before the trio of Kerby, Goldie and Captain Jim, after much talk about gags and script, and with a few rehearsal sessions behind us, were as ready as we would ever be for our first time out.

The story involved the Squad going around the country, dispatched by the Ministry of Agriculture and Sausagry. We were sent into areas that had recently been ravaged by 'bungy blight'. This was a vicious virus that attacked sausage trees.

Our duty was to combat the scourge, and plant our own Mark II, blight resistant tree, near to the outbreak. This always happened in the middle of the arena. Strange that! You can imagine the local farmer's relief at getting such help. We were quite self-contained as a unit. Complete with shovels, fertiliser and water supply, we were also well equipped to maintain our own security to protect our newly-planted sausage tree.

The sausage tree was now a substantial prop. We solved the problem of getting it into the arena by the use of two wheels, attached to an axle long enough to reach the extremes of the tree base. We then wheeled it out like a trolley.

The covers Deena had made hid the branches and leaves. Howard engineered a collapsible trolley that contained all our small props. He cleverly used strong plastic fencing mesh to keep its weight down. The sides folded flat when not in use.

At a later date Jim added a sophisticated bit of apparatus that enabled us to release the bungy snakes out of the tree's top. It was here we strived to have a balanced comedy act. Often we would see slightly tolerant and amused looks on the faces of dads with their children, watching this 'kid's stuff'. Then at the appropriate moment in the act, I'd point Jim's revolver and fire a couple of shots into the tree, and out would pop these snake-like bungies, right up in the air. With nobody within twenty feet of the tree when it was done.

Their faces were a picture. But they gave us credit for the effort. Some guessed we had sent the signal by radio. Howard was doing his bit too. He used his garage workshop to make a 'Nelson type' carriage for our ground to air cannon. Inside the cannon, (which by the way, was heavily disguised as a giant tomato sauce bottle, the squad's effort at camouflage) was a target launcher, our equivalent to an explosive charge.

This prop fired a string of sausages about thirty feet into the air, gently floating down by parachute, to be caught in an overlarge frying pan that also doubled as a mine detector. The only time it didn't work was when we forgot to put a cartridge in.

I remember a couple of problems making this prop work. It was not easy to load. The target launcher was a hand-held device for throwing tins in the air to be shot at by enthusiasts who'd rather not shoot birds. My tin would also help the sausages on their way.

My string of sausages were built on a cane spine to keep the weight down, with a rubber buffer to absorb the shock of the launch. The silk parachute had also to be folded correctly before being loaded into the muzzle of the cannon. If it opened up before reaching its required flight height, it would not work.

Whilst working with Pierre and the car, Deena constantly used to complain that it was a pity nobody heard most of what we had to say during the act. Thus the Sausage Squad had its own commentator, Captain Jim. He would announce us and proceed to tell the story as it unfolded on the field, so everybody knew exactly what was going on.

I had built a portable tape recorder into his sam browne belt with which to play a pre-recorded cassette that held the music for my strip dance routine. Jim would hold the microphone down to his belt and the taped music would be relayed over the loud speaker system. We also carried our own sound effects on it. At that time we were quite revolutionary! I never had any qualms whenever Jim went out to start us off. A thoroughly professional job always. A touch of class. Jim played a straight officer to our comic squaddies, and it worked well.

We turned our attention to Goldie next. He loved his big boots with peeping toes I had made. He wore khaki shorts that were also fly away trousers, for the finale. His helmet, khaki-clad, still had two gags in it, with water and balloon from the top of it. Howard who was not at all of slight statue, looked splendidly arrayed with his bare knees. I made him a corkscrew barrelled rifle to shoulder when we marched out.

Deena did all the costume work without a murmur. We were lucky to be so well served. She could do most things, but she must do them in her own way. I've stood for ages trying not to droop whilst she wrestled with under arms, gussets, waist bands and turnups. Then after Goldie she still had all mine to do.

I had a long coat of stretch material that covered all my other clothes. I would rip this off and underneath was a ballet with an enormous tu-tu. The ballet dress would come off revealing a Charleston dress, (these various items would be discarded by me to each appropriate tune from Jim's tape recorder.)

Finally I was wearing an old fashioned bathing costume with two road safety gags, front and back under its skirt. On my bottom was an unidentified hazard sign, a red triangle, and under the front, when lifted up, was revealed a 'No Entry sign'. At the end of the dances I would creep away and put on my bright red tunic and busby, whilst Howard held the stage .

My headgear for the entrance routine was a very large peaked cap with a black and white chequered pattern painted onto it. Under my large entrance hat I wore a green wig that helped the hat fit a little better. After my entrance I changed hats, wearing my soldier's busby, that had a crying gag in it. There was also a flash built in my belt at the back for the finale. There was a lot of work in it all and time was pressing on.

Our first date out was to be on Whit Monday in Hillingdon. Bert Layton from T.B.Phillips (Glos) booked this for us. I'd done all the previous correspondence for the car act through him, so he was delighted to have my own comedy act on his books.

We did nearly all of our agency booking that first summer through him. I don't remember that we got an enormous fee for that first show. £65.00 between three, but we were not dissatisfied with the return it gave us. It was a nice day and we didn't let anybody down with the performance.

Mind you, we had knocked off a lot of raw edges when we did as near a dress rehearsal as we ever did, in Howard's garden, a few days beforehand. That was uproarious. Trying all the various bits together. Brand new clothes, some not properly finished. I felt a few pins myself that time. Bess, Deena and Lynette were in stitches at our thrashings about, (even Lynette's pony said neigh, in the end!) A twenty-minute performance took over one and a half-hours to complete.

We knew it would tighten up after a couple of shows, but we were hoping to tie a few slip knots in it that afternoon. We had all aged a few years, but I never had any doubts we would win through in the end. We were enthusiastic, but nevertheless worried, but who wouldn't be? That we were 'The Super Sausage Squad' there was no doubt. The trio marched out into the arena that Whit Monday and almost took Hillingdon by storm.

We had recorded a grand fanfare of the Coldstream Guards playing their trumpets for our entrance on Jim's tape. It was magnificent but a bit too long. It seemed ages before the last strains died away. I suppose it was that we were just anxious to get on with it. And then we heard Captain Jim say finally, 'We present Kerby Drill and Goldie, The Super Sausage Squad', and out we marched, Howard and myself. The tape blared out 'When the Saints Come Marching In,' to enable us put on a bit of style.

Trying to fill a large field surrounded by the audience, with just two characters marching out in large boots, red noses and big smiles, takes a bit of doing.

I was more used to it than Howard but we put on a brave face and kept our peckers up by sticking together, coming to a halt together, in front of the Captain when the music stopped. Jim then inspected us, as per script, and away the story went. With Jim's voice loud and clear, it all came to life.

We kept the story logical. This way we could be out of this world, and very tongue in cheek, but without being silly. So when Jim asks me why I'm dressed like I like I am, not in uniform, I simply said 'I've been out on pass and have been dancing. He orders me to get dressed properly and 'take those clothes off'. I retort I'll do it if he gives me 'a piece of music'.

So the tape is switched on and I start undressing to the tune of 'The Stripper'. As I take off the big coat and large entrance hat, I hand them to Howard who puts them tidy and engages in a little dance of his own whilst doing it. And the music progresses to the next dance, a Ballet, then a Charleston and finally a Cha-Cha. It only lasted about three minutes but we really got off with a swing. Then as I ducked down to put my tunic and Busby on, Howard takes up the story.

Jim orders him to dig a hole for the Sausage Tree. I had made two trick shovels for this job, plus a fertiliser pot. The pot was rather like an overlarge silver salt shaker we used to see in the fish and chip shops of that time, half filled with talc for maximum visibility.

One shovel was hinged in the middle of its shaft. When used, it folded up, hitting you on the back of your head. The other had a detachable shovel section, which with practice, this metal part could be thrown a good few feet up in the air. So if all went well he could get three good laughs out of this business.

By then I was dressed again and ready for action. We were then ready to take the cover off the tree and place it in the hole Howard had 'dug'. Deena had made covers for all the props. So we kept the gags secret until we exposed them at the allotted time. The tree cover was very large and we used Velcro as a fastener for it. It took an enormous amount of material to do them all. We bought the end of a bolt of cloth from a furnishing store. A pleasant yellow ochre colour.

Cover off, we hoisted the tree in position. We then held a touching ceremony of breaking out the flag. I got out my trumpet and whilst Jim explained about the solemnity of the occasion, Howard was already pulling at the flag's lanyard. I can't play the trumpet and could only play a hell of a noise, that sounded like tum- tiddley-tum-tum, after which I had an old taxi horn built onto the trumpet, and did the last tum-tum on this. It was a good sound and always got a laugh.

The cord was finally pulled properly and the flag released, it being pulled into an upright position by the heavy duty door spring, it unfurled itself, fluttering serenely over the tree. Our single pink sausage emblem was finally revealed to all and sundry.

The trumpet had an interesting past too. I gave my friend Bill English a pound for it. It had been a good instrument but was coming apart at the seams. I did a thorough job soldering it together, also attached the taxi horn at the same time. I still can't play it properly, but the noises are a part our business, and you can't depend on anybody else for ' blowing your own trumpet'.

We dive into the story of the act when after raising the flag, and saluting it properly, Jim orders us to inspect the tree for signs of the dreaded bungy blight. A good look by three pairs of eyes, and lo and behold we sight the devils nestling in the top of the tree. Jim hands me his revolver, I aim and fire a couple of shots at them.

Jim lets the snakes out using the radio signal. It's a great moment. Pure clown business. Try the impossible and it comes off. I'm delighted at being such a good shot, and Howard is happy to be able to stamp around in his big boots, knocking the stuffing out of these things as they lay on the grass.

Jim's next order, 'The tree must be watered'. You can't give a blank look to an officer in charge from a distance of twenty feet or so, so off we went we to plead with audience in case someone had a spare gallon of water on their person? We weren't very successful. It always ended up with the Captain telling to us to 'go and find some then!'

We sprang into action. I went and got a 'dousing twig' and Howard shouldered a 'stand pipe tap'. We traversed the arena seeking underground moisture. Finally the 'hazel twig, dipped, and the tap was driven into the spot. Success! Howard tried the tap and water gushed from it.

I charged off to get a watering can. We mustn't waste water. So the tap was turned again and the watering can filled with the fluid. We marched over to the tree watering the base carefully. Jim explained that the tree flowered automatically at the first sign of the spray. (Well not quite automatically).

Howard pulled the strings that released the flowers, six of them, all different colours that added to the charm of the tree. I was still holding the watering can which had a rubber tube extending the spout. I had pulled this off and wandered idly about with it, Jim, said, 'Oh I say, Kerby's lost his spout. Howard then went over to the tap saying he was tired and wanted to sit down.

Jim realised he intended sitting on the tap and shouted out 'don't sit there, mind the pressure'.

I also reacted with a warning shout. This didn't stop Howard. Sitting down comfortably, he was busy switching on his water out of the helmet gag. When the water shoots up into the air, he jumps up with a yell and runs round the arena, near enough to the onlookers to give them a dousing. With a good run, and the wind blowing in the right direction, he would cover a goodly amount of the audience. The crowd loved it. We never soaked them. Just a splash or two, but it always caused pandemonium.

As Howard finished I would go over to the tap and pick it up, but not before I'd done a bit of jig dancing over it. In answer to Jim who would ask me what I was doing my reply would be 'a tap dance'.

'Guarding the tree', Jim's words. He explained that the squad was quite able to protect the new tree and started to comment on our arrangements. I would go over to the large cannon and with a flourish, take off its cover. About three feet long it looked like a formidable weapon from the dark ages. I would line it up with the audience. I always sighted it up onto the onlookers who I thought might react to having a large cannon pointed at them. Mostly middle aged matrons. These would generally have a good laugh at the goings on.

I would then shout out 'on a target sir'. Captain Jim would then outline the features of the cannon Howard was pulling on. 'It was a ground to air missile especially designed for firing at low-flying aircraft!' Howard pulled off its cover and revealed a very large bottle of a well-known brand of tomato sauce, about two feet long. During this action I went over to the trolley and picked up a giant frying pan.

Taking off its cover I shouldered it like a rifle and marched to a given point to catch the missile after it had been fired. We could not waste ammo. At the command of Jim, Howard fires. The missile, a string of sausages, flies into the air. Up about twenty feet and the small parachute opened up to enable it to float gently down to earth. I endeavoured to catch it in the frying pan. Sometimes I managed it, sometimes the wind took it well away, always I got a laugh and if I caught it, cheers all round.

Jim then spoke of the response by the outside world to the unfortunate bungy blight attack on the local sausage crops. Gifts from all over 'have been flooding in'. I walked over to the trolley and returned to the tree carrying a string of black puddings. Jim announced these were a present from the Mayor of Blackpool. I hung them on the tree. Howard then followed with some beacon sausages. These looked like a Belisha beacon. An orange sphere with black and white sausages suspended underneath. These were a present from the Minister of Transport.

I then followed with an inflationary sausage. It was a single large sausage rather like a red German variety. As Jim announced that this was an inflationary sausage, a present from the Chancellor of the Exchequer (he named him), I blew into the sausage. It really did inflate and Jim commented ' it goes up with the prices'.

Howard then came along with a giant string of three sausages. All were encrusted with jewels and spangles and shone in the sunlight as he walked towards the tree. (This was the time the Burtons, Richard Burton and Elizabeth Taylor were very much in the news. Richard was buying enormously expensive rings and things, showering his affection on his wife). So when Jim announced 'this present was from Richard Burton' it was always well received by the audience.

The captain's next comment was to say that this was the end of the presents. This statement didn't deter me from staggering on with a giant single sausage, about three feet long, with what looked suspiciously like a flying bomb fin sticking out of its end. A piece of brown paper was carelessly wrapped around its middle. I said 'here is the last one'. 'What do you mean', said Jim, 'that's no present, it's an unexploded sausage from the last war'.

Terrified I'd dodge about the field not knowing what to do with it. Finally I solve my dilemma by handing the thing to Howard, and running off. He is left holding it like a hot potato, and finally Jim tells him to put it down, away from the tree. He does so and he runs off too. You can't leave it there said Jim. 'Cant we', we said, from a safe distance. 'No', said Jim, you have got to explode it, 'get out the equipment'.

The equipment for dealing with land mines etc, were as follows. I come back with an ominous looking detonator box, painted red for danger. As I did so I unwound a long length of electrical wire from the box with an electric plug on the end. Howard then plugged it into the front end of the unexploded sausage, and we retreated us far as the cable let us.

I pulled up the plunger type handle, and with Howard, fingers in his ears, we awaited Jim's word of command. 'Get ready. FIRE!' I pushed the plunger down. Nothing. 'Misfire, we have a misfire sir'. 'Right, misfire drill then'. We bolted off to get a large pair of headphones and the frying pan. Howard placed the headphones over my busby and then plugged them into the contents of the frying pan, a large fried egg. It plugged into the yolk.

So off I went, looking more like a metal detector with the pan scanning the ground in front of me, about six inches above the grass. I didn't walk towards the finned monster. In fact it was a lot of pushing and shoving by Howard that made me approach anywhere near it. Finally I plucked up courage and started waving my pan over the actual sausage.

Howard had by this time picked up the detonator box, (still connected to the sausage), and started pumping the handle up and down with gay abandon. After nearly fainting in case 'it goes off' Jim orders him to 'stop it'. I then waved the detector pan over the finned sausage again. Jim asks if I can hear anything? I do indeed.

A loud ticking noise was coming over the air. The audience heard it too. I shouted out 'it's ticking' and turned to the crowd asking if there was a watchmaker in the audience? This thing's ticking, I turn my back on the monster and at that moment Howard really does throw the switch and the bomb blows up.

We used a fair-sized theatre maroon for this effect plus an amount of flash powder to make more smoke. It was very effective, dogs barked, babies blinked and iced lollies shot down young throats in surprise. In the ensuing excitement I disconnected my headphones and started rubbing my back side, it had been next to the blast. I also started to cry.

My crying gag in the busby worked well. I could throw a nifty tear a full twenty feet, mostly over the audience, whilst howling my head off. I blamed Howard too. 'He did it on purpose'. It was the start of us getting at each other leading up to the finale. I always enjoyed this sequence. We were all busy, with plenty of action and suspense with a good story line going ahead at a cracking pace.

The best gag was the loud ticking noise Jim had on his tape machine. It was a recording of a metronome in action. It was the perfect sound. The detonator box was a good looking prop too. Everybody had seen them being used in films whenever things were blown up. It wasn't our handle that let the bomb off but another switch carefully put out of the way to avoid accidental explosion. Howard really had to reach inside to use it.

After the fiasco of my bottom being blasted, Howard and I faced up for a bout of fisticuffs. Jim vainly tried to calm us down, I was having none of it. I challenged him to a duel. Jim 'Come on now you two, you didn't join the army to fight', but I challenged Howard to a duel. He chose the weapons, tickling sticks, and we indulged in a bit of knockabout fighting with long fencing props I'd made for the purpose. I get the worst of this as well, so in desperation I went over and got the big cannon.

Howard is very alarmed about this action but still taunts me, but from a distance now. I creep up behind him and surprise him with a bit of business that looks uncommonly like putting a hypnotic trance on him. It works too. He comes rigidly to attention and I gradually draw him nearer the big gun. Jim is alarmed by this time and is warning me with dire threats. I take no notice. I fire the cannon. A big bang and through the smoke a large shell flies through the air towards my victim. He sees it coming and jumps up, letting the shell go through his legs. It doesn't go far. It plops down on the ground about ten feet from where it started.

Howard now laughs his head off. Jim then gets onto both of us, saying 'it's a good job the shell didn't go off, it might have damaged the tree'. Realising it didn't go off then, I pick up the shell from the grass and threaten to throw it at Howard this time. He hides behind the tree. Jim yells 'if you damage the tree I'll shoot you both'.

This warning goes unheeded. I throw the shell at Howard, who is crouched behind the tree. Now he lets off a flash and a bang at the base of the tree. As the smoke billows out, he pulls the catch and the tree collapses. Jim is furious with us and drags out his revolver, pointing at me. I run away from him. He says 'if you think you can disappear in a puff of smoke you're mistaken, take that', and fires. I then set off the flash bomb concealed in the leather pouch on the back of my belt.

I jump up and down, beating out the fire, apparently caused by Jim's shot. Jim then turns to Howard, now already running away from him, and shouts out 'I'll shoot the pants off you, take that'. A couple more shots, and Howard pulls off his flyaway trousers revealing a pair of bright orange pants, with large black spots on them.

Howard then joins me covering up his confusion as best he can. I pulled out a small white flag and wave our surrender. Jim then announces that it seems as though the squad will have to have a lot more practice before we attempt to plant the tree again at the next performance. 'Ladies and gentlemen, the Super Sausage Squad'. We take our bows.

Chapter 19

Polishing the Sausage

After this we commenced to collect everything together after our first outing as the Super Sausage Squad! There is an enormous sense of relief after each performance. Elation if you have done a good show, but if something has happened that colours this feeling, a touch of gloom follows. But there we were, a successful show, well applauded. Our first time out, with a brand new act, we all felt very well indeed. Making sure we had not left any props out, we retired to our tent where after a short rest we started getting ready for the second performance.

We enjoyed our act. Every time out we thought of improvements and if we all agreed, would put them in for next the show, or at least try them out. An act is a living thing, it grows as performers grow, and we had every confidence in ourselves. How I wish I had a video of that first time out.

The basis of our success I'm sure was doing a story show out there in the arena. Keeping a narrative going, keeping the audience fully in touch with all the goings on. It also kept us informed of what came next. We could expand out there. Make full use of the props and polish up the business to get reaction each time out. The three of us were very compatible. We all had our responsibilities and got on with it. We had a happy season all in all.

When we had a three-day engagement in Gloucester, this was a fine chance for a bit of polishing up. Six shows one after another. We ironed out a lot of problems during those days. The weather was fine and we three stayed in Howard's caravan. It was very comfortable indeed. A strong contrast I remember to a motor cycle act also on the same bill with us. They had hired a large lorry that they brought their motor cycles in, and they slept in the vehicle for the duration of the date. I didn't envy them.

I'd taken my paints along too, and did portraits of Jim and Howard between shows. As we were there for three days we saw more of Gloucester than we normally see at a gala venue. Although we travelled al over the country to do these jobs usually it was all we could do to get there and back. We mostly only ever saw the show ground.

If Deena came with us, she could have a look around whilst we performed. But Gloucester was different. We met up with our agent Bert Layton and his family. It was all very pleasant. I enjoyed it, not a bit like work! Strange this business we call work. I'm one of those lucky enough to be doing exactly what they want to do, but don't tell anyone but I'd do it for nothing!

Howard had solved a pressing problem at this time. It was how to get all of our props to the venue. He had discovered a place that hired small box trailers that fitted our needs. They were light, and just big enough to stow our suitcases of clothes and props. I had a towing bracket fitted to my Vauxhall Victor. The trailers happened to be a similar colour to the car so we looked quite smart arriving on site. We could also lock it up securely. Before this we had used Howard's Land Rover to get around in. It was rather cramped and not always convenient to use but it got us started.

We suffered a minor calamity whilst using it to do a job on the American army Base at Mildenhall, Suffolk. Our practice was to load a suitcase or two on the roof of the vehicle, securing them with ropes. This day was very sunny and we could see the shadow of the van before us on the road. Then after a while, as we were passing Epsom we noticed the shadowy outline of the suitcase was no longer part of the shadow on the road before us. Oh dear! We pulled in and confirmed our worst fears. My brown case was missing. All my entrance costumes for the striptease, shirts, red tunic, busby and wig. No crying gag, belt flash or any of my contributions to the spectacular side of the act.

We retraced our tracks for a couple of miles, nothing. A quick conference and we had to get cracking and forget about the loss for the time being. We contacted two police stations. hopefully leaving details of the mishap and tried to make up for lost time to get there. It was a long way too. We arrived late past our first performance time. We did take the precaution of 'phoning ahead to let the Americans know what had befallen us. This we did this by hopping from one AA or RAC phone box to another, en route.

If you have ever tried to contact an entertainments officer in a large American town, for that's what Mildenhall was, a chunk of good old America plonked right into the Suffolk countryside, you'll know what I mean. We kept getting the guard room or general office and a voice would say, 'Hold on, we'll get him'. Getting later and later we would hang up in desperation. Twice this happened and both times the 'voice' never did 'get him', and just left us hanging on. Another conference, 'we'll just have to get cracking again'. So we finally got there.

A garbled message had been passed onto the man who had booked us. He didn't seem impressed. It's a sad thing about being an entertainer sometimes. So many excuses, deliberate lies, and ducking and diving go on that people just don't believe anything anymore, from an artists' lips.

We had decided what I could wear whilst chugging towards the camp. What a conglomeration. Fortunately my big entrance coat, big hat and boots were separately cased and were safe. We altered the story line to suit. What's that about, 'it never rains'? Well ,we were shown where we could dress. In our first letter to a 'booker' I always requested a dressing tent for the props and the trio, 'reasonably near the arena please'. Were directed to a staff canteen at least four hundred yards away. It was heart-breaking.

After my descriptions about the act, you can imagine we carried an awful lot of bits and pieces and to have to walk to the arena where we had to set-up was a major job. If there had been an arena, roped off, as is usual, it would have been a case of setting up there, going to get dressed and walking back to do the show. No such luck. The 'arena' was an area of grass and picnic well and truly covered with families of all sizes. From tall ones to tots. There were no stewards. No order.

Bearing in mind we used big bangs and flashes in our effects we were a little dismayed to say the least. The thought of leaving loaded gags about the place, whilst we were away dressing, horrified us. There was also another critical consideration that if something was accidentally set off we would not be able to re-set it in time, and we'd already lost a lot of business gags in the missing brown suitcase. When we requested help in sorting this lot out, I got the distinct impression that they were as rapidly going off us as we were of them.

Finally we got sorted out. We commanded a small flat-bottomed trolley and Howard hitched it to the Land Rover. We left Jim to put out the props the best way he could. The final blow came when we saw the 'public announcement system'. This was something we requested in our first letter. 'Could we please have a hand-held microphone with a lead long enough to go into the middle of the arena'. You can imagine how cynically this must have been read when we saw the P.A. system provided.

An ordinary radio of 1950 vintage was set up on the grass with a microphone jack plugged into the back of it. The lead was six foot long and when at full volume control, its speaker could be heard a full ten feet away, if you strained to listen. You can imagine how much of our finely thought out script was going to be heard by the milling crowds that day. NOWT. It would be coming in a half-foreign tongue too. Our colloquial speech was as hard to understand by the Americans as their drawls and nasal utterances were to us. This must read like an awful beef, but it was a very hard day for us then.

Although a great attempt at friendliness had at all times been frantically worked for on both sides, when it came to our departure the crunch came. They offered us half fee. The reason being we only gave one show and the whole fee was for two such performances. I pointed out that however lame our excuses about this might seem, they were in fact very true. We had come on a round trip of three hundred miles and the agent had to be paid as well. But in the end we didn't get a lot more from them and just put the day down to experience.

It's a very costly thing this item called experience. Sometimes it becomes a very bitter pill to swallow. Our pill that day was the size of a football. Strangely, we also had an example of the other side of being an entertainer presented to us. The big money side of the business.

Later on that evening, the show for the adults on the base was being given by a top band, 'The Tremeloes'. They had an enormous articulated lorry as their stage. It was decked up with thousands of pounds worth of electrical equipment. Light rigs, microphones and vast amplifiers. I got the feeling they wanted to be heard more than ten feet away from their listeners. The scene provided an exotic backdrop to our departure. Us crammed in the Land Rover, and a sad space on the roof rack.

When Deena heard about the missing suitcase she was very upset. All the hard work she'd put into the clothes now had to start again. I managed to scrape up twenty-five pounds for her to go to London and get some more materials. We had another gala date for the following week. I thought about re-making the lost gags. It wasn't 'til she got back from London with her purchases that we got a call from the Epsom Police. The suitcase had been found and handed in.

It had fallen in a ditch alongside the road we had traversed whilst we were searching. The ditch was deep enough to obscure it from the road. If we'd only stopped and got out, maybe we would have seen it. However a very nice person took it along to the police station. We would have heard far more directly if I'd put my address and phone number in the suitcase. It was in all the other cases but this one. I managed to collect it next day and go and thank the folk who handed it back. What a to do! Deena was happy with her new materials though.

During this first season out we were constantly altering and re-arranging the act. Considering all the difficulties we all had in establishing our own identities and developing the character of the squad, we had some good laughs too. Keeping a lookout for a cosy pub on the way home, for our pint of shandy, no eyes were sharper, and if there was a fresh sandwich available, well what heaven it was. If we all thought we'd done well this was the very stuff of life. One item ran through the trio, we were all performers.

During this year of 1970 it was still very difficult to make ends meet solely from road safety and entertainment. I was building still, and Jim was getting on well in his amusement machine busines. He asked me one day if I was interested in making a prize bingo unit for a local cinema operator, Vic Freeman. It was to be a fifty seater set up. I would do the woodwork and he would contract for the whole job, and do the electrical work himself. It looked good to me. At least a couple of months work. We got the job.

As I was new to this sort of entertainment I had to start looking around at various methods of arrangements to seat fifty cash paying customers, comfortably and in style, to play this particular game. We had several conferences about how to arrange the seating to suit the long foyer type hall, and to design an attractive layout.

Each seat would have two bingo cards which cost a shilling to play (5p). The lucky winner would receive a voucher which was exchanged for prizes. The more vouchers, the bigger the prize. I was amazed to find that the bingo parlour we'd built was only to be used during the refreshment break for the clients who were there to play cash bingo in the adjacent larger hall and part time cinema. But there you are, I'm not that sort of gambler myself, so it has no appeal to me. But the job did!

In actual size the fifty positions of play were about the size of a single desk position for say, a secretary or typist, about two feet per person. So it was all about a job, end to end, that would stretch nearly one hundred feet. They looked alright on paper, and all very neat. But when it came to making them, I was hard pressed to know where to put them all. I did the job at home. My workshop was not very large and as soon as I started to assemble all the little bits into big bits, then the fun began.

We had bingo units all over the house. Upstairs, downstairs, in the passage, and out the back. We ate and slept the various bits for what seemed weeks on end. We were all doing our bit. Deena was painter-in-chief. All the exterior surfaces were covered in Formica laminate. A nice pale blue colour set against a mottled soft grey, with the plastic playing cards black with brightly coloured little shutters that were manipulated by the player. It looked very smart. There was a little chromium trim as well and the whole set-up had a bit of class about it.

We could have bought a lot more parts to build into our job but we elected to make our own. Especially the parts which conducted the shillings into the machine to enable play. I made all the innards in plywood and with Jim's microswitches, we got a relatively trouble-free product. Vic Freeman was very pleased with the final result and when we had installed it, it looked very good. Jim got it all going, connected up to an electrical box of tricks he'd made that controlled each game and accounted for the money. It was still in use in 1977, though not in the same building anymore. The old Theatre Royal, Bognor Regis, had been demolished and it was moved to another former cinema in the town, The Odeon.

The last job we had to do with it followed a change in the Gaming Act. Previously limited by law to a shilling to play, we had now converted it to two shillings a go. The two shilling piece (10p) was bigger so it meant opening up all the plywood channels to take the larger coin. What a performance! I'm sure that many a show of mine might leave behind an intriguing spectacle for the cleaner upper. 'He's a strange clown, he drips sawdust'. If he'd known what else I got up to he'd probably have shouted 'House'!

The fact that I was entertaining more added, in a strange way, a little more enjoyment to the building side of my life. It's the variety I imagine. The old saying 'a change is as good as a rest' is very true in my case. That's why I'm enjoying having another change, writing this. Long may the ink keep flowing.

The seventies also triggered my interest in laminating wood. Working in Scotch pine, the colours and grains of this particular variety were what pleased me most. A good customer of mine, Colin Harding, from Barnham, asked me to design a tea trolley to match all the other pine claddings I had installed in his home. There was a finite size for it as it was to nestle comfortably in a recess in their kitchen.

With the new PVC adhesives now on the market and polyurethane varnish just out, I enjoyed designing it and making it. The new glues cut out all the rush you had with the old Scotch variety. One could take time assembling the various components instead of working against the clock before the glue went cold. I laminated the handle of the trolley, shaping it after the glue had set. At that time I did not know how this laminating, would become so important to me a few years hence.

The road safety work was now steadily increasing. One idea I had for the junior age groups was very successful. It used the powerful medium of RoSPA posters. These single idea posters were very compelling if you could get the children to really look at them.

I made a collapsible stand that I could display twelve of these posters on, after I had pasted them onto a cardboard backing. The twelve pictures confronted the children with their safety slogans intact. I then removed the slogans from their posters, having first cut carefully around the words in the pictures. I had elastic holders stretched across the posters to hold them in place initially. Each poster was numbered one to twelve.

The audience watched me take out the words. Then, with two teams of two boys and two girls already chosen in front of me, we tossed a coin to start. I shuffled the cards and held one up for all to see. Having a teacher's help, we invited answers alternatively from the stage and out front as to which poster the words were taken from. A score was kept. When each poster was complete with its wording restored, the teams joined the rest of the audience. I then took the posters down. We then gave a point for each poster remembered. Another twelve points up for grabs.

Of course the second part of the game was more difficult and it wasn't hard to imagine the rivalry engendered towards the end. So after a cheer for the winners, normal service was resumed. To sum up the road safety point of view, we got twelve good visual messages exposed and examined by the children in those ten minutes or so. It was a worthwhile and entertaining way at getting the messages home to the children.

We tried it out in the Lewisham schools and Ted Davenport, the RSO, gave it the thumbs up. I was rather proud of the stand that displayed the posters. I made it from broom handles and three by two timber. It was easily erectable, portable, and I've still got it. Going through my photographs of this set-up, I came across another that transported me back to my early concert party days.

In the fifties cinemas often put on short stage shows during the interval, continous film showings without a break being a modern invention. A friendly cinema proprietor who often used me as a lightning sketch artist at his Masonic do's called me one day to say he was putting on talent shows as interval entertainment. 'Would I care to enter, for a fee of course'!

He desperately needed a speciality act to break up the singers entered. Of course I wouldn't be in the running for a prize, hence the fee. The contest drew quite a crowd and of course he'd invited the press. In the report that followed the editor had selected a photo to head the item. A charming young lady called Winifred had volunteered to come up on stage and have me draw her name. The other person in the photograph was also quite presentable, I thought. Me! This episode could be headed 'shady goings on in a Swansea cinema'.

Whilst writing my quarterly episode for the Clowns International Magazine, the Joey, I had cause to mention the man who made my first clown costume. I've only had to buy one, since then Deena has always looked after me in this regard. He was a gentleman named Jim Robinson. He was a gentleman too. Living in Essex he had a caravan as his home and workshop. He called in one day after we responded to an advert in 'The Stage'. He took measurements and went about his business. He returned with a suit complete with a floppy bow tie. To my surprise and delight he'd also made me my very own fly-up bow tie which, to this day, is still one of my most reasured possessions.

For the younger audiences it's been a winner all along. Its working part of course being a old clock spring. The bow tie was attached to the collar of the same material as the suit. I used this suit right up to when Deena started making my clothes. My advice to all aspiring purveyors of comedy to the very young, 'get a fly-up bow tie!

Chapter 20

New Recruits for the Squad

At the end of the gala season, Howard, having helped us out with the initial launching of the act, then bowed out. His business was needing him on these important weekend days. His garage was on a main road leading to the beach and naturally very busy at the same time as the squad was out planting. It was great pity, Jim and I would miss the large, happy atmosphere he always enveloped himself with. Knowing he was going I'd been keeping my eyes open, seeking a possible replacement. I was always hoping we would find someone to complete the trio on a permanent basis.

My youngest son Michael had a buddy, Robert Oliver. They had become inseparable friends in grammar school when we moved down from Mumbles. He was about twenty, tall and married to Barbara. I put the proposition to him, asking him if he would like to do a summer's work for us. He was a gardener by profession, not self-employed, and so might find it difficult to do any mid-week bookings, I resolved to offer him a definite daily payment for his services. He would know what to expect and could assess whether it would be worth his while. To Jim and myself's delight he said he'd 'have a go'. It was very brave of him. He had never done any entertaining in his life.

I was amazed how Ollie, for that's the only name I really knew him by, fitted the suit and the boots. Like Howard he was tall and well set up and looked a good soldier for the trio. Deena had to do some minor alterations to his costume but on the whole he looked good. I tried to work out a makeup for him but as he fancied a moustache, a droopy one, most of it fell naturally into place. He felt he needed the 'tash to hide his youthfulness. It also gave him a lot of confidence. It's always amazing how a spot of makeup can be developed into a first class shield with which to face an audience.

It was interesting during rehearsals to see how the bits of business were gradually re-organised to fit Ollie's own interpretation. We had plenty of time before the summer season and began to meet whenever we could, feeling confident that we'd be ready and well-rehearsed when the time came. But life isn't like that, all comfy and cosy. A hefty spanner was thrown into the works in the guise of a telephone call. It was Geoff Winship, a well-known member of a famous circus family that also had acts to present in the gala field.

He asked us if we were able to do a TV recording for Yorkshire Television. Us being the Super Sausage Squad. It was to be recorded in The Queen's Hall, Leeds, in a couple of week's time! First of all I consulted Jim. We agreed it would be a great chance. I also 'phoned Howard wondering if he would be interested, but he and Bess had already booked a holiday on that date so he declined. So we asked Ollie. All credit to the lad, again he responded that he'd 'give it a go'. What a thing to ask a young man! His first public performance was to be for a television recording in a circus ring, for Roberts Brothers, in a major public hall.

What an outing this proposed jaunt was going to be. Jim had not worked in a circus ring either. Geoff Winship was to be ringmaster for the show and two performances we were to be recorded on the same day. We were to be included in the charivari of the first show and perform our act in the second. Geoff told us we would be allowed nine minutes. Nine minutes! Our routine lasted twenty minutes, so we got down to slimming it to size. This really was difficult. We decided to keep to the basic story rather than dis-jointed bits of business just for the sake of going for laughs.

We were also to be limited by the circus ring. Our stuff was ideal for what it was designed for, big open spaces, but with a captive audience sitting close by, I foresaw difficulties with our bangs and water gags. Both were on the large side, but with care we could overcome these difficulties. So we managed to prune down to the required nine minutes and rehearsed every minute we could. We had booked a small hall in Bognor for this purpose. It was early on in the year and not very conducive to do it outdoors, even if the weather allowed it.

Our first full dress rehearsal ran to around fifteen minutes, but with practice and smoothing out, we finally managed it in ten. We felt very confident and spirits were high. We set off in the Victor, trailer in tow, to Yorkshire and the Queen's Hall, Leeds. It was a long drive and when we arrived, Roberts Brothers Circus and ring were there in all their glory.

Animal cages abounded and there was a general warmth and horsey smell of the back-stage of a circus. I found out that also appearing in the show were old friends Jimmy Scott and Duke Dupree. Both of them I'd last seen on filming occasions. Duke in the Pat Boone film, Jimmy in the TV commercial. Jimmy was doing his clever chair and high wire spot. His 'high wire' was a rope stretched between two unsupported chairs. A first class tumbler was Jimmy.

Duke, working with his donkey, was dressed as a ballerina in an outrageous tu-tu which emphasised his bulk. He looked very funny. There were eight or nine clowns involved all told. Most of them not unfriendly towards us, rather just sceptical. We were an unknown quantity. Saying we were clowns but without a lot of circus experience between us, I suppose they thought we had a bit of a cheek. I suppose we did too. But I've never subscribed to the notion that to be a clown you had to work in a circus.

Pierre and I had experienced this situation once before whilst working on the Pat Boone film 'The Main Attraction'. The fact we were not doing a usual clown routine didn't help either. I have often felt this kind of antipathy towards me for not conforming. It's a favourite moan from agents and audiences alike, and some critics in the press, to demand something new. Then, when you tried to do something new and different, but therefore unfamiliar, you get no thanks.

We got set up and awaited our first run through. It was hard. Poor Ollie. He should have got a medal for bravery! He confessed later how much it had cost him in nerves, that first time out. Jim did a very good job with a re-arranged script and kept us all together beautifully. We began, did it all, and ended. I thought it wasn't bad. We got a good response from the audience that were mostly made up of technicians.

A bomb-shell followed though. The TV producer requested us to cut down to four minutes! They explained they were to have trimmed the time down to four minutes anyway. Unfortunately, our act was not easy to chop and change. Having already cut the story in half, and now more? We felt a bit dispirited.

When our turn came to do the act with the audience in, we went out and did our damndest. We got a very good reception and felt satisfied. The feeling was not to last long. Another visit from the TV wallahs. 'Could we cut down even more'?

We were asked to do the show in the evening. We tried again. This time we got as good a reception as any act in the show, from the audience there. Even so our act was not included when the recording was shown at a later date. We were paid and we returned home. Also not shown was Geoff's part as ringmaster. If it hadn't been for the charivari run-in, we might as well not have been there at all. But we weren't alone. Only Jimmy Scott with his chairs was shown when it came out. But there, all that work! What an experience! Ollie said it was something he'd never forget and Jim and I got a whole heap of new experience out of it.

We always hoped to progress through the years. It's no wonder the popular conception of a clown is one with tears in his eyes. If I had had any sort of voice I was, at that moment, in line to become the most convincing operatic Pagliacci of all time. I wonder what the great Caruso would have thought had his act been reduced to a fraction of its former self!

We had a very successful and happy season with Ollie. The act progressed and prospered but we did have one blip. It was at a show ground in Kent. An enterprising showman was trying to revive a previously annual happening, in that venue, of a few years back. He put on a very big bill. A high-wire motor cyclist thriller, a Western act and us, plus all the trimmings of a large fair. We were centrally situated and well advertised. Our trio booked into the Lion Hotel for bed and breakfast, and prepared to enjoy the event.

But it was obvious from the first performance that the audience was not turning up. You need quite a crowd to sustain a set-up this size. Whether the date was wrong, whatever the reason, the attendances were very poor. But there was no indication when we received our cheque at the end of it all that anything was amiss.

Shortly afterwards I got a short letter from the bank manager bluntly stating 'the monies duly credited to my balance from the cheque will now have to be returned and could I please sign here'.

At the time we were not exactly flowing in cash. I'd paid Ollie and the hotel bill, and it was only the fact that I was very much upset and annoyed, and was experiencing a 'hard done by' feeling, that I thought to take stock.

As a self-employed builder the first lesson I learned was that there was never any shortage of work. It was getting paid for it that counted. My earlier encounter with an 'eccentric' dentist in Mumbles who ran up a bill with me and wasn't going to pay, gave me the first fright of my business life.

This was in the early fifties but the memory is still vivid today. When your bank balance swings wildly from two pounds ten, old money, to four pounds, the threatened loss of this unpaid bill, amounting to fifty pounds, put the wind up me. By now my non-payer's business was already in the hands of a solicitor, and I eventually got paid, so I looked for allies to convert this somewhat rubbery missile of a cheque into something lodgeable into my account.

Being a member of Equity I thought to ask their advice, but I rang up the agent Bert Layton first. He was a Member of the Agents' Association it was decided to leave it a while to see what pressure could be directed from that quarter. We didn't have long to wait.

A letter arrived from the bank asking me re-present the cheque. With the soles of my shoes scorching and smoking from the run, I did just that. It seemed that somebody had bailed out my debtor. Honours were redeemed. The good samaritan was a member of his own fraternity, The Showman's Guild.

It is no joke when you read these long lists of monies having to be fought for by Equity from contractors who baulk at paying the artistes' dues either through business failures or downright fraud. Anyway, all ended well for me and I was very relieved.

It was during Ollie's year with us that we pondered on a second act for the trio. It was always a pity, when after doing a good show you were approached for a further booking the following year, to admit we had no second act to offer. So we lost business. I had a feeling for another story of our trio of clowns and it suddenly burst to the surface in a flash of inspiration. I rather fancied the title first, 'The Boiled Egg Brigade'. But that was as far as we got for the moment.

Jim and I worked out a couple of ideas for the main prop, which was to be an atomic egg-hatching machine. Jim was to do the electronics and had some grand ideas to propose. I was still, as always, looking for simplicity. Basically the squad, still with Captain Jim in command, would have the grand title of 'Brigade' bestowed on them. Whenever they made an appearance at a gala it would be to announce that an enormous egg had been found in the district, and the Brigade had brought their atomic egg-hatching machine to hatch it.

An allied string of supporting gags could be hung on this framework to bring us a presentation of about twenty minutes. So we let the ideas settle and percolate slowly in our heads until moments of inspiration would erupt like volcanic burps of comedy. These would be assessed by us all, during our long return journeys in the Victor from our tree dates. These were great periods of discussion and conjecture whilst driving home.

These journeys were also great trials of tiredness. As Ollie didn't drive, Jim and I were taking it in turns. Sometimes only hopping along the motorway, stopping at each service station in turn to enable a few minutes nap to charge us up for the next twenty-five miles or so. There weren't the number of service areas then as are now.

These were the night periods. After the show, dead tired and wilting, the one consolation on return journeys was the stop for a motorway meal. Boy did we enjoy those fry-ups in the early hours! We always had a plateful helped down by comments about our performance or other happenings at the show.

One journey was never to be forgotten. We had been to Northampton and on the same bill as an escapologist. This brave performer was duly placed in manacles and such like, then put into a man-sized canvas bag which was then padlocked at the top.

With the proverbial roll of the drums it was then all up to him to escape! There was an expected pause whilst 'things appeared to be happening' when it became clear 'things were not happening'. Muffled grunts and violent movements indicative of a struggle, resulted in the bag doing an impression of a large Mexican jumping bean that had had too large a meal. The assistants were getting worried. Very worried.

We were watching from the dressing tent. The audience were watching too. The commentator, to build up the suspense, had warned us all how tremendously difficult this task was. It was beyond his capabilities to stretch the adjectives he'd already used to describe the daring and complexity of the feat, to include the unheard of suggestion that it might indeed prove impossible! More grunts and movement from the overgrown kit bag.

More illustrious escapologists of the past, like Houdini, had boasted in their memoirs that in their time they would actually get free and go for a stroll, or enjoyed a cigarette, whilst the tension mounted in the audience. They mostly operated behind a curtain or screen. The paying customers could only guess what was going on.

We didn't have to. We could see! There was no screen in the arena. We could watch the pulsating sack magicing the release of its occupant. Only it wasn't. It seemed ages before someone went and had a hurried whispered conversation with the writhing sack.

We all watched, fascinated. The commentator's throat must by now have resembled the Gobi Desert, as it had dried up long ago. After the whispering to the bag the assistant came racing towards our tent, looking for the key to the sack padlock. A short while afterwards the escapee came in, still handcuffed. It appears he had forgotten to secrete the handcuff key, and not being able to get to the padlock key, also left in the tent, he was stuck!

We all had a good chuckle about it. The unfortunate artiste is a great friend of mine and I'm sure he won't mind me relating this incident. Once or twice this early morning meal of ours nearly came to disaster. Trying not to laugh with a great mouthful of sausages and beans is nearly as dangerous as escaping out of a sack!

It was also during this show that the army gave a mock demonstration of its attack capabilities. The bangs they used put ours to shame. Great big thunder flashes followed by enormous clouds of coloured smoke. Talk about a phoney war. This coloured smoke enveloped everything. It could have been better timed for our escapologist friend. A finish that ended in a puff of smoke might have saved his day, and spoilt our night's chatter.

One evening whilst watching the ITV magazine programme for the South of England 'Day by Day', I saw an item involving a clown who lived about fifty miles away in Ringwood. He was billed as having a motorbike in a suitcase. He was called Sammy Sunshine. In the few minutes allowed him he was interviewed about his 'smallest motor cycle in the world', as claimed for it by its manufacturer, anyway.

Staggering in with a suitcase he gave it a kick start and the case moved off on its own. A very good gag indeed. Opening up the suitcase he extracted a miniature motor cycle, similar in style to the ones used by wartime commandos. So off he went round the studio, a big chap dwarfing his small bike and making a good impression all round.

Prop-wise, I noticed he had to struggle a bit getting the bike out of the suitcase and made a mental note that he'd have to do a bit more work on it afterwards. I made a note of him as well. I had not yet got his real name as I didn't catch the beginning of the programme. But a few weeks later, whilst working a gala in Portsmouth. I met him doing a spot there.

He told me his name was Sam Rowe and on the strength of the TV appearance, the show organiser, who also had seen him on South Today, booked him. He was doing an act in the arena, on his bike using a set-up of belisha beacons and a zebra crossing. He was also doing a walk around spot so he didn't get to see the Sausage act.

Afterwards, I met him in the dressing tent and introduced myself. We chatted about clowning and the International Circus Clown Club. Saying I was already a member I promised to send details, feeling sure he would also be welcomed into the Club. I complimented him on his TV appearance. He told me it all happened so quickly he was on before he knew it. Hence the tight fit of his prop.

But it was a grand idea and I had seen him handle himself on the show. He was a natural fall-about clown and the audience loved him, and to do an arena show single-handed needed great skill and courage. Jim had seen Sam on the bike and Sam's wife Marion, had seen us do our act. She was as enthusiastic about our show as we were complimentary about her husband. It was quite an event meeting each other like this, because it is not usual for two clown items to be on the same bill. Consequently Jim and I had not met many other clowns in all our travels.

We only had one performance to do that day so Sam didn't have our second turn out to watch, but we exchanged addresses and kept in touch. I noted he was self-employed too.

This self-employed business was a major impediment for Ollie, not being his own boss. He was gardener for a small local estate, and I'm not sure whether his employer would have taken kindly to him taking time out to don make-up and a red nose. I was always extremely careful to ask whether Ollie could accept a mid week date, before saying yes myself.

Jim was self employed by now, the owner of the amusement machine business he'd been working for. Deena and I always had plenty of faith in his abilities and so we moved heaven and earth to secure him his chance to buy the business. Our house was used for this purpose, offered as collateral against a sizeable loan from the bank.

It was not a cut and dried affair. Another person was also bidding for the company and every time the asking price went up we suffered anxiety problems. In the end when the final amount was decided, we took a deep breath and hoped for the best. Deena and I have always been like this together. We have always decided on the most important issues and got on with them. Afterwards we would deal with the consequences.

It started when as a newly-married couple when we sailed into a building society office to see about a mortgage. We sailed out again, badly bruised above the collateral line. It seems if you have no money, no assets, 'We are very sorry. We dare not take any risks lending you any.' Mind you, a young girl just out of college and a young man just out of the army perhaps wasn't a most promising situation to be in to go hunting a loan that would, on average, take twenty years to repay. In the end we only became property owners because we built the house ourselves.

About this time I was being noticed for my road safety work. I was televised in front of a nursery school in Southwark and later filmed at a school in Salisbury. Both items were shown and I enjoyed doing them immensely. The rush trying to get back home to view them on your own TV set was always a problem. But it was nice to be thought interesting and good enough to be on the telly! It's a shame this was before video recorders became commonplace. I have no visual reminders of these very early days.

When Vic Golds, R.S.O. for Southwark, started giving me work in his schools, it was for very low age groups. He said there were others he could use for the school age children but he was interested in pre-school age groups and influencing young mums.

Tufty was very much in the picture at this time. Encouraging the mums to read these stories to their offspring was another tool to be used in the battle for safety on the roads. Working without the proverbial red nose and makeup was, to his mind, the best way to use my particular talents with these younger children. Vic would also book me at Christmas time so my appearances would not only support the road safety message but also provide the basis for a party in the groups.

It was whilst working for Vic I first attracted attention as a solo perormer, from television. A crew from London Nationwide came to film me working the schools. To be recognised 'in my own right' like this was a big boost, the extra TV money was handy too!

After the summer season came to an end we thanked Ollie and he decided that he'd better not try another season in case it jeopardised his day job. So Jim and I were back at stage one again, in need of a third man. We both decided to ask Sammy Sunshine if he would be interested in joining us for the future season and we were very pleased when he threw in his lot with us. Sam Rowe, ex-Navy like Howard, with two children Ashley and Andrea, and his wife Marion, joined the trio.

We invited them over to Bognor for a 'conflab' and we had a nice weekend together getting to know each other while sorting out problems of costume and going through scripts. We agreed that the bookings for the gala act would take precedence over other work coming in that all three of us would each agree each booking. This would make everybody responsible for all decisions and none would feel they were being 'steamrollered' by the others. Sam also had his building business to contend with. All was then agreed, and we looked forward to being able to build up the act into a top-line gala attraction.

Chapter 21

The Sausage Takes Off!

During our weekend together, Sam, Jim and I sorted out the future as far as the act was concerned. The whole set up was rather like a co-operative with the same agreement as we had with Howard. Bearing in mind that Sam had quite a strong character of his own to bring into the trio, we were confident of future work. We had plenty of brochures left and they were still very effective in selling the act, but as soon as they needed re-ordering, we did a bit of pasting up on the front picture. To save money, Sam's face was added to Howard's body! They were very similar in build anyway, both big chaps. We also had some full colour photographs taken that were a hundred per cent Sam. These pictures were very successful and got us plenty of work.

With Sam living fifty miles away, we adapted the system I'd used when working with Pierre. If we were working over to the left of England, around Bournemouth and away to the West, we would pick up Sam from his home. If we were working North or East, he would come over to us, leave his vehicle in Bognor whilst we all piled into our car for the journey.

There was one problem. One you would not have guessed in a million years. Sam was a bad traveller. Even in the navy, his bouts of seasickness caused him untold discomfort. Travelling by car was also upsetting for him. It was alright when he was driving himself, but when Jim or I drove, he was very queasy. It's a wonder what we will all do for our art, isn't it? Talk about having to grin and bear it, there was no alternative. Mind you, we all suffered a bit sometimes when the windows were down to help him manage.

One of Sam's jobs in the service was a boy bugler. So out went my trumpet and Sam blew his bugle in the flag raising ceremony. There were lots of slight adjustments to allow the new squaddie to expand in his role. He introduced his own ideas in the use of his props. We rehearsed all winter and got everything running well before going out in the field.

As a matter of fact, before doing our first 'sausage' together, I asked Sam to work with me on one of my regular Christmas jobs. In the last few years around November time, I had helped Father Christmas arrive at his grotto in the Army and Navy store in Chichester. I was offered the job again, so I invited Sam to join me.

The store arranged for a couple of vans to follow Santa around Chichester, en route for the store, with us handing out balloons as a promotional item. Then when all the procession was done with, we said cheerio to the gaggle of young shop assistants, Santa's helpers, and we would do a couple of shows in the store for all the children we'd managed to attract to the event. We found we worked well together. We were very complimentary to each other.

Sam was Sam and you couldn't miss him. He had a very large personality that children loved. His speciality was magic. So, with his magic and my drawings, we put on a very varied show. It was a great success and for some years afterwards we repeated this combination often for A & N.

Once we toured with a gypsy caravan and horse. On another occasion we roamed the streets of Chichester with an elephant. All great fun that only came to a sad end when the town centre was pedestrianised and processions were forbidden.

After the new trio had performed their first show, we were all pleased with the result. As soon as we could, we re-arranged the story line to include Sam's bike. This was to be in the shape of getting a message back to H.Q, with Sam as a dispatch rider. With Jim, we arranged a routine based on the old idea of a verbal message getting slightly distorted by the journey.

'The enemy is advancing on all flanks, send reinforcements' was the message. It finally got delivered as 'we are going to a dance, send three and fourpence'. We were aware that this was an old joke but it allowed an expectant audience to be drawn in when Sam finally delivered his version.

So when Sam told Jim he was the dispatch rider, Jim said 'where's your motor bike'? Sam pointed to the suitcase, gave it a kick start and it ran away from him across the field. It always got a good laugh from the crowds watching.

Opening the case, he would take out the bike, still pop popping away, engine running, and after making a slight adjustment to the handlebars, away he went. A towering figure in his big boots and tall helmet. His large frame dwarfing the machine, which was barely eighteen inches high. Around the arena he would roar. It travelled upwards of twenty miles an hour. It was a great leap forward having another bit of business that travelled around the perimeter of the arena, close to the audience.

We did this move also with the water out of the helmet, getting close to the audience whenever possible. Now we had another contact maker. Whilst Sam wobbled and swung around, Jim was yelling at him that 'he hadn't passed his test yet,' and to 'come back this instant'. It was all great fun. Sam had one handlebar he could disconnect from the bike and would wave this in the air as though it had come off accidentally. In the end, after traversing the whole arena, he would come to sudden stop, dive over the handlebars and looking a very sorry sight, he limped up to Captain Jim to relay the message, obviously 'concussed.'

Shortly after I made him a prop that resembled a bale of straw to tumble over when he finished. It came in very handy once when we did the act in the middle of a town, on tarmac, not quite so soft as grass! The bale was placed by Jim who would regulate the layout of the show, decided by us beforehand. This also gave Sam somewhere to park his bike afterwards.

This bit of business tidied up the whole act in another way too. Jim was always complaining about the arena being strewn with props and how untidy it all looked. We had no ring boys or stage hands to follow us around. So while Sam did his ride, I was released to tidy up. Transferring the used props back to the trolley, picking up covers and generally having a good look around to prevent anything being mislaid. As Sam staggered over to Jim, I also managed to collect his suitcase and loose handlebar and place them out of the way. Small items can soon disappear in grass.

About now, my Victor had done over 100,000 miles, and was in need of major engine repairs. It had done me well. Half of the back bodywork was new owing to two mishaps absorbed doing all those miles, so it still looked good going about.

One bump was from a BBC van that wasn't watching out at the Elephant and Castle roundabout and went into my rear. This was sorted out by their insurers. Another time, during a very wet day, en route for Salisbury, I was going through Southampton when a van in front of me suddenly braked. I had the fright of my life. I braked hard, but carefully, and just stopped, sliding the last yard or two gently within an inch of his bumper. I was just in the middle of a sigh of relief when, with an almighty crash, someone bumped into my rear.

It nearly shook my head off. I looked out to see who had caused it. The chap who had done it also looked behind to see who had given him a push. It was all caused by a naval officer three cars behind me who ploughed into us all, concertinering us all like a pat of butter. He accepted responsibility and his insurers paid for a new tailgate and allied parts. However, my friend Charlie from Vicker's Garage had a word, telling me it was about time I got myself another car.

He had done his best for me all these years. In fact, he had always looked after me admirably. I was very seldom unable to work through transport problems. So Deena and I had a word. Blow me down, I was working in London a day or so later when one evening she told me on the 'phone that she'd found the very thing we wanted.

We had both decided we now needed more than a car and were thinking of a motorised caravan. The one she saw was a Volkswagen Dormobile conversion, J registration. The price shook us and I was dubious whether it could be managed, but it was.

We got a hundred pounds part exchange for the Victor and had to find another thousand pounds to complete the deal. Our new vehicle had only six hundred miles on the clock and looked beautiful. Cream exterior, lift-up roof, orange curtains, cooker, sink-unit, double bed and two single bunks and a lovely driving position. I remember how pleased I was not to have any water problems, as the engine was air-cooled.

The real reason we got a caravan was I was knocking myself out coming back from London each night. It was a killer, as I have mentioned before. Deena said she would rather I stayed in London overnight in the van. So it was. I came back mid-week for a change. This worked quite well and the pressure was taken off me but it was a sacrifice for her. She hated being alone and if the boys had not been still at home at that time, I doubt whether I would have gone any further with my school work.

I was bound to do the very thing I didn't like about the entertainment profession. Travelling. The staying away from home, the nasty bit as far as I was concerned. I'm not an entertainer who likes being away, but doing the same act requires a change of audience, otherwise the work dries up.

As it so happened, having the mass of traffic on their doorstep, the large centres of population were having to do something positive for accident prevention. Hence the RSO came into being. One of the pioneers in this field was Vic Golds, for Southwark. As his office got under way, it became clear there was a limit to how much a few people could do on such a large problem.

Soon entertainers, always looking around for mid-week work, adjusted their routines and, adding a bit of road safety lesson, were getting wages from the RSO's budget. Clowns also got on the bandwagon, me as well, and as I progressed and became more proficient, the recommendations that followed kept me very much at it full time. I was now working in most London boroughs south of the Thames, and around the country. So the move to a caravanette was logical. No lodgings to worry about, a real mobile home that could also accommodate Deena whenever she could manage it.

Over the years, this turned up some unexpected happenings. Once whilst working for Percy Kemp, RSO for Grays in Essex, I parked in a disused fire station. All the comforts of heating, cooking and toilets saw me very comfortable of an evening after work. As usual the evenings needed some filling.

I had my paints with me so I set myself up for a self-portrait in motley. With nobody to interrupt me, trying to put down an image of myself as reflected in a mirror proved very successful. Later when the BBC made a film about my work, this picture was featured by Jennifer Jeremy, the producer of 'Look Stranger'.

There were a couple of occasions before I changed from car to caravanette that I remember very well. I was working in the midlands for a short tour of the local schools when in one bed and breakfast, the sausages for breakfast were definitely off. Another time I was booked into a good class hotel but the visit coincided with a strike by the staff. The brussell sprouts served up for dinner must have been the frozen kind. They were nearly as cold when served up. The change of vehicle altered all that. I became my own chief cook and bottle washer!

Staying up in London did pose another problem. There were very few caravan sites in central London. On the first night I stayed in a central car park in Catford, Lewisham, but it wasn't long before the police came and said no.

So that's how I came to be staying in safe council depots overnight, awaiting the arrival in the mornings of a member of the RSO's office, to accompany me around the schools. So eventually I was in Lewisham with the dustcarts, In Islington in a highways depot, in Southwark with street-lighting, then in Gwent in a heavy goods vehicle training centre.

I knew lots of night watchmen. Most did not know I was a clown. Nearly all enjoyed having a bit of company overnight. The new camper van was a bit noisy when I had the roof up. The gaily coloured awning was thoroughly draught and water proof, and I had plenty of headroom, so it was quite snug.

The variety of the public authorities' responsibilities always surprised me. They varied widely over country. The messages coming in were intriguing. Mostly, street lights were out. Sometimes traffic was the culprit A collision with a vehicle, and lamp standards may be left in a dangerous condition. A night gang would probably be informed by the watchman who got a message from the bobby on the beat. A blockage in the drains. Warning lamps surrounding a hole in the road may be vandalised and more might be needed. Dead animals, maybe road casualties, needed to be removed. The list could be as long as your arm.

I am reminded about the snags of buying a non-British vehicle at that time. Spare parts can cost the earth. In the end we acquired a 'universal' tow bar from a reputable company that claimed 'one part fits all'. I believed them. Fortunately it fitted perfectly. Unfortunately, some months later, we found we had to remove it again every time we needed to repair the engine.

When I asked Charlie put a tow bar on the van, he also believed it, and got one from his normal suppliers. It did the towing bit very well. The snag being that the van's engine was at the back. Any engine problems to deal with afterwards. It made me very careful about buying 'universal' spare parts afterwards.

The new van also meant a lot more comfort at galas too. We could brew up and eat at any time. If we had to start out at four in the morning, Jim and Sam could get their heads down whilst I took first turn at the wheel. Now with three drivers, and taking it in turns like this, lengthened all our lives, I think.

Sam was also changing to a camper too. He chose a Bedford Dormobile. This move enabled him to take his whole family on certain jaunts. He now had no need to wait for the day of the gala before setting off. A very nice fringe benefit this. He had more relatives than any other person I knew. He was from a large family himself and there always seemed to be someone he hadn't seen for ages, wherever he went.

We had very varied galas to do our first year out together. With Ollie we had done a booking in Scotland at Dunoon and now we had another one up there in Newton Stewart, Wigtownshire. The 'Argyle Gathering'. It was a long way up there too. During the in between performance times, we all had a good time there. A small circus was also on site. Circus Markus. We watched the evening show and were amazed at the versatility of the owner and other artistes. Talk about doing the lot between them! This is an enormous understatement. We thoroughly enjoyed their style and flair.

Their sheer personality and showmanship made our single offering about a sausage tree seem very small beer indeed. But they were very generous with their praise of our efforts. As Deena and Sam's family were with us, we were all enjoying the break.

I remember going into a small pub there for a drink that night. During the afternoon a pipe band had given a display in the town square. One of the band was in this pub. A giant of a man, kilt and all, playing the bagpipes. It was deafening. I had not realised until then how powerful a source of sound they can be. He was well and truly playing for all the drams he'd got lined up for his consumption by his grateful audience, whilst pausing for breath.

We crept out to another pub. This was charming. It wasn't a public house as we knew it down south. It was someone's home. We all sat around a table and chatted like a large family. Deena was delighted with the informality of it all, and enjoyed her tipple enormously, a straight lemonade.

The Scots liked our humour too. The sly digs and tongue in cheek comedy suited them down to the ground. We got a good reception and thoroughly enjoyed their appreciation of our efforts. We only did one performance. A six hundred mile round trip for twenty minutes work seemed extravagant, but client and performers were well satisfied and the trip was almost a holiday for us.

Then Sam and I then teamed up for Christmas work, large works' parties and the like. Most firms split their young guests into five to nine year, and ten to fourteen years age groups. The older ones would probably be taken to a pantomime and the younger ones entertained by performers such as Sam and I. As we were both familiar with this work, and had done this before we'd met, we helped out on each other's jobs, bookings permitting, from then on. I made him a large pair of boots for his own work and Deena made him a clown suit. Marion was also very handy and soon built him up a wardrobe to cater for all these different venues. Sam is also a stand up comic and was kept busy doing cabaret spots.

I can only do cabaret work if the audience is all in front of me. Watching the back of an easel is hardly entertainment. Also my non-drawing clowning is not the kind to sustain a sophisticated and possibly well dined and beveraged audience, to my own satisfaction. Sam was good at it though.

Increasingly now we were getting on with new act, 'The Boiled Egg Brigade'. I had solved the problem of the finale. This was now to be when after all our hatching of the giant egg, our little chicken, patiently sitting on top of egg, was to be blasted fifty feet in the air.

I had found a way to propel it into outer space. Crudely speaking, I was going to blow it up with a large theatre maroon. I was going to build the egg around a bomb box, and when fired, the maroon, placed directly under the chicken, would provide 'lift off'.

When Fred Jackson made the iron box he welded bolts on it for me to build up sufficient wood around it to be fashioned into the egg shape. A three inch tube led down into the box. Here would sit our chikadee. I made a delightful prop chicken. Very robust but pretty. The legs sat cosily at ease by its sides. A charming picture indeed.

Then I let the bang go. The chicken shot up into the air, up to the required height alright, but the legs went everywhere but not with the chicken! It looked awful. I'm sure the children wouldn't have liked that, so the legs were not replaced. Instead I reinforced the base of the hen with thick rubber and layers of plywood to absorb the impact of the explosion, and tried again.

This time it looked very funny. When I examined the prop afterwards, I found it needed re-glueing in parts, but it wasn't unreasonably damaged. I settled for that. I'd just have to carry some glue with me to do any running repairs needed. What the folk in the park must have thought, when early one Sunday morning, these noisy chaps kept firing a chicken in the air.

We had decided that the hatching unit should be guarded so I built an anti-aircraft cow. This man'o-war creature we named Bamber. I'll not say more except that her eyes, looking large and appealing, reminded us all of a very popular TV quiz master. So the name stuck.

Bamber would be chocked full of gags. Its horns when lifted off, would become a field telephone handset. It's tail was a handle that when turned, produced the sound of an air-raid warning. This was because it was attached to a genuine WD siren from the last war, used by air raid wardens locally. There were two snags though, it took quite an effort to get it going, then it was very difficult to stop. When going full blast, the handle would likely break you arm if you weren't careful.

The siren was also heavy and this, along with batteries to work the 'phone, made the whole cow a bit of a handful. It was placed on stout pram wheels with the front and back legs being fixed to the axles. The cow's armaments were to say the least intriguing.

Rotating a hand operated wheel on the side of the cow rotated its four udders lazily upwards from their undercarriage. Now pointing skywards between the animal's rear legs, we could fire a single teat, or a double one when required, to become projectiles to bring down any 'attacking aircraft'. It was a great gag and looked very funny. We used proper anti-aircraft drill practice to heighten its absurdity even if we never hit a plane!

It brought the house down. To see a cow's udder, under command, swing up from its rear, point skywards and at Jim's command 'Fire One', launch a single teat hurtling towards the heavens, was hilarious. Then, 'Fire two', and a double firing sent two more to follow the first. When it returned to earth, the fallen ammunition, when picked up, could also be milked. I had placed bulb containers in each teat which squirted milk when I stroked them.

The cow's head was made a long time ago. It was an experiment I made with gummed paper for a cow in pantomime. Perhaps Daisy in 'Jack and the Beanstalk'. Its shape was outlined in wire and soldered together like a cage. The gummed paper strips were stuck across and around the wires, always following the shape.

I set two halves of a Sorbo rubber ball to form the eyes. They were most appealing with giant plastic eyelids and lashes. It was a very pretty cow and surprisingly robust. Its mouth was open showing a warm red tongue. To prepare it for gala duty I covered it with bandages cemented on with glass fibre resin.

Having already remodelled its ears and horns to become detachable to resemble the telephone hand set, the whole cow was then covered in sandy coloured velvet, head as well. The colour was just right, it looked like a true Jersey cow. We had recycled the material from a former creation, a camel. This was made in our Butlin's days when we had two spare redcoats to man the humps!

We arrived in Harrow to do a gala when the latest wonder of the entertainment world, 'The Wombles', were also booked to appear. Or at least one Womble. It was a real eye opener for us. The children were lining up all over the place to be photographed with him. What a way to make money. Anyone could have been in the suit. When we did a show, all three of us had to be present, and seen to be so. 'Fings ain't what they used to be'.

Chapter 22

Hatching a Very Broody Egg

One stroke of luck as far as doing so many jobs to earn a living was concerned, was that road safety work was more in demand when the dark nights were with us. Similarly, there weren't many outdoor events going on then. I do remember two night jobs that came 'out of the blue', so to speak. In the 'The Model T and Pierre' days we were approached by Richard Burton's brother, Graham Jenkins, from Port Talbot, Wales. 'Could we do the car act as interval entertainment at a fireworks do?'

He was in charge of Council entertainments at the time. The M4 motorway was not ready then, so we went over the top using what is now called the Heads of the Valleys route. I don't know what the lorry was suffering from at that precise moment, but it certainly wasn't at all sure whether it could get itself to a point where it would be all downhill to the recreation ground arena. We did make it in time and asked our hosts about lighting and microphones. There were no loud speakers on the ground and the lighting was, wait for it , two hand held gas searchlights, dating from…we never did find out.

These lights were about three feet in diameter and eighteen inches deep with a large handle on each side. They were proper searchlights, but of the mobile variety. When it was time to do our stuff, it was pitch black, except for these two lights. Of course, the gallant holders of these glass fronted tools of illumination didn't know the act and were therefore also 'in the 'dark' as to where to point the beams. We were the clown act, but the antics of our two-footed 'super troupers' swinging their beams around and we two entertainers trying to be seen, were, I think the word is, hilarious.

When Pierre shot up in the seat, he became invisible! One minute the beam was on him and the poor operator had no reason to suspect he was shortly going skywards, so the light stayed below whilst Pierre went up. When the doors fell off, where were they? If we had thought about it, a few roman candles might have saved the situation. The pits were open then. If we had had a few miners' helmets with the lights on, as well as motley, that would have helped. Amazingly though, the crowd thoroughly enjoyed it and we were paid as per contract.

The other bonus job heralded a return to Wimbledon. Not the lawn tennis venue, but the greyhound stadium. Again the perimeters of the track were floodlit where the dogs ran, and when we went out to do our stuff, it was up to us to find the lights to work by.

Back to the Boiled Egg Brigade. The cow was nearly finished so we explored other antics for our brave trio to contemplate. A popular counter measure to a land-based onslaught was a gas attack. To simulate this I devised a giant wedge of cheese of doubtful age, stuck to a very large cheese dish. I used to lift the lid of the dish beneath Sam's nostrils, whereupon he fainted full length, flat out, toes upright. It was not until Jim suggested he needed the 'kiss of life' that he would suddenly 'recover' and spring back to life. It was a good laugh. We used to have a genuine WD gas rattle that was sounded prior to this bit of business.

The main prop of course, was the atomic hatching machine that powered the chicken that was sitting contentedly on the egg, quietly hatching away, whilst we guarded and tended it.

It was about three feet by two feet and three feet high, and had four wheels for mobility. It was be-decked with a flashing beacon and lights that blinked on and off when the machine was switched on. There was a small umbrella-like section that clanked up and down in unison with the electric pulses going out to the chicken. From the broody bird leading to the machine were two impressive brightly coloured coiled electric cables, connecting the bird and egg to its power source. Batteries.

I made three flat batteries that were exactly like the blue Ever-Ready variety we used in our torches at school. Well known and much used by boys in their flashlights. One battery, a small one, was twice the size of normal. The second one was twice the size of that. The third one again doubled up in size, about two feet tall. All were to scale and looked very real. We gradually increased the power to the chicken by starting off with the small one and working up to the large. The story was tied up in this trio of batteries.

Another important piece of equipment was the one I made to collect water for the chicken. You can gather from this there comes a time when the chicken needs a drink, just like the tree in the other act. I found it helped to run the story line by developing the chicken script like we had developed the sausage tree story. The chicken must be set up, guarded, watered and fought over. A perfect set-up for the Brigade to bumble along in. Start, middle and finale. Not wanting to use the tap and divining twig again, I opted to make a giant carpenter's brace and bit, complete with large drill.

The brace looked beautiful, made in one inch copper tubing and twice the size of my own brace. The principle was the same as used in the tap. A siphon tube was used to produce the water which was stored within the hollow body of the brace. When pressurised using a foot pump, the water could be released by a tap in the handle when required. Sam would locate the place for me to drill for the wet stuff and shortly afterwards a jet of water shot out from the top of the brace's handle. It went up a fair way too, about twenty feet, looking quite spectacular like an oil rig blowing its top. Some of it might even find its way over the audience. Accidentally, mind you!

When we wanted to stop it, Sam would remove the drill having first carefully slid a large boot over the 'hole' in the ground. This would only stop it for a second or two before it would squirt out of his helmet. Off around the arena he would go, so that the audience could get a closer look at the phenomenon. Sometimes they would get wet as well! It was a similar sequence to the sausage act but was so successful, using different props, we thought we'd be forgiven for the repeat.

We enjoyed the lark and our efforts didn't really wet anybody. Just a fine spray, plus a large amount of cheek by us. Everybody loved it, it was the sight of someone running towards them spurting a jet of water that caused all the excitement among the audience. With the younger onlookers, I always found they would be most upset if they didn't get a drop for themselves. Funny things, people. Funnier than clowns!

To repeat the successful idea of raising the flag of the brigade, I made a new flag pole. Deena made a new flag, a single egg in an egg cup, on a plain background. Instead of springing up from the tree, this flag unfurled itself very sedately. Like drawing the lounge curtains, sideways. This allowed it to unfurl correctly even without wind. It was also constructed to allow me to let the flag and post down rather abruptly on my head, in the final duel with Captain Jim.

To enable Sam to plant something again, I made some flowers that opened by hand. We decided that after he had banged in the H.Q. (headquarters) sign he could also 'plant' a couple of flowers. These were quickly assisted into a growing mode by use of an oversized hammer. He belted them with it, walloping them into the H.Q. garden. Talk about green fingers!

It was necessary to fertilise the ground prior to planting too. The way Sam sprinkled his plant food willy-nilly and with gay abandon was very funny. Spreading clouds of white fertiliser everywhere (chalk dust), plus a little puff or two under his armpits, he always got a laugh. Jim would comment at this stage, 'Ooh look, he's a Johnson's baby'. (This referred to a TV advert for talcum powder that was popular at the time).

We had thought to ring the changes with the guarding business. We would prepare for a sea-borne attack by sailors of some sort. So, as a diversionary measure to a frontal attack, the enemy would have a large notice dangled in front of them announcing 'Free Beer', with an arrow pointing in the wrong direction. If this move failed we had another scheme dreamt up by the Brigade's own 'Department of Novel Tactics', by going at them from a tangent, or different angle.

We had a roll of artist's canvas that opened up to reveal an enticement that most sailors could not resist. It was a life size picture of a busty blonde secreted from a saucy seaside postcard, and copied in minute detail. We would let this canvas unroll at the appropriate moment, on the command of Captain Jim. It was all very colourful and fitted in with our policy of visual novelty always. Although the Department did add, there was a risk of it not working if the opposing attackers were thorough gentlemen where the fair sex was concerned!

So briefly the story was this: The Boiled Egg Brigade would be booked into a district to deal with a large egg, supposedly found there. Kerby Drill would still turn up outrageously dressed and would disrobe to concealed music. Sam would then set up the H.Q. We would erect the flag pole in a grand manner and assemble the atomic hatching machine. The egg would be revealed and placed on a nest and connected to the hatching machine. The chicken would then be ceremoniously placed in a broody position astride the egg. We would then connect up the smallest battery and switch the machine on.

Everything would then spring into life. The lights would start flashing, instrument needles would swing wildly, the beacon would light up, and up and down would go the chumper and chump away merrily along the wires to the chicken. Pulses of movement, in a regular rhythm would surge back and forwards. All was well with the world.

Sam had an enormous stethoscope with a plastic funnel on its end to test the egg's temperature. This we did at regular intervals. Captain Jim would then order us to search for water. The chicken must have a drink. Out would come the brace and bit and the whole water business would be carried out.

Nearly at the end of this, a raucous warning would come from the egg. Something was amiss. As we ran over to it, a large flash would come from the battery and the pulsing would stop. Jim would explain that the small battery had failed and so we then fetched the next largest one. We connected this up to the machine and hatching was restored while the brigade demonstrated how we would guard against attack by other nations eager to capture the prize egg.

First we dealt with attacks from the sea. The gas attack from the cheese dish, then the beer diversion followed quickly by unveiling the busty blonde bombshell.

Then Bamber, the anti-aircraft cow, would be put through her paces showing how we would deal with enemy aircraft. For this demonstration, Jim himself would set the scene. A lovely cow being quietly milked into a spotted bucket by Kerby Drill. As he leaves the cow with his now milk-laden container, a telephone would ring. It was the big silver bell around Bamber's neck that did this bit. (It was an ex-ambulance bell and was a corker).

Jim would order Sam to see who it was. He lifted the cow's horns and spoke to Brigade H Q. It was an aircraft alert. Sam yells a warning and goes to the rear of Bamber and turns his tail in a clockwise direction. As he did so, the siren sounded across this idyllic scene and the rest of the troupe springs into action. Captain Jim raps out instant commands, Kerby Drill goes to Bamber and jockeys the cow into position facing south, the direction from which the expected aircraft were approaching.

'Up three hundred, traverse right, Fire one'. BANG. Up goes teat number one. 'Fire two'. BANG. Up goes the double teat. The orders are crisply carried out and the enemy attack thwarted. Before Sam and Kerby can start to congratulate each other, the hatcher's alarm screams out a second warning. Rushing towards the patient chicken another flash emits from the battery and the hatching machine grinds to a halt again.

So the last and largest battery is connected. We switch on again and sure enough all is well again, but not for long. A strange series of noises emanates from the machine. Its excruciating sound throws every body into panic. Sam blames Kerby, Kerby curses Sam and Captain Jim is about to put them both on a charge. He reckons it's a mistaken battery connection. We shout 'It's not us, it's the battery, it's too large. It's going to blow up, take cover'! As soon as we scuttle away, a terrific bang comes from beneath the hard working chicken. Up some fifty feet into the air goes our now spinning flying fowl, hurtling from his hot seat, bruised bum and all.

Captain Jim, entrusted with the momentous task of hatching the giant egg, sees promotion prospects fading and chases Kerby, who seeks shelter by hiding behind the flag pole. It's not really wide enough to conceal his bulk. Jim fires at the flag pole, a direct hit. The flag pole crashes down on Kerby's head. Dazed he can only watch as Jim chases Sam away, firing as he goes. Sam's trousers are shot off from under him and the duo surrender to their patience tried officer. They are forgiven and orders are issued for the Brigade to prepare to try hatching the egg again in the second performance. So instead of being clapped in irons, the trio go off to claps from the audience. Hopefully!

Making the extra props caused few problems. Once I get an idea, the making of them just seems to follow on. The carrying case to put the egg in, because of its weight, had a rope handle at either end. It looked like a little packing case. But when the lid was turned over, there was the nest for the chicken, fashioned from some greenery plus a few twigs, it looked quite a respectable residence for our brave fowl.

Making the egg was quite labour intensive. I have wondered since how much time we spent dreaming up and making these ideas work. First of all they are mainly 'one-offs'. Nothing to copy. There would be no surprise or novelty if this were not so. So you feel your way forward, hoping that what seems a good way of raising a laugh can be brought to fruition, and made robust enough to do the next performance, and so on.

To 'launch' the chicken we were going to explode a large theatre maroon, (firework), inside the wooden egg, encased in its own steel compartment to withstand the blast. Because of this the finished egg, when shaped and painted, ready to do its job, was quite heavy. It was in view all through the act so it couldn't very well show handles. It didn't help either that the gloss paint finish made the egg slippy to grasp. But in the end it was worth it. I still have it as well as all the other props I've made. I'm very proud of them. They are our tools in this business of making people laugh.

Deena made a new set of stripping costumes for my entrance business. For the egg I did a Spanish dance, with a short bull fighting episode with Sam. He held up a mock pair of bull's horns and taunted me. I made a special wig, out of string, with another chicken sitting on top of it. This one was made of felt. A tube ran up inside of it and I did the crying gag through the chicken's own eyes.

After the striptease routine, my working costume was fashioned in bright blue with white webbing and a belt pouch at the back, similar in style to a soldier of the Crimea War. My final underneath costume was a blue and white striped stretch material and contained two gags. Painted on my bottom was a skull and crossbones, and on the front was a popular catch phrase of the time 'I'm only here for the beer'.

Sam was clothed Scottish-style in a red jacket with loud plaid kilt, bare knees and large boots. Getting the tartan colours loud enough to be seen clearly from a distance was a slight problem. I painted a twice full size plaid onto an existing kilt. It looked very effective. A sporran-looking ancient distemper brush waggled from his waist.

Jim of course, still a captain, was dressed as for the Sausage. With a squad like this, he will be lucky to retain his three pips for when his pension comes round! So the B.E.B. was ready to do business. We accepted bookings for the following season. So beginneth our second gala act. It had taken us three years to get the first act up and running with a settled complement. This had taken half the time.

Also at this time I was doing more painting. Three of us from the Bognor Art Society decided to hold a week's exhibition in nearby Chichester. The hall had to be booked a year in advance. It cost fifty pounds for the week. My friend Phil Lake was a lovely artist of the old school and like me was keen on portraiture. His skill though lay in the slow build up of colour, as distinct from mine, a slap bang wallop style, more impressionistic, according to some purists! A third painter was John, a water colourist.

Unfortunately, it wasn't to be for him. A few weeks before opening, he died. It was a shock for us all. We were relieved a bit when his widow decided to carry on and show his work. The fourth member who joined us was a lad from Elmer, Bognor Regis. Matthew Hillier was still at college in Wales. His forte was wild-life paintings. He used gouache, a kind of refined poster colour. He was very talented and already being sought after by dealers.

Getting works framed, sorting out stewarding rosters, ordering wine for the pre-view, kept us pretty busy. As you can imagine if it had been in gala season it would have been very hectic indeed, but it was in the spring. Deena and I, with our vacuum flasks duly primed, plus eatables, enjoyed our period of chatting up the visitors and we didn't do badly. I realised a long time ago that I was never going to set the world alight enough to get a living out of painting.

One thing did surprise and sadden me though. On the day the public came in, the dealers entered, studied Matthew's work, did their business, if any, and turned around and walked out. Not a glance in our direction. Hey ho, back to the drawing board!

During that season we got a four day booking for the Sausage act. It was at a trade fair at Newton Abbot, at the racecourse. It was like heaven being able to take time, enjoy our work, and discuss ideas all at once, together. The weather was glorious too. We enjoyed a new experience here. SONY, the Japanese television manufacturer, had a stand in the fair. They were showing off their latest range of video-tape machines. The salesman co-operated with us and we recorded the whole act on tape.

They then produced a very good recording of us at work and used it to play back to customers on their stand. It helped us no end. We could sit back and view our own efforts dispassionately for the first time. It was only in black and white, colour on portable video was quite a way off yet, and afterwards I bought the tape from them. I still have it.

One bonus was they came into the dressing tent and watched us dress and make up. I thought there wouldn't be enough light under canvas to do this, but no, their cameras did not work like photographic film and we were very pleased with the result. Even Sam, semi-dressed, was presented as though we were at the Oscar's Ceremony.

The fine weather continued and as Sam's family were with him and Deena was with me, we were more on holiday than on a work site! One morning , up bright and early, (I have always been an early riser), I wondered just how fit I was. I likened it back to the time in the army when I could only run a mile or two, without finding myself in the queue to see the medical officer! That was years ago, so as a test, I decided to run round the racecourse. It was a steeplechase course so I had to run around the inside perimeter unless I wanted to take the jumps as well.

What a job. It seemed miles and probably was. I gritted my teeth and plodded on. Half way round, I contented myself with the thought half had gone and it couldn't get more painful. Couldn't it? The end came in sight, I had done it. Not having told anybody what I was attempting, there were no welcoming crowds. In fact, having to tell people that I had done it seemed to me afterwards to have been a sad insight into my advertising capabilities.

There was one consolation, if I had not managed it, and I was forced to give up before my tongue had finally disappeared down towards my stomach, I would have had no explanation or apologies to excuse myself with. That was well over thirty years ago. Now the very mention of Newton Abbot makes my new heart valve and two bye-passes quiver violently!

Chapter 23

Fading Out the Gala Acts

Reading back a bit about my epic run around the Newton Abbot racecourse, I realised that being a gala clown had kept me quietly fit. To be able to run about an awkward grassed area for a full twenty minutes in an arena, kept you on your toes. To manage four, forty five-minute shows with my school schedules each weekday also helped to keep the pulse racing and the arteries clear. Of course performing was the easy bit.

With the sausage and egg stories includes taking the props to the show, dragging them out in the field and placing them, doing the pleasurable bit, then humping them back again to set up for the next performance. With the school shows, I did have a bit of help.

With children, my thrust was always visuality. Words needed to be backed up with items that caught the eye. Some of my props were necessarily bulky to be large enough to be seen from the back of the hall. My easel was now fashioned in the shape of a tree. It was all wood and blooming heavy, so I was very pleased to have help.

So, set up in school A, do Infant show.

After a cup of tea at playtime, do Junior show.

Have a school dinner, move to school B.

Repeat programme as morning,

Load props back into van.

All very healthy stuff. But wait, what about the backroom staff. The other day I came across one of Deena's checklists for the two gala acts. These revealed the very loving care and lubrication that enabled three hulking brutes to gallivant around to their hearts content, field-wise, in the secure knowledge that when wanted, all the bits were at hand.

Captain Jim's uniform. Sam browne belt, revolver, holster, etc, etc. Sammy Sunshine's uniform. Helmet, big boots, etc, etc, Kerby Drill's two outfits, dresses, wigs and headgear, etc, all in their respective suitcases, cleaned and ironed where necessary. Tree, egg, cow, chicken, bangs, and props all accounted for. Over a hundred items, each act, each time out. And without pay! How lucky we are with our womenfolk.

Insurance agents were reluctant to insure our lives. They said it was because of the danger of working with bangs and flashes and doing stunts of a dubious nature. My own thoughts on this was that they probably knew how much we got paid and just wouldn't stand the risk of us all starving to death!

Sam's son Ashley, was at this time considering his future. He was very interested in photography so we encouraged the lad to do us a good turn. Jim hired a movie camera and with reels of colour film, Ashley filmed us doing the Sausage Squad, here in Bognor Regis. We also taped the sound. I intended to fit one to the other afterwards, but even so, we now had a coloured version of the trio doing their stuff.

He did a very good job for us. Knowing the action end to end by heart, (and from back to front as well I should think), he was able to be sure of pointing the camera in the right place at the right time, action wise. The fact that it was filmed in my home town was also a bonus. Many local people appear in the audience. Some of these were friends of ours. It was at a Lions Fete. The weather was kind to us and all in all, everybody was happy. Since then Sam has kept us in touch with news of our young photographer's progress. He is now an award- winning producer working for BBC, ITV and the cinema. Look out for the name Ashley Rowe.

During the evenings in the van, away from home, I was doing more painting. At the time I was working in oil paints. Nowadays, I'm more for acrylics. These dry more quickly and as they are water based, you don't have to put up with the smell of turpentine or its substitute. These wet oils took quite a bit of looking after in the confines of a camper van. I made a carrying case that held six paintings, separated from each other while they dried. These paintings proved invaluable as extra income when sold at local exhibitions. Thus the camper van was not only my home on the road but a mobile studio as well.

The portraits I painted of people I met on tour stayed with them. How sorry I am that this was before I started using the camera to record all my works. There was a time when an art teacher wisely said to me 'When you have painted your first hundred faces, you will have a decent idea of what to do on the next one'. There was an occasion when the situation was offered me to do something about this gem of advice.

In the Bognor Art Society, a friend of mine was making a great name for himself, he was Dennis Frost. He worked in pastels and was published later on. At the time, Dennis was working in a holiday camp just doing the faces of campers for a living. He came to me one day saying he had a second camp wanting a resident artist for the season, would I be interested? Would I! There was a problem. I had no knowledge of pastel painting, and I couldn't do the job in oils.

The speed necessary to turn out a product for sale, using another medium, was not really on. Then there were more compelling arguments for me not trying: a wife, two children, mortgage, and of course I would be in camp during the summer, building weather. Otherwise I would have jumped at the chance.

Dennis and I used to swap subject photographs to paint. We had similar inclinations as to what made a good subject. It was very sad that he should die so young. I have a page out of one of his books in my studio up on the wall now. It's of a be-whiskered Chelsea Pensioner, showing his age and medals, and the sympathetic conception of an old soldier that only Dennis could see and portray.

A Sunday newspaper recently held a competition to paint a portrait of the Queen for her eightieth birthday. I decided to have a go. Now can you imagine 'little old Hal Brooks' being granted a sitting in the palace by Her Majesty. Neither can I!

So my submission was done from a photograph. A short time before the same newspaper had published a supplement commemorating Her Majesty's Jubilee. I took it to my local Middleton Art group and asked the twenty or so members to choose a photograph from these pages. They chose the one I also favoured, and I painted it.

It received raved notices from my family, artist friends and creditors. Its first public showing was at the Tamarisk Centre in Littlehampton, West Sussex, where I am also a volunteer piano player. A Council inspired establishment for the over fifties, it also provides dining facilities for the members. I play whilst lunch is being served.

Our art group was having a two day exhibition in Arundel that weekend, so to draw attention to the event, I set up my painting of the Queen on a chair by the piano alongside a small poster advertising the show. (Littlehampton is quite close to Arundel, so it could have attracted a few visitors).

Well, I was surprised at the interest it aroused. Two things could sum it up though. One, the sight of a portrait of Her Majesty who was shown smiling and in a good light, and two, that the artist was the same eighty-odd year old chap tinkling the ivories and helping their digestions with tunes from a bygone age. A very happy combination.

Not wanting to see the painting go, I put a prohibitive price on it. A bonus was to come the following week with a nice photograph of me and the painting being displayed in the local paper, 'The Gazette'. Hey-ho, recognition at last. My masterpiece didn't get anywhere by the way!

To quote a favourite introduction from the famous Max Miller, 'Now here's a funny thing'. Every Tuesday morning I have to take my 'one a week' pill. This one is to help me get on with all the other pills I take daily. Instructions on the bottle read, 'to be taken first thing with a full tumbler of water. Do not lie down or eat anything for half an hour'. So, leaping out of bed, I stumble downstairs to take my pill with a tumbler of luke warm water, and then sit down to get over the shock of the leaping out of bed bit.

After I've run out of curtains to draw back, I wander back to see what I'd written the previous evening. There was a faint plopping sound as I leaned forward to investigate. I realised I had a nose bleed, when the red showed up on the paper. This is an unusual experience for me, and I suddenly recalled seeing a film about Chopin. Whilst he was belting out the Revolutionary Study on the joanna (piano), his plops showed up on the keyboard. Just a few lines previously I had been writing about the very same instrument, not expecting my own blood to kick-start this old memory.

It struck me, in a quiet way, that there is a slight difference in our situations. He could have stopped playing and laid down to stem the flow. I was forbidden to do so for another twenty minutes yet! I must admit I don't like these quandaries so late in life. It also reminded me of the Billy Cotton incident in Jersey. My plops onto to the makeup girl next to me when the piano blew up. I survived then and I'm still writing this ages after! What luck. Now back to the past again.

When I was working in the London boroughs the heavy traffic was a constant problem. At nine o'clock my 'looker-afterer' from the RSO's office would drive ahead of me to escort me to the first school. He would duck and dive all over the place, with me in hot pursuit. I normally got made up ready to work as soon as we reached the school. There was always a hazard whilst wearing the red nose, and driving. You could feel eyes being distracted and sometimes a screech of brakes was heard to remind you someone had taken his eyes off the ball.

Most of the time we could get a meal in the school we had just worked in. The children were used to you and sitting down at a smaller table with them put you firmly in your place, just in case you had any exalted ideas of fame! Other times we ate in council canteens. You can imagine some of the comments when I walked in. I can honestly say most were friendly and complimentary.

There were some anomalies with me doing regular visits to schools. I got to know the head teachers quite well, but most of them never saw me as myself, my clown face being the only one they knew. I think this might have added a wee bit to my success with their young pupils. My charm, as my artistic friends continually draw attention to, is not in my relaxed appearance at all. This they say, presents me as a somewhat miserable looking b****r.

It was brought home to me once and I was quite taken aback when I was shopping in a Woolworth one day. A woman who passed me suddenly said, 'So this is where Kerby Drill does his shopping.' It was a local headmistress who recognised me out of make up.

I am very pleased to be able to melt into the background once I take my nose off. On the subject of noses, it took me a while before I developed my own brand. In the first instance we shaped a table tennis ball to fit our proboscis, Pierre and I. Experience goaded us on to get a nose that looked good and stayed put.

The trouble with clip-ons is they soon become full of perspiration, and besides, they distort the sound of one's voice. A nasal twang would be handy should I get a booking in the Bronx! No, I solved my own problem by filling up a red plastic clown nose from a joke shop with plastic foam. After shaping it I stuffed it into the nose, glueing it in with contact adhesive. Then I shaped it smooth with a hot poker. I then secured it my own 'rozzer' with spirit gum. It's tricky removing it, and often it brings tears to one's eyes, especially so if I've been too generous with the sticky. After removing the gum with surgical spirit, I used to have the 'baldest nose' in road safety!

It had taken us three years to get the sausage act running properly. The boiled egg brigade was supposed to have increased our business. It would have done if we had been able to do both acts at once, for double the money. But two acts and only one set of clowns! I was never the impresario type so didn't even dream of letting anybody else do our work. We did do the two acts one weekend.

The Sausage on Saturday, the Egg the next day. Having to come back to change over props, and all the extra travelling, nearly killed us all.

It was my fault really for not thinking ahead clearly. Fortunately the two events were reasonably close. If one had been too far away it might have forewarned us. None of us were pleased this day. In fact we did very good shows and were offered work afterwards, which is really the only true indication of a satisfied customer. But we learned a harsh lesson.

Since we started the gala acts, Jim had sacrificed his summers to help me out. So when it came about that he wanted to expand his business, it was agreed that we rest both gala acts. I approached Sam to see if he wanted to do a double act with me instead. But after four years of gallivanting around, with his children growing up, and not to be always away in the summer, he decided to give it a stop also. So there it was, no gala acts to offer. A rest.

Deena was very pleased. Since my first going out with Pierre in 1962 with the crazy car act and then with the two later acts, she had been responsible for the clothes and cleaning all the way through on her own. It was an enormous task and she contributed more than her share at making it all a success. But the worry of it all was very wearing. She was glad that we'd done it but was also pleased to stop it for a change. All the check lists, all the gettings us off at all hours, and the preparing of meals, now ended. Time for a huge sigh of relief.

I was not so happy for a very different reason. We were now a really first-class gala act and we always topped the bill or were supporting very good attractions all over the country. We were very much in demand and our money was going up every year. I would have preferred to have upped our fee considerably and so cutting down on the cheaper bookings, still doing the really worthwhile jobs willing to pay for our services. This way we could have seen how much we were really worth. But it wasn't to be. Losing a large part of my summer income I decided to do a solo clown act for small arenas, and did reasonably well. I did miss the big stuff though!

Another thing that happened that took our minds elsewhere. South Africa to be precise. Our youngest son, Michael, always wanting to join the merchant navy to get away for a while, finally got an assisted passage to Cape Town. Deena and I had many anxious moments. We had no doubt about his ability to look after or fend for himself. He was a first class bricklayer and I knew the value of his trade was world wide. So he would always be in demand somewhere.

When we heard he'd arrived there safely we just had to let him get on with it. There is no substitute for experience, especially of growing up. I can remember the quizzical looks my dad gave me when I was verbally putting the world to rights at Michael's age. They have to break loose and learn for themselves.

One of the perks about working with the road safety departments is that you can be observed by other sections of the council also. The parks and entertainments especially. It was only a small step from the schools when they are open, to the parks, when they were closed for holidays. I was now at liberty to accept this work, and I did.

I had been noticing some of these summer audiences. To get a quiet smile of enjoyment from my young clients is a great joy. Doing a show on grass and sometimes on asphalt in big housing estates, requires that you hold the young mind's interest to the point that they put up with any discomfort to stay and watch. Not like school this. They have only to get up and walk away and you are left working to an empty space. We have all ages too, from babes in arms with their mums, to toddlers and upwards to fifteen years or so.

I was very careful to put everyone at ease whilst watching that the older child did not intimidate the younger children. They would all have an equal opportunity to become part of the show. Children have a fierce sense of justice and fair do's all round. I try to preserve a child's dignity whatever we do. To put on a programme to interest so wide an age range, my solution was to use mainly short items, with plenty of visual interest, and that requires a little thought and dexterity of mind.

I only tell one joke. I might remember more but I only tell one. I don't think jokes as such go down well with children so well as an apt comment about a prop that they can see. My joke is a riddle and I use it as a warm-up encounter. Whenever you enter a park you can bet your boots you are observed.

My camper, driving onto grass, signals the magic or puppet man, and wherever you stop they sit waiting for a show to start. It's maybe only 2pm and you start at 3pm. Never mind, what's an hour to a youngster. I have stock answers to their offers to help me. 'Thank you for asking but I have to do it in a special way.

You can watch though. Getting out a length of rope I lay it on the grass, the distance I want them from the van. This gives them something to think about and to tell later arrivals. Invariably I'm asked do I do Punch and Judy. I always say 'No, you've got a clown coming today'. Magic word 'clown' to children. So the buzz is passed around and helps them over a few more minutes. They don't associate me with the clown at this stage with my glasses on. Putting out the props I don't much look like one either.

On most jobs, the council provided a helper who knew the venue. Mostly my assistant would be an active pensioner, who would also act as liaison man between me and the council. They would do a couple of hours a day for the whole of the holidays. I made many friends amongst these folk and always introduced them properly as 'uncle' this, or 'auntie' that. I would add that they 'would be here each week at the same time, with a different show for you to see', urging them to bring their families and friends along.

One particular week I had 'Uncle Ted' with me and we were doing circuit No. 1. I had a list of ten parks to do in five days from Monday to Friday. One at 11am and another across the borough to commence at 3pm. There were three circuits comprising thirty venues in the borough of Lewisham and so three of us (entertainers) were working daily to cater for all our young patrons. I rarely met any of the other entertainers as we were all working at it the same time.

I had several bits of business to make contact with our growing audience. A kind of warm up. I break into a song. It's not a pretty sound. Startled, the children give me an old fashioned look. I ask the children if they like my voice. The comments can be very funny sometimes. I ask if any of them like singing? If I get a volunteer I get a bit of hush for their efforts. It's here I might say I know a riddle and come out with my joke.

Here it is, 'Why did the chicken cross the road softly'? There are many chicken jokes and we get lots of answers back. So I say, 'He crossed the road softly because he couldn't walk hardly'. I am always amused at the cross section of reception I get. It also helps 3pm to come a little nearer. About six minutes before curtain up I dive into the van, get changed and I go out to greet 'my public'.

Chapter 24

I'm on the Telly!

In fifteen years the family had outgrown No. 1 Argyle Road. We needed more space. But there was a snag. The house was blighted, marked on council plans for road 'improvements' which would turn our house into some sort of traffic island. Because of this we couldn't sell.

There was another dilemma. Jim, studio and all, didn't want to move out in the traditional manner. What to do. Then Jim had the idea he would buy another house, and move us out.

He went to the council to apply for a mortgage to buy No. 1. He knew with the dreaded blight he wouldn't get one from a building society. The council said he couldn't have a mortgage because the house was blighted. He said something like 'but you've bloomin' well blighted it'. But it made no difference.

Within months, however, a solution beckoned. The council finally abandoned its plans to build a road round us and the planning blight was lifted. Jim could now go ahead with his plan to move us out.

One evening while working away, I 'phoned Deena. She was very excited about a house she'd found. As always, it was Deena that found our next abode.

The owners of 'Alvine Cottage' were elderly folk and had over the years poured a great deal of work and loving care into making it the beautiful place it was. I was doing the Tufty Clubs in Southwark at the time, but by my return at the weekend, it was settled.

A cottage in Middleton-on-sea, about three miles east of Bognor Regis. It had fine large gardens back and front, far larger than where we were used to in Argyle Road. I could put my van off the road for the first time since having BNY 13. We had a fairly large garage too. The motor caravan was too high to get in so wonder of wonders, I didn't have to think about building a new workshop. I set up in this garage instead.

So the van stayed out in the cold. It was very nice being able to wash it and

Kerby, Jim and Sam, The Boiled Egg Brigade

Sam, Jim and Kerby, The Super Sausage Squad

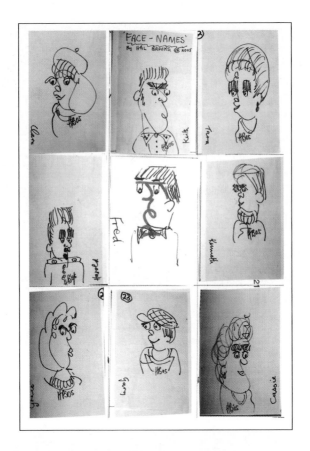

Face Names, Fred in red

Soft foam birds for playgroup game

Kerby, clown sculpture and water drilling brace

A diversionary ploy against seaborne attack

My dressing-gown and Landcruiser, in between schools

*Sisters Coral,
Bettie and Deena*

*With Bernard in Army and
Navy Stores*

Working early children's parties

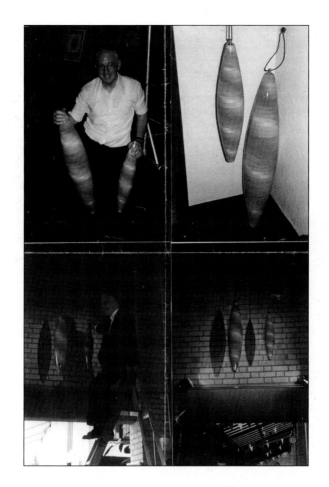

Me installing sculptures in The Regis Centre

SPINNERS

These mobile sculptures in Laminated Pine were made by Hal Brooks of Middleton-on-Sea, and donated to the Bognor Regis Centre, with grateful thanks to Olbys and Keith Jay for their sponsorship.

Summer 1981

Plaque noting the occasion
PS - I have omitted picture 108, as it's virtually identical to pic 106

A young charmer in Arundel

My stage easel

A happy London play group

A bed table and
needlework box

My family dresser

Two fish sculptures

A young admirer of the Crane sculpture

The Welsh Dragon, Clown and cardboard dog, Boxer!

Oliver in car, George in plane. Our grandchildren

Making Billy Bulb

Some garden ornaments

Zita, three times a winner

ZIPPO'S *clown piano*

An American performers prop

At a Craft Fair

*Mayor Cosgrove
opens my exhibition*

*The suspect 'sausage
bomb'*

The Tufty puppet set-up

Deena, friends and visitors

Our recycled 'Summer House'

Inside

Being built

A selection of pine Name Sculptures

A paper knife for Grace

Musical Jane is a canoeist and skier

More Name Sculptures

For an Egyptian snooker player

This young lady was fond of anything Dracula

Some of my Paintings

The Queen at eighty

Popov, the great Russian clown

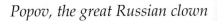

A Dutch baby

Boxer's cousin, Draughty

Kerby by Hal

see to its needs off the road though! It was after Christmas when we moved in and I really was having to clean the van, even if it was only to see what colour it was. I was preparing for a tour of Lewisham schools, so I had to be tidy. Jim had taken over our old house and so we were all settled now. Michael was living in Brighton at the time with some of his friends.

Just a day or so after there was a telephone call from a BBC Television Producer, Jennifer Jeremy, asking for Hal Brooks. Jennifer was executive producer of a programme on BBC2 called ' Look, Stranger'. I had been in touch by letter with her many months before about the programme. It appeared that with the economic axe falling left right and centre, it was not certain that any more episodes would be filmed, if any? But there she was, on the telephone, saying it might be possible for her to come and see me work. 'Could it be arranged?

The two weeks tour I was about to do gave her this opportunity. She came and watched me doing an Old Age Pensioner Club first, then the next day she saw me do a junior school. Jennifer wanted to see me do an infant show and so stayed and had a school dinner with me. I was due to perform in the first period that afternoon. Afterwards she said she would like to film me for the programme. It was a matter of urgency for the schedules to be kept for inclusion in a new batch of 'Look, Stranger', programmes. This time round it was to be introduced by Rene Cutforth.

So it was arranged that they would film on two days of the following week. Ted Davonport, RSO for Lewisham, London, for whom I was working at the time, helped to 'oil the wheels', asking for permission from school heads, club presidents and nursery matrons, to allow us to film in their establishments. We were welcomed everywhere without exception. In fact everybody was tickled pink about the venture. I was extremely flattered and pleased to be asked.

BBC 2 had always produced quality products to my mind, and it was a national network channel. Not the largest audience by any means, but it meant that my friends and colleagues all over the country could look in if they so desired.

The format of 'Look, Stranger' was about people not doing a run of the mill job. An unusual way of earning a living so to speak. The camera would follow the subject around watching their daily routines. Some aspects of my entertaining, and in particular my road safety work, was to be revealed in this programme about 'Kerby Drill, the Road Safety Clown'.

We had filming to do at a nursery with an under-fives audience first. I had only to do what I normally did on these occasions. I kept my fingers crossed for a reasonable chance. The children were a joy and very responsive. A hand-held camera was used to obtain some marvellous close-ups. No notice was taken of this intrusion and we got lovely natural reactions on film. With the modern cameras there was no dazzling with powerful lighting. We had a lovely show and I was pleased to be over the first hurdle. The producer seemed very satisfied and Geoff Mulligan, the film cameraman, a very nice chap, gave me a thumbs up sign.

The next shot was of Ted and Terry Martin, (one of Ted's road safety colleagues whose area the nursery was in), carrying out the props to my van in readiness for the next show. The final shot was of my van pulling away, off into the distance. That concluded the morning's business.

We were all to meet at a local club for OAPs later that afternoon. When we weren't visiting a school we were usually invited to a council department of something or other to get a meal. In the borough we had a number of places with a canteen we could drop into. Me in clown always caused a bit of a stir on these occasions. All good humoured though.

Before becoming RSO for Lewisham, Ted Davonport has been a London bus driver. He'd seen the world we have to move in traffic-wise, from very close quarters. So it was, in my tours for him, he guided me into any establishment likely to encounter traffic, to emphasise the enormous problems of fast cars, lorries and the like that could pose a threat. Hence my arrival in this neck of the woods, the middle of the metropolis, where if you were an old aged pensioner every vehicle seemed to be gunning for you every time you tried to cross the road.

When our mature audience was told the BBC would be coming with their cameras that afternoon they all buzzed about with excitement.

National television visiting their club. Unheard of!

I was introduced to Rene Cutforth, a very well-respected figure indeed. On radio and television he was widely known. He said he would be interviewing a couple of adults from the audience. There was a small stage, a piano, and a tidy audience of nearly a hundred. The stage had been well lit by the 'sparks' and Geoff's rostrum camera was set-up, left of centre, half way down the hall.

My easel was at the ready and alongside were my props ready for action. For grown ups, these were fun items and an assortment of RoSPA posters with which to illustrate my talk. I had a locking mechanism to stop my drawing board turning around. I then hung these posters from it. They were then high enough to be seen by everybody.

The Royal Society, RoSPA, published safety posters highlighting all manner of accident hazards. The ones on road safety were very potent, and I made full use of their graphic messages. Afterwards I usually held a general discussion, when particular local items and grouses could be aired. Ted would bear the brunt of the criticism and provide answers if needed.

There was an air of expectancy and a touch of excitement amongst the rows of club members. I always enjoy the lovely unpretentious atmosphere in these mature gatherings. So different from school shows. They have reached retirement, seen their families grow up, and know most of the answers. Ted introduced me and I proceeded to amaze everybody with my accurate forecast of where the next shower of rain would fall. Very nearly on them!

The children always get a drop but not these folk. Most wear glasses and a joke can easily become an irritation. No, the rubber bulb of 'rain', secreted in the handle of my small umbrella, was only used on this occasion to demonstrate how accurately I can send a small squirt of water from the end of my umbrella. It's annoying when the little copper tube leading from the tube gets blocked up, but all is well when I blow down it to clear it and get an eyeful in the process!

Taking off my large entrance coat off, remarking 'I've just bought it from Mick Jagger, Boy George, or Gary Glitter, or whichever extravagant, outrageous public figure had made headlines recently', I find a couple of interesting items in my jacket pocket.

One is a 'spring onion' I had recently made for Delia Smith. (She had a cooking programme showing on TV). She complained of spring onions being in short supply during the winter months. 'My 'spring onion works anytime'. Then I would let the spring loaded prop vegetable fly out of my hand.

My next comment was about a 'word I've just had with Chancellor of the Exchequer. He suggested using my inventing skills to seek a way to help us all with the rising cost of living.' I show my new pound note, which I stretch to twice its size, saying 'my new note goes a little further'. A painted copy of a pound note onto a strip of three inch corset elastic sufficed here.

Not great gags, but fitting for my audience. (An irony about this, is of course, is the demise of the humble pound note). I do a few drawings on my easel for a further establishment of my credentials that I'm a bit more than a made up face.

There are so many people who cannot seem to be able to draw, that on the face of it, it's clever.

With my audience settled, they expected something funny from a clown, I succeeded, and now to the serious business of the visit. I get rapt attention for a quarter of an hour or so. I have made my posters into a kind of large book that I let each page unfold for discussion. From sixteen to sixty five and on, we all agree there have been significant changes to the 'bodies we call me'. Slower and possibly not a little unsure. Eyes seem to be the most shared problem. Balance, it sometimes takes you unawares. And hearing problems.

My posters give us a chance to see how all these changes can affect us when dealing with traffic. We took it all for granted once, now it can't be shrugged off. 'So watch out. Please'!

Then I go over to the piano to run a song quiz. About twenty popular oldies and modern songs, with Ted keeping score between the 'boys' and the 'girls'. I find a few notes on the piano is all that is needed to make contact across all ages, and we were soon well into the quiz. Suddenly I was aware of a hand-held camera taking close up shots of me playing. Well, that shook me. Only playing by ear, I don't need much to move me from playing in a confident manner, to absolutely forgetting even the key I'm playing in.

I spent a few shaky minutes whilst I wondered where he was. I daren't look round. I got over it, but it could have been awful. You can't see terror when you've make up on but I was very pale beneath it, I can tell you. Although I didn't use it for the filming because I had to sing them, I had written some road safety parodies on popular old time songs that go down well with OAP shows. A couple of lines I remember from one on 'The man who broke the bank of Monte Carlo'. 'As he walked along the pavement with his nose stuck in the air,' it concluded with, 'It was the man who broke his neck down at the corner'.

Afterwards we were warmly thanked by the club president and were helped to a second cup of excellent tea and extra biscuits. I didn't notice Rene doing his interviews but he was well satisfied I'm sure. If he'd chosen somebody like my mum (a real working class Londoner), he'd have had no difficulty in getting their views on the proceedings.

Next day Jennifer decided to film only the junior show. I still had to do the infants though as we were still running to my itinerary. After my entrance business for the infants show my main thrust was about finding a safe place to play, away from traffic. I used my puppet set-up of Tufty to get home the need for finding a safe place to cross the road. Choosing the zebra crossing I could get Tufty to select the proper belisha beacon from a selection of mis-shaped ones. Once we'd got the right one, and made the lights blink properly, we could all blow the lights out. Magic from concealed switches. Good fun, but learning too, in an acceptable way, for my young audience.

I always changed my performances in natural breaks. Generally infants first period, and juniors after play. Most schools only had one main hall and after me it was then the dining hall, for dinner. With the production team at the ready I started the juniors show. As always the first thing is to establish that you are funny. I'm well-prepared for this. Apart from what I look like I have at least nine chances of getting them on my side. Umbrella and rain business. Entrance coat, big boots, small replicas underneath. Glove gags, separate fingers, one on elastic, and main glove four feet long. Putting on jacket, props in pocket, a fish and snake gag. Overall about five minutes of work to make myself acceptable.

Starting with safety at play. I have a football inscribed with 'Play with this in safe places' on its front surface. I pinched this idea from a drawing I'd seen in a Tufty book. I adapted it so that the whole sentence can be seen at a glance. Painting this message on a spherical surface was quite a tricky problem. I still have the ball but it could do with a spot more air in it nowadays!

I carry the idea a little further with a drawing on my easel, using three different sized balls which I developed into a drawing of a cowboy sitting on a horse. The 'nag' is saying the same message, in a balloon coming from its mouth. As I'm working in a school my easel is a blackboard surface and so its white chalk only. With the OAPs I used a stage easel with paper and coloured chalks. It's more messy than white chalks, but worth the extra hassle.

A short session of appropriate posters to hammer home, 'the safety at play' point, and it's time for a little more comedy. A large dark brown cardboard container holds a selection of items I have gathered over the years is brought to the fore here. A plastic tube that can mimic a police siren. A puppet of Mr Punch on a stick with bells all around his collar so that I can sing 'jingle bells' to him at special times. I have put a trumpet mouthpiece onto an old fashioned London taxi horn that can be blown as I let a string of sausages fly out.

All good quickie stuff. To finish, I have a special flowerpot holding a 'pop plant'. This can grow eight feet when I choose to let the extended point 22 blank cartridge off, with a bang, courtesy of a target launcher. Back to work!

An important part of my message to the seven year olds and upwards is to slow down. Quite a different approach from when dealing with OAPs. The tendency amongst youngsters is to be impulsive and too quick off the mark. With the elderly slowness can be the problem.

I used to emphasise how important it was to be aware of stepping off the kerb. With a bit of exaggerated clowning and mime I used to bang home the message of pausing at the kerb. Not a great big stop and over long examination of whether there is a car a half a mile away, but a pause to think of the next step that will take you into the traffic. We dwell on the time it takes for a car to pull up. It just cannot stop as quickly as you can. So watch out!

Time now for a little more fun. Having someone up from the audience whose birthday it was we'd have a bit of a laugh drawing a face on the board from their name. If it was a girl I would also ask a teacher to choose a boy to help me. I ask him if he'd like to be a clown when he grows up. Most boys say yes to this. I then suggest how they go about impressing someone. First, dress tidily. I help a little to show how, with bit of work with a feather duster. Asking if he's ticklish, I try him under the chin. Whilst doing this I spot a 'whisker'. Out comes my 'electric' shaver and I give him a quick once over.

The shaver is a converted cycle horn. I finish the job and reward him by doing his name as well. A big clap for the lad and back to business.

I already have my easel on which to hang the song sheet, containing road safety words that Deena had written to be sung to the tune that's all the rage of the moment, 'I'd like to teach the world to sing'. Coca Cola had been plugging their product with it constantly on television, so I don't have to teach them the tune.

After explaining my son Jim plays the guitar, I thought they'd appreciate hearing him sing it first. I switch on the tape recorder, held high for them all to hear. Jim's got a pleasant voice and it goes down well. I then go to the piano and after a one, two, three, four, off they go. 'If every boy and girl....'. I have two verses up on the song sheet and it goes without a hitch. Afterwards, I compliment them on their singing and suggest they deserve a good round of applause. This they give themselves, heartily. We discuss the points raised in the words of the song just sung. I then turn over the song sheet to reveal a third and final verse. Back to the piano, one, two, three, four, and they all belt out the last verse.

I thank everyone there and hand over, normally to a headmaster, this time to a headmistress. They then would generally sum up the proceedings, thanking me in the process. Thumbs up again from Geoff, and I sigh more with a little relief. Filming can be tricky and sometimes it takes a lot of repeats before everyone is happy.

It was decided that Rene would interview me then. The headmistress kindly lent us her office for the job. I had not spoken more than a few words to him since we met. Rene explained it was a deliberate ploy on his part. He wanted freshness from me on the interview and he'd always found that if things came up in conversation prior to the interview, they could inadvertently be left out of the finished product. I agreed. He talked very easily and guided me through the paths of conversation skilfully and in a kindly manner.

He left me plenty of places where I could ride my own hobby horse. It fascinated me. I didn't know what sort of discussion he'd had with the producer, or what instructions had been given or requested, but I know I thought at the time what a workman-like job of work seems to be being done here, and I was pleased to be a part of it. I love the whole experience of film making.

During my telephone calls to Deena of an evening on those two days you can imagine the questions I got fired at me. She was excited about it all. 'Did I wear a proper shirt for the interview'? (I was still in clown), 'did I comb my hair'? My hair, its always a problem. 'Yes, Yes, Yes'. I had managed to do all the right things and felt more confident being turned out nicely, on her insistence. She is a marvellous manager and knows me through and through. I get well looked after.

I also gave her something to think about too. 'We will be filming up in Alvine Cottage next week for two days'. Gulp! Most audible even though 80 miles of telephone cables were separating us. 'Yes, they will all be coming over on Tuesday and Wednesday'. Cameraman, lighting engineer, sound engineer, producer and continuity girl / secretary. 'You'd better get some coffee in'! By the time the 'next week' had come round, we'd heard the details of the rest of the filming.

One day shots of the interior of the house and activities. One day driving around district. To give some ideas of my other activities we were to show some of our gala work. As luck would have it, a few weeks earlier, I had done a couple of shows in Chichester for a teacher friend of Jim's, Teresa. So I suggested to Jennifer that we ask the headmistress if we could use her children to make up an audience and for me to do a shortened version of the Sausage Act. So this was arranged.

On the Friday I was already booked to assist the Lady Mayor of Southampton in inaugurating new pelican lights in Shirley High Street. We were to accompany school children to the lights and show them how to use them correctly. Jennifer said she would like to come and film this extra outdoor activity. So this was also arranged.

When I got home that weekend we all had plenty to talk about. Jim said he would help me show off the sausage props. We rehearsed a shorter version of the routine and to make a show of it for the children, I'd do a short entertainment for them afterwards to round off the afternoon.

But for the moment other things were very pressing indeed. We hadn't been in the new house more than a few weeks. There was so much to do it wasn't true. But I had made a start in the kitchen and decided to try and get that room finished in the short time available.

So on the Friday evening when I got back home from London I stayed up and decorated the ceiling, after repairs, with two coats of white emulsion. Next day I papered the walls and bought tiles for the floor. On Sunday I tiled the floor. On Monday I finished the sink unit and on Tuesday the film crew arrived. Phew!

It was a different team. I only knew Jennifer amongst them, but they were all very friendly and we soon got to know each other. Deena looked after them very well and they all appreciated her efforts to make them welcome. Our drive was packed out with their cars and neighbours were starting to wonder what it was all about, with these newcomers.

Chapter 25

Getting it on Film

The new film crew, Sussex based this time, was sizing up the situation. Jennifer had a good look around and discussed with Deena and I what we could do to show our activities and interests. It was decided I would be shown maintaining my props on the bench and doing a bit of woodwork on a fitment I'd just made for the kitchen.

In the workshop, my garage, which was crowded out with all sorts of bric a brac and strange shapes, an inseparable part of our prop-making facilities, we strove to get a camera in and lit by the sparks. Talk about a gallon in a pint pot!

I used my puppet of Tufty as something to be examined. He was built on the lower part of the Bendy toy, his feet! Deena had made a hand puppet of him. With my hand up his back, I could discuss things with him standing on my other hand. He could only squeak, but of course I could interpret for the boys and girls. He has a beautiful fluffy tail, which looks quite real. I also did a small repair on another puppet. This was the papier mache head of Daisy Duckling, a very appealing Miss indeed!

After testing the lights on the belisha beacons I was interested to hear Fred discussing the extra bits of film he'd shot with the producer, who thought these film clips could be used to good effect when she came to editing the whole. On occasions like these I'm all eyes and ears, like a bit of blotting paper, soaking up the interesting bits to relay afterwards to any interested listener. Also, sometimes to not very interested, but polite listeners, not wanting to appear rude! We all like to appear experts sometimes.

Then we moved into the kitchen. I, suitably wearing my carpenter's apron, was to appear to be working on a fitment drawer. The whole structure was a surround in knotty pine, to contain the sink unit. With a few curly shavings suitably arranged on the floor to accompany my controlled sweep of the smoothing plane along the drawer runners, I hoped it wasn't going to be a long shot. The drawer already fitted comfortably and each extra stroke tended to make it looser. Any way we got it in one, Fred and I were working well together. I was really enjoying all of this.

Showing off one of the gala props, I demonstrated one from the egg act. Using the large brace and bit I 'drilled' our lawn hoping to strike water! Surprisingly, I was lucky and was rewarded with a fine jet out of its top, making sure of course that Fred didn't get any!

Then Deena got a shock. She was being very attentive looking after us all when Jennifer told her of her plans to include her in the film. Well, this upset the apple cart. She was very willing to do her utmost in helping the project along, but she had no idea she would be required to do more than show a smiling, helping face to the camera. She had a few moments of panic, I'm sure. But she is a natural and rose to the occasion beautifully.

It was decided to film some of her fancy dress costumes, with her, me and Jim modelling them on the lawn. Younger son Michael popped in to see what was going on and very nearly got roped in too. Deena put on an Anne Boleyn costume. Jim was attired in the Lawrence of Arabia outfit and I humbly put on an old fashioned bathing costume. These shots were not included in the finished film but they caused many hectic moments in the making of them.

After this Deena had the full attention of everybody focusing on her actually working on the props. Under lights in the lounge, she was filmed furiously turning the handle of her Singer sewing machine putting a lining in a clown jacket. Fred, using a small camera, got so close he was very nearly hemmed in himself. It was hard work and used up masses of nervous energy, but the lighter moments always seemed to arrive at the right time to relax the tension. Then Jennifer told her she was also going to interview her next day. I got the impression she wouldn't get much sleep that night.

Deena never wanted to be out front but she didn't get any choice here. The producer was very understanding and her patience and kindliness towards us both gave us the necessary encouragement to do our best and persevere. After the interview she was desperately trying to remember what sort of answers she'd given to questions asked. It was frustrating, but we'd just have to wait for the broadcast.

I was then asked to do a bit in the Land Cruiser, (my motor caravan at the time). Fred with his camera thrust through the driver's window, peeping in on me making a cup of tea and getting myself to bed, and generally giving an idea of what is standard practice for me whenever I'm away, working alone, without Deena to look after me. As it was in broad daylight with all the curtains drawn I heard Fred say he was doing something with a blue something or other, to simulate night time. All very technical but I just did as I was told. Whilst we were in the van I also donned my makeup for another sequence.

In a moment of thinking about the shots involving using the motor caravan, I wondered whether Dormobile, the makers, would be interested in knowing about it. So I wrote to their Folkestone works, somehow knowing that they would bound to be interested to learn about one of their products being filmed for BBC2.

I had a very nice letter back thanking me for the information. A few weeks later they rang me up to enquire if I would appear on their stand at the Caravan Club's Rally in my capacity as Kerby Drill, to entertain their customers' children over the Spring Bank Holiday. This was to be held on the racecourse at Stratford-on-Avon. It was a great success and I met a lot of their colleagues and made many friends. It's strange how work begets work. This was also a long way before the showing of the film. A nice bonus I thought.

Then we worked on shots of Deena the gardener. Our garden is large and I can take no credit for it. She is a great doer of work. She was filmed hoeing and raking and a pretty picture she made too. Not yet a gardening expert she was worried that she'd done it right. She needn't have worried. A pretty gardener doing her bit, who would notice the way she holds the rake. I didn't, anyway.

I think Jennifer did her job wisely, interspersing Deena throughout the action. A welcome change from me popping up all the time.

Next we took some travelling shots in the van. Me coming out of the drive going off on a job, and over the shoulder shots of me driving into Bognor. We took a lot of film in Bognor but these were not used in the actual film. It was a pity. I would have loved to see Bognor's half-pier included. Everytime we tried to film our passing of it, some member of the public would wave to the camera team at a critical moment. It may have been a bit of a lark to them but it was very frustrating to the producer, spoiling the spontaneity of it all.

The day afterwards was set aside for the Chichester school children. This was to enable filming to be done of the gala props from the Super Sausage Squad. Jim's teacher friend Teresa was there to welcome us and the headmistress was extremely helpful. We explained that it would take us all morning to set up the props and filming was laid on for after lunch. We were fortunate that the weather was kind to us. It was overcast but bright.

Jim was still Captain but the squad was reduced to one, me, so we selected props that the could be profitably used by just the two of us. No Sammy this time. We put the Sausage tree up, had the large cannon and sausage firing gun, and allied props to support a short story line. The children loved it. Jim supported me well and Kerby Drill was outrageous as the 'squad'.

Most of the gags were caught on camera and they all worked for us on cue. The bungy blight jumped out of the top of the tree at the right moment. The guns went off well, the parachute opened to let the sausages float down to earth in an orderly fashion, to my waiting overlarge frying pan. And when Jim shot at me for the finale, my belt flash blazed obligingly. All in all I was pleased with our performance. The teachers and children were excellent. They enjoyed it all and their reactions were captured by our sound engineer. It was most impressive.

As all this had only taken about fifteen minutes to run through, I carried on with a show to extend it to about forty minutes. I thought it unfair to have all this palaver of school attendance and organisation for a measly fifteen minutes. So I did some drawings, played a few games and tied up the loose ends. Fred also filmed this extra bit as well. I thanked the teachers and children for playing their part so well and they trooped back to their classrooms.

Jennifer wanted a close-up of the belt flash. We set up to do it again and lo and behold the flash wouldn't oblige. We tried again. No go. Jim traced the problem back to a break in the wire leading to the battery. We repaired it and finally got the shot it in the can. By this time it was past four o'clock so we called it a day. We went back to Alvine Cottage where Jennifer asked me some supplementary questions to fill in the gaps.

The hot coffee Deena made for when we got back was very welcome. We had all got chilled in the school playing fields and we were grateful to come in from the cold. With the microphone suitably placed and me in the best chair, I was ready to respond to the questions. Jennifer explained that I wasn't to repeat the questions. She wanted me to be 'sparked off' by her comments and to just go on talking, but including a semblance of the question asked in the answer.

Then the sound engineer butted in, 'There's a noise'! We all listened. It was the faint sound of a motorised lawn mower. Not loud but insistent. So Deena and I went off to seek its origin. About four doors away we found the mower himself. We explained what was happening in our house and he agreed to rest a while.

We would let him know when we'd finished. I remember how impressed he was to know the it was BBC TV. So, back to the questions.

I was keen to try to include points I'd forgotten to mention to Rene Cutforth, like giving credit to people who had helped me get established in road safety. I'd forgotten to include Walter Davies from Gwent. He had been very supportive of me and it was he who published our version of the 'Teach the World to Sing' with road safety words. I was not wholly successful but I did try.

Attempting to explain to friends what and why lots of stuff was left out, is difficult in these situations. It's a strange business this filming lark. Seemingly wasteful in some respects, it remains a highly specialist one. The end product must be entertaining, informative and digestible. Having to tell children that although they were filmed, it wasn't possible to include their bit after all, is never easy.

The following day, Friday, was spent in Southampton. I was to attend a school's birthday party. The Lady Mayor was in attendance. The plan was for me to present my road safety show to the school as part of the celebrations. Afterwards the Mayor and I were to take parties of children to the newly installed pelican crossing in Shirley High Street, and instruct the children how to use them. These new crossings had lights that were quite different from belisha beacons on zebra crossings. There was no controlling the beacons. They flashed night and day regardless. The new lights had button switches to press when you wanted the traffic to stop, allowing you to cross the road safely. We were to instruct the children how to use them properly.

After my show in the school we started to shepherd the children in batches towards the new crossing. Jennifer wanted to film us doing this so Fred was filming from the opposite pavement. The weather was good. Weren't we lucky? I was walking along wearing my big Tufty coat, big boots, with umbrella held aloft. It wouldn't have looked as funny if it really had been raining. I enjoyed it and the children did too. Passes-by were enthralled to see our unusual crocodile snaking along the busy shopping area.

About eight out of ten adults enjoy a remark or two on occasions like this from me. Nice banter! The other two people don't 'see' me. You can't imagine how successful they are at not noticing a clown in full make up, outrageously dressed, walking past in broad daylight. But there, they have a right to their opinions. I learned a very long time ago that clowns are not everybody's cup of tea, so I don't ever force my attentions anywhere.

So with the filming finished Jennifer and the rest of the team bade us goodbye and departed from Southampton. Being all together for four days we somehow got used to film making. But it was over for us. They could now get on with the rest of the job. Putting pieces together, selecting and sorting. We'd shown and they had seen, so, cheerio.

My job wasn't over though. Basil Henning, the RSO for Southampton, had arranged for me to visit a protected workshop in the afternoon. We thought that as the BBC camera crew was coming to film us that day, we would arrange a selection of the sort of road safety venues we were used to doing. If they wanted to film different aspects, this would be an ideal opportunity.

Most people in the work shop were very young minded and not able to earn a living in the hurly burly of normal life. It's a very happy atmosphere. Most of them are very friendly and open in a childlike way. I love working with them. I did my best to help them remember my points about keeping them free from accidents. I did it with my usual awareness of what was going down and what wasn't.

I used the children's props but reinforced it with a song quiz and sing song. The drawings went down well, and we had a good half-hour show. It was a complete change for us all. The staff were very understanding and I felt our visit was well worthwhile. Also while I was there I recorded an item for Radio Solent, the local BBC radio station. That went out the same evening in the local news.

Deena had also come to Southampton with us but as I had to go to the school first, she was to be 'otherwise engaged'. The Southampton police had kindly arranged for us to have lunch in their canteen. Being treated kindly as VIPs, she was asked if there was anything she especially wanted to see whilst I was doing the shows. Anyway, she was whisked off in a police car and treated to a tour of the docks. The Queen Elizabeth II was berthed there that day. She had an enviable ride and saw never to be forgotten views of the great liner. Some people get all the luck!

The end of the day came with many thanks from all sides and we left for home. A sad footnote was, that all the filming done on that day was a casualty in the film's final assembly. It wasn't seen. Not a mention. This is what I mean about explanations!

After the filming we were exhausted. We spent the weekend molly coddling ourselves and relaxing in front of the television. The anti-climax to the past two weeks was very strong indeed. It had been something special and we talked about it endlessly. It was very nice for once to being slightly larger fishes in our own small pool.

The film was to be shown in June, that same year. I remember how I made the entry in my financial accounts. 'Fee for BBC Look Stranger film'. It would only be my accountant who would see it. I imagined a loud chorus of 'So what' emanating from Swansea, where he was. In the past I had seldom got the urge to include the fact that I had just made a wardrobe in knotty pine for Mrs Jones in my books!

Meanwhile we were having problems in our new house. We had a very large elm tree in the front garden, and it was infected with Dutch Elm disease, which played so much havoc in the sixties and seventies. We knew it would have to come down as it overlooked the road. Deena was afraid that strong winds might bring a branch down on some unsuspecting car or young horse rider who happened to be passing at the time.

We had been approached by a felling gang who wanted sixty pounds to trim it down to safety. I was hoping to do it with Ollie and Michael when we had the time. It wasn't to be, and one evening during a telephone conversation to Deena when I was working in Gwent, she said the worry was too great. The wind was ferocious and please could she have it felled. I agreed it would be for the best.

When I got home it was reduced to an enormous pile of branches, trunks and twigs. The place was choc-a-bloc, but it was safer on the ground. The fee for the work was saved later by burning the wood all through the winter. It's a lovely thing a log fire, and elm burns well. I also got a lot of satisfaction sawing the logs. I made a saw horse and cut a barrow full or so whenever we needed it. The bark was so thick and plentiful that I kept it separate and fuelled our Ideal boiler with it. We used the larger lumps to create a dell in the garden. It looked very pretty.

Our neighbours Ruby and Dennis also had their elm trimmed at the same time. The felling lads had got ours down without a hitch, but when they lopped a large branch from theirs, the blooming thing fell on our front gate. I had to put it back together as though it was a jig-saw puzzle. Then our boundary fence had to be rebuilt. More expense. A hundred feet long, it was quite a task. A small bonus from this was the small wicket gate I put in to enable us to visit our neighbours more easily, saving a long walk right round.

Son Michael did a fine job, concreting and crazy paving an area for me to turn round in. It was too dangerous to reverse out as we were on a bend in a rather busy road. Then we had a visit from the Portsmouth Water Company. They said we had a leak in our mains pipe. This meant either digging up the whole garden including the new concrete to find the leak, or put a new one in entirely. I chose to renew the pipe from the road to the house. Michael and Ollie dug the trench alongside the drive, for the new pipe, and I filled it in. It was over forty yards long. Finding the connection in the road was a nightmare too. This was 1976 and the famous drought of that period was at its height.

Another unwelcome inhabitant was occupying our loft space. More deadly than the bungy blight this time. Woodworm. The roof space had been a paradise for them for a long time and it had to stop. Our cottage has a mansard roof. The pitch was similar to the one I had built in Potters Bar. About 45 degrees. Plenty of headroom and once I had time to board it out, would be an extra room and a half of space for props etc. But the intruder had to go first. I got an estimate for the job to be done for me. Eighty pounds! On top of all the other expenses this was out of the question, so this had to be a self help job.

Deena volunteered to go up and brush it clean. It was a filthy undertaking. Dust from the years had settled and it wasn't easy to get it up. It cost forty pounds to buy enough woodworm killer and spray. So complete with goggles and mask I did battle with the tiny grubs doing their dastardly work. Apart from a single light bulb and a few glass tiles there wasn't a lot of light either. The roof timbers being dry and unplaned were a perfect recipient for the spray. They soaked it up, so putting an end to the pests when they nibbled their way to the surface to fly off and lay their eggs elsewhere, round about June. Now at last we had the house to ourselves.

Chapter 26

Moving In

First exit the woodworm, then a little time later when the sprayed loft air became breathable again, I surveyed the roof space for possibilities. The ceiling joists were not comfortably safe enough to walk on and the gaps between revealed the lathe and plaster ceilings of the bedrooms below. There had been an attempt to put in insulation, but it was only an inch thick, so I decided to board it over.

I had a bit of luck here. The builders' merchants from where I bought my timber from had lots of off-cuts from purchasers who did not want whole boards of plywood and chipboard. The bits that were not wanted I noticed took up a lot of room, so I made an offer for them. They were pleased, I was pleased, and so that's how my loft floor looks more like crazy paving than a traditional one. Nailing the bits down would have been too violent a procedure, so there's an awful lot of unscrewing to be done, should anybody want to see what's underneath!

Then up went the spare props and fancy dresses, plus a few paintings I wanted to keep. By doing this we gained a lot of room downstairs to boot!

It was against this background of pay out, pay out, that I had to face up to the change in expected summer income. No gala money to look forward to. When it means losing a third of one's income over the year, I thought I'd be back to building to make things up. But it didn't quite work out like that.

A year or so previously I had done some work in a play group scheme organised by local authorities. It was similar in scope to the 'holidays at home' idea put out just after the war. Organised play would be provided for children in the summer holidays.

I was offered four weeks work in the Torfain area of Gwent. It was a combined effort between the entertainments and road safety departments. I would put on a normal parks' programme, but include a sly mention of road safety to keep the children alert to traffic dangers whilst on holiday.

So in the event I was busier than ever. I had also decided to do a solo clown act for gala work. Not for the main arena this time, so I got myself out a brochure to send to agents looking for this kind of work. I survived the summer.

It was during this period that we found out that the 'Look Stranger' film was to come out in August. Jennifer rang us up saying that the film was about to be dubbed but she was having difficulty with the copyright of the music I had used in it, 'I'd like to teach the world to sing'. This was a bit of a setback, and unexpected too.

Walter Davies, RSO for Gwent, and I had taken a lot of effort to get the Coca-Cola people, whose jingle it was on TV, to let us use the music. When we'd had a letter finally saying as long as we only used it in conjunction with my road safety work it was all right, we thought we were covered.

When Jennifer had then approached the publishers of the music they knew nothing about this arrangement and she couldn't move any further until the matter was cleared up. I got on to Walter and Jennifer, and sent the resulting correspondence to the publishers. It appears there were more than one or two people needed to give their permission and one was at a film festival on the continent.

The dubbing date grew nearer and I was worried. It would have been a great shame to have it cut out of the film. It had become a cornerstone for the junior age group of my shows.

Finally Jennifer got an answer from the legal side of the publishers who agreed that if we would sign over our rights to the road safety words to them, we could use the music in the film. So Deena's words were sold to them for a shilling. Five new pence.

We had never sought to make money out of my road safety work, except wages for performances given. But it was rather sad that we should have to disclaim ownership. Deena didn't mind though, she felt the same as me in wanting to be able to keep the song in. So it was signed and sealed. Jennifer did her dubbing, adding the sound track, and the film was finished. I still have the contract of sale containing the shilling sellotaped to it as a memento.

Jumping forward forty years to the present, to help me with this writing I sought out the contract. It was that much older, the sticky had long worn off the sellotape and released the coin from the paper. Wondering where it could be I was very relieved to find it nestling at the bottom of the old envelope. We had managed to hang on to the money even if we had had to give away our words!

The first date for transmission given as 24th of August. I pondered over writing a letter to alert all my friends. Whilst I thought about what to say there was a phone call from Jennifer. 'Hal, I'm sorry that date has been changed to August 25th', and to a different time as well.

So I decided to leave the letter for later. A good job too because the date was later changed back again to the original date. But this time it was finalised for the Radio Times, so we could reasonably rely on it now.

Turning my mind to the letter I thought it well worth while to make it a short hand-written copy to each county RSO. I simply stated that I was to be on a BBC2 programme called 'Look Stranger' on such a date and that some of my work on road safety would be shown in it. 'Yours sincerely, Hal Brooks'.

The London boroughs already had plenty of knowledge about my work. I had no doubt that the film would do me proud. The integrity of Jennifer, Rene Cutforth and the BBC2 themselves were enough to guarantee this.

I had hoped it would be shown in term time then I could have alerted all my head teacher friends as well, who, when they had heard about it, also wanted me to let them know.

I got quite a few letters back from the RSOs thanking me for the information. I was treating it like a show date because, in this instance I equated RSOs with entertainment agents. These people had the power to engage me to work in their area. A kind of nation-wide audition.

Most replies were of a friendly nature. One or two pointed out that I was not the only one doing this work and that they also had someone like myself doing similar work for them already. Another response was 'Sorry, we will be away on holidays but good luck anyway'. But most were encouraging. They would make a note of the date and also let their colleagues know about it. It was still three weeks away.

We let the family know. Deena's sister Coral let Tredegar know. Heady days, Coral has always been one to sing our praises. Wednesday at 8:25 p.m. was to be the climax. I was working in Pontypool. After my afternoon show I was away smartly to get home and watch it with Deena. Jim in his efficient way had hired a video machine to record the programme. Getting home in good time I found Deena on pins. A nice snack and a hot drink and we were settled. The front door locked and telephone off the hook, the two of us waited. The moment arrived.

A grid map of the British Isles was flashed onto the screen and moved towards Sussex. The square nearest Bognor Regis enlarged to reveal a close-up still photograph of me standing on the porch. Squeals from Deena, she was halfway up the armchair by now. And so it continued. What an incredible half-hour. It fled by. Then it was over.

We were both very pleased and happy with what we saw. The end was still on the screen when feelings started to return. We were both wondering what we might have left out, not wanting to hurt anyone's feelings.

As soon as I replaced the telephone it started to ring. Friends, business acquaintances, family, we were flabbergasted by the interest it aroused all round. We rang Jim and were pleased that our two boys had seen it all right. Later on Jim came round, and while he set up his machine, Deena brewed up and we all watched it all through again. We bought the tape hoping one day we might be able to afford a video player of our own so we could watch it whenever we wanted.

Back in Wales to finish my tour of the playgroups, I remembered how tired I was when finally getting into bed on the Thursday evening. It had all been a great strain on one's constitution. The summer ran its course. Playgroups, parks work and a couple of solo gala jobs took me again to September and to schoolwork again.

I'd got new venues as well after the film. Four important new areas of work. Devon, West Yorkshire, Middlesbrough and Hartlepool. This itself produced problems, mainly of cost. I was caught up in the inflationary spiral as was everybody else. These longer journeys meant that to keep costs reasonable I decided that I would have to stay away for two weeks at a time.

It wasn't possible to come home for the weekend. The mileage was against doing that. A six hundred mile round trip would soon reduce me to a physical wreck. We got over it by my going up and doing the first week on my own, then Deena would come up by coach on Friday and stay with me for the second week. We would then return together and have a week at home.

This was a natural progression for us. Long ago I'd decided that I just couldn't ever see myself ever being able to stop work and retire at a certain age. For one thing I have never earned the sort of money that allowed us to provide much for our old age. Being self-employed it was supposed that we should be able to amass a fortune to retire on. With no pension in sight, other than the state one which was covered by my weekly stamp, we decided that it would be saner to start retiring earlier. So I worked a three-week cycle. Two weeks for wages, the third one for us at home.

To make two weeks money last for three is no more hardship than living on a pension, and I enjoyed being at home for a whole week. Another reason for not making a fortune was my changing professions more than once. Going self-employed for a start kept the coffers low until I got established. Changing to entertaining was another pause before earnings caught up again. Back into a woodwork and crafts after stopping touring was another. Not being a one job man, Deena has had to put up a lot with my erratic earning ability. But I am the luckiest of men, I can assure you. In a few weeks from now, 16th November, 2006, we will have been wed 60 years. Our Diamond Wedding Anniversary, complete with a card from the Queen.

The longer trips brought a bonus too. We saw more of the country having the odd weekend away together. Deena loved visiting new places, antique shops, museums, markets and such. The scrap books she started keeping then still brings back those moments when viewed today. Mind you it was a good job she didn't mind wandering around on her own. With me in the schools all day it would have been awful had she not had these other interests.

We made many friends on these tours. It also became clear that wherever you go, whether it be humble or grand, there are always places of interest close at hand to be explored. I had to always bear it in mind that this girl of mine never married an entertainer. As a carpenter I was always back home at night. It was the other bit I took up that involved all the travelling.

It was about this time doing a stint in Lewisham, early on a freezing cold morning, that I thought about getting all this down. I'd never done any serious writing before. I was not what you call a grammar school person. Never having passed an exam, except in the army, I was prone to put full stops and commas down with gay abandon. I still do. But in the quiet of an evening in the camper van I warmed to it. I wrote for over a year. Only in the evenings, on my own, in the van. Over one thousand three hundred pages in all. If I hadn't done so, this final attempt at a memoir, would not have had so many details from so long ago.

My advice to you dear reader is, even if you only do it for your family's eyes, get a few things down to have something to work on in your old age. The most important thing to realise is that you can do it sitting down!

My new areas of work had marvellous things to offer as it turned out. The RSO for Devon, Leonard Newman, was a charming person. He gave me the impression of being the squire of his county. There was nothing he would not do for the young citizens for whom he was responsible.

There was a delightful happening on this tour. During the week I visited a convent school. The teachers were all nuns, dressed in their habits. Deena and I were invited to a school lunch there. This was no ordinary occasion. The dinner table was beautifully covered with lace tablecloths, and the convent's silver tableware graced the pristine surface. The whole occasion was absolutely lovely. The nuns were most kind and courteous to a humble joey and his wife. Torbay was known as the Cornish Riviera at the time. It was certainly a very warm and friendly place to us.

West Yorkshire became a metropolitan borough around this period. The new boundary took in Leeds, Bradford, Huddersfield, Halifax, Dewsbury, Keighley, Ilkley, and Wakefield and more. There were five RSOs for whom I could be working. The person in charge of road safety overall was Gemmill Alexander. I think he was in the colonial service before this post. Anyway, it was he who passed me on to the local RSOs.

On one of my tours he invited Deena and I to his house for dinner. He and his wife were a charming couple and made a great fuss of us. During a lovely meal I disgraced myself by knocking over my wine glass and spilling its contents everywhere they shouldn't be, but things were graciously tidied up quietly by Gemmill. It was a great evening and it was very nice to meet the man who really appreciated my work.

One of my first trips up north was to Bradford. The RSO was Mr Ford, and as things happen in the workplace, he was called Henry. He and his wife Betty were very kind to me. Betty was a local magistrate and Henry was also steeped in local affairs.

The towns and dales of Yorkshire were an eye opener for me. I had been on the wild side of East Yorkshire in my army days being stationed in Kilnsea, and working out on Spurn Point. Now West Yorkshire was unveiling itself to me. It became clear to me that out in the wilds the weather could be as varied as the countryside.

One weekend when Deena was with me, Henry took us on a tour that was punctuated by every kind of weather. Wild wind, pelting rain, brilliant sunshine, snow, hail and fog. All in a couple of hours. Our ability to see what was happening outside the car, a large Volvo estate, was only made possible through excellent windscreen wipers, and a proprietary brand of liquid additive, mixed half and half. The washers on my van and of previous vehicles I had used to hump my props around in were no match for Henry's.

Another story about the elements in this part of the world. One of my overnight parking spots was in Elland. It was nestled beneath the M62 and you could see the lights of the motorway traffic from there of a night time. It was a depot for the gritting and vehicle maintenance.

Most of my stays there were in mid-winter. It was wild and woolly to say the least. There was nowhere to plug in my extension lead to get electricity into the van for heating. My only source of comfort was from the gas rings on my stove. The heat never got down to my feet.

If the weather was bad it usually meant early nights under the blankets. Sounds nice and cosy but if the temperature was really down, all night there would be the constant business to and fro of the gritting lorries. I'm a good sleeper but the fact that it is deep in my memory proves it wasn't the easiest place to get a good night's rest in preparation for doing four shows in the schools next day.

I also had a the few quizzical looks from the council workers there. You could agree with some of their thoughts that 'it's a funny way to earn a living'. And I will agree now. The word funny in this context, bears no relation to the same word to describe my antics whilst working. Funny that!

Henry's home was in Ilkley. I often parked in his driveway which was quite steep. I was off the road but pointing upwards. In Mumbles I had been quite used to pointing downwards in BNY 13, but there was plenty of space around it. The whole street. This Bedford motor home was a lot wider than the old Ford van but I could get in and out alright because the Dormobile had a door in the back, similar to the ambulance bodies they also made.

Henry's patch contained so many places of interest. One such place that enthralled Deena one weeked was Howarth, once home to the famous Bronte sisters. I got the feeling whilst there that the sombre atmosphere of the place had well and truly percolated into the stories the sisters had invented. There was also a cemetery there, of course.

Quite a different experience was on offer for the hungry, not very far away. An original Harry Ramsden's fish and chips shop. Nowadays in Yorkshire and elsewhere, it has proliferated and become well known as a leading fast food chain. Then, in the seventies, it was word of mouth, based on quality, taste, value and service, that made it stand out.

In Bradford schools more than elsewhere I encountered the mixed race element. Some schools were a third coloured children, others a third white. A fantastic experience to put across a road safety lesson there. All children's eyes are appealing. To see all the different kinds, looking deeply at this chap with a red nose on who was talking about crossing roads safely, was something to behold.

Most were learning a strange tongue. What they thought of me and my utterances I would have loved to have known. I did have one universal contact maker to help me though. Comedy. And, more importantly, you knew when you had got through. Children are generous with their laughter.

Talking to head teachers during these visits, they assured me that they all thought this unusual lesson of mine had been well received by my young audience. Also that they had plenty to refer back to in later lessons. All the visual images I left could be explained in detail afterwards.

One of my pensioner shows in Bradford was unusual, in that it was in a theatre, on a proper stage. It always made a nice change dealing with adults. I revel in such situations. 'There's nowt like a good audience'.

Some schools I visited in the Yorkshire area also had some lovely surprises for a travelling entertainer. The head teachers were always very proud to show off the talents of their charges. It was normal practice at morning assembly in one school for the band to accompany the children singing.

The band, all pupils, was a remarkable achievement for the dedicated music teacher, who nurtured this enterprise and conducted the performances. They had a very good piano in the hall too. I remember I managed to have a play on it myself. I would have liked an instrument in my camper for consolation whilst being away. Then, to have a piano handy meant something with an iron frame. Very heavy and bulky too. The modern portable keyboard was still a few years away.

Whilst working with Pierre, in my early clowning days, I had often toyed with the idea of a musical clown act. It always frittered away with the thought of carting a piano about. It was just too much for us.

There were acts of this nature about then. A well known one had a major fault as far as I was concerned. No-one was able to supply a bit of real recognisable music from their prop instruments. But I was only ever confident enough to get by on a piano to make such a thing feasible. Nowadays with printed circuits, there's no end of things you can do with hardly any weight at all.

Later on I was to make Zippo's piano for his trio. But as they were also using it as a vaulting horse, with three hefty performers pouncing upon it, I had strength to think about rather than other things.

One school's art teacher I remember decorated their hall with full-size clown paintings, cut out and hanging around the walls, in preparation for my visit. She was very talented. I ventured to ask what would happen to them afterwards, and she kindly let me have them a week or so later.

Then a few years later at subsequent Clown Conventions in Bognor Regis, Deena and I encouraged the local school children to decorate the Regis Centre in the same way. Awarding prizes for the worthy ones.

Another art teacher made me a painting sheet from her drawing of me, after a visit. It was better than my own. The fact that my act always included me drawing something or other was always a marvellous bonus to me because of the many spin-offs it engendered. A drawing is often as good as a speech.

I was talking to my friend, and clown, Ben Lester, on the telephone one day, and he told me how he also used drawings in his children's shows. I had another thing in common with Ben. We both have been connected to a car act over the years. Ben was also an engineer. One of the early comments I used to make on being a clown was that sometimes I felt more like an engineer than a supposedly funny man.

As you can imagine, travelling the schools, I was a visitor in many teacher staff rooms. I always knew when I was in Wales. Rugby football. The place is a hotbed of enthusiasts, the ladies as well as the men. Passionate discussions in which I could, alas, not join in. I'm a soccer man myself if I am anything at all, and it was in my army days that my interest even in this game was finally dealt a lethal blow.

I volunteered to play once in a recreation period. It was not the game that I remembered playing with friends in my youth. I knew that I had been called up for war, but not against members of the same army! I was appalled at the aggression. It seemed as though the field was occupied by armoured carriers, or even tanks. I never volunteered again. It's a great shame really, but when the opposing team is kicking everything except the ball it's time to retire and fall back, or in army rhetoric, retreat.

Chapter 27

Turning to Crafts

I am now coming to the end of the words I wrote in 1975. Up to now it's been easy to enlarge on what had already been put down over forty years ago, whilst my memory was keener.

Now, events seem so far away. Looking up ancient calendars, old work books, contracts from gala agents and road safety departments, all have to be scoured for relevant bits of information to bolster up my recollection of events. Also I dearly want to make it readable.

Now with these longer journeys away I was painting more of an evening in the van, instead of writing. With a good seed catalogue I got to be a dab hand at painting vases of flowers. I could compose these pictures without upsetting my tranquillity after a hard day's work.

I also developed an interest in designing names. I treated the actual letters in a name as building blocks, creating unusual shapes and ones that could also be made up in wood, mainly plywood.

My third week at home gave me the opportunity to get back to the bench and do a bit of woodwork. After all, a long time ago I turned to entertaining as a break from building. Now I was having another break, this time from entertaining. Back to my seed skill, woodwork.

During these evenings, with pen and pencil, I filled many an exercise book with my ideas. Some very fanciful, some eminently practicable. I had always been a great supporter of the crafts movement. On all our travels, one road sign that nearly always caused us to divert for a while was 'Crafts Exhibition'.

Early in our marriage when money was short, I used to make unusual calendars in varnished plywood. A pretty ribbon to hang the next year's tab on and a loop to hang the whole thing up. Then over to Deena who painted small posies of flowers, butterflies, or small animals on them for decoration. The fact that we haven't got one now means they must have been worth the half a crown we charged for them.

It is little known that when we first met, Deena in college and me on the island, it was she who was the artist then, sending me drawings in her letters to me.

Another time in the sixties when we belonged to the Independent Order of Foresters, a small number of us formed a craft group. My speciality then was making brooches. I had got from somewhere, a dried seahorse. I pressed the small long gone creature into a tray of putty and made plaster casts of it. After decorating and mounting them on brooch blanks they sold very well.

Also in these evenings on my own, inevitably I was thinking of what I would do when the schoolwork stopped. Four shows a day and carrying around your own theatre, for that is what my work routine really amounted to, wasn't easy. Like gala work there are not many helpers about to ease the pain of taking everything out, doing your act, bringing everything back, and then preparing to do it all over again.

I needed a good night's rest to make it all work. It's strange that the heavy physical work is not so wearing as the amount of nervous energy required to deal with people, whatever their age.

Viewing work programmes over the past years, patterns emerge. I was not working for any RSO other than of the male variety, in the London area. A little farther out the districts of Alton, Caterham, and Petersfield, all had a lady in charge.

Sally Stroodley, RSO for Alton always had a grand Christmas party in a public hall for the younger members of her domain. We all celebrated in company with me and Tufty. Very joyous occasions too.

In Calderdale and Middlesbrough there were two more. In all my dealings with these council employees of either sex, I rarely got the impression that they were doing this job until a better opportunity came along. The men and women for which I worked had the same dedication to their jobs, which tallied with mine.

The road casualty figures were not just statistics at the end of term, they had a real impact on our working lives. Once or twice the school I was visiting had just suffered such an accident which had affected the whole school. You can imagine the sort of impact it would have on a village community. The whole area would be traumatised.

I have been noting some dates where the RSO added another dimension to get the message across. One time was in Salisbury. I was carried about for a short tour accompanied by the Michelin Man. With him wearing his suit resembling a few car tyre inner tubes, which inflated his appearance somewhat, we waved to Saturday morning shoppers during their road safety week. On this tour the BBC local news was on hand to show me on film in one of the schools.

Another time up north in Middlesbrough, Deena was with me when we were paraded through the town in Chitty Chitty Bang Bang. This was the first time I had seen the car used in the making of the hit film.

It was the prop car made for shots of Chitty running on the road. A beautifully imaginative job. Other models had also been made to represent various other properties, such as the flying version.

Some years later whilst attending a craft fair east of London, I met Pierre, my former partner, at the same event. He now owned the car. The third time I saw the car it had Pierre at the wheel attending a clown convention in Lincoln. Deena and I graciously accepted another lift from our friend.

When you're working on your own, small incidents can assume giant proportions. One Saturday morning I had just arrived at the Middlesbrough Park where other road safety attractions were gathered. I was already in motley. I got out of the van and the door closed, with my keys inside, locking me out.

It's times like these when your whole life flashes before you. I panicked a bit, or more than a bit. All the props were inside. Chatter, chatter, amongst the welcoming crowds, then out stepped a guardian angel who also owned a Bedford vehicle. He tried his key, and it opened up for me. A real stroke of luck.

The RSO of Middlesbrough and RSO of Hartlepool had clubbed together to give me a week's work in each town. My overnight parking space in Hartlepool was a vast empty concrete area where until quite recently all the North Sea oil rigs had been built.

A town on the coast there, is Seaton Carew. It's what I called then a small seaside resort. Just like our own town of Bognor Regis was at that time. We enjoyed our second week's stay there. An ice cream and a walk on the beach was a very welcome change for both of us.

For the second week Middlesbrough was quite different, with heavy industry all around. A very imposing bit of evidence of past attacks from a seawards direction were the enormous cannon on the quayside and promenade. The coastal areas were very different from down south.

Away from the schools work I notice I was not lacking in interesting jobs. It was 1976. I remember one job, for the Navy shore establishments. You might think that with all the discipline that abounds around a service establishment, that the children's parties would reflect some of it. You'd be wrong..

From the behaviour of my audience it seemed it was a well-established practice to let the children do as they liked. A great shame really. A few bullies pulling rank can be great spoilers. A similar situation presents itself when a mum who has booked you for a birthday party leaves you to a room full of children without an adult present, then joins all her friends for drinks whilst leaving me to get on with it. A similar sort of thing.

An unforgettable sight once was to see twenty or so large beautiful sheep dogs bounding into the arena at the Northampton Show. I was doing a solo clown spot and Deena was with me. We met Stanley Unwin on that date. A lovely man to be on the bill with. It was nice to be getting gala money again.

On a weekend in Wakefield after touring the schools we went into an antiques fair. A sculpture of a rearing horse caught our eyes. Cast in spelter and painted black, it attacked the money in our pockets ferociously when we walked out with it.

One time we visited Barnsley Market. We both liked these brief visits up north, especially when something was happening locally. They were a sort of sweetener for being away. We thought they were well worth being away from home for. We found the world's biggest pie dish hanging up on the gable end of a house, awaiting the next festival. I didn't ask about the amounts or constituents of the filling. I'd have loved a taste though.

Once attending a jumble sale, we soon realised we were not in our local area. The South, with plenty of retired folk about with money enough to buy a house for their latter years, had a lot better class of jumble. They would relinquish more, sooner, than what we found up North. This was well before car boots, table top sales and the abundance of charity shops.

Whilst touring Leeds I enjoyed a visit to the shopping mall that housed 'the cyclist', a sculpture by Rowland Emmett. He had collected around him craftsmen of varied talents and I marvelled at his design and their work to present a fascinating image for a casual shopper. What a draw to the visitor.

At the back of my mind I had thought one day that son Jim and I could do something in a similar vein, but on a smaller scale. With his skills in electronics, and my imagination, I had a yen to make shop window displays, for hire.

The attraction of something moving will always catch the eye of passers-by, luring them to stop and gaze in the shop's windows, and possibly getting them inside to buy something. Automata have been around for ages, and I fancied doing my own thing. Looking back it seems that other things kept the fancy from becoming fact.

I noticed I was getting plenty of parks to do during these summers. A couple of Butlin's dates at Bognor as well, for short periods over Easter and Christmas. I was lucky to get these odd dates, but being on the doorstep and known to the management was a big help. These bookings also offered the opportunity that I might be working on a big stage such as the Gaiety again.

There was another spin-off from coming to Bognor. The opening of the camp in 1961 saw a couple of folks from Southampton staying for a week with their children. It happened that the dad was secretary of the sports and social club of the electrical manufacturers, Mullards, now Phillips.

Later that year he booked Deena and I for their works children's party, at Christmas. We must have impressed because I ended up doing the job there each year for another twenty-five years.

After this length of time, Deena kept saying I should give someone else a chance. At the back of her mind was the thought I was being kept on out of friendship. Mind you, I did venture to remind her that this is the third or fourth club secretary I'd dealt with. But to help ease her concern I thought of a way to resolve the matter.

So one year, as the date they liked having it on was quite clear from earlier years, I took another booking on 'their' day. It was for a group of disabled and children with learning difficulties. At least these children never complained, unlike the frustrated sports' secretary who had to search for another entertainer that year. Whoever it was he got, he never lasted. I was back again the next year.

In the beginning it was Deena and me that did the job. There were over two hundred children to cater for before and after tea, so when Deena retired from the business, I always took someone along with me. These included, in turn, Pierre, Sammy Sunshine, Bingo, Goldie, Tricky Nicky, Smiley, Ken Rowden, a magician, Pancho Pete, and of course whoever was resident Father Christmas for that year.

From speaking to friend Ben Lester these long runs of children's parties are not uncommon with clowns. He himself had a longer run than me in his career, over thirty years in fact. It is very likely that we are bound to provide variety for a mixture of ages. Plus making them laugh. Variety is the key to dealing with our young clients, variety and visuality.

When we moved to Bognor Regis the local newspapers reported our joining the local community. Shortly afterwards I had a telephone call from a Mr Basil Shippam. He was very well known for his sympathetic dealings with older boys and he ran a boys club in Chichester. His family business as purveyors of potted meats, was a household name.

'Have you and your wife anything to offer lads of nine and upwards? The club held an annual party known as 'Sausage and Beans Night', which he wondered if it would be a suitable venue for us.

Deena and I had started running a lucky dip show in Butlin's for a couple of years now. It was a game show with prizes. The games, played on stage, were tailored to certain ages. I explained that this would be an ideal 'after beans night' entertainment. He booked us. We did well, got subsequent bookings and became friends.

A popular summer pastime then was beach entertainments in the school holidays. Basil was interested in my road safety work and so I intended to ask Shippams if they would sponsor me for this summer work, with a road safety slant. Very sadly, Basil Shippam died shortly afterwards. Later on I received a letter from the company which baldly stated that 'all Mr Shippam's interests died with him'.

Then a major customer, also based in Chichester, began to show up in the dates columns about this period. It was the Army And Navy department store. In the beginning I knew it as Morants Of Chichester.

A very talented window dresser, Jane Windsor, was my first contact. She and her lively assistants had me in for the occasional mix and mingle job. I remember on these occasions we never knew where we would be dressing. In the alterations department, in the stock room, in where ever we could get sometimes.

I made myself an easel that could be wheeled down to the town centre for me to do name drawings of Christmas shoppers. Our shop girls would feed us with balloons to give out to the children.

I had to carry a car battery to provide power to the light Jim had rigged me up on the drawing machine. It added quite a bit of weight to the contraption, but it was very successful.

We also gave a helping hand at the time of the City's Christmas lights switch-on. Each year I assisted the important personage who was to perform the ceremony. I remember Patricia Routledge doing it one year. I was already hooked on Hetty Althrop, the down-to-earth lady private detective from the North of the BBC series, so it was a real pleasure to meet my television heroine in person. I also remember others who didn't quite hit it off with Kerby Drill.

I wouldn't call working in the store the usual run-of-the-mill mix and mingle. On gold card nights, wine was laid on and it wouldn't surprise me if some of the customers were driven to do their Christmas shopping in their Rolls Royces.

These special shopping evenings were usually on Thursdays and most times I had Bill English, Smiley, with me. A first class accordionist, we used to stroll through the various departments, Bill doing the serenading whilst I did all their names, and most of their children's, although the evening was adults only.

One problem with the store was its position. Although it was right opposite the Cathedral, it was a good few yards away from the Town Cross, where most of the shopping crowds were. So Bill and I had to be the highly visible representatives of the store doing as much luring as we could. Not quite down a dark alley, sort of thing, but it was very important clowning never the less.

For many years we had as many as twenty dates to do from November to Christmas closing. During this period, our league position of all the stores in the group for business was always up high, and twice, top. The manager, Mr Hodgson, was very supportive of our work and Jane did an excellent job putting us in the right places.

Then in ninety-six it all changed. Whatever caused the upset, clowns were out. The management changed, Jane retired, and we got no more work from the new set up. But Bill and I had had a good run. We'd made many friends and both of us really enjoyed working with them all.

On my breaks back from the schools I enjoyed being a member of the Bognor Regis Art Society. Often I would don makeup for them and sit for a few hours whilst being painted as a fully paid up member of the clowning community.

Sometimes I'd dress up another member and then tutor the group in portraiture. I often did this with other groups as well. A favourite ploy of mine was to take my own models. These invariably were two very pretty children, Casey and Tina, my grandchildren. They loved all the fuss.

Sometimes I managed to set up and do a quick one of my own, explaining methods at the same time to the class. Now the two girls, with children of their own, Oliver and George, still have some good visual memories in paint of those happy times.

I came across an old certificate of public liability insurance for 1977. In it concern was expressed by the insurer about me using 'explosive devices'. With the Model T and the other gala acts I had never bothered about this before. If they had had a rundown on what we got up to, our premiums would have been more than the work was worth.

However, after cutting out major bangs and flashes from my engagements, I resolved to try again. After all schoolwork and children's parties can be more peaceful, somewhat. Or should be!

My 'pop plant' had to be negotiated. It used a target launcher and an extended blank cartridge to provid motivation for the pretty plant prop to grow to eight feet in the blink of an eye.

In the end it was agreed the pop plant could be launched as long as there was 'no person within eight feet' of it, excepting me of course. Before this I 'aimed' it for a child to catch, or not. So it was I was re-classified as a 'children's entertainer and schools lecturer' on the document, and with the new rules agreed, it was deemed unlikely that any of my future audiences would 'die' laughing! Such were the perils inherent in our job.

Another thing that turned up was my membership card of the International Circus Clown Club. I had joined with Pierre in March, 1968. We used to regularly attend the AGMs in a church hall in South London. The lovely ladies of the Dalston Church looked after us very well.

My impression of the club then was of the definite divide between clowns doing the children's parties and the circus members. A very mixed bunch. The major travelling circuses were still very much in evidence then, but the situation was changing rapidly.

Jack Gough, a railwayman and an ardent member, was our secretary. It was his dedication that was holding all of us together then. A lovely man who dutifully put out the newsletters that kept us all informed. I rarely saw Jack in motley and never saw him work.

It's a strange business. Mostly we are working in strange isolation. The formation of Clowns International, and later on the clown conventions, have given most of us a public face, and to each other as well.

The engagement books show a period in the late seventies when I was also asked to do some home safety work, for the London boroughs mainly. Once again there was a marvellous source of information on the subject already at hand.

Most councils were putting out leaflets, posters and other information that were particular to the circumstance of their borough. But I also got a lot of my posters from RoSPA. As with their road safety posters, they were excellent. It was a great help for me to build a home safety talk around the very visual subject matter printed on these.

As with road safety it was a matter of balance to get the comedy element right to match the age and content of your audience. Having proper lighting in vital areas like staircases. Watching out for loose carpeting and floor coverings that may slip or trip. Somehow as you get older your feet don't seem to come up as high as when younger.

Watch out for wet spots on bathroom floors, especially if your grip is faulty and can't be relied on. Balance, and sometimes the lack of it can be a real killer sometimes for the aged. My eldest sister Floss was a victim of her own bathroom. A fall there with so many hard edges about to hit against can easily prove injurious, or even fatal.

You might say, well, all these things are well known and adults won't thank you for going on about it. Not a bit of it. As with road safety these lessons have to be said constantly and any helpful new way of presenting them, is welcome. A reminder or two interspersed with a laugh occasionally was a pleasant and effective way to get the message across.

The Health and Safety professionals thought so anyway. My wages had to come out of their budgets.

During my tours of the country I have been witness to some sights that linger long in one's mind. During a spell of severe weather in Wales, in hilly terrain, during the day of our visit to the village school, we were aware of a funeral taking place. Plenty of snow and ice about. The main road was passable but as soon as you departed from it, watch out!

The church was up one of the hills. We watched as the hearse made valiant efforts to get up to the cemetery, to no avail. The deceased could not be laid to rest that day, and the ceremony had to be postponed until the weather broke.

Compared with the ease of recording items on video today, it was not so easy whilst I was gallivanting about. Mrs Hill, from Petersfield, booked me to tour the schools in Horndean and District, an area in between Chichester and Portsmouth. In the Rowlands Castle primary and junior school I did both shows, as per normal, which was much appreciated by the kind headmaster.

The children were very responsive and it was only when I was packing away he came and told me he had recorded both shows on his tape recorder, and presented me with the tape. The large hall was not a favourable place to do it in but as it is the only record I have of all my school shows I treasure it.

With the gala acts, when a story is unfolding scripts are very necessary, give a word or two. But I have always been an instinctive performer. Routines gradually build up and alter according to the situations at the moment of delivery. I never wrote down one script for any of my road safety acts.

I was prompted the way through a forty-minute performance by the props waiting to be used. It never became mechanical. Now, I'm listening to the Rowlands Castle tape desperately trying to piece together what I said at the time. Thirty years is a long time ago.

Since then, during my search for material to include in these writings, I have tried to locate the man to thank him again. He wrote the school's name and date on the tape but not his name. After such a long time he will know I tried, I hope, if he ever reads this.

Also during this tour, I will always remember a very sad occasion during one dinner break, when a dinner lady asked me if I painted portraits? If so could I paint one of her little boy as he had recently died of leukaemia. Asking if she had photographs of the boy, I said I'd try. Most of these were black and white and the only coloured ones were taken when the poor lad's appearance was being altered by the drugs and treatment he had.

A friend and photographer Mrs Stevens agreed to enlarge these snaps for me. Whilst waiting for them, her shop was only across the road from me, the poor lady died suddenly. Such was the upheaval for the business these snaps were never found and returned to me. It was an enormous blow to me. They had been entrusted to me by the mother, so it will always be an unhappy memory for me.

I carried on until I had a decent painting of the young lad. I had the feeling I hadn't quite 'got it' when I showed her my efforts. Just a feeling. The Mum was however most grateful for the picture, but how much happier it would have been, all round, if we had still got the prized photographs and I could have been completely satisfied with the result for the poor grieving mother.

I now have in my hand a letter from Vic Golds, MBE, the RSO for the London borough of Southwark. I am remembering back to the early sixties when Vic helped me get started in road safety. Pierre was very busy doing his teeth routine in schools, and was unable to accept a three-day road safety tour of Southwark schools, so I said I would stand in for him.

I had time to prepare a decent routine and make appropriate props, and found I liked doing it. Later I wrote to Vic. Could he please give me a further week's tour for expenses only. A show date.

Whilst carrying out this event I was keeping a weather eye open to see if any other London area R.S.O, had looked in to see my show. I had written out extensively informing them all just where I would be performing at such a date. The ploy worked, and I got bookings to present my own acts.

So Vic was the one who gave me my first chance. Uncle Hal was in business. The Kerby Drill bit came later. 'Dear Hal, I am sorry I was unable to see you doing your last tour in Southwark.....'. Yes, in the months prior to this I had decided to cease my school work for a more relaxed life in crafts. I would be working from home. At fifty seven, woodwork would be far less stressful.

It would be a while before I finished all the work already contracted for, but the decision was made. Now the local press announcing my arrival in their district for a further tour, would also announce it would be my last. Some papers did more and were very kind and generous in their farewells.

I was getting on famously with my new woodwork. The ideas kept flowing and I had started making what I called name sculptures. People's names in wood, personalised by their hobbies, professions, or any other talents they had.

For example, one of my first commissions was for a Ron, who was a keen tennis player. By standing the letters R O N on top of each other, I gained enough height, about three inches, to place a small tennis racquet alongside the name. It's not hard to imagine the racquet was far more of a problem than the name.

The main difficulty was the stringing bit. I solved it by making use of embroidery cotton to form a look-a-like fabric that I cut to shape after the glue had dried, and had stiffened it somewhat. I got twenty pounds for it. I was earning again.

How did this Ron know about me? My youngest son Michael, a builder, had teamed up with friend Ollie, a past member of the Sausage Squad, and a gardener. They had rented a shop in Aldwick, Bognor Regis, as the headquarters for their business. In return for allowing Deena and I to have the window space for our crafts, we would look after the shop.

With Deena's peg bags, crochet work, tea cosies and all, I was allotted a space for my woodwork. So began a new episode for the Brooks family. In the Craft business now!

Chapter 28

The Latter Seventies

'Here we are again', just like the old song. Another changeover for the Brooks family. No abrupt change this time, but a mix of old and new. Wages were coming in from schools but were starting to dwindle, and I was keeping a sharp lookout for replacement cash and new opportunities.

From the records I was as busy as ever, what was different was the source of the money. My new paymasters were not solid types using cash from councils' coffers. This is what I was going to miss from now on, regular no nonsense cheques. But as with all my past changes, I was supremely optimistic in my ability. Just as being at home on the stage I knew I had come back to my first love, making things in wood. And no ordinary things. I'm not using just any old bit of wood, but blocks of a special nature, made up by me.

By glueing two pieces of finger thick pine together with the grains going in opposite directions, I made what is known as a laminated block, like plywood, but thicker. My blocks made of two pieces of wood, relatively weak in themselves, became extremely strong and stable at the glued joint. It was this that allowed me to design my work as I pleased, and the overall thickness once glued together, was quite wide enough to stand up on end, without support.

If it seems that what I'm describing now has just popped into existence, nothing could be farther from the truth. Since I finished recounting past events in the camper at night I have been working out these ideas over many months. The third week at home had allowed me to try out new ideas that I'd sketched in the exercise books in anticipation of this moment.

Through it all has been my love of Scotch pine, the colour of the grain, and its ease of working. The very first bits made when I started were small brackets of elaborate design and doubtful strength. These would be no good for holding up the shelves in the kitchen. My aim was always towards the artistic element, hence my path towards practical crafts was clear.

Our shop was called 'Home & Garden Crafts'. It was not on the main road, but we were opposite a busy garage, a wholesale stationers, and the post office was quite close. But of course we had no money to do an extensive publicity campaign. What we did have was a Crafts shop, the only one in Bognor at the time. Deena also put some of my paintings up as well. But it was obvious there had to be a bigger field to play in. So back to the travelling again. Mainly Saturdays and Sundays to craft fairs, but with a big difference, we slept in our own beds at night.

At first, we just had a table display. Gradually I made our table set-up more craft-fair friendly. A screen for the back of the stand hinged open to about eight feet. From this we hung curtains and used the background to display Deena's goods. Under the table was a relic from our theatrical shop days, the cash drawer. I used green felt to cover the whole area. It showed up my wood in a friendly light. I came to use the same green colour for all our bits to add a uniformity to our stand. Then another slimmer table to present my woodwork on, that stood against the screen.

A crafts magazine was also in its infancy at the time, it was called simply 'The Craftsman'. It kept us informed of various fairs, prices for tables etc. We also came to be great friends of the couple who originated the magazine, Angie and Paul Boyer. It seemed a group of us craft workers all grew up together then.

Trying out new venues and promoters. I venture to say the craft industry was taking on a new look about then. When I started putting all my writings together in preparation to seek an agent and publisher, I rang Angie to tell her of my intentions.

It was very nice being in touch again after so many years. I sent her some photographs of what I'd been up to. She kindly sent me the latest edition of their magazine. It is now entitled Craft and Design. Wow! What a difference from when I last saw a copy of their creation all those years ago. Now a beautiful full colour imaginative magazine so different from when I, in black and white, graced it's front cover. Whereas I rarely saw clowns before, we crafts people were always running into each other.

So what an exciting time this was. From my date book I was still being enticed back as Kerby Drill on occasions such as a 'Cyclerama'. An RSO booked me into an event where hundreds of children and their bikes were in a park for instructions on relevant subjects of safety. They could also get their name punched onto their vehicle, in case it was nicked.

Cycling proficiency was just being introduced then and they could acquire a certificate of competence to hang in their bedrooms. It was a proper fun day with a strong press presence. The local papers were very generous with their photographs. I thought it was a very worthwhile venture.

I note I had to go up to Southwark for Christmas parties too. In the past these nursery schools had me for free, my tours being paid for from council coffers. Now two headmistresses joined together to pay for my journey up. Miss Cronin and Miss Selby, were to my eyes the perfect answer to anxious mums who had to go out to work.

Their schools catered for two large separate areas of housing. They were council establishments with adequate staffing and the children attending them were the lucky ones. Being well looked after sympathetically in purpose-built nurseries. A marvellous start in life for them.

I saw such a wide variation in the provision for pre-school children then. Lots of playgroups were run by the mums themselves, on a shoestring budget, but with plenty of enthusiasm and determination. Others needed more support. Once, while I was doing my stuff in one playgroup in central London, a letter was received from the local council advising funding had been stopped. They were at their wits end as to know how to carry on.

Another Tufty Club I used to visit was hard to find at first. The whole housing estate was off the ground. The ground floor was on the first floor so to speak. There were shops up there but at that time they were in an awful state of repair and largely boarded up. There were lifts but if you were out of luck it was up the steps with everything. In fact the sole places of normality were in with the children I was visiting. The following year two other heads paid for a visit. Morning in one nursery and the afternoon in another.

In Bognor there was a very lively group of volunteers who raised money for seafront and Christmas lights. They called themselves 'The Illumination Fund,' and son Jim was a keen member. One Sunday afternoon whilst on a visit, he was giving thought to raising the fund's profile, when he suddenly said 'What we need is an illuminated procession.'

The fund's mascot was a cartoon-like character called 'Billy Bulb' and I was given the job of building a giant light bulb that could be towed in the procession. A song about Billy also followed, and he rapidly became a focal point for the fund and Bognor itself. The shape of an electric light bulb is definitely not an easy one to produce, especially for an eight foot high Billy! So in good prop making fashion I looked around for something that resembled a bulb shape, and lo and behold, I found one in my builders merchant's yard. A great big glass fibre septic tank.

It proved to be big enough, strong enough, and wouldn't rust. It was still a bit too heavy for me to move about on my own, but I had plenty of help. When it was finally set up in the front garden I could work all around it, making all the bits that would transform our Bill from something that you would normally bury in your back garden, into a figurehead for the fund.

Using mainly thick-ish card and gummed paper, the feet, hands and bulbous bottom were constructed. The nose was reminiscent of a highly imbibed clown, but was not red, just huge. Other members of the team arranged the wheels and the towing bits. It looked very good, and I was pleased that the crowds lining the route for the first procession on a Bank Holiday Sunday, were very happy and responsive.

After the cavalcade of lighted cars, lorries, and all sorts of entries paraded through the town to the West End Car Park, prizes were awarded for best walking exhibits etc. I don't know if he got a prize, but Howard Goldsmith, Goldie, a founder member of the Super Sausage Squad, made himself a pair of illuminating spectacles that he could switch on and off whilst doing a spot of collecting and rattling the old bucket.

The car park was packed solid. Suddenly I heard Jim's voice over the speakers reading out the latest figures on monies collected and other allied items, finishing off by announcing a grand fireworks display. I, and everybody else, wondered where he was speaking from. It was my first experience of someone using a radio microphone. Twenty-five years on and everybody's using them it seems, but it was a mystery to me then. It was his firm, Sussex Automatic Machines Ltd. that picked up the bill for the fireworks. In the ensuing years my first construction of Billy was transformed by a coating of glass fibre resin. He's still about somewhere, One thing's for sure , he won't have rusted away!

Around this time also was a very popular movement of Town's twinning with continental neighbours, Bognor Regis was no exception. Our chosen first was to a French town, St Maur des Fosses. As with such happenings on these occasions mutual gifts were presented to each of the Mayors involved. I was asked to produce such a present from Bognor. I submitted a couple of designs to the committee, and when one was chosen, I made it up in pine using my laminating technique.

The design was based on the fact that there was an R on two ends of Bognor Regis. One at the end of Bognor, and the second at the beginning of Regis. With the Bognor in a vertical position and Regis on the level, I had two thicknesses of the letter R, so two thicknesses of laminate made up a base, which was ample to enable the whole nine inch high sculpture to stand upright without assistance. It worked to everyone's satisfaction, including mine.

This was a bigger job than just a name sculpture. Mind you the quirk of the two Rs was an enormous bit of luck. A few years later I used the same design feature for a similar present to a second twinning. This time it was a German town, Weil em Rheine. Meanwhile my design was also used as an embroidered crest on a neck tie for raising funds.

When I started woodwork again I made all my sculptures myself, entirely by hand. Using a process called piercing, I just needed an electric drill, and a coping saw, which was a shorter, more robust kind of fret saw. In the beginning my name sculptures were slightly smaller.

The craft fairs turned out to be good providers of sales and orders, which I posted on when finished. I devised a way of making boxes of thin card lined with strips of polystyrene. That looked attractive, and protected the sculptures in the post.

The source of the thin card was the trays Sainsbury stores displayed their premium tea in. Grey on the back and white on the inside. Every week during the shopping, I would collect these trays, if they were empty. Whilst living in Bognor my local supermarket was a Sainsbury store in the town. Middleton-on-Sea is half-way between Bognor and Littlehampton, and when we moved there we found parking more convenient for doing the weekly shop in Littlehampton.

When a new Tesco opened there as well, I became a devoted collector of their recyclables. I must own up to being well-served by all sorts of free items from the supermarkets in my working life. Cardboard, bubble wrap, potato sacks, paper and plastic, and of boxes of all sizes.

Under nearly every craft table then could also be found cardboard boxes for keeping the crafts in. This was well before the age of the plastic containers of today. Under my telephone table in the workshop is a bank of drawers that are thirty years old or so. The drawers themselves are used lettuce trays. Only about five inches deep, they serve well for my drawings, letters and photographs.

Each time out now we were meeting with craftsmen who were members of this and that craft groups and Guilds. They had banded together to help and protect their interests whilst struggling to earn a crust.

Some groups demanded certain standards to become a member. Others saw the advantages in numbers and were not quite so fussy who was selling on the next table. My first association was with people who were enthusiastic about an idea or project that they found they were good at doing, and looked to sell a few items on. But this was completely different from my 'sea-horse' days, and now, with wages and other costs involved this was more serious.

Renting a table at a good craft fair could be expensive. Transport was nearly always a must, with consequential expenses involved. Most of us doing the craft fairs then still had day jobs for security, hoping to bolster earnings through the fairs.

My first dealings with a Guild came by way of an invitation from the members of one, the Wessex Guild. Their area of operation was half in Hampshire and in Sussex. Our fairs were mainly towards Portsmouth, rather than Brighton. A very friendly group of people with a wide range of skills to offer. The Queen Elizabeth Country Park liked our work and we were invited to display there.

I remember our first time. We had a fine spacious marquee to ourselves, about fifteen members or more. Deena and I were of course in our camper van. Early morning in the park, wet with dew, and chilly as a result, it seemed out of this world. Although the A3 was nearby with Petersfield the nearest town, we felt we were cast back in time.

Next to us a blacksmith was using the heat of his forge to do what we were doing on our stove, brewing up. Being decently advertised we all did well. On the last day of our stay we celebrated with a wine and cheese party. We had experts to hand. Cheese makers and wine producers amongst our members. That was a night to remember, and we made lots of friends.

One of our members Eileen, really fancied one of my spinners. In particular one in a dark coloured wood with flecks of silver in the grain. I had priced it at forty five pounds. She told me that she had a fret saw in her garage, that hadn't been taken out of the box, and she asked if I would make a swap, I consented. I was not into mechanical aids just then so I wrapped it up well in plastic and put it down the garden, more about this later. I remained a member of the group for a number of years.

It was during our shop days that Deena was also taking the opportunity to buy in stock that complimented our own efforts and provide a variety of other goods that a good crafts shop needed. It was mostly crafts people themselves that came in to try and sell their work through our shop. Offering sale or return sometimes.

We didn't like this way of doing business ourselves. I understand the pressures of trying to get your work known but to stock someone else's shop like this was a step too far for me. But there, we were in our premises on the backs of our lads out building and cutting lawns. Talk about luck!

Not far from us just past Goodwood is Singleton, the home of the Weald and Downland Museum, a collection of re-assembled buildings from the past, in a wonderful setting. In a marquee there was a craft fair, an upmarket one. The Guild of Sussex Craftsmen was one of the elite craft guilds in the whole of the country. Nearly every county had a collection of skilled workmen who had elevated their crafts to a higher plane. Some of their work was in fact sheer artistry, but as it was made by hand, it usually came under the heading crafts.

We went to have a look. It was an eye opener for me. The skills displayed took in furniture and tile making, weaving, needlework, jewellery, wood turning, glass painting, pottery and more. There were coppersmiths and silversmiths and all variety of skilled trades. It was all serious stuff and expensive, commensurate with the care and time invested in the products. No cheese or wine makers whatever the quality. This was real craft business, and this is what I wanted to be a part of.

I had taken a few photographs of my woodwork and was encouraged to seek out membership details. Examples of your work had to go before a selection committee. I am reminded of this by an article in the Brighton Argus stating that I had been accepted. What the paper did not say was that when I took examples of my work over to the Ditchling Craft Shop as required, I didn't leave them packed up and hidden from customers already in the shop as instructed.

Michael the shop owner wasn't best pleased when I put some of my pieces on the counter, and attracted the immediate attention of his customers. I didn't see any harm in it, but it was oafish behaviour. I hope he and his potter wife Jill have forgiven me.

I must say I didn't find the new company quite as friendly as the Wessex Guild. Perhaps it might have been the fact that I was an entertainer. I know that sometimes the clown image is not conducive to being taken seriously. However, as soon as I started exhibiting with them, I felt increasingly at home.

At first I was at a disadvantage to the other members of the group, which was linked with COSIRA. These are the initials of the then Rural Industries

Association. The other members were looked upon as rural. The Guild took in East and West Sussex, and Bognor was considered to be built up and urban, so some prestige fairs were denied to me.

One of these was held annually in Michelham Priory. A beautiful setting complete with moat. As luck would have it the rules that precluded 'urban' craftsmen were quite soon relaxed and I was allowed to participate.

Michelham was a five day event, and the Guild marquee had an established craft following. Most of our members went home of a night so there wasn't the same camaraderie as happened with the Wessex folk.

But Deena and I loved it. I painted most evenings. We loved the ducks, wild fowl and other wild things that stalked the ancient abbey. One or two members did stay overnight, but not to socialise. They stayed for the fishing. Enormous carp prowled the moat and lake amongst all the reeds.

It was about this time I was doing a bit in the Bognor Carnival. Goldie and I were doing some collecting when a new clown turned up. Trevor Pharo, 'Bingo the Clown'. had just settled in Bognor with his family. The main thing that struck me at the time was his Coco-style wig.

Trevor wore a full makeup and to see his hair stand up like it did was quite something to be remembered. I had never bought a wig, generally using a covering that resembled my own hair. I was always looking out for fake fur hats at charity shops or wherever. Taking out the lining, made them fit snugly to my head sufficiently enough to support my clown's hat which I had sewn on. It was well forward on my head so needed to be firmly held.

Later on, I got generous help from large kirby grips used in the fashion of all women seeking to fix a wave or secure their hat. Strange how I came to get to grips at last with my differently spelt clown name. Nine times out of ten the captions under the many press photos of me over the years spelt my name wrongly. Until I was able to explain on subsequent visits I was more often than not 'Kirby Drill'. I was too darn clever in thinking Kerby as a name would immediately denote the edge of a pavement, it didn't.

My first wig was one Pierre gave me. It was threadbare, on its last legs, and tinged with a strange green colour. But it was a proper wig.

Nowadays, sadly with thinning tresses, I have to use so many grips to keep my wig on that if I didn't paint them white I'd look like a pin cushion. I did find Pierre's old green wig jammed tightly on my head, stopping my large entrance hat from slipping off during the opening march into the arena of both the gala acts.

After the carnival Trevor and I got on well together and we gelled easily working with each other. He was a travelling salesman in graphic design and a real live wire. When it came to going after things he was excellent. It showed up in later years with the amount of work he put in getting the International Clown Convention going at Bognor.

Back to getting the money in. We were doing quite well in the shop but there was a cloud on the horizon, and it was heralding a major change. When we arrived in the sixties, Bognor was chugging along merrily. It was enjoying good summer seasons.

Our local entertainment venues, The Esplanade Theatre, The Rex Ballroom and Theatre Royal had all gained a little impetus from Billy Butlin opening up. The summer season stretched from June to early September, a reasonable time for Bognor's summer season based economy to gird its loins ready for the visitor-less winter months. Later bookings at Butlin's also helped to keep things going. But times were changing.

With the shop on our minds we began to realise the season had only been coming alive in July and now, not yet into late August, it was already falling away. The season was drastically shortening. It was general too. I thought we were all in for a dose of belt tightening, and so it came to be so. Being 'round the corner' our passing trade lessened considerably with less visitors.

Bognor had also acquired two more shops very much like ours, and the apparent success of the lads' business venture, also based in our shop, prompted the landlord of the property to put in ridiculous demands for rent increases which we would have found impossible to sustain. Just as we were beginning to make a go of it their demands forced us all to have a rethink. We decided to close. It was a great shame.

Changing business patterns also meant the small independent shop was rapidly becoming a thing of the past. This thought was rammed home to me on a visit to neighbouring Chichester. A really bustling market town. But although the small tobacconist there seemed the same as always, on closer inspection, I realised it had become a part of a string of enterprises. Big monied names behind small shop fascias. The novelty of the small shop with its attendant variety of purpose was being phased out. And that's just what had happened to us.

Never mind, for the boys, they never did their actual earning in the shop, so their business continued. I was still very active on the children's' party front, and the craft fairs were not affected, so we soldiered on.

One of my regrets when trying to get work for our gala acts in earlier times was I never could get a showing at Ardingly, where the South of England Agricultural Show was held annually. I wonder if it was because of the bangs we used in our shows? Very disturbing to some people and very definitely so for dogs, cats, cows and horses. Anyway I did try without any success but now it was on the menu that I would be able to have a showing of my woodwork there.

The Sussex Guild has its own marquee at the show, always held in June, for three days. It was a great thrill, and my first outing with them for a major event. Exhibitors were allocated parking in a separate field quite near to the marquee. So, arriving very early on the day of opening, Deena and I unloaded the van, parked it up, then got back to sorting out my work, for my first appearance at Ardingly. Alas, with no red nose.

Chapter 29

Getting Mechanised

The showground was laid out and most of the tents, marquees and stands were in position when we got there. It's a very big showground and they had been building up for over a few weeks now. Apart from the permanent buildings on site like toilets and club amenities for the Society's Members, it was mainly grass covered, except for the main road and small service roads leading off. One of our members was already parked close by our tent in his caravan. He was allowed a free space to keep an eye on our patch overnight. Later, I took it in turns with him for a couple of years. We rarely experienced any upset or trouble though.

The marquees containing the floral displays were very big. The permanent buildings to house the livestock were already filled with some of the finest farm animals in Sussex, and beyond. In our first year I didn't manage to see the main arena that I had been trying to get a gala booking in as it was well away from us. It catered for the show jumping and other entertainments. One of my friends had performed there, the high wire act 'The Derricos'.

Another marquee a little to the side of us housed the 'Rural Crafts Association'. These were craftsmen of similar standards to ours but maybe not resident in Sussex. Most of us had met each other over the years and were friendly rivals who respected the other's talents. Indeed I had joined them at one time.

As they exhibited all over the country I had thought it was a good opportunity for Deena and I to visit other places and shows, but every time I put in for a show I got the reply that there was no room. Full up. They favoured craftspeople who would book more than a single show or shows. The situation hardly changed, so it was pointless.

By this time Deena had rigged us up with an apron that went around the table, sides and front. So I thought we were already tidy before we joined the

Guild. However, some comments were pointedly made about stands looking 'scrappy' or 'unprofessional.'

I was showing letter and name sculptures in pine, along with some of my more inventive pieces, spinners and timber sculptures. My number sculptures were mostly in hardboard where I used the extreme one eight thickness in many layers to form quite large sculptures

I did learn one lesson whilst doing shows at Ardingly. The enormous numbers of visitors to the show did pose a problem, especially when we had a shower of rain. Being a natural showman I always felt the urge to entertain with something that catches the eye, and attention, but with a packed marquee I dared not be too active showing off what I had created from a particular nine by nine block of laminated pine. It was easy to create gridlock demonstrating my more unusual pieces that showed wood could be made to behave in very 'un-wood-like' ways.

Whilst using my fret machine I had wondered what if I made an extended cut in the shape of a spiral. The answer had turned out to be a piece of wood that behaved like a clock spring. You could easily get a log jam around your table, and beyond, if suddenly you lifted the middle of your wood up about twelve inches or so and then let it down again, without it breaking. My laminating process allowed me to do just that. The long grain on one side supported the short grain on the other. However, an untrammelled slow procession through the tent was essential when crowds dominated the scene.

When it wasn't so busy I would leave this apparent elastic type sculpture on the table. I had two pieces of nylon twine attached to it. One length prevented the wood from being pulled up beyond twelve inches and the other was a simple loop you could put a finger through to lift it. I invited children to have a go. When it was up, you could see through the wood to a small sign that said 'Peep Bo!' It was a real winner with all who tried it.

I sold some pieces from the table but my aim was to get orders for name sculptures, to be made at home later. I charged a two pounds design fee, for a series of as many ideas as I could dream up based on the information provided about the recipient. At the top of the list of wants for inclusion would be all the sports, hobbies, professions, their ages, anniversaries and trophies won for all manner of endeavours. If a job was carried to conclusion I deducted the design fee from the cost.

Most times I could manage four or five ideas. Sometimes I came up with a dozen. The basis for charging was mostly the same. The name itself would cost so much, then each extra feature added would be priced separately. If the recipient was say, a golfer, these extras might well include say a golf club, golf ball, or a flag on green. It really amounted to how much the person was prepared to spend. Some just had the name done, other customers would have everything I'd thought of included. If they had then they would receive a piece of my work that would grace any mantle- piece, display cabinet or desktop. A very personal gift, signed and dated on the base.

Nearly everybody in the Guild had a 'rent' piece for sale. Something inexpensive for visitors to buy as a keepsake. The wood turning members usually had a nicely turned wooden biro pen. Useful as well. It helped pay the rent for the table.

Others had their own solutions. I did not have anything to offer under about four pounds. One of my cheapest names was Ada, it was one of my simplest and one of my favourites. Even then I had to charge £3 for it to get a return for my effort, and there aren't many Adas about, I can tell you. So in the beginning I didn't take much money over the table in the three days.

Back to Eileen in the Wessex Guild and the spinner she wanted from me in return for the saw 'still in its box in her garage'. There were times when I thought it was silly my ignoring it down in the back garden.

In Littlehampton Market, a dealer called Malcolm had a second-hand tool stall. I was a regular customer of his, seeking out bargains, sometimes amongst a load of junk. The things that attracted me most were tools with boxwood handles and the like. These types of handles mostly denoted quality tools. I bought an awl from him of best Sheffield steel, years ago. It's still one of my most used and valued tools. An awl is simply a sharp prong with a handle on it, used for poking holes in things. I've never used it as such but it's the nearest instrument I've got that could be considered a weapon!

I asked Malcolm what he would give me for the saw. He came and looked and offered forty five pounds, I wanted fifty, so no. Having uncovered the saw to show him, I took a closer look at it myself. It had been made in Canada. A heavy industrial one with a beautiful iron casting that allowed you to cut up to 24 inches in depth.

It was practically of an age for a museum, but when set up in my garage workshop and I got used to working it, I didn't know how I had managed without it before. My stubbornness about doing everything by hand dissolved when I thought of another application for my new tool, a cheaper line of products in plywood. Simple, nicely designed names for children's bedroom doors and the like.

In the beginning I used my existing designs, but later I extended the range. What's so different from before you might say. On my machine I could cut six thinner plywood names at a time. I could now sell something for a pound. The next time we exhibited at Ardingly I got a great thrill by serving my first child customer. He could at last afford me. The saw had made this possible.

It had another feature that I hadn't used. A small tube delivered a continuous puff of air to blow the sawdust away from the moving saw blade. Jim helped me go one better than this. We connected a vacuum cleaner to draw the sawdust away altogether, so a minimum of dust was floating about in the air. Even so, I mostly used a mask as a further sensible precaution. It was a bonus as I now had a source of clean sawdust whenever the vacuum was emptied, such a wonderful resource for any workshop, especially for mine.

I developed a very handy instant weld that I could use on all manner of materials. I used to demonstrate it in my clown workshops by standing a wire nail in a spot of instant glue, then sprinkling a bit of sawdust on it, according to how robust you needed the weld. After it hardened, you could repeat the process, adding another layer for more strength. The finished join having the appearance of wood.

Looking back now it has just dawned on me how strange it was that I chose to use two layers of pine to make my first name sculptures, then to move to a machine laminate, plywood, for my second bite of the cherry, which grew into a collection of over sixteen hundred designs.

Although the craft tent is not a permanent establishment like a shop, it still throws out the same sort of problems. A family flows around your table, each child seeking their name. We have product in stock for four out of five names requested. Result four smilers and one glum face.

To remedy this, for a small amount extra and postage, I'd agree to send the 'missing' name on later. This meant it had to be designed and made first, so adding another name to my growing list. Deena and I never refused a request, which is why in the end, we had drawers full of boys and girls names, all colour-coded for our benefit in finding them for a quick sale.

Popular names and the rarely asked for, including traditional names with unusual spellings. These plywood creations I called 'fun names'. Later I added 'picture names'. These designs were more elaborate, built around a country cottage, bird singing in a tree, a castle with ramparts and a flag flying from a tower, and a duck swimming in a moat. All are encompassed in a plywood picture nine inches by six with the child's name prominently featured. For these we charged three pounds each. So pretty soon we were earning our way again even with the change of direction from touring schools.

Another important change was also coming along. It was to do with son Jim. He was getting into quite an exciting new business. With a partner they were developing ideas that in the first instance I would describe as a sort of 'bringing Times Square, New York', to Bognor Regis.

My compelling memory of that place, through watching films, was seeing the news being sent around a block of buildings by electric signs. Electric bulbs would form words that made up a continuous visual message. These lights were computer controlled and our boys were aiming to become the controllers. There was one important difference. Jim's would be on a trailer and mobile. It could be towed to any location, deliver whatever was needed at events in sports arenas, race tracks of all sorts and anywhere where up to the minute items of information would be required. They worked very hard to produce the blocks and lines of bulbs necessary to bring their lightboard about.

It was on a Saturday afternoon. We were all in their small workshop where they were building up to demonstrate their progress. This trial frame of lights was about a yard long. Suddenly they sent 'Hal Brooks' across, in lights. Such a great thrill. Fortunately we had an instant camera to capture its image. It couldn't capture its impact though, or the excitement.

Shortly after this I was up to my neck working on our first full length, working 'Leaderboard' display. Jim later registered the name for their business. He designing, me making. It was too big to put together in my workshop, so the decks were cleared in the dining room. Protecting the dining table with thick card, our board finally grew into a sixteen foot container of over two thousand small light bulbs that could transmit readable messages across its surface. When it was finished we just squeezed it out of the window. Made in half inch waterproof plywood it was very strong and could well look after itself.

Then came all the paraphernalia that had to be made to enable it to function. All sorts of switch boxes to house the heavy electrical equipment required to handle such high voltages safely. This couldn't be run on number eight batteries.

Over the years I spent a lot of time updating and altering plant for Leaderboard Ltd. It became a very good customer of H.D. Brooks, Builder and Decorator, for which I was very grateful.

Chapter 30

Crafts and Clowning

One of the things that kept me in good stead over the years was the knock on effect of pleasing customers and then being employed to do work for them in other circumstances. To be a children's entertainer you had to meet the parents. If you'd done a good party a follow up might mean a bit of work on the building side. Most of my working life I seem to have been wearing either a red nose or an apron.

I came to the attention of Michelham Priory when I first exhibited with the Guild, showing my woodwork. Five days is quite a long time to show in the one place. Ideas put forward amongst our members suggested we put something in place for the many children who came to see us with their parents. Clay modelling, drawing, painting and the like were put in place.

When I suggested I do a clown show for them, they jumped at the chance, rewarding me for doing so by adjusting my table price. It became a regular thing. More so, the Priory asked me to do more clowning for them throughout the year. So my bank holidays also became teddy bears' picnics, May days and other celebrations. At busy times there was a problem at the Priory. There was only one entrance across the moat through a stone entrance that may well have had a portcullis in olden days to protect the monks. It took quite a long time to get everybody in.

So for a period before opening time I was outside keeping everyone happy, being Kerby Drill, until things slowed down to a gallop. Afterwards I did two shows for the kiddiwinkies in the gorgeous grounds, either side of lunch. I did this for many years and became close friends with the administrators and staff. Once I was even told mums would ring up to enquire when Kerby would be there. Deena and I used to get this whilst working for Butlin's, especially from the parents of children going in for the talent competitions. It was very heartening to know.

It was right back in the sixties or so that I first came into contact with the Goodwood Estate. From the office of the Duke of Richmond and Gordon, I had a letter asking if I had anything to offer as entertainment for the retired estate members' Christmas party. To add something different to my show I also took another member of the family with me. Jim. Not yet in uniform as 'Captain Jim' and still at school, he sang a couple of songs with his guitar accompaniment. Since then, over the years, I have entertained for numerous other members of the estate, mainly at their children's parties.

The racecourse side of the Eastate was also expanding facilities for youngsters at their new 'Family Funday' race meetings. There was a creche with toys and entertainment. The main looker-afterers were two ex-teachers. I did two shows during the day for the children and later I brought Bingo in to help me, owing to the expanding popularity of the exercise.

Bingo and I did a mix and mingle and walkabout session amongst the punters too. The beautiful setting of the racecourse amid the Sussex Downs was magical. It wasn't called Glorious Goodwood for nothing. Mostly the weather was on our side, but on off days we could go under cover. The main summer festival was a riot of good neighbourly banter with a strong Irish accent.

In later years of course Jim was also at the meetings, but this time with his own firm, showing winners and betting odds on his electronic displays. To this day he is still attending meetings at Goodwood, Chester, Cheltenham, Newmarket, Ascot, Aintree and others, as well as all sorts of other sports events. It is a long time since Hal Brooks, in lights, swept across that first experimental display we'd built in that small Felpham workshop. Once when his mother was at the races, he surprised her with the message, 'Happy birthday mum'.

For a couple of years I exhibited at craft fairs held in Goodwood House. It was a great draw for visitors but the beautiful fittings and furniture were not at all accommodating for our craft tables. We were confined somewhat. Later, the problem was solved by holding the craft fairs in marquees.

Another job I did at Goodwood was for a dressage event. This top line competition was being sponsored by the international cosmetics manufacturer 'Clinique'. I worked in a large tent to entertain the children of the visitors and employees.

It's a good job I was a clown. The employees and customers of this firm were straight out of the fashion mags and Bond Street. I felt a bit scruffy by comparison but at least I knew I was clean, if not in fashion. The dressage itself was also an eye opener for me. The precision and discipline of both horses and their riders were really something quite exceptional.

Inside the marquees where the firm's products were being shown and sold, I found the sales ladies were very warm and friendly to this clown. I expect some of their children had put a good word in for me. Deena was a very grateful recipient of the many freebies given me as samples when I got home of an evening. They all despaired of improving my make up. No matter how much the advertised magical properties of their products did for the ladies, my red nose got in the way!

One weekend I was entertaining in Goodwood, West Sussex, and also exhibiting in Ardingly, East Sussex, on the same two days. After getting Deena settled for the crafts I had a long dash over to produce a few laughs on the other side of the county before returning to Deena at night. This wasn't a full showground do, just a crafts and country living event, held in one of the large cattle sheds. Hard work though!

As members of the Sussex Guild we enjoyed exhibiting in many exciting venues. We had an exhibition in the Towner Gallery, Eastbourne. It was set up and chosen by the gallery's officials and it firmly got me off on the wrong foot for any subsequent similar shows.

The preview with drinks was very convivial but I couldn't find my work. In no way can my pine sculptures be called large and the six pieces I put in were all over the place. Not prominently displayed either. They were meant to be shown as a group selection of my methods and ideas. Instead they had been used to fill gaps in between other people's work. I was very disappointed and disillusioned by things out of my control.

In the event, that was the one and only time I put myself forward for such a venture. It might seem churlish but I expected the same sympathetic consideration to be given my work as to the favoured pieces picked out by the selector for prominence. It was a Guild exhibition after all.

Happier times were to follow. One of these was when the Guild was invited to hold an exhibition in Chichester Cathedral. My pieces took quite a few hours to make, but this great monument of devotion, skills and sacrifice took centuries to complete. We would be showing in a place oozing with the patience, skill and hard work of countless generations of craftsmen like ourselves. A very humbling thought. We would be judged against the standards they set.

Not being a religious person I had nothing in my work so far that I thought would be fitting for such a solemn setting. A germ of an idea came to me through thinking of a painting that my eldest brother Charlie had done many years ago. The subject was a popular rendition of the end of World War One, of the peace and quiet when the guns fell silent. The sad sight of a fallen comrade's 303 rifle stuck in the ground with his steel helmet slung by the chin strap over the rifle butt. Charlie had painted it for some reason or other but I lost sight of it after he died. Rose took a lot of Charlie's writings and things. Perhaps one of her children have it even today. It was only a small picture, but very moving.

My sculpture, only about six inches high, was the five letter word, peace. The letters placed to be read downwards on a base resembling a grassy place with a rifle stuck into the ground with its bayonet half buried, alongside. The helmet hung as in the painting with its dome and steel rim creating a perfect place for a nesting dove. This was my first bit of work.

For the second I cut sixty small crosses out of tempered hardboard, a type which would varnish up to a deep rich brown on completion. The cross was of the kind associated with a religious meaning. From these I made a spiral sculpture about seven inches high. By glueing them one by one on top of the other, but in a slightly rotating position, it developed into a spiral. To make sure it was kept vertical I erected a piece of thread in an upright position on the bench for me to follow. Sounds complicated but really just needs patience to do.

My third and last sculpture was quite different. Made from one piece of my laminated pine nine inches by nine inches, I cut a series of hoop shapes about a quarter of an inch thick. Starting with one nine inches across I then cut out the next one from the remaining wood, which was about eight and a half inches in diameter, and so on, down to three inches. So the rings decreased in size and fitted snugly into each other.

Afterwards I drilled a tiny hole in each end of the hoops, I threaded them onto a steel wire which was fixed upright in a base piece of pine about four inches in diameter. Each ring then could revolve around the wire, which incidentally, was a single cycle wheel spoke. These spokes were always made of high grade carbon steel, and so just suited my purpose. To hide the spoke where the inner three inch hole was, I made a slim cross with a spoke hole right through it. The threaded nut of the spoke I buried into a wooden knob shape that when screwed back on, held all the bits together.

As with all non selling shows we took turns at stewarding the event. We could then answer questions, hand out cards, and generally look after the works whilst the public were about. I enjoyed these times immensely. One morning the Cathedral choir was rehearsing. The purity of the different ranges of voice in such a resonant setting was a never to be forgotten moment.

It isn't easy filling in details of happenings so long ago. For the parts needing remembering I have been lucky enough to call on my friend and past guild member Sam Fanaroff. A master metalworker specialising in working copper, I much admired his work. Sam was like me, not one to copy. It was a label that could be reasonably applied to all our members. Originality and excellence, to our best ability. From a humble start on the bench I often wondered how my woodworking dad and brothers would have viewed my work, and the company I was keeping.

What a good situation in my life, doing what I loved, woodwork, and still managing to mix it with my other passion, entertaining. And now after putting this all down on paper, I've developed a real liking for writing. Lucky me.

Chapter 31

Out on the Briny

I kind of got used to entertaining in all sorts of places. Front rooms, school classes, parks, theatres, hotels and conventions, and on the backs of lorries. But much as I was attracted to it, not much on board ship. The last place you'd expect a craft exhibition to be was at sea. But, there we were on board a Townsend Thorensen channel ferry, showing our wares on the briny. We were being used by the ferry company to add a new dimension to the many other attractions they were constantly dreaming up to entice passengers on board. We were paid a small fee as well as being able to do ordinary business on the voyages to and from France.

We had a few hours ashore for shopping and a visit to a vineyard where the growers presented us with two bottles of wine, as well as taking orders for further custom. The liquid was a bit harsh for me, and Deena hardly touches anything, but I found it very pleasing with a large dash of lemonade added. I thought that was nice, and the sea was in a kindly mood.

A few months afterwards we were surprised to be offered a similar trip, and who should be the organisers but BBC Southern Radio. With a full compliment of paying listeners, the craft show sailed again. There was further visual entertainment this time. On one of the other decks, there was also a selection of classic cars from Lord Montague's Transport Museum, in Beaulieu. Deena's sister Coral was with us on this occasion, and they both enjoyed being photographed in one of these special vehicles.

Harking back to my days with Pierre and the Model T I thought my past had caught up with me. We hadn't long been doing the car act when we were booked to perform at said Lord's residence. We were to entertain at a steam rally there. Just as a ballet dancer should be wary of dancing on a corrugated tin roof, so we should have given some thought to what it would be like to do our act on ground that had already been roughed up a bit by these mighty steam rollers.

Life on the ocean wave it was not. Henry Ford's gift to the travelling public, now over fifty years old, didn't enjoy it a bit. The heavy bar that held our driverless car in a safe circle, threatened to jump out of lock. It could have run anywhere then. As a very raw performer in this gala business at the time, I was very pleased when that part of the act was over and I was able to get back into the car and take control again.

At the end of the show, when our teeth had settled back into an ungritted state, we met Lord Montague and his young son. They were both very interested in our prop. It was a show date and we were only on expenses of twenty-five pounds, but funds were very sparse in the Brooks' household at that time, and we needed the money. Expecting to be be paid on the day, we were disappointed. The company kept us waiting over a month for the cheque, and when wages are slow to come in, slow payers remain writ large in the memory.

Writing about surfaces to work on, Pierre and I did an interval entertainment at a stock car meeting. For readers who may not know of this sort of self-inflicted torture, I offer a few words of explanation.

Old banger cars, suitably rigged to give a degree of protection to the driver, race against each other, with very faint rules to go by. I would re-name it as 'murder with intent'. I'm glad we didn't travel more than twenty miles an hour whilst doing our act.

Our second voyage was less calm. On the car deck the wind was lashing the spray against the protective canvas sheets, and as always in these situations, I felt a little less brave. However we had a well-known radio presenter with us who tied the whole event together. Everybody enjoyed it and we did good business in the circumstances. I was a lot slimmer too when I disembarked, and had let the air out of my rubber ring.

Looking through documents from earlier times I came across some from the Business Names Registration Office. I remembered when I changed my name for the Butlin's holiday programme from Harry to Hal, because Harold Manley was being already called Uncle Harry that year, and the programmes had already been printed. I notified my Midland Bank branch about whose bank account these 'Butlin type Hal Brooks' wages cheques should be very carefully diverted to. Mine.

So here were documents proclaiming that I am Kerby Drill, and that any monies in the way of cheques made out to ' The Super Sausage Squad' or 'The Boiled Egg Brigade' etc. could also be very safely greeted by the bank clerk who sees to my account, in the clear knowledge that not the slightest hindrance will be offered, by me, to their safe passage.

One memorable exhibition the Guild held was in Hever Castle. Deena was over the moon to walk in Anne Boleyn's footsteps in this historic place. Like Michelham Priory, it had a similar serenity about it. We showed on a normal Castle opening weekend. There were conducted groups of visitors being shown around as well as groups of foreigners with their own interpreters and guides. There were also two groups of Japanese folk being shown around, all of whom had been given a see-through umbrella.

Just as our countenances must be a puzzle for them, so theirs were for me. A lot of interest was being shown in my work when the older man who seemed to be the leader leaned over the table and said, 'Ah Mr Brooks, and how many students do you have?' I was very flattered, but carefully I explained, that's not how things worked in our country. I was very much on my own.

In the beginning though, I was one such student, looking over my dad's shoulder to watch every move he made, and listen to his advice. Charlie was first to do it then Fred, then me, and how lucky we were. In the fifty or so members of the Guild I knew of two or three who also taught skills to earn more for a reasonably stable living as tutors in adult evening classes. Others had their own teaching arrangements with private classes. Only Sam Fanaroff, coppersmith, had an apprentice.

What the leader was asking was, how much interest is taken of people with special skills to be afforded help in passing their talents on for the good of the country as a whole? Very little I'm afraid. Both my boys had very definite other interests to follow. But I would have jumped at the chance to co-operate with any government initiative in that direction.

As it was, employment regulations, responsibility for wages, insurance and the like simply put it out of the question. What a waste. In my experience there must be many people like myself who could not generate the sort of profits out of our work necessary to be able to employ someone on their own without outside help. Ah, well!

Another group of visitors I remember, at Hever Castle this time, were from an International Money Marketing concern. There were guests from all parts of the world there. Coaches of them would arrive about eleven in the morning to all sorts of goodies.

They were being hosted in London hotels. The marquees erected to accommodate them for the next four or five hours were rather like canvas palaces. Fully floored with interlocking wood panels, equipped with portable kitchens for preparing meals, and amply staffed. The food we had was also of a very high standard. Apart from the magnificent castle itself and the gardens, our group generally had a bee-keeper complete with hives, needlecrafts, and other skills that fitted in with the rest of the estate, and of the period.

I always did well at these dos and my commissions often went abroad. As well as the crafts, we usually had a display of falconry, and once we had a jousting company to gallop off with the fair maid, rescued from the evil Baron's clutches. Eventually new specialities were found to offer the guests, but we had had a good run. And in another sense too, it was quite a long journey to Hever from Bognor.

In the late seventies there was much excitement about a large sum of money to be spent on a new civic building in Bognor Regis. To be called the 'Regis Centre', it would have at its centre a real theatre and assembly hall. I watched the development with interest. It was of an unconventional appearance and shape, and not unlike an industrial building, at least it seemed so to my eyes. Since I invented my spinners I always had it at the back of my mind that I would try to find a suitable site for one to be on public display. The ideal position to my mind would be a quiet corner secluded from the hurly burly, a place of contemplation.

About six feet long it would be suspended by a steel wire that from a short distance would be hard to see. The motor for driving it round slowly would be hidden. Nothing spectacular in the shouting sense, just to come across it and see the bands of natural light from the side grain of the wood gently flowing down the curved surface, and seemingly falling off the bottom as it rotates.

Mind you the chance of it ever coming about was very slim. But, I thought, there was nothing to stop me trying for something a little less ambitious. I approached the council to see if they would be interested in accepting two smaller spinners for our new building. It was through their good offices that I met the architect and visited the as yet unfinished building. We got on well and he showed me around. A large modern style mural painting already adorned a major wall. I couldn't find one quiet corner of the sort I have described earlier. However not to be put off I sought helpers in getting the job done.

There were three components needed, materials, mechanism for turning the sculptures, and someone to foot the bill. I would undertake to make the spinners as my contribution, and supervise the whole enterprise. My timber suppliers were A. Olby and Son from Bognor. I had opened an account with them when I first arrived in Bognor in 1961. This was a time when the shop assistants had to know their stuff. Nowadays with the way it is all laid out in the DIY shops it's the buyer who has to know what everything does. I wrote a letter to David Olby, the managing director of the company, explaining my hopes and intentions. He kindly agreed to supply the materials required. Alf Hanson, the timber department manager, was a great help to me in sorting out a few pine boards of character and colour for this particular job.

It was a great firm that also played a caring role in Bognor by employing many people some with impaired abilities. My attention was caught very early by a portrait of David Olby's father, hung in the shop. It was by a member of the Royal Academy, R.O. Dunlop. When I joined the Bognor Art Society this distinguished painter was the club's president.

I came to know him at our exhibitions and once saw his studio in Barnham, a not very elegant large shed with a corrugated iron roof. He once explained how the small paintings he was selling for eight pounds locally, saw to his household bills. The oil portrait in the shop was not a pot boiler. It was a present, commissioned and paid for by his employees, on an anniversary of the founding of the firm. It was a bold, strong portrayal, and I liked it very much.

I was already known to the person from whom I sought the financial backing, Keith Jay. Keith owned a top quality furniture shop in Bognor. Some time previously we had been neighbours in the small row of shops in the forecourt of Bognor Railway Station. He also agreed to be a part of my scheme and support the idea. Strangely enough Keith's father Sam was also a very public spirited member of the community. He started by supplying a vehicle to assist in the transport of patients to local hospitals which had grown in stature over the years. The minibuses are fondly known as 'Sammies'.

The third person I sought help from was a locksmith and engineer, Ron Biggs. One of my building jobs had drawn me to the workshop he had inherited from his father. It could also have been the fact that he owned a twin to my fret machine, at the moment in pieces awaiting reassembly by him. I was amazed at his array of machinery. There weren't many types of engineering he couldn't do there.

From my teenage years at ENV, with dad, I have always held any machinery for working metal in very high regard. It wasn't easy to coax Ron to make the brass apparatus needed to suspend and turn my spinners. At the time he was up to his eyes in making and flying model helicopters, a passion of his. He had devised a special bearing to support and to facilitate the rotation of my wooden sculptures which, although not enormous, were relatively heavy. He produced a very elegant solution quite in keeping with the beauty of the pine spinners.

Jim then sorted out a pair of electric motors to turn them. My original spinners do not rely on motors for their motion. Suspended on nylon twine they just need a twist to get them going. The wood winds itself up, then unwinds, and so on, until all the energy of the first shove to start them has run out. A simple system.

The Regis Centre was now finished but one final bit of argy bargy came about. We had decided the sculptures should be installed on an elevated section of wall that could be seen from either end of the concourse. What about the electrical point needed for the project? Who was to pay for its installation? In the event the job was done and we never received a bill.

A plaque to commemorate the event was ordered and also paid for by our trio. A circular disc about six inches in diameter of stainless steel, beautifully engraved, naming me, Olby's and Keith Jay as the people responsible for its installation, dated summer 1981. The switch-on was dutifully reported in the press. A photograph showed me halfway up a pair of steps with a large grin on my face. There should have been another photo of me, when with all the frustrations that came with the project, I felt like I was going up the pole, rather than the steps!

Sadly I have to report what happened twenty or so years later. The local council having withdrawn funding, handed the building over to a large brewery. A group of volunteers managed to win support for running the theatre part of the building and the brewery cut the Regis Centre literally in half. The seafront side now houses a pub and a restaurant. Our bit that's left holds the theatre and concourse. The large hall and our café was swallowed up in their conversion. My spinners were on the wrong side. We made extensive enquiries to the brewery and their contractors without success, subsequently my son Jim was told 'they had been binned'. Fortunately the plaque was found and I still have it. So from being up the steps it seems I was now also up a gum tree. Sad isn't it? Three cheers for the photographs, at least we can prove my work was there once. I've got my grin to prove it.

The large picture mural has also gone. One glimmer of hope for future visitors is an embroidered mural made by a local Women's Institute Group, also in celebration of the old Regis Centre. That is still there. Thirteen years later the volunteers continue to keep the theatre open, against all the odds. Son Jim is presently the chairman of the charitable trust that runs it.

As the gala acts had led us to many new venues to perform in so the crafts business also enticed us to some very colourful happenings. Deena and I both loved the steam rallies. A barber from Rustington was the nearest organiser of one such steam rally in Parham that we first attended. We watched this grow to a very sizeable event.

Another was at Netley Marsh near Southampton. We attended this one regularly and met some of our clown colleagues working in their arena shows. We saw Ben Lester and Pierre at various times, with their car acts. Later on I started doing my children's show in lieu of my table cost in the crafts tent. Deena looked after the craft side of the business, whilst I did so. I think I also managed to get a fee as well after I proved myself.

It was a very happy three days gathering with all the steam buffs, veteran vehicles, and individual collectors of all sorts. Fairground organs, fairs, working steam farm machinery of former times, beer tents and evening entertainments. At that time 'The Wurzels' was a favourite act. Once I remember I stood in for an evening performance and did a drawing spot. It went down quite well amongst the hog roasts.

The daddy of these rallies was of course the Great Dorset Steam Fair. I had read about this steam event for a long time but in the beginning I knew it as only one word, Stourpanes. The name itself conjured up all sorts for me, and after seeing it first time I was not disappointed. We also watched this one grow to the enormous show it still is today. It was difficult to see where the great sprawled out event finished.

We were very friendly with the craft tent organisers and it wasn't long before I was also doing a children's show here. Once when we arrived, not being aware of the rule about no entry on site after 6pm, I was in deep trouble. What with the van being choc-a-bloc with craft tables and props there was no room to sleep. I had got used to being able to unload in the tent before nightfall. There were lots of traders having to wait overnight to enter the site and the organisers were in no mood to make any exceptions.

However, a quick conflab was arranged for the officials to decide if we could be helped. In the end I drove back out and was given a guided dark night journey that took me for miles right round the site, to creep in by an adjoining farm gate. By the time we had got all the van contents out and had safely put them in the craft tent, we needed no rocking to sleep that night.

This five day event was used by the Showmans' Guild to show off to the world their finest rides, side shows, and sometimes a full circus. The night scene was particularly exciting. The areas between all the stands and rides usually had a large steam rollers awash with electric bulbs pumping out light from their generators. Their whirling fly wheels causing the whole engine to shake whilst doing so. Large wedges of wood were thrust under the rollers to keep them captive whilst working flat out.

What used to fascinate me was how silent the actual steam power was. Plenty of hissing from the various valves, but the real noise was the result of what the power of the steam compelled the metal bits to do, to produce the light and power. Close up it was a kind of bright magical inferno. Possibly terrifying to the timid, but exciting to the candy-floss munching crowds.

One ride was nearly silent, except for an occasional shriek. The tall helter-skelter doing its job of delivering its mat riding passengers, with a swish, out onto the grass verge.

Early rising meant that you could have a good look around before the gates opened. The American Army enthusiasts showed off all their vehicles of war, including fire engines past and present, parked in orderly lines. I recognised one type that we'd driven about in when working on the Handy Andy commercial, with Pierre.

Groups of travellers, or just pretend ones, displayed beautifully decorated horse drawn caravans seemingly from all over the world. Every day all these groups of vehicles would circle the arena according to the programme times. Over the loud speakers a commentator would say what each vehicle was, its age, the name of the owner and person who resurrected or rebuilt it for its new life of rallying. Wonderful stuff for the devoted onlookers.

We would have our water delivered on site by tankers. The lines of individual loos, mostly blue in colour, were conveniently convenient. It was also one of our most lucrative fairs. Great crowds during the day, and another influx after 6pm. The weather in early September was generally good. The date of the fair of course being decided by crop time. Harvests had to be got in first to clear the site for us lot. Once or twice we battled with the weather. Getting off site problems due to mud were readily solved by enormous tractors giving a helping hauling hand, to get us onto firm ground. Then away we would go, looking forward to the next year's rally.

This was also the time of year for our Guild Annual General Meeting. We usually met on a Sunday in Hassocks, East Sussex, not far from Brighton. Not every member exhibited, so this was the one time we all got together. Each member would bring some eatables and a pleasant meeting could be interrupted by a little stuffing of ourselves and a chin wag. We had some good cooks amongst us.

New members were introduced and the business of the past year gone through. Possible new venues were discussed and difficulties that had arisen during the year were dealt with.

In one meeting the discussion was about applying for charitable status. It seemed that as our Guild was organised at the time, should there be any dramatic downturns finance-wise, like becoming broke, the brunt would fall on our small committee. We needed the protection of being a formally constituted company, together with the advantages to income of having charitable status. This was duly voted on.

The Guild only organised a few events each year, too few for me to earn a living with. There were of course plenty of craft fair organisers that did it for a living. They would book the venues, set up the events and rent out the tables. One of these was a man Anthony James. He was a professional opera singer, and when not working abroad he organised quality craft fairs. We did a lot with him and became friends.

I was impressed how easy it was to find his events. He would always put out special signs on road junctions for the stall holders. This solved a very real problem for me.

He spent real money on advertising so we invariably had good attendances. He bought a couple of pieces of my woodwork and used these sometimes in local shop window displays to gather interest. Not all other promoters did this kind of preparation, or were as professional.

We turned up once to a show in Basingstoke and the 'setter upper' had handed out a few leaflets announcing what was on only that morning. All the table holders soon got fed up with talking to each other, instead of customers. As a matter of fact he actually did us a favour. I was told of a major craft fair that was recenty started. It was held in a well run venue at Viables. Next year and many times afterwards we made regular bookings there.

The Christmas fairs were very good for us. I even ended up doing my party pieces for them. The combination of my clowning and craft work did us well over the years. I remember once though there was no call for my entertaining. The fair was in Dorking Halls. Who should be there but Smokey, Ron Townsend. Smokey was an accomplished musician, an accordionist. It was a lovely surprise to see him working. It was then that he told me he'd done road safety to children well before Pierre and I started. He was also an established clown entertainer long before me.

Later on I was to have my own accordion playing partner. Clown Smiley, Bill English, also an excellent musician and singer. We have both pulled a little away from the stage now, but in former years there's no doubt I could not have had better musical back-up.

Chaper 32

Stuck in the bath

The period from 1980 to 1984 was a very busy time with crafts and just enough variation of jobs to keep me fully employed and happy. It was very heavy work manually for Deena and I, in so far that every outing was rather like moving shop. The hours were very unsociable too. Just as it had been with the Sausage and Egg acts, it was often very early rising with long journeys. But at least then, my beloved wasn't dragged along every time we had a date.

Now we only had ourselves to get up and go, unload, carry in, set up, work all day, then reverse the procedure before we got home to cook and eat a slap up meal, before crawling up to beddy byes. If we'd had a good day, the 'good day' feeling stayed with us right up until we dropped off to sleep. If we hadn't had a good day it seemed a heavy price to pay for the privilege of being self employed.

The carting around of sixteen hundred different names and sculptures was not to be lightly undertaken. Often we would have parking problems. Even if you could find a space, the venues were nearly always in a high tariff region. Charges were skyrocketing. A bigger problem often was the journey from van to table, which seemed in many cases more demanding than the assault courses of my army days.

A new customer requiring my red nose came onto the scene about now. Courts the furniture people. It was a kind of mix and mingle in store on special promotion weekends and bank holidays.

I went prepared with short games and drawings to supplement the large reservoir of plastic balls that the children were romping about in, during normal shop times. The larger stores were increasingly seeing the wisdom of giving the children something to do so the sales assistants could tackle the parents unhindered. The plastic balls were also a sign someone in the toy market saw a niche for their products. Plastic for toys was the new material that was to dominate in their manufacture.

One of the very early companies for whom we used to do the works parties in Wales was Mettoy. Their primary material was metal, as befits their name. As well as our fees this firm always provided Christmas toys for our two children as well.

This work in the furniture store helped this entertainer a lot. With children of all ages, temperaments, size and abilities to entertain, between my offerings and their inclinations it worked well. I enjoyed my stints with Courts, over quite a long period in their different stores. Pleasant places to work in, well paid, and promptly too. I would have liked to have indulged in their merchandise, but there wasn't much chance of that owing to our precarious way of earning a living.

I am always reminded of my mum's first purchase of a new piece of furniture, a Berkeley armchair, when I was nineteen. Strangely enough it was an armchair that was one of our first buys when we got married, but it was nothing so grand as mum's. After the war everything was controlled materials wise, and carried the government logo, 'Utility'. Thus the wooden arms of our new chair were bare. It was still very comfortable though and it was years before it finally left the Brooks' home.

The date for this next bit is easily remembered. February 1980. I made the front page of another of the prestigious crafts magazines, 'The Woodworker'. A friend of ours, Sylvia Hayes, was a local journalist. She had written an article about this unusual combination of clown and carpenter. She herself also had a very special combination of talents, being a retired dancer, and a former member of the world-renowned dancing troupe the Bluebelle Girls of Paris.

Sylvia had taken a series of photographs to accompany her article. In one she had me reclining in a deck chair in our back garden, very comfortably thank you, umbrella aloft, size thirty-two boots to the fore, and a smile on my face that almost made me look handsome. I expect you can guess which of these shots I used to paint a self portrait with. I show it wherever our group exhibits even now. Anyway she got published and it duly got noticed I was a carpenter clown.

Each year, The Woodworker held a wood carving competition. That year the subject was 'clowns', and so my picture was on the front cover with Sylvia's words.

The Woodworker Show was held in the old Wembley Conference Centre. At this moment in November 2006, it was in a state of metamorphasis, in due time to rise again with as a centre befitting the twenty-first century with a brand new stadium to boot.

I exhibited myself a few times at the Woodworker Show. It was always a joy being looked at by fellow craftsmen and wood enthusiasts during opening times. Some were from overseas. I have snaps taken by these folk of me and my stand, with some very complimentary remarks made of my works.

One year I got there with no voice. A cold had put paid to my vocal chords. Some unkind people would say, out of hearing, I'm glad there's something that will shut him up! But it was got over by a series of messages on cards and the help of neighbourly crafts workers. This was prior to me coming to terms with the fret saw from Eileen, so at that time I had no fun names or any workings with plywood. Most of my work was in pine.

All my pine products were finished in varnish to protect them and bring out the colour of the wood grain. There were two main manufacturers. Ronseal and Ruskin's.

While at this show a gentleman came over and spoke to me. He was very complimentary about my work, and I in turn extolled the virtues of Ronseal as a finishing agent. Later I saw the same gentleman on an exhibition stand. It was Ruskin's, Ronseal's rival. I realised I had been talking to Mr Ruskin himself. A few years later I did start using their products in my other calling of prop making. And very good stuff it is too. It was very nice meeting him though.

On returning home from one such event I became very worried. Whilst driving back I realised I was not at all well. What with cramps, aching joints and stiff and painful fingers on both hands I reported to my GP, a Doctor J. McLaughlin, who has looked after me since we moved to Middleton. He sent me to see a specialist in Worthing. He confirmed what was already suspected. It was rheumatoid arthritis. There are several kinds of this disease that attacks various joints and causes painful inflammation. I had the kind that attacks the hands.

When I was in hospital with a damaged knee after falling over, many years ago, whilst running behind buses and lorries, the doctor told mum I had rheumatism. It seemed a bit out of place then. I was only twelve. Now it seems the early signs were already showing. A treatment of steroids followed and luckily I responded. However, much worse was to follow for our younger son Michael. For us, it was the beginning of our darkest and most worrying time.

Michael and his long time partner Hazel, were about to go on holiday to Greece when Hazel, always observant where Michael was concerned, noticed that a mole on the left side of his face had changed. Thankfully she insisted that Michael had it removed before they went away. We are eternally grateful for her persistence, because on their return from Greece, a letter awaited him to report at once to the hospital.

From there it was a roller-coaster of despair and worry for us all, as it was a particularly nasty form of cancer, and a big operation was duly performed. This was not completely successful, and the ensuing very big operation, which saved his life, was performed by a fantastic surgeon, who will always be our hero.

Many months of convalescence followed, waiting for the scars to heal. Hazel was told that with due care and watchfulness Michael would be alright. Thus it was that life took on some sort of normality again, in spite of a few scares spotted in time by the wonderful Hazel.

They are fortunate to have two lovely girls, Tina and Casey, from Hazel's first marriage, and their supporting help, especially from Tina, the youngest, who has always regarded Michael as her 'Pa', has been invaluable.

Back to my troubles again. Being washed by another person, armed only with a flannel, was no real solution. I longed for a bath. So it was decided we would try. I got in alright and I got a similar feeling I had from an experience whilst in hospital a few years before. Complete and utter relief plus the water was lovely too. Then I had just had an operation for haemorrhoids, commonly more known as piles by the ones who couldn't spell it.

My first bath after surgery was a relief that was way past explanation. The nature and the whereabouts of the operation put an end to nature's habit of relieving itself whenever necessary of excess flatulence. The warm water unleashed the pent up pressure likened only to letting a car's tyre down. I seemed to shrink a further three inches lower into the bath. This settling down, ever so gently, produced a look on my countenance of such sheer joy, and relief, I have the feeling many would volunteer to be in the same situation just to experience it.

However, I had just managed to get into the bath virtually unaided, but it was quite another tale getting out. With sore joints and no grip left, I was immovable. My poor wife was very much aware of the fact that her beloved had become a thirteen stone slippery ailing person who denied all her efforts to be prised out of our lovely Victorian cast iron piece of bathroom furniture. Normally water would lubricate movement and be welcomed for this quality, this time being wet worked against us. Letting the water out plus diligent rubbing of towels found me nearly dry but still stuck. With the various strategies we tried it was over half an hour before I was set back on terra firma again. So for quite a while, until my grasp returned, it was back to the flannel and calling out for my back to be washed.

The fact that steroids came to my rescue was not the ideal solution to my problems by any means. Having a serious condition requires using heavyweight measures in tackling it. The strong measures used to gain control again now had to be phased out. So a period of withdrawal was needed, otherwise the drastic treatment itself might begin to cause problems in other organs. It turned out to be a very difficult process, for me anyway. Halving the dose for a while, then halving that further, and so on, took months. Now and again warning signs meant going even slower. But, and it was a big but, I had the use of my hands back, free of pain.

Over the years now, except for the occasional flare up, I have enjoyed good health again. I am now ticking over nicely on a very low daily dose of my powerful ally, steroids. I have nothing but praise for the N.H.S., and the care given by the medical staff.

We visited some very famous and well known places during this period. Another historic fair we did was at Penshurst, Kent. The event was organised by the local scouts, although the significance of this was not fully taken on board until we found ourselves under canvas, in good scouting style, and not in the welcoming portals of the stately home.

Further into Kent we did a couple of years at a hop festival. Seeing the oast houses I incorporated them into my designs and was rewarded with several commissions from customers who chose name sculptures which included this feature, a reminder of their beautiful county.

Whilst growing up, there was a time when large numbers of working class families regularly holidayed in the Kent hop fields, picking hops and getting paid for it. Quite a few were from North Kensington, where I grew up. The camaraderie of these gatherings was also a big draw for them. There are not a lot of places where a group of cockney types could mould into an enjoyable shindig. And the hop picking attracted all sorts.

Most of the historic houses we saw possessed a beauty all their own, built in wonderful countryside when their owners didn't much have to tolerate the planning laws and regulations of today. It was the classic case of 'if you owned the fiddle and the fiddler, you would certainly choose the tune'. The wealthy demanded excellence and could afford to employ the best artisans. A proud statement to the talents of the past.

One such stately pile house we went to was Longleat. We were put in a large marquee in the grounds, overlooked by the house and within sight of the lake. It was a perfect setting. If you had to walk there from outside the estate you needed to allow plenty of time. The grounds seemed vast to me. There was no shortage of customers though, they had already paid to see the house and we were an extra free attraction, similar to the ferry jobs.

Early one morning a tall person from the estate came and had a look at what we had to offer. It was the late Lord Bath. He was attracted to my work and requested me to do a sculpture for his wife Virginia, and his daughter Silvi. After he gave me all the details of what he would like included in my designs, he paid me I remember, with two old crumpled and well handled pound notes, then left. Virginia was very fond of King Charles cocker spaniels and if possible 'could he have some reference to the dogs along with the name'? He also left the design for Silvi to me.

In due course he received my designs and once selected I got on with it. There was one hiccup. His lordship rang me to tell me I had spelt Silvi in my designs with a 'y' instead of an 'i'. I changed the design accordingly.

Having three 'I's to deal with in his wife's name, Virginia, I carved a small cocker spaniel's head on one of them to represent the dot of the 'I'.

My commission completed, I posted both sculptures to Longleat. Within days I had received a cheque and my invoice back, bearing a hand written message stating,

'Thank you, very satisfactory, Bath'. July 8th 1981.

I was increasingly being asked to give talks on my woodwork. The first was for a meeting of Women's Institute area delegates. Then followed two more for the W.I., one in London, and another in the De La Warr Pavilion, Bexhill. It struck me that other W.I.s might also be interested, including those much nearer home. It transpired that one had to audition to get on the list of approved speakers. Off I went to Chichester and demonstrated my prowess to the local selection committee, and was put on the list. You don't have to hold your breath whilst awaiting an engagement as the W.I.s often booked a year in advance. The pay is negotiable and reasonably prompt in coming.

My antenna went up a little higher and I added other subjects to my offer. In the end my 'how I earned a living as a clown' seemed the most popular. Others on my woodwork and 'how to become a lightning sketch artist', did not get quite the same response.

The W.I.s had a strict rule that forbad pressurising members to buy things. Here arose a snag. Showing my woodwork provoked a lot of interest and led naturally enough to enquiries to buy. My solution was to hand out my card if requested that could be followed up after the event. This proved to be an acceptable compromise and I sold a number of pieces that way.

On one journey to a meeting Worthing way, I had transport trouble. I had to get a taxi to finish the journey, arriving late. Luckily the talk was well received, except that the order of the day was upset by my delay. The all important tea and biscuits became somewhat dislocated from normalcy. My causing this was akin to committing a cardinal sin.

Often in our business an entertainer will subsequently take another better paid booking somewhere else on the same day, knowing full well they would not be able to get to the next date on time, so turning up late with some excuse or other. Unfortunately this practice 'tars us all with the same brush' and an unconvinced member complained, in writing. She intimated to the gaffer in Chichester, who was by now a firm friend, that I was trying to sell.

In all my work producing name sculptures only once did I manage to include the subject's surname in the design. I had previously made a name sculpture for the gaffer. Her husband was a keen fisherman, so as well modelling his name in a fishing position I had also managed to work their surname in the turbulent waters. She was well pleased with the result.

This counted for nought though in matters W.I. The gaffer explained the rules of the organisation were 'set in concrete'. I appealed, but the verdict stood and I was taken off the list of the approved! It was such a shame because a large proportion of the members come to the meetings for more than the cup of tea and a chat. Talking to and engaging a group of articulate women was always to me a highly enjoyable experience. I was also not a huge consumer of biscuits nor did I take sugar.

The cost of the taxi back to my abandoned vehicle was more than my fee, but after alerting the A.A. I eventually got home. I might have been better off not to have turned up at all, but that isn't my way. My reason for lateness was genuine, nevertheless I got the boot. 'Just like that', as Tommy Cooper used to say!

To say I was unhappy to ban me from W.I. audiences was to put it very mildly.

Many years on now, I'm looking at a postcard dated 29.2.2003, which says, 'A big thank you from all the ladies of the Working Group of WIs whom you entertained so wonderfully yesterday (a talk on my woodwork). Also our grateful thanks to your Jim for being your chauffeur. Hope your journey back was stress free. Thank you both, Sally Clinton.'

At this point I was well past eighty. I remembered how much I enjoyed the venture. It was like being given a new lease of life. We had a full and very appreciative audience of mature women who must have noticed I was less sprightly now.

Another plus happened that afternoon. Jim recorded my performance on video, the only record I have of the very many talks I have given over the years. So thank you ladies for providing this late opportunity.

There were also large annual craft shows dotted about the country that we regularly visited. One was held on the former Lord Louis Mountbatten's estate at Romsey, a class show, it was a joy to be a part of it. Another was the New Forest Show held in Brockenhurst, and I was invited to attend, and was pleased to be awarded a silver certificate for my display.

We met other craft workers here that we already knew. One, Maureen, a seamstress whose work was often to be seen in our craft shop in Aldwick, had a distinctive theme of children at play sewn on her wares. A feature of this show for me were the cider makers. Beautiful stuff that added a glow to everything around, including one's legs. They got such a soaking sometimes that they imparted more than just a glow, rendering them useless for balance and walking on. Legless is the term used, I think. Strong stuff this!

Appearing regularly on our regional ITV station was a meteorological expert and forecaster named Trevor, affectionately known as 'Trevor the Weather'. I received a commission to portray him as a subject for a name sculpture. A design was chosen by the studio and made up. It was to be presented to him on air, at the same time I was exhibiting at the New Forest Show.

There were several retailers of electrical goods also showing on site and a friend of mine alerted me when the local ITV news was on. I dashed out in time to catch it on a television set in their marquee. I was expecting some sort of presentation to be made after his forecasting spot, him being such a popular personality on the programme, but it wasn't to be so. The announcer held up this small item of my woodwork saying something like 'and here's something that's been made up for Trevor'. No explanation, and no Trevor present. I still don't know to this day whether he ever did get it, let alone if he liked it or not. Very disappointing. My account was settled in due course and that was that.

In the design of Trevor's sculpture I used an open umbrella to represent his initial T. To indicate rainfall a large drip was formed on one of the ribs. A small cloud had a smiling section of the sun peeping over it. The base holding everything together was a choppy sea with a grinning fish half out of the water. If Trevor ever got it, I hope he liked it

Two experiences at the New Forest Show I remember. One nice, one nasty. A visitor to the show came and introduced himself, we were both in the same business, workers of wood. He said he had a great admiration for my work but there was a big difference between us. He was not exhibiting and told me why. Whereas I was happy dealing with many commissions for small amounts, he was quite the opposite.

He took great care in choosing the wood he be worked on. Nothing but the very best to be had. He was pouring in his skill to get the absolute utmost increased value into the job, selling through an agent or gallery.

I really hadn't given the matter much thought then. We had such a different approach. He only worked in wood, but I was keen to explore the possibilites of other materials, like chipboard and hardboard. I enjoyed the variety. I loved the changing scene on the workbench. Not so much a flitterbug, but restless with the new ideas that constantly came into my head. Wasn't I lucky?

The nasty part of being at New Forest was due to a police decision on the exit plan after the show ended. Instead of going out the way we came in the exit route used a forest track instead of a road to form a vast one-way system. This route did not qualify to be called anything but a forest track. It was awful. Miles of it too. The forest might suit the wild life, but I can assure you that the wildest folk in the forest for those few hours were us drivers of cars, lorries and caravans, wondering if our springs would survive the very rough treatment they were experiencing. I never did that show again.

A friend of mine, Nigel Purchase, an artist, kindly let me show a few of my pieces in his Chichester Gallery. It wasn't a success, as my novelty is movement. A lot of my sculptures needed a gentle push or twist to show their true potential. I suppose I should have sought out the same kind of help as with my public sculptures for the Regis Centre. When at craft fairs no such problem existed, because Deena or myself were always on hand to demonstrate.

A few years later we were in Woking, doing our stuff. I was holding up one of my table spinners at the time, when a voice behind me said 'Oh, I'd like one of those'. A female voice gently said 'Well, get one dear'. I recognised the voice. It had not long ago been delivering the Christmas Lectures on BBC2. It was Professor Alan Laithwaite.

Both Jim and I were keen on these lectures. Broadcast over three or four days, they consisted of talks and demonstrations given by an expert at the very forefront of their particular scientific subject. Professor Laithwaite was the authority on electro-magnetism and the inventor of the linear motor that powers high speed trains today, allowing them to 'float' above a special track. He was also an expert on gyroscopes.

He was a large man whose shape and bearing fitted exactly my perception of what the head of an experimental universtiy department should look like. A proper professor. Both he and his wife were very likeable people. As well as ordering one of my spinners, he was also interested to see all my designs and ideas. Living in Surbiton at the time, when he retired, he came to live in Bognor Regis, and we became friends.

Raising the profile of his campaign for a local radio station was a constant for son Jim at the time. To this end he devised a putting contest to raise money and awareness. To add extra interest a prize was offered for the best mechanical putting machine.

There were several entries and Professor Laithwaite generously adjudicated. He also calculated that the way the putting competition had been sequentially organised meant that it would take eight months to complete. With only one afternoon available, changes were hastily made. Later he also kindly contributed to Jim's science programme 'The Brain Exchange' which took to the air on Radio Bognor some time later.

One evening I had a telephone call from the professor. He would like to come and see what I had in stock that would make a suitable birthday present for a forty-year-old. It was for a close friend of his. Prince Charles. heir to the throne!

Chapter 33

Royalty and The Guild

It was while I was in the Sussex Guild that I first got 'aquainted' with royalty. The big news was that Prince Charles was going to attend Ardingly for the South of England Agricultural Show. We were discreetly told he would be visiting our crafts marquee, possibly talking with some of us about our work. I was to be one of our members to have that honour. Came the day. If the presence of more than a usual complement of police wasn't a pointer that someone of import was expected the activity inside our tent was.

These large plain-clothed rozzers had a more than casual look around to see what we had under our tables, in our cases, and I wouldn't wonder, in our pockets as well. Uniformed coppers holding eager inquisitive hounds in check, or nearly so, finished the job. The inquisitive flowing movement of these guardians of the peace then gently flowed out of the tent to do their business in some other spot where the royal footsteps would shortly tread.

A period of expectancy then followed. Charles entered out tent later than stated in the itinerary shown to us previously. It appears he had been delayed in another part of the show, by a presentation of some sort. I bet you've guessed it. I was the last to be presented of our lot. Whilst chatting to the next table an aide appeared, whisper, whisper, whisper, and they departed. I know I've already I've used this couple of words to sum up various parts of this epistle of mine but here goes once more. Ah well!

It doesn't take much of a stretch of the imagination to think if only I had had a few minutes of his time to give him the same demonstration I'd given the honourable professor, in Woking, he might have recognised the two pieces of my work now to be chosen by his friend, for his fortieth birthday! What a to do.

All the 'nearly got there bits' came flooding back from previous years. Pierre and I getting on ITV and BBC. Being in a film with Billy Cotton. Filming with Pat Boone and Co. Being a subject for a thirty minute feature for the BBC Look

Stranger series, and so on. I won't mention being blown up in Jersey as at least that did make the national press, and of course it was more of a direct hit than a near miss. You can't help but laugh at the way things work out sometimes, and in Jersey I was in stitches. Seven of them in my forehead!

Anyway back to the visit of Professor Laithwaite and his charming wife to see what I could suggest for a suitable royal birthday gift. When you come to think of what a person like Prince Charles would have been presented with from all over the world on occasions, I should have been chuffed, and I was, very much. There was only one snag. At the time I could not betray any confidences of my customers so was unable to talk about it. This is the first time I have gone into any details.

I had never thought much about giving specific names for my large sculptures. I should have done so. It would have made it easier to identify them in writing. One of the pieces was designed for the Cathedral exhibition, with a cross in its centre. The other was a continuous saw cut contained in a way that you could wobble it to amuse onlookers. I understand they were well received, and successful.

Another time I came within touching distance of the Royals was a fun day put on by the Variety Club of Great Britain. A lot of disadvantaged children were bussed into the grounds of the Mansion House for a day out amongst us clowns. They were feted and fed and we all worked hard to amuse them. The Duchess of Kent was the big draw. She was the guest of honour at a luncheon party put on by the Variety Club as a fund raising event.

I enjoyed the food put on for us working outside amongst the youngsters. But my very large clown pockets could not have stretched to the price of a ticket allowing me to eat inside. Mind you, she was worth every penny the paying guests were forking out to sit down with her. I admired the lady tremendously. A true worker for valiant causes. The money raised was to be ploughed into even more of the Sunshine coaches that had bussed the children in for the do.

I did notice the sterling work being done by a group of clowns greeting the generous paying guests as they arrived. And I noticed Mr Woo played a leading role here. Afterwards we were awarded beautiful certificates to commemorate the event, and saying 'thank you' for our co-operation.

David Barnes, 'Barney', got in touch again. 'Would I like to take part in the Children's Royal Command Performance'? I was unaware of such an event but didn't hesitate to accept. The performance would be held in the Victoria Palace Theatre. The BBC booked us into a London hotel the day prior to the show. Trevor, Bingo the Clown, took us both in his car and that made it very acceptable. I always disliked driving into the city.

Princess Margaret was to attend. Prior to the star-studded stage show being put on for our young audience, our party of about twenty 'funnies' were told to line the stairs leading from the foyer to her box, providing a guard of honour. The press and television crews were very busy on the stairway, causing it to be somewhat crowded.

It all went off without a hitch. Unfortunately, I was on the blind side of the cameras up the stairs, so the looking in Londoners were quite unaware of my efforts to look terribly 'in earnest' whilst holding my umbrella high above Her Royal Highness as she climbed the stairs.

Doing a mix and mingle job amongst the occupied theatre seats, I did notice the television boffins had anxious looks on their faces. An enormous net of balloons hung overhead, and every now and again one would pop off. The young audience loved it, the sound boys were not amused. So the balloons were let out prior to the show being recorded.

None of us was invited to do anything on the stage that night. Strange that. Most of us were fully paid up members of Equity and professionals to boot. Perhaps it was because we were more widely referred to as children's entertainers, and after all the show was the Children's Royal Command Performance. When the show was on, we discreetly hunted around for any sandwiches that might be available back stage.

A few weeks before, the Winter Olympic Games had thrown into prominence a young daredevil skier who had literally flown into everyone's heart with his giant leaps for English sport. On the Richter scale he had barely avoided dropping off the bottom, but his courage was highly visible to all. It was 'Eddie the Eagle'. A lovely name to have bestowed on a lovely lad. He had been one of the celebrities of the moment gathered to provide an added attraction for the cheering masses that occupied the theatre seats.

Eddie was in the same state as we were, hungry. We met him in the darker depths of the theatre, also on the prowl for grub. A nice lad, and a joy to meet someone who had done something you know you could not have done yourself, even if it had been by 'Royal command.'

There is lots of manoeuvring about in these eighties and nineties of mine.

Unlike the running order in a theatre, my memory has a job keeping on the time track. But one thing is certain, all these things happened.

So much seems to have been our lot to work through that I wonder how we found the time to do it all. One answer might be in the date of the 16th November 2006. Deena and I had then been wed sixty years. The diamond slot.

The cottons, wood, opal, silver and gold have all relentlessly been overtaken along with the rest of the wedding anniversaries. I've gathered a few splinters on the way. Once was when after much aggravation on my part my lovely girl threw a hock of bacon at me. I don't remember whether it was smoked or not. It all ended, as usual, in laughter.

We were coming up to momentous times with the Clown Club. And things, they are a changing! So sang Bob Dylan the troubadour. The folk singers had always to put happenings into songs. After a lot of strumming of chords, a preliminary bedding down of the subject, out comes the real message. And that's what was happening with the International Circus Clowns Club. It was slipping into reality by becoming Clowns International.

No longer was the bulk of us having any tie with a circus, in our country at least, let alone touring the summer months away from where we lived. And the modelling balloon industry was beginning to expand quite nicely thank you. The magic shops were also doing well. There was no way of stopping any entertainer putting on a red nose and declaring himself a clown. More importantly I think is the realisation that lots of people like me were having to be part timers.

In the beginning I remember at my first meetings with the club, I was loathe to stand up and air my views of the current trends, because I had this feeling of guilt about not being strictly bound to get a living out of clowning. Especially for the amount of wages that had to be demanded to carry you from one engagement to another.

The television programme Kilroy had us on their programme. His method of creating a discussion for television was presenting two sides of a current difficulty to argue it out in front of the cameras. The invited audience were supposed to be a mix of circus folk and us. Us being the children's entertainers primarily. But there were no two sides in the studio. There wasn't one full time circus clown with us there.

All the front row were microphoned up and our every word was heard. Members without a mic pinned to their lapel had to wait for Mr Silk himself to thrust the one mobile mic under their noses, for their comments to be heard in a meaningful way. We all liked dressing in a way that put us apart. A made up face and red nose, our object was to create laughter. All over the world my fellow clowns were doing this, but it seemed to me we were working in isolation, and we needed to get together.

So we did what other groups in a tight community had always done, we had planned a grand get together, a 'convention'. The first person I heard mouthing the word was Trevor Pharo, clown Bingo. Once uttered the momentum started to build. I can only relate what was happening in Bognor.

We were not a big town but within a radius of twenty miles or so we had quite an array of non-circus clowns about the place. Bingo and myself were all for the convention being held in Bognor. Butlin's were keen, and they also held out the prospect of being able to accommodate all the visiting clowns.

The local council was supportive, and in the event even the police were encouraged to put on red noses, as a mark of solidarity. Bognor Regis was already in the top register of sunshine resorts, and Royalty in the past had proclaimed its healing attributes, hence the Regis bit.

Anyway we were certainly not an unknown backwater, and not too big. We had a very good chance to include the whole community in the venture. It was solely for that reason Trevor and I put so much effort into its beginnings. The fact that we were living locally meant we got called on for all sorts that required a body on the ground.

The first official convention programme had fine photos of the organisers, Bingo, Barney and Doni. David Barnes, Barney, had plenty of experience organising large groups. Don Stacey, Doni, was a journalist for the Worlds Fair, who could make himself heard internationally. Trevor Pharo, was a business representative for a graphics firm, and had enough drive for all of us. My part was as a co-opted member to deal with schools and raise enthusiasm for the 'Grand Clown Parade from the Bognor Regis Station to the Regis Centre', as stated in the programme.

It didn't quite work out like that. We all assembled in town by the library for the great walk. We were lucky to have Councillor Mrs Margaret Tullet as Chairman of the Arun District Council that year. A delightful person who was an enormous help in bridging the gap between officialdom and the humble citizen. She became well versed in putting on a red nose as the celebration progressed.

We all met frequently. Our friends from Butlin's, the police, council officials and the clowns. One name that stands out for me, was Roger Quinton, a council officer, who looked after my immediate needs and helped me do the school rounds to bump up interest in the convention. My ploy was get the children interested and excited, then along would come their families as well.

Deena and I composed a letter that we sent around to all the local school heads, briefly setting out the marvellous occasion that would soon descend upon Bognor in the guise of a hundred or so clowns. It stated these funny men from all over the country and beyond, had chosen Bognor Regis for their first convention, or get together, and hoped all the good citizens of said seaside resort would join in the fun and entertainments.

'To enable the children and adults to join in as well, we would like them all to take part in the Grand Procession on the Saturday'. It would make its colourful way through the town to the forecourt of the Regis Entertainments Centre where our President, Ron Moody, would do the honours and officially open the celebrations.

'We hope the children will want to dress up and join in. To this end will you allow me thirty minutes of your school's time to show how easy one can dress as a clown without great expense'.

We sent this letter out in plenty of time for the head teachers to make arrangements for the visit. Using the same technique as for road safety, allowing them to select an afternoon or morning visit on a day of their choice, within the period I was touring. Trevor saw to the financial arrangements to spend two weeks work, doing so.

The first time out I managed to gather seven schools to visit. Next year I spread the catchment area wider, and so on, with each subsequent convention. In the fourth year I was invited to over twenty-five schools, such was the interest shown.

The show I took round to the schools had a similar formula as with road safety. Comedy to gain interest before putting across the real purpose for my visit. Using specially made props I suggested funny items for them to copy if they had no ideas of their own. How to make wigs. Jolly up old footwear. Use patches with stitches that could be taken off afterwards if necessary. Making a red nose by cutting out a space in a red coloured table tennis ball. Encouraging mums and dads to put on a bit of makeup. Better still getting all the family to take part..

Reading this now it's hard to realise that in 1985 there were very few joke and party shops about as there are now. Not in our area anyway. I took a few noses with me. Some with elastic attached as well as the clip on types. Later I left a couple of pages of ideas for the art teachers to add to their own instructions on the subject of dressing up and being funny. Jokes on a stick sort of thing. Give them something they could do whilst walking through town. Wavers, whistles, and the like. Carry a school banner, let everybody know where you come from.

The school visits paid off. We had a very good turn out for a first time. I made myself a stop and go symbol on a broom handle to control the children en route. I led from the front. Out went the clowns, the bands, the stewards, and we followed. A small but very pretty children's marching group, wearing white curly wigs, leading. It was enchanting.

Up London Road through the town to the Regis Centre. Crowds all the way, cheering, waving, laughing, some grandparents crying. We slowly wound our way to the Place St Maur where Ron Moody and the organisers, plus distinguished visitors, awaited us in an open-topped bus. I was still busy seeing to the various schools' children and keeping us all together while the greetings, speeches and other formalities proceeded.

Then a lovely surprise, Mrs Highly, headmistress of Climping School and her husband, also a head teacher, drove into sight in their well worn estate car loaded with soft drinks and biscuits for the young marchers. A much welcomed surprise. She had organised this on her own initiative, unbeknownst to me. Anyway, she taught us all a lesson and in subsequent years we made provision for it to be a properly organised part of the programme.

Starting in 1986 I was able, through the generosity of local shopkeepers, to organise a small gift for each child as well. The fact that in the district we had an internationally known company of seaside rock makers, Lewingtons, to call on, helped.

I made myself known to them and they kindly did up a batch of rock with the name Bognor Regis, printed in red letters right through. That in itself is an achievement that takes some licking! They never called it a batch, to them it was a boiling, and for us it was at a much reduced price. In 1987 they supplied us with rock bananas. Each year we changed it where we could. Any of these sweetmeats left over we used as prizes for other things.

Being an art fanatic and a member of a local art group I suggested to the committee I ran an art competition to bring in that section of Bognor talent. They agreed. With the generous help of my friend Keith Jay, I had one hundred pounds in cash to use as prizes. So with ten prizes of ten pounds each to offer,

I enlisted four judges of standing in the local 'arteries' to adjudicate. With no exhibition space or stands at our disposal, the entrants were to arrive outside the Regis Centre at a certain time, complete with picture, to be judged.

What a cheek. But with the weather on our side and the informality of it all it was a real success. One important reason for this was the work of Mr Scott of JP Printers Ltd., a Bognor firm that supported us all through with their free posters. Our local tradespeople really did all I ever asked for in some way or another.

The following year we got art display stands from local groups and lined the shopping arcade with them, so didn't have to rely on the weather being kind to us.

On display in the Regis Centre was a marvellous model circus owned by the Silvers family. I remember Trevor telling me that he'd worked hard to get them there and it was a great success.

In the weeks before the convention, Trevor, me, and any clown we could rope in, held workshops over the weekends in the Royal Hall, for the local children. Whether we helped any potential youngster to become one of us, is hard to say, but they were very enthusiastic and enjoyed the romp. We threw in a bit of a show as well, to capture their interest. After that very hectic start in following years we were more organised I did a spot on the theatre stage for one of the first convention's children's shows.

Anyway there was no shortage of volunteers. Deena and I thoroughly enjoyed the gala shows. All the other trimmings such as the civic reception, our closing conference and Annual General Meeting all went well. Of course to me it was wonderful meeting all our clown friends from all over. A very rare occasion, until we held this, our first ever convention. Even then it was only short encounters. They were all busy doing alfresco entertainment about town, in hospitals and public places. Everybody worked hard to make it a success, and it was. And there was no doubt we'd all be doing it again next year.

But before that, Bognor town forked out for a very pleasant lunch for all the organisers and co-opted members, in a hotel in Pagham. It was a very nice thank you to all of us who helped make the convention work for Clowns International and the town itself. The amount of publicity, the television coverage and world-wide interest it had aroused was a perfect justification for the title of Clown Town. I know Trevor put up quite a few notices to that effect, that might have been frowned upon if permission had been asked for first.

So the event went down in history. That is not to say the whole story has been told fully. This is me and Deena's part in it. It's time someone drew all these events together while most of us have some teeth left and have not been driven gaga by all the regulations we now have to observe. I am very lucky I came on the scene when I did. I'm not sure if it could have ever started at all in today's climate. Indeed I'm not sure whether all my school work involving the children could be fitted in now, with the current strictures of today's curriculum .

From my work records it seems as if the pace of life itself had increased in pace and quality. Ideas for new pieces of woodwork came flooding in to me on the workbench. My fun names in plywood came into being about now. Apart from just names I also started what I called 'small and large' miscellaneous designs. 'Shut the gate'. 'Please, no smoking'. 'I love you'. 'There's no place like home'. 'Bathroom', and a great seller, 'The Loo'. All nicely presented and reasonably priced. It wasn't long before I cottoned onto the appeal of football clubs. Liverpool was favourite for a long time. Each of these designs sported a football somewhere. In Liverpool of course it was the dot over the i.

In pine also things were happening, I did a series of nursery rhymes, all free standing. The Humpty Dumpty one was a tipper lorry tipping debris from a brick wall, with parts of an egg clearly visible in the rubble. The name Sinbad was being transported by longboat with himself at the tiller. The dot on Christopher's i was a robin.

Not back slapping humour by any means, but adding a smile to a design as extra appeal. For one major exhibition I did a selection of the Royal Family in pine. I was told the Queen's name, Elizabeth II, had the wrong crown over the i. (I had a Victorian one it seems). The Queen Mum's was set against a view of the Castle of May. The design I did for Charles and Diana enabled me to suspend a small heart by a nylon thread, to represent the i in Diana.

I was still making props when the idea for a different sort of bouquet was worked out and made. The prop flowers had room to allow a few fresh flowers to intermingle with, and so keep a sense of reality about them. Of course, hidden in the wrappings was the inevitable target launcher, primed ready with a blank cartridge to send the bunch upwards at the appropriate time. A good prop to be used at fete opening ceremonies. A warning in red letters though to let the recipient of the bouquet know in advance of the outcome and what will happen when an obvious friendly gesture results in the fete being opened with a bang.

My birds game came into being now. It was a simple game with five birds that hadn't yet learned how to fly, aimed at four-year-olds and playgroups. By sitting the birds on one end of a stout but small see-saw arrangement, then belting the other end with a semi-hard mallet, the birds were launched up into the air one by one after all and sundry called out, '1,2,3 Fly'. One of our helpers was to catch them in a basket. 'We mustn't hurt them if they fall back to earth, you see!'

The real point of this being I tried out working in plastic foam and coloured felt to make the missiles. There was Olly Owl, A Dragon, Clara the Duck, one called Carrot Nose and Beaky. Using a contact adhesive to stick the foam and the coloured felts together, they could be used in any front room or church hall without causing damage of any kind. I found these materials very useful for other games also. They were colourful, light and very hard to damage. It was the beginning of my interest in using other materials, with non-wood sculptures in mind.

Chapter 34

Using New Materials

I had been making carnival heads for a number of years using cardboard and wire netting as a base on which to apply papier mache for the finished surface. Modelling the overall appearance as the head progressed. For this work I amassed a quantity of cardboard I could draw on when needed. The bottom panels of lettuce boxes were ideal. Each visit to a supermarket added to my stock. Deena also was instructed on which boxes to choose as well. Unstained and without ventilation holes punched through. It was whilst I was cutting these bottom panels out I had an idea for the sides of the boxes.

A garden ornament that would spin around in the wind. First I cut out strips of cardboard about three inches wide by twelve inches in length that were tapered at both ends. I then pierced a small hole in the centre of each piece.

By fixing a cycle spoke upright in a board, I then threaded the pieces onto the spoke, glueing one side and then advancing the next piece slightly in a clockwise fashion past the previous one, and so on, producing a screw like effect. Building this to about thirty pieces high I then left it for the glue to set, repeating the process five more times.

A good few years before this, Deena modelled some small wire figures complete with clothes and uniforms. I made the wire skeletons for her to work on. Friend Fred Jackson, the blacksmith, had supplied me with some copper coated welding rods which enabled me to solder them together.

I now used these rods, about a yard long, to thread all the bits onto, glueing them together as I did so. Ending each end of the rod to form an eye, I hung it up in a tree on a short length of nylon cord and watched it rotate in the breeze. When the wind stopped winding it up, it unwound, just as did my pine spinners. I had to twist the wooden ones to start them going. The garden ones were going one way or the other all the time as long as there was a breeze.

I made no attempt to make the first ones weatherproof. Later I did so by putting a layer of cloth over them, as one would put on a coat of papier mache, using a PVA glue. To keep the weather out I varnished them. I did a whole series of these using different shaped layers of cardboard.

A disappointing moment came when I attended a craft fair and saw a wooden one for sale. Coloured wooden slats could be folded flat or arranged like a screw. The seller explained he'd bought them in to re-sell and the idea was hundreds of years old. There seems nothing is new in a world where some civilisations had been up and running for thousands of years before ours had even learned to walk properly.

There are far more people with jobs that have regular working hours than us self employed, but it would be a mistake to think that people like me are able to work, or not, as the mood suits us. Life is not all that it seems. I never really stopped working. The time of day was not set in stone when I was at the bench fiddling about with some idea or other. Much of the time there would be far more than just one thing to think about. The working day would be spent on any job that was in hand. No finish, no cash. That rule applied to everything.

If you failed to make it to a children's party, craft fair or anything that required your presence, or if you turned up late, reductions in your wages were usually the result. Transport then, be it by car, van, cycle, or shanks's pony, was the number one priority.

Whilst building, my vehicle was a tool carrier. Whilst clowning I was moving different tools. Props. For school visits it was the same. When I changed from a Fordson van to a camper van, the garage that was seeing to my needs locally closed. As a result some redundancies came about for its employees. One, Peter Trent, decided to go it alone and I was one of his first customers.

Pete looked after my camper and kept it going for me for years after. As well as being a self-employed motor mechanic, he was also a part time fireman and, over the years, if there was a 'shout' and I heard the clanging of bells, then sirens, my fingers were always crossed for my four wheeled steed. Behave yourself, Pete's busy.

After the convention I was back on the runs to fairs and giving talks to earn the wherewithal. Some of these jobs were kind of different. A Cow Pie Rally in Dorking. Young Farmers Club in Crawley. Penshurst, Bentley, Liss, Hever Castle, Chertsey, Aldershot, Corn Exchange Brighton, Guildhall Portsmouth, All were points of the compass where duty called. Some were regular visits, others, one-offs.

One ploughing match we attended was remarkable for its weather. Arriving early for the competition in fields which had just been harvested, we found the competition already underway. The sun was shining and spread out before us was an idyllic scene. Tractors ploughing away. Furrows as straight as could possibly be wished for by the toiling drivers.

Then the public arrived and the weather began to play play more than a trick or two. Down came the rain, and the surface of the ground became a slippery nightmare. Flanders and Swan's rendering of their hit song 'Mud, Glorious Mud' immediately sprang to mind, followed by cries of 'oops' from the more polite, but slipping visitors. In general we were always able to deal with the vagaries of our British weather, but you can't put a ploughing match in a marquee.

Our set-up now was changing to suit our expanding business. In the early days we just had a table, a chair, and a cloth to cover it all. Now there were two tables and various other bits to position. My two-tiered system of drawers that held the myriad of fun names. Larger drawers for bigger designs. For fun names we had four drawers each for boys and girls. There were other compartments for more rarely asked for or names with obscure spellings. So if our rented space was, say, eight feet square, then three sides would be formed by pull-out drawers and boxes holding stock.

I had purchased two rolls of clear plastic tubing. From these I made up sachets eight inches deep with the name of the contents marked in black for boys and red for girls. Each contained about four fun names. Only one would be finished ready for sale, with a red dot on its back to denote I had cleaned its edges.

The unfinished names had just come off the saw that left jagged edges sometimes. As we sold one I would clean up another to replace it. I had a small working table that took only about three square feet of floor space. To anchor it for safe working I used to sit on its in-built seat. Thus while Deena sold stock I worked to replace it, adding that visible hand-made touch to our stand at the same time.

We felt we were an asset to any show in so far as it we provided a constant demonstration of craft work. Deena also had a sideline for the ladies. Hand crafted Art Noveau style pewter jewellery from France, a leftover stock from our shop days. Of course we didn't sell bought in items at craft events organised by the Guild.

There was another use for the sides of the lettuce boxes. Apart from buying paper bags to put the plywood goods in, I also carried a stock of pre-cut pieces of cardboard, to put in with the fun names. A safety measure well worth the trouble to reduce possible breakage on their journeys home.

A very important part of selling the thousand or so designs we carried, was letting our customers know we had them. I had recently taken an armchair apart which had been covered in a kind of artificial leather. I then re-formed this hide into a belt about twelve inches wide that revolved around the two large rollers. On this I printed all the fun names in stock and other items for sale. I still have it, and when sometimes I glance over the myriad of names on its surface, I wonder just how we ever did it.

Along with the roller we needed displays as well. Cutting six pieces of card just larger than our name-sized paper bags, I sandwiched them together between two continous strips of felt, leaving an inch of felt between each card. Glued in on both sides, the cards provided backing on which to attach the fun names.

The whole thing could then be hung like a banner from the back screen, displaying six names or so as examples. We used strips of masking tape rolled up, so it was sticky all round, to attach the names on the display, and the spaces between the cards allowed the whole thing to be rolled up, with the fun names inside, for storage.

It was soon coming round to our second clown convention. This time, as in our first year, the event was to be held early in the spring. Later on and the circus touring season would have already started, and some of our members would not be able to attend.

The second year programme had a page of thanks for the people who had made such a success of our first time out in the conventions game. Also a nice picture of our pipe smoking president, Ron Moody, with fresh photographs of Barney, Bingo and Doni, the organisers.

There was also a mention of yours truly, Clown Kerby Drill, with thanks for 'his hard work in enthusing teachers and school children in the area'. Another big thank you for the teachers and children for their participation in the event. Nice paragraphs that nestled amongst the list of credits due to all the other hard working members from the council, Arun Leisure, Bognor Chamber of Trade, Butlin's and others that had co-operated so successfully in 1985. Bon voyage for the 1986, event coming up.

We increased our catchment area for the school letters in our second year.

No doubt the publicity of the first event had been well circulated and the increase in interest showed itself by an increase in requests for a visit by myself.

The basic show I took around was the same except that I altered my prepared drawings for those schools that had seen me the previous year. A prepared drawing is one that I had practised beforehand and could be reasonably confident of a good result. Name drawings taken from my audience of course I had to work up in the moment. We had some new additions. The Art and Craft Show 1986 was far more structured. Keith Jay came up trumps with another hundred pounds for prizes.

Ken Ford, a local artist who ran the Downlands Arts Centre, gave a special award for the 'Most Imaginative Entry.' His prize was a free course of attendance at the Centre, which was held in the Old School in Felpham. He was also one of our panel of judges. That year the subjects were, 'Clowns', 'Clowning', and 'Crazy Car or Vehicle,' with free entry as before. To show an example I made a small model car out of cardboard which could be extended like a trailer to carry a stick of Bognor Regis rock. It is now resident in our clown museum.

Deena and I took on the schools together for the first four years. So much happened in this period. We had four different Mayors, a change in council personnel, and folks on the committee came and went. With continuing support from the council and officers, Dick Coen, Roger Quinton, Alan Caig, and all the staff of the Regis Centre and the Tourist Office, the event grew in stature and importance.

Each time out the convention and procession grew and grew, with increasing schools support it blossomed into an international event. There was so much to appreciate in those times, but my greatest pride remains the Saturday march through town with all the clowns and children. It was the crowning moment for me, involving as it did most of Bognor town, and for me the most memorable part.

Each year Deena and I devised a different competition for the schools to get their teeth into, and each one caused us to work very hard sorting out the rewards. We decided giving rosettes and certificates was the most effective way to do this.

I found a supplier in Bristol to make two sizes of rosettes for us. Large ones for schools' achievements and smaller ones for individual awards. In the end we were ordering these in their hundreds. I had two or three places where the entries could be put on show. In the Regis Centre itself, the windows of the tourist office and sometimes in Boots the Chemists window, in town.

Once I encouraged the children to do life size pictures of clowns to hang on a coat hanger. That year the entire wall space of the Regis Centre concourse was covered with the children's work. What a job putting them all up that was. I had left Deena to go round the schools first to judge and collect them, not forgetting taking them down afterwards and returning them. But what a sight it was to see.

Another year the children were set a task of designing a birthday card for a clown. A further task was designing wrapping paper for a clown present. The one competition that I remember every detail of was to make a clown egg.

I made about six examples to show what could be done, on my visits to schools that year. Explaining how to blow the eggy contents out of the shell before you decorated it. How to use a defunct toilet roll tube as a very reasonable substitute for a body. How to use all sorts of bits and pieces of everything imaginable to dress said clown or clowness with. The response was incredible.

It also bore out my belief that the key to involving the community in our event was to work through the children for the best result. Obviously the older children were more skilled and able, but there were some marvellous efforts by the younger ones too. However, when we saw entries described as the work of a Jimmy Jamjar, or a Penelope Pincushion, with their ages given as five or six, the parental input was quite obvious. But it would have been a foolish person that would point a finger.

The Tourist Office windows looked out onto the forecourt of the Regis Centre, so with everybody helping we made a great display inside that everybody could see. Bognor Regis is regularly top of the U.K. sunshine league, known by the weathermen, world-wide. Blessed with its fair share of sunshine, some of which fell on the Tourist Office windows, a fault in our choice of venue for our display of our egg-based clown figures began to emerge.

There could have been any number of explanations why my explicit instructions about blowing the egg out first did not reach the ears of many of the competitors, but it was soon an unmistakable fact that this was the case. Also I had noticed that by the weight of some entries that even boiled eggs had been used by some.

First came an uncomfortable feeling as you entered the Tourist Offices that something was amiss. Each day increased this feeling. We had a good spell of spring sunshine that finally produced a pong that could no longer be ignored.

It must have been a strange sight, seeing us behaving like sniffer dogs, from the outside, rooting out the culprit eggs that caused the terrible smell. I can only say that in subsequent years the staff looked very closely at my requests to use their windows for displaying the current year's competition.

I photographed all the eggs in their respective school groups before returning them. With every competition I did this, so I have a very good record of what we achieved during our four years at the reins. My only regret was not having a flash on my camera at the time. Relying on a light meter in our lounge, my studio, the photographs are not as bright as I would have liked.

For one of the conventions I loaded Jim up with plenty of film and he did a wonderful job for me recording the gatherings and the walkabouts. We were very lucky to have started the conventions when colour photography had become the norm. The manager of our local Boots, Mr Bageley, was a great supporter of the event, and did us proud developing the pictures for me. My one regret is not having much in the way of photographs recording the Regis Centre's concourse walls covered with the children's paintings and drawings.

Another idea we put into practice was a clowns auction. At first we did it to support local children's charities. I did the rounds of the shops for items to be included in the sale. I am looking at my receipt book for 1986 so it's not a big deal for my memory here. Peters Newsagents, St Mary's School, The Body Shop, Homar Water Softeners, Glade Infants School, Boots the Chemists, W.H. Smith, Presto Supermarket, Elmer Post Office are listed. Just a small selection of the many that donated items. The event was later developed to include clown memorabilia and a much wider net spread, for future auctions.

The local weatherman, Les Allat, who was also a great good doer in our area, supplied me with the names of four local charities that received a cheque from the proceeds.

For one of the years I painted pictures of twenty clowns or so, as a gesture of support. Some real, some out of my head. This was also the year of small stickers advertising the event for lapel use. Also I had some mini certificates printed on which I drew my face names for one and all.

Kooky, who organised the clown's workshop programme, asked me to host some sessions. The most successful one was on prop making. I remember explaining the operation of one of my favourite discoveries, the target launcher.

This used a blank cartridge to fire an empty tin can into the air. Intended for taking pot shots by the shooting community, I had used it in a number of props requiring something to be launched skyward with a bang.

I explained my own Pop Plant, that could grow about eight feet in an instant if the fertiliser used is a sort of gunpowder. The main body of my talk though was about the growing range of adhesives available, and which I found most suitable in bonding the many materials like leather, felt and plastic sheeting that needed to be stuck safely together when making props. Afterwards the response of the older clowns, who like me, had mainly had a go at making their own props, was very heartening. I was on their wavelength and they said so.

I also did a workshop on my working in schools. Using my puppet routine with Tufty to explain that although the comedy element was important, it was the teaching element that was the reason for going into schools, enabling you to receive wages from the RSO's budget.

Three lovely surprises came to us during this period. Deena and myself were awarded two civic awards from Arun District Council. The third was given to me by Clowns International. An Honorary Life Membership. All three were given in gratitude for the work we did with the children.

During the conventions I didn't have time to do any al fresco work, but I was able to contribute to some of the stage shows. Some in the Royal Hall and others in the Alexandra Theatre. I loved working in the theatre. It was just the right size for me. You could really get a grip on the audience. Young or not so young. Out of convention time I worked a Saturday morning show for children with Malcolm the Magician, a local entertainer. We worked alternate weekends.

Since the Regis Centre opened in 1976, I've been a regular performer there over the years. Always a supporter of the venue through thick and thin, and it's had a very checkered existence. As the councils of Bognor and Arun have played havoc with on and off funding, so we've had to fight to keep developers from building flats on the site.

After closing for a short while, it re-opened as 'The Watershed'. To help popularise the newly-named centre I lent them ten of my large, full size copies of the impressionists' most popular and well known paintings as décor. I remember this well owing to the brick walls on which we had to hang the paintings. They were a beautiful cream colour, but as tough as old boots. Trying to drill them for a rawlplug was agony.

But when they were up it was well worth it. There were copies of works by

Manet, Van Gogh, Lautrec and others by Renoir, which included 'The Dancer', 'Two Circus Girls' and a full size 'Umbrellas'.

The battle to keep our only remaining entertainments venue has gone on ever since. The Watershed became The Hotham Arts Centre, and now it is The Regis Centre again. The latest plan to build 168 flats on the site only being thwarted by the credit crunch.

Run now by a charitable trust, Arun Arts, the Regis Centre is putting on more shows, and even cinema, than it hosted under council control, and it doesn't cost a penny on the council tax. This must be a big embarrassment for the council that still claims 'it isn't viable and should be demolished'. What a turnaround. 'Tis all a far cry from the heady days of the first clowns convention.

I have every confidence that it will enjoy continued success in volunteers' hands. But I would, wouldn't I. Son Jim is the chairman.

Chapter 35

Jim's Studio and Hiring Paintings

Looking back before the first convention a couple of items need a mention I think. Striving to get notice for the coming of the clowns, press interest spread to radio and TV. One morning I had a call from the BBC 'Today' programme on Radio 4.

'We are interested to hear about the new clown convention and would like a couple of minutes air time please?'

I knew that Bingo had been contacting ITV and commercial radio for this sort of response for a while now. So silly me, I mentioned this to the caller. I might as well have hung up then. The mention of their great commercial rival ended all interest in my nuggets of knowledge about what was going on in Bognor. They never rang back.

We did have more success with television and we were invited to appear on the 'Wogan' nightly magazine programme on BBC1. About a dozen of us turned up at the Wood Lane Television Centre. I took my 'pop plant' prop along to surprise the great Terry with, and it did. Also on his programme that night was the famous American singer Howard Keel.

As 'supporting' guests we were firmly put in our place by the management. Although it took not inconsiderable expense and effort to get us all there, we got nowt for doing so, and never got a sniff of the green room facilities. I don't think they even indicated the presence of a tap so that we could get a drink of water.

I could have imagined a rather shy invitee on the programme being overlooked in the hurly burly of the studio. But our lot, outrageously dressed, large footed, heavily made up men wearing wigs and mostly with spherical red noses on, being overlooked or forgotten about, seemed odd to say the least.

For one convention opening ceremony I made up a puppet clown figure about eighteen inches in height out of plastic foam that I called Brian. He

Leading Barnham School

Deena as De De

Deena, Tina and me

Deena's clown shoes

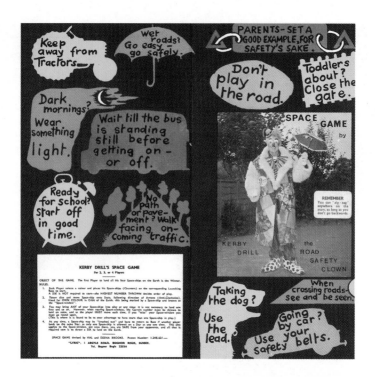

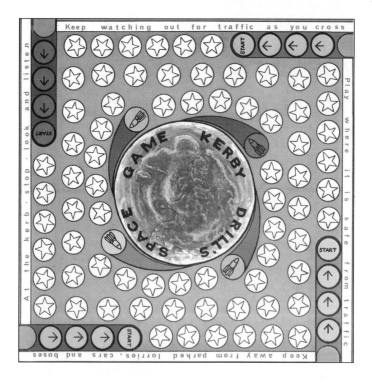

The board game I patented

With my 'nurse',
Tricky Nicky

Bingo, Smiley, Jim and me

Some popular plywood designs

My painting of Pierre and Verco (Arthur Pedler)
in Chitty Chitty Bang Bang

Pine candleholders

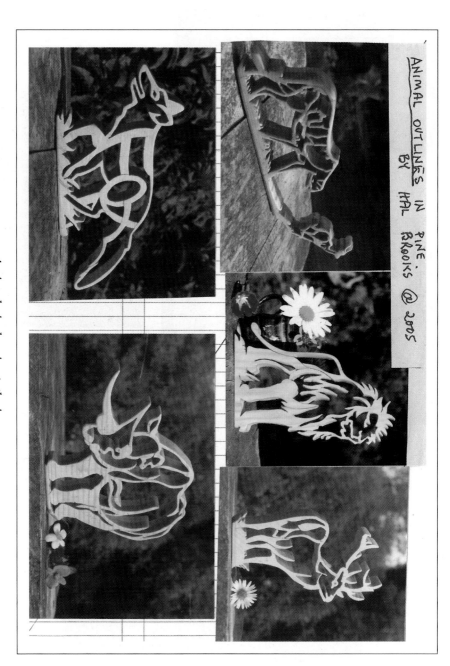

Animals in laminated pine

More pieces in pine

A spinner for the Professor

My three pieces for Chichester Cathedral exhibition

Pigeon for Ronseal

HAL BROOKS

Guild craft table card

With TV presenter Peter McCann

An owl for Wilfrid

Me with pick-up sculpture

On the cover of
'Woodworker Magazine'

Announcing 'Look, Stranger' in
Radio Times

On the cover of
'The
Craftsman'
magazine

On the cover of
'Independent Forester'
in Canada

Made for a Millwall
supporter

Popular 'I Love You' plywood Fun Name

A school shield

More plywood fun names

Baby Austin trophy

Bognor rock carrier

*With musician 'Smiley'
Bill English*

Dancing jig dolls made for Jim

Horse 'Trier' ridden by 'Major Blunder'

Diana clowns around

THE Princess of Wales had a fun day out at sea yesterday, and among the characters she met aboard the QE2 off Cowes, Isle of Wight, was Kerby the clown. She was attending a party for 400 underprivileged children who cheered her as she came aboard. The Princess wore a peach seersucker skirt with matching fitted jacket.

Onboard QE2 with Princess Diana

More of my Paintings

Self portrait and others

The weather

Light and Sight

Michael's farmhouse and barn in France

The two of us

Some of my 'Impressionists'

Top: Number Sculptures
Middle: Name sculptures, Claire likes cats and frogs
Bottom: Two American visitors wanted mementos of London

Some more of my 'Impressionists'

The Plum

The Loge

A Bar at the Foilles-Bergere

reminded me of a friend of that name. The business was this. Ron Moody would announce that Brian could only squeak rather like the sound of a miniature taxi horn, so he would interpret for him. Standing Brian on his hand, with a squeaker buried in the puppet's torso that Ron could tweak, he announces that the small clown was a poetry lover and could he please say a bit on this auspicious occasion. He had learnt the poem 'If' by Robert Louis Stevenson.

The fact that Brian was made in two parts was not revealed to the waiting crowds. The lower torso also concealed a target launcher, plus tin, plus a blank cartridge, plus Brian's upper torso, the head, on top of the tin. The action to go as follows. A few squeaks from Brian and Ron interprets.

'If you can keep your head when all about you are losing theirs', whereupon the said interpreter pulls the plunger of the target launcher that should catapult Brian's head in the air, with a bang. After only a brief period of rehearsal prior to the opening speech and instruction by Kerby Drill, Ron's hand slipped and nothing happened. Slight pause, try again.

'If you' and so on, another misfire. Ron being the trouper that he undoubtedly is took a more robust view of the whole procedure the third time. 'If you can keep your bloody head' - Bang. Off went the clown's top half high in the air.

The gag was well received and through the perseverance of our intrepid president. He then got on with the official opening of the convention, to loud and prolonged applause. If this all sounds a bit made up I have three sequential photographs to prove it.

In the first photo Ron turns to crowds assembled just below him with an 'about to start' expression, holding Brian. The second shot looks as though Ron's got his gander up. The third photo shows Brian's head firmly in space, presumably going up to meet the poet himself.

What also was a surprise to me when I recently uncovered the photographs was that at the time I was wearing my nice new clown suit that Deena had made for me. It also revealed me to have been quite near enough to be fully aware of any well deserved expletives aimed at the maker of the prop, during the first and second attempts.

Music has always been a part of my life and so it was no surprise that it found a decent home for itself when we moved to Bognor. Jim was playing the violin and I was never far away from the piano. With money he earned for himself humping campers' suitcases to their chalets, he bought a drum kit. Shortly afterwards he indicated a desire to buy a guitar.

True to the Brooks' tradition he wanted the best, a Gibson. It was a lot of money then but quality always costs more. He earned the money and paid for it himself. Interest then blossomed into Irish folk music and to this end, jigs and reels. We spent many an afternoon modifying the bridge of his violin to help with the fingering required for the speed of some of the tunes.

While all this was going on his desire to record the songs was growing. Learning the business of electronics in Portsmouth Polytechnic was also a daily matter. So it wasn't long before the first recording equipment appeared in our house. Not a large affair at this time but sufficient to attract all his music and folk-minded mates to descend on us.

A musical afternoon would be something like this. The control would be in Jim's bedroom. The drums set up in another room and various other performers dotted about the house, all microphoned up with headphones on. The vocalist was in the hall downstairs.

They could all hear each other but poor Deena and me, we only got fragments. Every now and again the vocalist would belt out a few bits of the lyrics seemingly willy nilly, amongst all the cables connecting each to the other about the house. It was later when we moved out and Jim had the house to himself, that finally we built a proper studio, and a separate control room.

The middle bedroom became the studio. The small box room was used to enlarge the control room. I was engaged in making new windows, triple glazed, and soundproofing doors, walls and ceilings. A massive job all told but when we finished it became the home of Airship Recording Studio. Later still, it became the Radio Bognor, then South West Sussex Radio, with regular transmissions throughout the day. But Jim should tell the rest of this story. I only did as I was told!

One interesting thing came out of the soundproofing of the walls of the studio. After covering them with insulation board, the whole area was covered with an insulating felt. To break up any reflective sounds the felt was held in position by thinnish wood battens nailed slightly apart from each other. The battens were about six inches longer than needed. This resulted in me having about a hundred off-cuts six inches long. It is exactly this sort of situation that sparks off my imagination.

There must be a use for them somehow, so hang on to them 'til I could be inspired. If this takes time, years in fact, there is room for them somewhere on a shelf. I used to muse about other people's workshops as seen sometimes in magazines. Everything neat, tidy, precise arrangement of different size chisels on the walls. So different from my own.

Later I decided to glue these off-cuts together into a cube. Using my laminating process, I placed each layer at right angles to the other and made a solid block from which I carved one of my nicest sculptures. It bears the name 'Evolution'.

Just a little something for nothing. Jim had to retile his roof. Whilst there was easy access to those dizzy heights, he painted his six chimney pots different colours. It's something to do with the genes I think!

It was after the fourth convention Deena and I decided to step down from the schools programme and let others, with possibly fresh ideas, to take the strain. There was no denying that we were feeling the strain a bit. To save any embarrassment to anybody following we decided to take a holiday whilst the fifth convention was on. Deena had always been very interested in the Potteries and their wares, so off we went up north. This time, without the ties of any road safety programmes, we could holiday together.

Making for Stoke-on-Trent we visited all the factories that offered inspection. Of course though it was essential to hold the convention early so it wasn't really the time of year to seek the sun and do a bit of paddling in the sea. In fact the further we went up the colder it got.

The weather was reasonable though and we really enjoyed the Wedgewood Factory. It was as well organised as you would expect a factory with that heritage would be. The 'how it's done' processes, and the nitty gritty of many hands on making things, have always been my number one interest. Quite different from my own way of working where I alone am responsible for every part of the process, from idea to finished product.

The Colport situation was different. I remember a brick circular kiln of yesteryears, being in the forecourt. The beauty of their decorated vases was quite outstanding. The prices reflected the amount of time the pieces cost to make. Well above our pockets then.

We were in our Landcruiser at this time and needing somewhere to stay overnight we saw a sign indicating a camping site. It was off the main road and without thinking anything amiss I just followed. We were gradually climbing and finally came to said site.

Being out of season we didn't expect trumpets announcing our arrival. It was obviously a farm with plenty of ups and downsey bits. We finally found the owner who said yes, his was a camp site, and we could put up overnight. When we saw the facilities we should have turned round and gone straight back to civilisation.

Now getting dark we decided to brave it. We were pretty well independent in our van and, as the only one on site, we got on with cooking a meal. By now it was very dark and the wind was getting up. With the radio on for entertainment, accompanied by the howling of the wind, we wondered what we had let ourselves in for. Getting colder, even before it started snowing, it provoked stories by the Bronte Sisters into the consciousness. If one of their heroines, Cathy, had been out there, she would surely have been better off in the van with us.

We had two plusses on our side. Deena thought I was the bravest of the brave and I thought she was too. So we were well supported. I was not surprised how quickly the weather could change up there, I'd witnessed similar in the Yorkshire Dales, but now we couldn't just drive out of it. We were stuck for the night. As a matter of fact we were stuck in the morning too. When daylight finally came, ice and snow abounded.

We didn't argue about the cost of our stay, we just wanted to get going. Then was revealed the biggest problem of all. I hadn't taken much notice of the fact that it had been uphill coming , by how much, I was soon to discover when I got back on the road. What surface was underneath the snow and icy patches on the road I never found out. All I knew was our tyres weren't reaching that deep. It was only a mile or two but it was a nightmare every inch of the way back to sea level. Our intention had been to get away from it all, and one thing was for sure, our thoughts were now very far away from clown conventions.

Nevertheless, we enjoyed our few days away and the journey back, but Deena and I were always reminded of my stock reply to questions about the camper. I suppose it was inevitable that on seeing our lovely van, people used to say 'I bet you have wonderful holidays in this', whilst I was touring the country's schools. I mostly said, not unkindly, 'No, when I'm on holiday I go home.'

One day, for some reason or other, I painted a copy of the Mona Lisa. It was not earth shattering but Jim liked it and hung it in his bedroom. He suggested I do more. So on an impulse, my love of the impressionists came to the fore. Van Gogh, Manet, Lautrec were top of my list. I looked for what I considered to be the easy ones first. How simple I was. It is not until you try to emulate the talent of these artists do you come to realise their massive achievements. Anyway I started with Van Gogh's 'The Schoolboy'.

I realised doing the Mona Lisa that my drawing was never going to be good enough to accomplish the task unaided. So, not having a camera obscura, or even knowing how to use one if I had, I took colour transparencies with my camera, then I projected them to the actual size of the original paintings, drew in all the lines and every bit of information I could possibly glean, from the image displayed on my board.

I was working in oils at the time and was using a white oil primer, two coats, on my hardboard. I have only ever painted on this material. Only once had I painted on canvas and this was on a second hand one from a jumble sale. At the back of my mind was the thought that I'd know when my painting was of a quality that was worth the extra expense.

Such a silly thing really. One of my best and favourite paintings is the head of a tiger. It stares me in the face on the back of a length of wallpaper, after using blocks of school colour. I can paint in an entirely different way in these circumstances, completely free of inhibitions. I'm either barmy or mean, and I don't know which.

Back to my copying. After very carefully looking at every inch and making sure I haven't left something out, I switch off the projector and remove my now as near perfect a copy as I can get. And that dear friends is one way of getting a good drawing to paint a true copy of the great master himself. Mind you, you still have the painting to do.

To isolate and fix all of the marks, my first job is to fully paint in the picture with thin paint so as not to lose my drawing. Also I added a little terebine in the mix of turpentine substitute and linseed oil that I use as my medium. About half pint of it in a very useful plastic container that previously held Christmas nuts.

You can imagine a few sharp breaths from the purists about now, but the method has served me well over the years. After the painting is finished and dried, I apply a coat of artist's picture varnish to bring out the darks. The medium I used dried very flat and required that.

I no longer paint in oils. Fixing my copy now that I'm using acrylics, I paint over all the drawing with a diluted white so you can still make out the drawing underneath. If you have used pen or pencil to get so far, it will prevent smudging.

I would hazard a guess that Van Gogh's 'Schoolboy' wasn't at all happy about school. It wasn't the most popular one to start on according to my nearest and dearest, but I love it. It's raw I think.

My next Van Gogh was 'The Seated Zouave'. Probably another reason why

I tackled these two first was their size. I could manage them in the box room which was my studio, it being only about ten feet by eight feet. Bookshelves and a chest of drawers soon cut down the working area, but I learned a long time ago how little space you actually need to do some things in a working life.

My 'drawing office' downstairs, pause for a smile, is only thirty inches by twenty. It is a drawing board that is held securely in my ten inch quick release vice. Mind you the vice is fixed firmly to my work bench which has now grown to be ten feet long. A pair of compasses, a twelve inch ruler, my three foot Raybone rule and a rubber or two, a variety of pens, pencils and other markers, just about accounts for the vast amount of drawings and designing I have done over the years.

And so I continued painting my favourite subjects. I did a 'Sunflowers' early on, the one with Vincent's signature on the vase. Jim liked to see heaps of paint piled up, so not having Van Gogh's genius, I helped out a bit by palette knifing the drawing first with Polyfiller where I thought the bumps should be. I soon found out I should have done the bumpy bits before priming, because its surface was as hot as hell. By hot (should you not paint yourself) means it's very difficult to move your paint about with your brush. You can liken it to painting on blotting paper. These bumps saved a lot of paint though!

When we moved out of Bognor I left the Challen upright piano for Jim to use. To help me out with my entertainment work I fancied an electric keyboard that would be mobile enough for children's parties. This day we had gone to Chichester to see what was available. The journey never came to much because what I would have liked cost far too much. On returning to the car park, which was situated at the rear of several businesses, Jim spied one John Fenton, a person he knew, coming out of the rear of a shop's premises which were obviously being renovated. It was being turned into a restaurant.

In goes Jim, me following, chatter chatter chatter, Jim was 'selling' the idea of using my paintings to use as décor for the place. I always carried photographs of what I had painted, and John was smitten. So a business was born. The hiring out of my copied paintings for rental. So soon twelve paintings graced the walls of a smart bistro café called 'The Brasserie' in the heart of Chichester, when it finally opened.

In the meantime there was plenty to do, like framing. I had only framed small paintings until then. We went to an industrial estate in Worthing to see what was on offer professionally. The prices took our breaths away. Most of my pictures needed at least three inch framing for a decent effect, not the skimpy stuff you can get away with on water colours.

Down at the timber yard I viewed the stock mouldings available. Two offered me hope. One was a handrail, the other was the weatherboard that you see at the bottom of your back door, a drip board. Both sections had to be rebated to take the hardboard painting. But both sections looked very well, made up as picture frames.

We had a bit of bother sorting out how to decorate them. Deciding they should be gold in colour, we experimented with different makes of gold paint. In the end we arrived at a mix of two colours. A gold paint made for radiators, that looked far too brassy, and an antique gold of another make, came out well together. We used this mix throughout the collection.

Fixing them to the walls was a stroke of genius on our part. We had been concerned that they might be a target for thieves. Suffice to say, when in the hanging position, they were secure against the wall, and needed a screwdriver and the know how to take them off again.

There was one overriding problem that confronted a copiest like me. What to copy. I was never going to be able to see the originals when I needed to, so it was from books and their photographs I made my choice. But there was a snag, which photograph to use. The colours varied so much from printer to printer, which one to take as gospel? So it was a constant search to see what was on the library shelves at every visit, so I could decide which print to use.

I remember long after this I came across a picture of 'The Gypsy Girl' by Manet. I did not know of the painting before. I loved it, and made a copy for myself. Usually when describing the works of the impressionists, I find the authors use the same 'stock' pictures each time. For Van gogh you have the Sunflowers, for Renoir you have The Luncheon Party. And so on. You see a few printer's errors too. I have seen two books about Manet showing his portrait of Emile Zola. One with the subject looking to the right, the other to the left.

The amount of cropping of the subjects shown can be quite ruthless. I can remember painting 'The Luncheon Party' by Renoir. In the first instance I had difficulty in finding the extreme left hand side of the bearded figure of the picture I chose to paint. The cropping resulted in my having to use several different volumes to gather all the detail I needed. I have now painted this subject three times, counting the smaller one of a more suitable size to fit over the fireplace in a customer's lounge, before I started painting full size.

We were holidaying somewhere for the day when I spied a shop selling poster size copies of the Renoir. It contained what I saw was a full rendering of 'The Luncheon Party'. It was as a very happy customer I walked out of the shop that day clutching a copy. It has been on the back of my studio door ever since. A hard look at it reveals fourteen hands and fourteen faces, fifteen if you include the dog's. A real masterpiece if ever there was one

My own feeling about all of the paintings I have done of these masters, about fifty overall, I am truly humbled. Although the task was never easy I really enjoyed doing it. Still having the great majority of them, my only concern is where to put them in a cottage that is bursting at the seams. These were painted for me and although at this moment, none are out earning their keep, they are also not for sale. Jim is far too busy to see to them out working, and I'm fully occupied writing it all down.

By the way, he's also taken on another job for me now. Helping me to put it all this on computer to fit the modern age, for which I'm very sure I was not meant. Attending adult learning classes to learn about my PC has been a real struggle on my part but I'm slowly getting the message. For this I must thank the council staff and all the tutors, not forgetting our local mobile library bus. I am truly grateful for all the sympathetic help I have received locally, from friends and other helpmates, photographers and family.

Chapter 36

Meeting Princess Diana

About this time I had a nice job offered me by Sammy Sunshine, aboard the liner Queen Elizabeth II. It was just after a refit and before going back into the cruise liner business. About forty clowns would join the ship, along with lots of children, for a trip out to the mouth of the Solent. There we would be joined by a helicopter flying the Princess of Wales, Diana, out to meet us. On coming on board for the return trip, we, the laughter making cargo, would entertain the Princess and youngsters for a couple of hours on the way back.

With eats on the way, a party atmosphere, and seeing the Royal personage close up, it was a very pleasant experience. The impression I had of the lady herself was of a very warm personality, well used to getting on with children.

The voyage was coming to an end. The photographers were frantic to get disembarkation pictures and somehow I found myself amongst them. The bunch I was with chose the spot where she was going to get off. I think the rest of the clowns were on the other end of the ship, probably to stop it tipping over, such was the excitement. The next moment I found myself next to Diana, the only clown. With all the press men shouting 'look this way, please', 'Kerby use your comb', Diana and I looked at each other and then we flowed on to the exit gate.

The next morning very early a friendly reporter from the Brighton Argus, Les, rang me up saying 'Kerby you've made all the London newspapers.' And I had. Me and Diana. Clown and Princess. One of the newspapers had doctored the photograph and erased all the crowds milling about us to allow Diana and Kerby Drill to have centre stage. Nice wasn't it? A good one for the family album and this book.

I experienced a truly professional occasion on being booked to give two shows in the Worthing Pavilion. It would be my normal children's show, with parents in mind. The big difference for me was that I had never been singularly publicised before. Now I was to play to people who had actually paid to see me rather than a show I was appearing in. It was on a percentage basis with the theatre that I would get my money. The more bottoms I put on seats the better I would be paid. The percentage was 75% of the box office takings to me, and 25% to the theatre.

The second show was fuller than the first one I remember. But apart from the money, it was being king pin in a lovely seaside venue that I loved. It was the right sized auditorium for me, and being well supported by all the staff, a memorable event. I loved it. No records were broken money wise, but it was well worthwhile to me anyway.

Just down the coast at the Windmill Theatre, Littlehampton, I did some afternoon shows for half term. The weather plays a big part in these ventures. If the weather is too good you can't expect the children to come indoors readily for entertainment. The sandy beach and swimming can take a strong grip on the movements of families. The local council paying for me to be there, was always to be applauded from my point of view. They would have been criticised if there was nothing to do if the weather played up.

Over the whole week it was very worthwhile. Only once was a problem thrown up that could only be managed by me. Showtime two o' clock, and at least six children had turned up. Ages ranging from four to seven years. As these were spread about somewhat, with the help of a couple of usherettes we formed a small group down the front, near the stage. After doing the bits I normally do from the stage, drawings, funny bits etc, we all moved onto the stage for games as though it was for a birthday party at home. A great success according to the audience. A little harder than usual for me but it's a good illustration of how well prepared one has to be all times.

My props are very good tools for these occasions. I have never quibbled about taking extra items along with me just in case. Of course in some front rooms, if the children are in there first, It's difficult finding a place for all my bits. You really have to watch out where all the small hands of your audience are, and be careful where you put your feet. Especially if you've got your big boots on.

Interspersed with all these goings on I found time to be having a rest in various hospitals whilst undergoing treatment and repairs for two hernias and what I can only call a re-bore through my prostrate gland, which was in a way increasingly becoming more than a wee problem. The test for the rate of flow was simple. A nurse considered whether what you were doing in the bucket constituted non-harassment by the said gland to your normal performance. It was, and the kind surgeon said he would open up a new vista for me.

After the operation, with a catheter in, I was to soon to be seen walking the ward, trailing my bottle on a little trolley, as though I was taking Fido walkies. Every now and again a nurse would stop to admire my little load, taking notes of its changing colour. The wine term Rose was liberally used to describe the hue. Life goes by at such a rate, but what if we hadn't had the National Health Service that has kept me going through thick and thin. I have fought for and supported it all my life and now I'm indebted for all its work for me and my family.

Becoming a lot thicker on the ground then were the modern shopping malls. It was blossoming into being a nice little earner for us clowns. Who better to entertain the shoppers that thronged the multi-layered shopping precincts, than someone doing a spell of mix and mingle. This term, used by us when we are wandering amongst the crowds jollying them along and supplying a laugh or two in the process.

My main tools for this job are usually a pad of paper and a handy to get at pen. The pad contains a hook to enable that enables me to hang it on my pocket when not being used. The drawing faces from peoples' names is always a winner. In my pockets are close up gags like the elastic fiver 'that goes a little further.' If there's cricket being played anywhere I carry a ball with a large eye painted on it. An invention of mine, 'it finds its own way to the wicket.' It's always a bonus if you can come up with something topical to raise a laugh.

Another rule is don't stick outside one shop. Every shop has forked out a bit to get you there and shopkeepers get upset if they don't get a look in. I always make a point of going in for a quick chat and a laugh. I enjoy this sort of work and the argy bargy that goes with it. I find an apt comment in conversation can be as entertaining as any joke. Its up to you how successful you become. These malls don't go away and satisfied customers are generally your future clients. So about now I'm very happy with the mix of work coming in. It's quite a mix too. Craft fairs, parks, steam rallies, race courses, children's parties, regattas, and theatre shows. Life is never dull.

Chapter 37

I'm not getting Rich!

Looking through my bookings for 1990, at the time it was quite obvious that it was very much to be a re-run of the previous year, just as busy, and with many of the same shows turning up. A few place names are different but the vast amount of my bookings were repeat business. How I didn't get rich beats me. When you are contented with your lot, the thought of hiring a business manager is the last thing you'd think of doing. But I was wrong. I'm not complaining, but to be properly self employed, you do have to make more cash than is just necessary to pay your way.

Then my strong philosophical streak kicks in. Weighing up your lot with someone turning up each day at someone else's bidding and quietly working to retirement age, or not so quietly in some cases, always caused a shudder in me.

I've always been happiest making things rather than making money. Pierre once told me 'you'll never go hungry with all the things you can do'. He was right of course, but only up to a point. He went on to make money which could in turn earn interest in a bank account. My bank wouldn't accept my pieces of wood. Shame really. But that's life so lets get on with it.

One deviation to the norm came in June. The fees for attending the Guild's function in the South of England Show were getting beyond me. None of our friends of the bowler hatted brigade ever accepted us as a contributing element to the overall drawing power of their show, but only as highly skilled money-spinners using excellence for monetary gain. (I always thought we should have been paid to attend). I never knew anyone to get fat on crafts. The few who attracted fashionable prices were greatly outweighed by the rest. We pay a high price for putting the amount of time and effort into our wares that we do. I can hear a few comments to the effect, 'then it's about time you got a proper job then'.

At the same time time as the South of England Show was another, The

Cornwall Show, so I decided to go there for a change. I got in touch with the organisers, only to be told the crafts tent was fully booked. We could exhibit though, but must bring our own set up. At that time a square tent about the size of a small room was available to me, so I adapted it to fit the side of our van. All was ready and we set off. I soon realised it was very different from exhibiting in our own county.

It was a very long way. The main roads were still being modernised then. Motorways soon petered out, but we made it eventually. The pitch we had booked was quite near the swings and roundabouts. Quite enjoyable really. Getting set up had its moments, but my carefully constructed canvas awning was user friendly and we were quickly in business. Not a bit like a craft tent, more like a market trader, out in the open.

It turned out the crafts tent was more like the Rural Crafts set up than our Guilds. There is no doubt we would have had a far smoother ride had we got in with them, but there, it was something new for us. The weather wasn't at all bad and we enjoyed the evenings. Being near the amusements we had more than our usual share of interested children. Not being in a car park we were more a part of the whole show.

The journey back was more traumatic. The police created a one way system out of the show ground and we had a similar run of twists, turns, and narrow passageways that was reminiscent of the New Forest Show. The van took a bit of damage and it seemed a longer journey home. We survived it all, and it was just one of those occasions that got chalked up to experience.

Looking back in my records of the period, I noticed the large amount of drawing and correspondence I had to do. Much of this was preparing designs for interested customers I had recruited at the craft fairs. I had collected a flat fee of two pounds from each to discourage time wasters, and by return I sent them drawings illustrating my ideas for their personal sculpture, together with the costs. More than three-quarters of the people contacted in this way ended up buying something from me, and the rest seemed quite happy with the system.

One cheeky item, however, caught my eye. A request for the return of the design fee because the sender didn't like what he'd received. In view of the fact that I rarely provided less than four alternative designs in a range of prices, plus a self-addressed envelope to return my drawings in, I didn't feel much minded to recompense the so and so. His returned drawings are still in my loft with the others.

My envelopes were a soft cream colour with a clear rubber stamped return address, so I could easily pick out possible jobs from all the dross that one got targetted with through the letterbox even in those days.

One name gave me a tinge of pleasure. Nile. I had not heard of anybody called that before so I was very pleased when my design of the four letters, cut through a small pyramid of pine, was accepted. It is not always that the design chosen is my favourite too. Of course cost must be a limiting factor in many cases, but with Nile, our choices matched.

A difficult task was to carve two Army cap badges. The difficulty of carving them was outweighed by my disappointment at the photograph I took of them. Something must have been amiss with the light meter on my camera at the time. All I have been left with are very dark images indeed, hardly visible.

Another woodworker who became a good friend, had a small joinery business, making all sorts of furniture. He asked me to do his fretwork, mainly fascias, for his cabinets. He was pleased to have met me at a craft fair and I was pleased to have a filling-in job. It wasn't without its difficulties. My machine could cut in depth up to about twenty-four inches. His fascias were much longer than that. It was no dawdle but I managed, and it was a great help to my cash flow.

I must say as a designer the little quirks in spelling came in very handy sometimes. One request by a girl electrician demonstrates this very nicely. She wanted a door sign for her room, 'Jack's Ohm'. I was delighted when she accepted my design, which was in the shape of an electric light bulb. At that time I'd not met a lady electrician before.

Another help for a designer like me was if I could miniaturise an item that fitted my idea. So golfing requests sporting a tiny golf club, golf ball on a divot, plus a flag poking out of a hole on the green, were all grist to the mill. The flag was also handy for denoting birthdays, anniversaries and the like.

Tennis, squash, and badminton enthusiasts were always captivated by a small racquet complete with pink stringing. Cricket was also a popular game to depict. The three stumps of a wicket and bails, to support a leaning cricket bat, about two inches long, and a ball amongst a few tufts of grass. I could marry many names to these.

The cycle, tandem and motor cycle rider caused me many hours of very careful work to portray their hobby or sport. A subject of these meant a machine less than two inches in length. To suggest spokes, saddle and handlebars in these dimensions you have to keep your wits about you I can tell you!

Builders provided a lot of work. If the name required had a letter with a flat top, for example, 'Ted', it was easy to tile the top of the T as in a roof. Once I hung a plumb bob from the overhang, for a building firm. The use of a nylon thread solved many such problems. Small trowels alongside a small brick wall came in handy for bricklayers. Carpenters tools looked very attractive when reduced. Smoothing planes, claw hammers, nails and screws, nuts and bolts, all added novelty and charm to my wares.

The use of a nylon thread to suspend dots over the lower case 'i', was a great help to me. Always looking for novelty in presenting my ideas, it added great charm whenever I could use it. In my Diana and Charles wedding design I formed the dot as a heart shape to represent love.

A present for a young Thomas had the lad sitting on his capital letter 'T', crouched over, fishing. Suspended from his fishing line was his 'catch'. The letter O from his own name! It dangled gently, quite separate from the rest of his name.

Years afterwards, meeting his mother, she reminded me of it, also telling me that Thomas now had a family of his own. She lived around Bognor it seems. Another common occurrence when you have been doing children's parties over the years, is for an adult to come up and say 'do you remember coming to our Freddie's party'? I must say it's very pleasant to be remembered with affection.

I never found a satisfactory answer to a little girl's christening present. With the boys I had several actual vehicles to use. A name on a lorry, train or boat was a very acceptable cargo or load to announce a baby's arrival in a family. Did I forget the pram?

It was when I started making plywood names and what I called 'large miscellaneous', that I gathered some unusual requests for my imagination to deal with. 'Amorous Acres' was one, from a very Reverend. 'Gone to the Pub' needed no input from me really. For a student, 'Room Sweet Room'.

The most popular amongst the standards were generally wife generated for hubby. 'Potting Shed', 'Bolt Hole', 'Workshop', 'Music Room', 'I Love You', 'The Nut House', as populated by squirrels. It was my practice of not refusing any reasonable request that, on looking through my book of all names in stock, that accounted for over sixteen hundred designs. Phew!

I now have volumes of photographs of my name sculptures. How lucky am I to have grown up in the age of being able to record images so easily. The achievements of Joseph Grimaldi, the forerunner of clowning, are only recorded in the words of his contemporaries. Cameras weren't invented then. Contrast with this the exploits of Charlie Chaplin, a modern clown, whose work is preserved on film for all to see.

Around this time I caught sight of an advertisement for a sale of paintings in London. The auction house was Bonhams. The catalogue showed many copies of impressionist paintings for sale. Jim took Deena and I up to London on the sunday morning for a viewing session. The range of paintings on show were very interesting. There were a few copies of the old masters but not so many as I was given to believe.

I enquired about the possibility of my entering some of my larger works, but I got the impression they were not at all happy at encouraging this. However one painting for sale was a copy of 'The Bathers', by Seureat. This interested me in so far as my own copy of this subject, was of a similar size. Not full size, which is very large. My own work compared very favourably to the one on display, so I thought, as did Jim and Deena.

On returning home and after the auction had taken place, I rang to enquire the price it had fetched on the day. Seven hundred or so pounds. This was very useful in allowing me to gauge what my paintings might realise in another sale if given the chance. But as I was out numbered in wanting to put one in for a try out, I didn't pursue the exercise.

Younger son Michael, apart from feeding me with his woodwork jobs, (he was a fully-fledged builder now), was also working a lot on the continent. Later he and his partner Hazel bought a farm in France and decided to live there. It needed a lot of work doing on it. We had helped in its purchase, so when it was time to finalise the business, Deena and I went over with him, along with Hazel, and made a holiday of it. Whilst appreciating its possibilities, they were under no illusion about the task they had undertaken.

A real challenge, it needed an enormous amount of restoration before it could be habitable, and was going to need a lot of effort and labour. But with a great deal of hard graft, the coming years were to prove the project to be very worthwhile.

Les and I built our houses on a corner plot of ground in Potters Bar with nothing to spare around the edges. This farmhouse building alone was the size of our whole plot. A barn was slightly larger, and an adjoining field, also part of the property, was the size of a couple of football pitches. Possibly a little more potential! But Les and I were two, Michael was on his lonesome.

When we came to Bognor from Wales most of my entertainment jobs were booked through outdoor event agencies. After the gala work ceased I started getting local parties through Bognor agent Jock Campbell. It was one of these dates that put me into a nearby beach holiday camp. Mostly on Bank Holidays and Christmas, I was booked as a supplement to the normal staff who were playing the 'redcoat' role as in bigger establishments, such as Butlin's. It was during these excursions that I fully realised how lucky Deena and I were to have got our experience in Billy's camps in that golden era in the fifties.

Those days of massive numbers of holidaymakers, large supporting staff and programmes to match, meant we came on the scene at just the right moment for us. The greater commercialisation nowadays and the increase in franchising of different bits and pieces, I feel there would not be the place for our sort of entertainment and approach to the job. There is too much shouting and overall noise levels for my comfort.

Sammy Sunshine gave me a lot of work about now. He had got the ear of an agent, or perhaps he himself had done the digging, but Esso Petroleum were in the market for clowns at the pumps. We had a very unlikely companion on the forecourt, a tiger. A fantastic costume but the designer forgot to include adequate ventilation. I thought it was a good job this animal only worked from ten until five, with breaks for removing his head for a breathe of fresh air. The lad inside must have been to RADA because he didn't let it interfere with his performance.

I'm glad I was only giving out balloons, and tightening the odd nut or two with my oversized clown-type spanner. These jobs were well paid weekend efforts. Foul weather was kept from me by the awning protecting the pumps and customers. Our 'tiger' wasn't so lucky, he had a roving commission that took him kerbside most of the time.

There were a couple of differences that separated our performances. He had no lines to remember and didn't even have to look pleasant if he didn't want to. Only when he took his top off had he the need to care.

John Fenton, owner of the Brasserie Restaurant in Chichester, sold up and moved on. The new owners came in with their own ideas regarding décor. We'd had a good run, but my paintings had to come out.

It was to be a few months before John surfaced again. He was to open a new restaurant, this time in Rustington, about a dozen miles away. The new restaurant was to be called 'Santorini'. Again John wanted us to provide the décor. We were able to properly light the paintings this time. We had a dozen pictures all told and a mention in the press.

Things went to plan and eventually John sold Santorini to a very pleasant married couple, a Mr and Mrs Woolley. Although we offered a new selection of my impressionist paintings, they wanted everything to stay exactly as it was. However, as we will see later, this was not to be the last of our involvement with John.

We also had another venue to consider now as well. One of the travelling salesman who regularly did business with the restaurant happened to be a freemason. His lodge, Charmandean, was in Worthing, and he arranged for us to hire four of my paintings with which to decorate their lounge bar. This lasted for a few years. Every now and again Jim and I would change the pictures, if they wished. So it seems as if the old adage, 'business begets business' was also borne out in our case.

The conventions also provided a couple of interesting bits of lively business too. At one time, we, a group of C.I. members in all our glory, attended a holiday exhibition up in the smoke to publicise the convention and the attractions of Bognor as a premier holiday resort.

There was another occasion when we did the same on the platforms at Victoria Station, flaunting our placards and giving out hand bills and a few laughs at the same time. All helped to keep the publicity pot boiling. After all, not only did we have this exciting collection of clowns coming from near and afar for their convention, but Bognor Regis also held the hours of sunshine record on the U.K. mainland.

There was a slight stumbling block showing up in my personal well being around now. My hearing was such that I was increasingly having to say, 'pardon me, what did you say? more frequently than I would have wished. My doctor prescribed a hearing test, the thrust of which was for me to indicate when I could hear a faint buzzer, attached to a meter reading that gave the audiologist a score.

I was lacking in some areas of sound recognition, always worse if I was listening to multiple sounds at the same time. The follicles in the ear had been damaged and nothing could be done about it medically. I either had to invest in a hearing aid, or get used to saying 'pardon'.

I learned a long time ago about this handicap when dealing with customers who were in a similar situation. Always to keep your voice up, and if possible talk to that person in a direct manner. This was especially so in the young. At one children's party nobody thought to tell me one child was deaf. I was very upset about it because I could have done so much more in seeing that the child understood what was going on. You can nearly act words.

A friend of mine, Philip Lake, was a fine artist, but his ears were very much less use to him than his brushes. Once, towards the end of his life, whilst visiting him in a nursing home, he was having no joy at all with his hearing aid. I had a go at adjusting it myself. I was horrified to hear the distortions of sound that he was having to put up with. This was a good few years ago and the technology has come a long way since then.

As I'm still around and kicking I can do my own update. Early this year, the kind N.H.S. fitted me with two digital, beautifully moulded assistants that snugly fit in my ears, bringing the whole gamut of modern sound straight into the places where I have been led to believe, you must not put anything in smaller than your elbows.

I then understood how Philip managed to keep his concentration on painting as he did. Like me, his passion was for portraiture. In the monthly get together of the art group of twenty or thirty painters, he just switched the darn thing off and got on with it, without distraction.

The early nineties threw up a couple of interesting jobs. One was in an american college situated halfway to Arundel on the Ford Road. Called the New England College, it looked like any other campus when I arrived. I was booked to do childrens shows on a fun day. Fortunately I had enough youngsters who had come because their parents worked there. My bits went well and later I wandered off to see what the adults were getting up to.

I distinctly got the impression that I was in a foreign country. Whilst doing gala shows in the american camps years earlier, it had felt just the same. Not to be put off by the similarity of language, and sometimes that needs a bit more than the normal concentration to be comfortable with, no, it's very strange. At least I found it so. I don't remember the experience as being pleasurable, and that's not making an unkind comment. Why exactly it felt weird to me, I just can't explain.

I was invited to exhibit in the Newbury Show. The craft tent was by invitation only. The organiser saw me at the Woodworkers Show. It was quite a big event with a similar compilation of events, rather like The South of England Show at Ardingly. The standard of exhibitors was very high. One stand really impressed me. A leather worker. The hand made suitcases looked a work of art in their unstained appearance.

I had competition with my names here. They were made up on the spot, using a different method from mine. Whereas I pierced my letters if necessary, such as in 'a's and 'o's, my 'rival' cut in with a very fine blade and so sawed the innards out, in just one continuous saw cut. A similar saw cut as you would do cutting out a jigsaw puzzle. My names were stronger, but he was doing very well, charging by the letter. He was using chipboard whereas I used plywood.

On the first visit, I parked in the wrong place. Stopping in what looked like a convenient spot, we didn't notice our mistake until darkness came. We were next to a large electricity generator. Although it was supposed to have been sound proofed, nothing could dampen the continuous throbbing it gave out. We moved the following evening. We did very well here. It was a joy exhibiting in the same sort of quality crafts as I was used to in the Guild.

A promotional job I did once that was to be remembered for rather strange reasons. I was working in the Bognor D.I.Y. shop 'Do It All'. Deena visited me for a short while and amongst the festivities for the customers' entertainment was a competition involving a mini-car. How many balloons were crammed into the car? Her estimation was the winner. The prize, a garden table and four chairs in white plastic, complete with sunshade.

When we brought them home then, I had no thought of who would be using the four 'sit-downers' most in the years to come. By strategically placing the same chairs, two out front and two in the back garden, I can flop out in most places in my domain any time I want to. And I want to most of the time these days.

Three sad dates have come to light in this sifting of mine. Ron Haubner, sister Rene and younger brother John all died. When Ron and I went to Perivale to open the shadow factory during the war, we were both young bloods, straining at the leash to prove we had become grown-ups. Both of us had been nurtured by our fathers at E.N.V. Engineering Ltd. in Willesden.

He, like me, had diligently watched his dad bringing us into our trades. His Czech father, a brilliant toolmaker. My dad, an all round carpenter, a man of many parts from London W10. Now the pressures of war had thrown us into a second edition of the London firm out in Perivale, with the same surnames, doing the same jobs. Haubner and Brooks, toolmaker and carpenter, the young and new old firm!

Ron had probably heard me mention my sister Rose. Who could have predicted their marriage a few years down the line. Their two offspring, Jack and Jo, both using their hands in probably gene-guided skills. Jack, a toolmaker, of his grandfather's ilk, and Jo, arranging the hair of the rich and famous, in her West End salon.

I will remember Rene always as being two years older than me, with her hair in a fringe. Her straw-coloured locks, streaked with darker bits. I was always 'er Arry'. In our street, amongst most of us working class Londoners, there weren't many aitches going spare when we were growing up. Rene and I were never going to be the intellectuals of our family. I never knew the results of my eleven-plus and I don't know if Rene ever sat for one. One thing that bound us all together without many words being spoken, was our love for each other.

When Deena was carrying Jim and we were thrown out of Enfield, it was Rene who found us our two rooms in No.400 Portobello Road. A lovely girl and a friend indeed. When she married George, a London bus driver of the old school, she had the right person to look after her. Their daughter, Irene, after her mum, had the same sort of face as our Rene. Round and plump. The sort of shape that seemed to make eyes twinkle. That's how she came to be known as Twink. I still call her that.

John was born John Munt. When mum's younger sister Dode died, he and his sister Audrey were taken in by relatives. Mum had never adopted John formally. She always said he would make his own mind up about that when he was old enough, and he did. In his teens John became a Brooks. You could detect that, at an early age, John had got a lot of Wingrove, his mum's maiden name, in him.

At fourteen when I was still making cowboy trousers out of sacks, John had a printing business going in a shed in the garden, printing all the neighbours' stationery. He was always coming up with something. He traded in Green Shield stamps, getting enough to buy his first car with them. When dad died we all sold him our share of the house to enable him to stay there.

Later on he acquired more property. The Wingrove business sense was strong in John. I always remember him as a very kind and generous person, like, I hope, the rest of the Brooks's. When he married Beryl, a very quiet and gentle person, she was the perfect match. Their daughter Sara is very much into the modern way and reminds me of John's earlier adventures into the business world. She is fully engaged in a computer-run business.

John and Beryl were very keen on travelling about and were long standing members of the Youth Hostel movement. Deena and I were looking in a book about collecting one day when an article on John revealed itself in its pages. Mentioning he was a keen collector of the movement's memorabilia there was a nice photograph of him to accompany the item. It was he who obtained my prints of wartime Rackham Street, showing the bomb damage.

After having a week of aching joints I was awaiting my turn in the health centre to see my doctor when a familiar face beamed into view. Mike Monk, retired manager of our local leisure centre. In our conversation I told him I was hard at it with my memoirs and that I noted he'd ordered gymnastic trophies from me, enough for five consecutive years, rather than get them in dribs and drabs. I didn't like to say it, but it occurred to me he might have thought I'd pop my clogs sooner than later. I can't remember how I looked at the time. For sure, pretty miserable, but I thought not on the verge of breaking apart.

These smaller trophies were in place of my original one that featured a young girl gymnast on the bar. The original was held by the winner for a year. These were for keeps. When he departed from his office he was told to clear all the trophies that had accumulated over the years. He contacted the infant associations that had grown now to national stature, and they jumped at the chance of having them as a part of their own historical beginnings. I was extremely pleased to hear this. I always regretted selling so much of my work. Silly really, isn't it?

Chapter 38

Seeing the Real Thing

My twelve months of 1995 contained some interesting highlights, one of them being a visit to the National Gallery in London. The sight of Van Gough's Sunflowers, with a century year's old paint, looked very lack-lustre to my eyes. I get the same feeling now seeing some of my own paintings with only thirty years old paint already toning down.

I think I know the reason. In my early days of practising the art, I always used the cheaper student colour oils. Not knowing how Van Gogh's paints were made up, and the binding oil used in them, one can't compare his to mine. But I know enough to realise when he put his brushes down, the flowers must have leapt out at you.

The nearest I got to getting a similar result was when I did a painting using scenic artist's pigments, mixed by me, with linseed oil. Not an easy thing to do. The mixing bit I mean! I didn't pursue this method because at the time the cost of enough dry colours to make up a palette was beyond my pocket.

The sight and size of 'The Bathers' was an eye opener to me. My copy is only a third the size of the original. One of my most difficult undertakings, but I love it. It graces one of son Jim's walls now. Looking at the gallery brochure and enquiring why other favourites were not shown, the reply was 'they were in for maintenance'.

It was a fabulous but tiring day out. My legs had been playing up more than a bit. Before we left I was amazed at some of the books in the Galleries Bookshop. Here were some class illustrations of paintings that I would dearly have liked to have had by me in my copying days. It was only the price tag on most of them that restrained me from coming back home with an armful. I did purchase the official transparencies of the galleries collection, just in case!

The most memorable and startling experience of the day happened in The Courtauld Gallery, along the road, a little later. The stairway up to where the paintings were hung, I remember as being rather a tortuous climb. When we entered the room, Deena, Jim and I had the surprise of our lives. There, side by side, were the 'The Loge', by Renoir and the 'Bar at the Follies', by Manet. It was just like walking into our house. I had both these pictures up in the same order, hanging side by side, on our staircase wall. Both were full size copies, in oils, and if I say so myself, not bad representatives of the originals.

Mine were obviously not so valuable as the ones we beheld that day, quite a bit of difference in fact. Well let's agree, more than a bit! But the amazing coincidence was a priceless memory for our intrepid trio.

I wanted for a long time to get to see the originals of my copies, to see how close I got to the paint colours rather than the drawing. After all the printer had decided on the reproductions I chose to copy, not the artist. I was not displeased. A little later in the library I came across a volume that contained some very clear details,of Renoir's brushstrokes, and I was humbled. Even after getting the colour and drawing right, this mortal is still a very long, long way from the emulating the genius shown by the masters.

In one sense I suppose one's brushstrokes can be likened to fingerprints. I can see with my own eyes the enormous difference between my working on a portrait, from a photograph, and someone who has the subject in front of them. Painting from life allows much better interpretation of colours and all the interesting bits that go to form a likeness.

There was a reference to me, 'delivering sculpture' a little later. It could only have been to an open art exhibition in The Worthing Art Gallery. Not liking having to be selected as a rule, I wanted to give my clown an airing. He was accepted, and when I went to the preview I was disappointed once again. I conceived him as being viewed from ground level, and there he was nearly three feet in the air on a podium. To my mind raising it up thus actually belittled the sculpture. It was obviously not what the selectors thought. I always had it in mind to be viewed by a child and from a lower level. Oh to be consulted sometimes! It appears you have to be in another league to be so.

'Tommy the Terrific', another of our clowning community, asked if I could simplify his main prop to make it more user-friendly when going from job to job. He used three full-sized kitchen doors in their frames to perform his routine. I proposed to amalgamate the three separate items into one manageable frame. With the help of my mechanic friend Ray Woolven, we did just that.

The outside door had four panels hinged with strips of strong rubber. These four panels could swing both ways. They could also be 'dived' through, as indeed Tommy did in the act. That door frame was hinged to another door frame at the bottom, on the sill. A strong catch held this door frame and panelled door securely closed. At the end of all the business, Tommy would kick the catch whilst lying on the floor. That released the whole lot down on top of him.

Buster Keaton, the world famous non-speaking silent movie star, did a similar gag with the front of a house. The entire wall came crashing down on him, but he made sure he was standing in the front doorway, with the door open. A terrific gag slightly larger than Tommy's.

I never saw the act performed and the the props never came back, but I've since seen Tommy alive and kicking. I also made chairs and a table for an american performer's balancing act. All these props were made for people working in Zippo's Circus. Martin Burton, 'Zippo' recommended me to them as a prop maker.

A while before, Martin gave me the task of building an upright piano that his trio of acrobats could use as a vaulting horse. There were several other requirements as well. The keyboard was to fly out on command. A vase of flowers must shoot up in the air, woodworm fly out, and at the end of the act, the piano must seem to fly to pieces with a bang.

The American gent demonstrated how he mounted the four chairs on the top of the table, balancing one on top of the other, seemingly in a ridiculous position, without breaking his top vertebra. Deena and I watched fearfully whilst he accomplished this on our front lawn. All exciting stuff. And I was in my element doing it. I would have loved to have known what my other trio of chippies would have thought of it. Dad, Charlie and Fred. If we ever meet up again I'll be able to show the series of photographs I took of the job as it progressed. How pleased I am now, that I did so.

An unusual request for the art side of the business came in then. Could I paint a picture of 'The Dallas Doll' onto a leather flying jacket? The Doll was, in fact, an American bomber plane. The bomber's crews always had their chosen names written on the fuselage of their aircraft. The picture to be copied included a 'doll', and she was blonde, busty and beautiful. She ended up astride one item of their very unfriendly load. A flying bomb.

The customer was very pleased and I was very relieved he was very pleased. The job had had its difficulties. It was a very expensive canvas to work on, very different from my usual inert and very stable hardboard. I was lucky with my choice of paints of those available. Acrylics, being water based, served me very well.

There was a blip in the summer programme in Bognor that year. Our famous Bognor Birdman was not going to happen. Lack of funds were to blame. Instead of an event of international importance, nowt. The seafront traders were very upset and organised a happening of their own. On the day these intrepid pilots of non-engined flying machines were due to have risked life and limb, launching themselves from Bognor's half pier, I was to be engaged entertaining some of the disappointed children on the beach.

John Mell, the owner of a yoghurt kiosk on the promenade, booked me to do some shows a few feet away from his place of business, as his contribution to the replacement fun day. Managing to park on the pebbles, performing against my back cloth on the van, I had good audiences throughout the day. The weather was very good. The following week the local newspapers showed some fine pictures of us 'filler-in' entertainers in action.

It was also near the start of 'Red Nose Day'. A day given over to the helping of children in desperate situations in Africa and other places. Bill English, 'Smiley', and I did a day in Bognor Town dangling our collecting receptacles under a wide variety of noses. I had made these from two plastic bottles that had in a previous life contained bleach. Empty of course. I modelled them as two figures. Bill's was a lady clown, mine a gent. The novelty plus our 'sparkling personalities' helped us turn in over a hundred pounds. Not bad for our first time out.

In the January I had made a note about taking my water pills. These are innocent looking tiny discs of what looks like chalk. Whereas chalk is a marvellous soaker up of moisture, these small things were intent on dispelling any superfluous fluids from one's own self. And by Jove I wish I was as successful at doing my job. From that day these little pills have dictated my movements from early morning, when they are taken.

The theory is that life started in the oceans, and when we came out onto the beach, we maintained the status quo by growing a skin to keep water inside us, as though we were still there. I really do get worried sometimes the pills will win and I'll just be drained flat. Judging by the size of my ever expanding paunch, I've a while to go yet. But it is worrying.

The year ended up mixing and mingling in store to such a degree that I was glad I'd accepted no bookings for the two days when they finally closed for

Christmas. I had counted twenty days with just two letters showing, A&N.

Perusing the year's wall chart of 1996 leaves me in no doubt that the writing of memoirs later on in life was far from my mind. The scribbles reminding me of this that and the other are now being scrutinised and pondered over to an extraordinary degree, trying to bring them back into the reaches of memory. The word 'radio' tells me I was helping in some way or other with Jim's local radio station venture, South West Sussex Radio. At the same time I was doing lots for his business, Leaderboard, building new switch boxes.

These were needed to distribute high voltages of electricity to the message displays. They were very heavy indeed and making them was quite a big job. The lightboards were always being updated, re-designed and repaired, so I know I wasn't sitting about twiddling my thumbs. Michael, the younger son, was also bringing quite a lot of work my way. I enjoyed being out on jobs with him and Jim whenever the opportunity arose.

As a self-employed builder, bricklayer and gardener, Michael had an extensive area of work coming in. Window frames, garage doors and helping out on greenhouses was a steady source of work I could help out with. My dad's dad was also a brickie, and a good one from what I was told. The work he did on the convent in Portobello Road still bears testimony to the old boy's skill.

I cannot see any mention of the Sussex Guild. For about twelve years I was member but it seems I was out of it now. By the same token Deena and I seem to have passed over lots of events, crafts and otherwise, from the previous years. It seems we were pulling in our horns slightly. Even though I'd left the Guild I was still very busy at Michelham Priory. Maydays and teddy bear picnics still showing up.

April saw us visiting the Cezanne exhibition in London. I must admit that of all his works it was the 'Card Players' that I really wanted to see. It is the only one I have copied and he seems to have been drawn to the subject more than once. The painting on display seemed smaller somehow. Whenever pictures are given more space, as in the Tate Gallery at that time, this seems to happen, to me at least.

There did seem to be differences from the one I painted from a book. It's a fine portrait of two card players, calm and serene, pondering over their next move. I had great difficulty sorting out the background to this. I never think twice about putting down a stroke or two to represent a feature in my own works, but it's not always easy to work out the intention of the original artist.

That's why a lot of ordinary folk think that our style of painting, impressionism, sometimes let's us get away with murder.

Another year and another public appointment change. The Mayor's parting gift this year from his colleagues was to be a sculpture by me. I'm was getting to know the Arms of the Bognor Regis Town Council reasonably well by now. All told over the years I've carved it five times on trophies and presentations. It isn't easy to do, but it does look nice in pine.

Councillor Ken Scutt, that year's recipient, was also the trainer and masseur for the local football team, so I used that as a facet for the design. Along with his christian name there was a figure in football garb with a cap on, holding a football in the air. I have often wondered how my works have been received. With pleasant surprise I hope. Anyway, I've not had any complaints.

If they ever get damaged I always do my best to restore them. One of my creations was left on the roof of a car when it was driven off. It was like doing a very complicated jig-saw puzzle. I managed it though, and gained a lasting thanks for doing it. I had something of a similar nature happen with a client's name sculpture whilst craft fairing. It was a double item with both husband's and wife's name in the design. About a year afterwards I had a request for an exact copy. The couple had gone out for the evening and when they returned they discovered their dog had eaten the original!

The Arun Leisure Centre had a trophy problem one time. A young lady gymnast was for a third year the winner of the same class. It was decided she should be honoured with a special prize to mark the event. I cut three copies of the pine trophy, a girl on the bar, in thin gaboon plywood, and set them a little apart. It seemed to introduce a bit of movement by doing so. With her name it came out well. A memorable name too. It was Zita.

We are lucky in our art group to be able to exhibit in a very desirable wooden hut, in a very popular visitors' spot outside Arundel Castle, the ancestral home of the Duke of Norfolk, a few miles away from Middleton-on-Sea. Our hut is only a short distance from one of the castle's gates. When I first saw it this wooden building was home to a table tennis club. No longer, it has just been refurbished to conform to more modern standards.

The hall is always in use for one exhibition or other and our group exhihibits three times a year. We have had many visitors over the years. A special one for me was a famous actress, Fiona Fullerton. She had starred in a Bond film, and was there with her family. Her hubby liked a sunflower picture of mine.

Over the years on subsequent visits they were very popular customers of our group.

They lived in a very nice building which was awash with wisteria. One year Fiona turned my painting of it into the subject of her Christmas card. It was such a pleasant surprise to see my work so nicely presented. Another commission was for a teddy bears' picnic. Here was a challenge, nothing to copy this time. Looking down at the year's work load there was also a request for me to paint a display of roses to fit a very elegant but pictureless guilt frame the customer already owned.

Over the years I have always done a bit of entertaining for the art group by drawing face names for the visitors coming through our show. I hate sitting about twiddling my thumbs. Nowadays I don't do so much painting and to help pay my way, I charge twenty pence for these drawings. As the visitor has no idea what a 'face name' is, I always do the first one free. This serves two purposes. It demonstrates the quality of my work, and mostly draws a smile from the beholder. It shows to my mind also that I am still an entertainer and purveyor of comedy.

As a keen observer of humanity the lessons I have learned through doing this are interesting to say the least. Some names still defy me today. My maxim here is 'when in doubt, be bold'. So instead of trying to soothe sensitive feelings I go outrageous and don't charge. A strange fact is most people, especially children, seem to like that better than if I'd produced a masterpiece. The twenty p's come in very handy at home too.

Recently my face names caused a problem reminiscent of our wet days at Ardingly, causing an obstruction to the flow of visitors around the exhibits. So now I operate from a small table tucked in a corner, and out of harms way, I continue to use lots of paper, supplied by friend Paul, and wear out numerous pens, doing what I still love doing, causing merriment in one way or another, drawing faces from names.

Nineteen ninety seven brought great sadness to us all. Deena's sister Bettie's youngest son, Christopher, died. Barely into his thirties, leaving a lovely wife Janet, and two very bright children, Elizabeth and Nicholas Acutt. Chris had tried for the RAF unsuccessfully, because of imperfect eyesight, but went on to become an expert in computers and software. A brilliant nephew and a lovely boy. How can families bear such inconsolable loss?

Funerals are as if a very heavy boulder falls into deep water. The ripples widen to reveal family members rarely seen, distant relatives and new faces unknown until then. All the wide circle of friends and business associates that a well-loved person gathers about them, in their lifetime. There is rarely a sad gathering of this sort, when any one person knows everybody present, and of course the one that did was no longer with us.

Littlehampton was in the frame for me about now with the annual town show, carnival procession and regatta day. I seemed to be a regular for their fun on the water day. I never seemed to get my van onto a flat bit of grass, pulled in as I was a few yards from where the River Arun flowed past. And talk about flow. The pace of it coming in and going out was extraordinarily fast. You needed a very good engine to get up river when the tide was going out and vice versa.

Being busy looking to my own audience, I never saw much of the antics that went on over the promenade wall. There were always plenty of goings on for the general public, but I always managed to attract a good audience. It was after I gave up my van and had to use a car that difficulties showed up. No dressing room, no scenic back cloth, and no shelter.

After taking these for granted for so many years the shock was tangible. When last I worked from my Vauxhall Victor estate car it was in the London parks. Much younger and a very eager beaver then. I suppose it's not very surprising really with a gap of forty years that some things would have altered slightly.

An unusually timed party always seemed to pop up in February. It was for the Methodist Church in Bognor. At a time when I would normally be thinking of taking a look at Easter props, it was Father Christmas again. A little late but the children never seemed to notice. The church had a proper small stage in the hall, and it was refreshing always to do a show in its rightful place.

I had always to keep a careful note of what I'd used the previous year. The younger ones were always about the same in number, as were the adults. The piano was something I always tried to include in my programmes. It was for this party I gave serious thought to a children's song quiz. Whatever the age, a musical quiz really does bring a group of people together. Pat Stinchcombe, the party organiser, was also a local councillor. We'd been friends for many years, we had both spent a lot of our energies in the cause of Bognor Regis. Our politics were different but as I always kept mine 'under a bushel' no one was bothered.

After a stint as Bognor's Mayor, hers was one of the parting gifts it was my good fortune to be asked to make. She'd had a finger in many pies, so whereas most of the other retiring gifts had a name, a civic symbol and a personal attribute, hers was a collection of them. I hoped she liked it.

It's always the same making things for third parties. Another person usually makes the presentation, so can judge the response. Ah, well!

Chapter 39

Someone Likes My Work

A short time after Christmas I had a telephone call from a Malcolm. He had rung before to see if he could come and see some of my paintings. At that time we didn't know what ones would be wanted for Charmandean so a later date was arranged. When I met Malcolm he told me a friend of his had been to Santorini Restaurant, seen my paintings, and told him that they included copies of Manet's works.

The friend knew of his interest in this artist's work. I showed him what I had, and afterwards he asked if I would paint him a copy of the Berthe Morisot portrait by Manet, twice full size. I saw no problem with this request. He had brought a book on the works of Manet with him, which he gave to me. So I said I would paint a copy of the Berthe portrait as illustrated in the book. We agreed on that and also the price. At that time I also had an unfinished 'La Loge' by Renoir, standing in the hall, and Malcolm said yes to that too.

I found the man a very pleasant person. He had a family and had just moved into a house on the outskirts of London. He was in business in the 'smoke'. After we said our goodbyes Deena and I looked at his cheque for six hundred pounds, and I hadn't done a stroke yet. He was the first person I'd met who was willing to pay a proper price for my work.

In the seventy odd years up to that moment, I can only think of two entertainment jobs that had, I thought, paid a proper whack for my efforts. These are my estimations mind you, and is there a slight possibility that I'm biased! But it was a great moment nevertheless. Here was someone showing the same confidence in me as I had always had of myself.

So setting to work for my new found patron it soon came to framing time. Jim had already bought a mitre cutting contraption which turned out to allow me to dispense with the mitre blocks of old. Fairly large sections of timber had to be cut and this machine helped enormously. Our association extended over a couple of years and a number of commissions followed.

As I write this into the computer it is just becoming clear to me how much work was involved, and how busy I must have been. Everything else was still going on. I couldn't have just dropped everything to do it, so it's not surprising that the exact sequence of works for my new patron are mixed in my memory, and why these reminders on the back of a door seem so sketchy.

Take one painting, 'The Luncheon Party' by Renoir. I think back now and I am amazed that the enormity of the task didn't frighten the life out of me! This one had to be drawn in the garden because it was so big. I couldn't project the image far enough indoors. So awaiting a dark dry night, with my board hung on the side of the cottage, I did the drawing bit. All those hands and faces. The picture I had to copy from let me down. I realised later that what I had painted to be part of the design of a fruit bowl on a table, was actually the tail of a dog the principle character was holding.

It was here I had a stroke of luck. Deena and I were out for the day somewhere, and a shop was selling poster-sized prints of all sorts of subjects for you to frame yourself. I spied one of the Renoir subject and it is still on the back of my studio door. Its size is roughly twenty four by eighteen inches, and looking at it, for the first time, I could actually see what was going on and was able to correct my painting. You've no idea what a relief that was, especially when I learned the young lady in the painting who was fondling the dog was the future Mrs Renoir.

Whilst I was working on this painting I knew I would also have to have one for myself. To help me with my own copy I took a series of photographs of the way I had tackled details on the first one. I also have a nice photograph of me and Malcolm in our garden, on the day he collected it.

When I come to think about it, the tools I used to carry out this task beggar belief. The suitability of my ragtail collection of brushes would never have been acceptable had I been doing woodwork. Strange that. I did improve later though. One of the reasons for this state of affairs was the kindness of other people. Whenever anything was being disposed off in my art groups, I was always considered as a recipient. Unwanted picture frames, old painting boards and all sorts. My friends all knew I was able to alter frames, rub down and re-prime the boards and so on.

When my great friend Phil Lake died I inherited all his books and equipment. A friend moved up north and decided not to paint any more, and I was given all her stuff. And I can't throw things away easily. One of the reasons why this is so is the nature of one of my other strings of work. Prop making. If I see a strange shape in whatever material, my mind naturally views it from the point of 'will it come in handy'? My workshop and garden sheds bear silent witness to this built-in habit of someone with a restless mind, and who doesn't need instructions on what might come in handy or not. I'll think of something later!

I had a problem with this new development. How to price my work. Jim suggested I charged by size. So by taking a painting that had been paid for already, I arrived at a square inch estimate for the ones to follow. It seemed to work well in my case and Malcolm seemed satisfied. As this also included framing, it all seemed reasonable.

You can see by this that I'm still very much a woodworker at heart. Looking at quite a different skill I am still thinking in time spent on the job, plus materials. I wonder how a professional artist would view my method?

Another Mr Jay, Anthony Jay, rang me to ask would I be interested in taking part in the next Bognor carnival. This was brother of Keith, both the sons of Sam who's efforts to introduce social minibuses led to them being called 'Sammies' to this day. A member of the Bognor Lions, who were organising the event, asked if I would help with the procession. Most years the whole event had a theme, and sometimes willing participants were very keen but often short of ideas for their entries. 'Would I assist if someone requested help'?

I was very pleased to work for the Jays again, as I had done for the previous thirty years or so. Anthony Jay was an estate agent when we first met. His wife Doreen and their two children, with Deena and our two, were always keen to participate in anything Bognor. The first experience Anthony had of Deena's skills of dressing up was a riot. His disguise as a copper on the beat I'm sure was largely responsible for the fall in the crime rate that August. It put the wind up me at any rate!

As it turned out the 'Mardis Gras' as it was to be termed this time, did not require much help from me. I wasn't idle though, I used the intervening period to build a big carnival head. This was to be different from the others I'd made in the past. The wearer's arms would be free for balance and safety's sake. The body would have facilities to change heads. The wearer would also be able to push a smaller identical edition of the figure up through the hat, on a stick.

Rather like a Punch and Judy routine, I was using the same gag as I used with my entrance boots. Taking the large ones off to reveal a similarly decorated, but properly fitting pair, for working in, underneath. We found a volunteer to don the head, leaving me free to work and entertain the waiting crowds along the route.

From my experience with this walk and other events using the same route, Bognor is at a disadvantage always because of the location of its parks and open ground being far from the town centre. With my experience of helping to organise the children's procession for the clowns convention, we had felt it was far too long a walk from the West End car park to the town and back. With the family element encouraged and masses of children involved, our much shorter journey made all the difference for us. Even though our procession was in March when it was often much colder.

In the morning prior to the afternoon's action, I spent a couple of hours at a table by the Lion's stand, in the town centre, drawing face names for all and sundry passing by, with a collecting tin by my side. The whole day was fine, and the charity that year received a well-earned boost to their finances.

Chichester being within working distance of Bognor meant it was not surprising really that I would be asked to do something for their Lions Club. One of their money raising schemes was a kind of open market-come-table-top-come-boot-sale down the main parts of the town on a Sunday. I did children's shows with my van parked by the pavement. Somehow or other it never seemed to gell. There was no comfort in the cobbles or the shopping area. My audiences were wide ranging in age too. These are my thoughts only. My Lion friends seemed well satisfied with my contribution to the day.

Something in Chichester that used to tickle me was, when working in support of one particular charity in the Assembly Rooms, I had permission to park in the Mayor's allotted space, just behind the building. It never came to a test of which of us had priority rights on those dates. We never bumped into each other, thankfully for me. My feather duster would hardly have been much protection against the Mayoral chain and Mace!

Leaderboard Ltd was working in Chester for a race meeting and Jim asked if we would like to go. It's a beautiful racecourse and Chester is a lovely historic City, so we accepted his kind offer. I'm not a racing man myself but Deena loves it. One of the family whom she grew up with, Rhyce, like my dad, loved a bet. His enthusiasm found a willing target in her. It's not as though she would know how to put a bet on, but she can pick winners. Years ago one of her hobbies was marking the newspapers' race cards one day and checking them the next. I can vouch for her high score. But she is no gambler and we never tried to get any positive results from this knack of hers. Had we tried we might have all become better off!

Now straight after this jaunt we had elected to attend an international clown convention in Lincoln, the first one to be held there. So after a lovely few days in Chester we set our sights on getting across England to the Cathedral City. I had taken the trouble to get a route map from the AA but it seemed an awfully roundabout way of getting there. Silly me, it looked so simple on the map. Straight across. It was, as a crow flies, but someone forgot to remind me I was no crow, and our van couldn't fly. Of course, Derbyshire intervened in our 'straight line' journey.

Although you could use a ruler to draw a straight line across you'd have to use a dressmaker's tape to follow the ups and downs of the road surface. It turned out to be a very stressful journey. Often I was unsure if my bottom gear was low enough to overcome some stretches of it. There was only one redeeming feature of this saga and of course it was the beauty of the county itself. A most remarkable few hours that we'll never forget.

The Lincoln Festival was the first one we had attended since the ones in Bognor finished. We looked forward to meeting up with all our mates again. Deena wasn't dressing up, just looking after me. Lincoln is also an 'upsy downy place'. We were parked on a very upsy bit, the town was down a steep hill. The weather was fine and of course the Cathedral was a highlight. We did alfresco entertainments around town and invaded some council offices, much to the delight of the staff there.

In the town centre who should we meet there but our old sidekick Pierre. Not with the Model T this time but 'Chitty Chitty Bang Bang', the car used in the smash hit film of that title. He owned it now. He was dressed for the part too, and invited us aboard for a ride. It very much reminded Deena and me of the time we were last in the vehicle touring Middlesbrough on a road safety jaunt.

It was a somewhat hectic but very enjoyable few days stay there. During the procession through town, Deena spotted an eye catching item in a shop window that she loved and dearly wanted to buy. Somehow or other we were not able to get there again to do the business. It took one of our family a long time to forget this!

When my Lincoln photographs returned there was a good one of Pierre and Verco, Arthur Pedler, sitting nicely in Chitty just waiting to have a painting made of it. I did just that and made Pierre a very happy Joey. At least I hope it did. I've also painted Arthur's portrait since.

John Fenton was active again, he had taken over another restaurant, in Bognor this time. 'La Bodega' was its name and it had already been operating in the bistro business when the deal was done. So after a clear out and clean up he wondered what we had to offer this time. Even with the Santorini still open we had enough paintings to fit the place out.

I used some of Manet's portraits of beautiful women. They were a smaller size which fitted the many faceted areas of the new venue very well. I had painted another 'La Loge' which we made a focal point. Also I took another Berthe Morisot from the painting called 'The Woman on the Balcony'. A detail that stood up well on its own.

Again sad news from the Brooks family. My eldest sister and last surviving family member, Floss, had died. A fall in the bathroom precipitated it all. Eldest daughter, youngest son, we always were close. A fine craftswoman, she excelled in dressmaking, and seemed always to take things in her stride.

One day mum let me have my own drawer in the chest of drawers in the kitchen. Most of the space was taken up with bits of material she and Floss had given me. I was never afraid to put needle to thread. My stitches though reminded me of Neil Armstrong's famous words, 'One giant step'. My stitches were of the same ilk and size as his footsteps.

Husband George always called her Florrie. I never thought to ask her if that had been her wish. I'm afraid to me she was only ever to be 'my Floss.' The last connection with the past had now gone. We will no longer be able to cobble up probable truths about family relationships with remembered scraps from us both. Being so far behind her in age she was always able to help me get a clearer view of our family history. Our Harry will miss his Floss.

Malcolm had collected his first commission from me and a telephone conversation had given me some idea of what he wanted me to do next. On a family holiday he was photographed with his two sons out skiing. He already had an enlargement of the photo and wondered, 'could I do a painting from it?' Of course.

You cannot stray too far away from an actual photograph but there's no doubt you can also enhance and dramatise, and so I did with this. I surprised myself as well, managing reasonable likenesses, and still retained the power of the snow clad mountains.

I also had a Lautrec to do as well. It was a copy of 'The Café at the Windmill'. A group of Lautrec's friends posed for this painting, most of them entertainers. Toulouse had also included himself and his Uncle Gabriel in the background. I really love this painting. This artist rates very highly in my scale of 'the greats'.

It might be that I feel my natural style is running in the same direction as his. I always call this picture 'the green lady'. The figure in the bottom right of this painting has a face tinged with green. It's the house lights of the café presumably that caused this. It's also interesting for another reason too. I've read that he added another bit of canvas to the original design to accommodate her. So was it an afterthought?

I have some sympathy here with him, if that was so. My habit of working on hardboard enables me to crop my paintings after finishing, or add a bit on, if I've misjudged the subject's position on my ground. Whatever the reason, without that green countenance a vital part of the whole picture I think would be diminished. I had a hard job painting this, I remember. But it didn't stop me from painting a second one for me. I wonder what these early painters would have made of hardboard. Sizes from eight by four feet, tough, with two painting surfaces to choose from. One disadvantage though, it cannot be rolled up.

My one regret about the work I did for my client was parting with the Renoir painting 'The Dancers at Bouganville'. The young country couple dancing. She radiant and he red bearded, made a perfect partner. I regret not doing another for me. My legs won't stand up to it now otherwise I'd give it a go. A small posy of flowers is strewn on the foreground along with dog ends of cigarettes. The touch of a genius. Apart from loving his work I now have something in common with him. Arthritis. Whereas he suffered cruelly, I am benefiting from modern drugs and the comfort that comes if you are compatible with them. Very fortunately, I am

After Lincoln, we thought about a suggestion made to us by Sheila and Harry Beatson, 'Uncle Fred and Beato, who were camped with us on that occasion. It was our first chance of getting to know each other, as we were in Bognor and they lived in Sheffield. They urged us to book in for the next Azores convention, which we did.

To be eligible Deena also had to become a 'proper' clown. So in good time we arranged for my lovely girl to become 'Dee Dee' in her own right. Colourful and bright like the other half of our duo. I always knew this character was waiting to be let out. And there it was. Perfect.

Before the trip she had been practising Portuguese to translate for me to ask the locals for their names. Not an easy task with a limited vocabulary, to appear friendly whilst intervening on behalf of this red nosed bloke brandishing a note pad and pen, just waiting a chance to amaze them with his artistic skills and bring a smile to their faces, whatever the language, culture, or time and place.

So that following year we made one of our very rare trips abroad. It was Deena's first flight. Our clown club secretary Bluey Brattle and wife, Joey editor, Jenny, gave us a lift to Heathrow airport. Without their help none of the following would have happened. To me, getting to Heathrow, parking and getting a subsequent lift to the terminal was a major undertaking in itself, and in no way possible by ourselves. On top of this we were invited to sleep overnight in their home, so we could get off bright and early next day. This saved me having to do a fifty mile drive before starting off, sort of thing.

Arriving at Lisbon airport we met most of the others also coming with us, before catching another plane to Ponta del Gardo, Azores. Here we met the man of the moment, Clown Pezinho. The one whose monumental efforts had brought about this convention, and other previous ones. Also greeting us were Sheila and Harry who had flown out earlier.

The four star hotel 'The Ponta del Garda' was our base for the festival. Very comfy, excellent food, and within walking distance of the town. I was seventy-eight by then and had had plenty of practice noting these important details! The weather was excellent, the temperature just right and about two dozen of us were very compatible with each other. A perfect start to what was for Deena and me a most wonderful and magical ten days. We were feted everywhere we went.

The first day was taken up by a coach trip around the island, And what an island. Mind you the whole area is volcanic and very different from Bognor Regis. Hot springs, bubbling mud pools, geysers constantly spouting steam, and holes in the ground serving as ovens for cooking purposes.

Mind boggling vistas across extinct, we hoped, volcanoes, lush with tropical vegetation. The beaches with faintly greyish fine sand. Over the rocks a type of lizard was scuttling about. To my eyes it was a wonderland. We stopped for a marvellous lunch. I remember the word we used when stillness was called for, or a body was needed to make up a picture, it was 'Panasonic'. And with nearly everybody having a camera there was plenty of shouting going on whenever we stopped to observe another feature being pointed out and explained to us.

This day we were tourists, tomorrow we would start work. Back to the hotel to sort out our programme and props. For from the next day on, we would be in motley and being gazed at by many enquiring brown eyes and such.

The beds and rooms were all we could wish for, and after breakfasting our first visit was to meet the President in his offices. A grand place and everybody was very friendly. He spoke excellent English. I don't know if any of our lot spoke Portuguese, but amongst our sprinkling of non English clowns we had Dutch, Swedish, French and a lively American girl clown called Giggles, also a couple of Geordies that even we couldn't understand. So it was a kind of regulated confusion.

We were given gifts and plenty of reading material about the Islands. Excellent photographs came out of it too. 'Look, this is me, that is the President.' Marvellous stuff for the folks back home. I did the President's name and anybody Dee Dee and I could nail to get a bit of practice before going public. Then we entered the outside world.

We were a colourful lot, all dressed up doing clowny things, and we moved in a loose group through the town centre like an amoeba. We flowed in a kind of circusy way. It was quite an extraordinary experience. So different from Lincoln. I loved it all. So warm and friendly. Every now and again, finding an English speaker, I came into my own, being able to complement my actions with my own repartee. I otherwise leaned heavily on my beloved to translate.

Our evening meals were gifts from the owners of the establishments we visited throughout our stay, it being their contribution to the cost of the whole festival. A large part of our hotel costs and flights were also subsidised by the local authority and businesses. We had a very good deal. I for one could not have considered the whole occasion if this had not been so.

The menus on offer reflected many of the local dishes available in the region, mid-Atlantic. Fish of course comes to mind, pineapples, bananas, and lots of other goodies. Once when I chose sardines it was news to me that they had been swimming off-shore just a short time ago. The size of them came as a complete surprise. My only knowledge of sardines until then came from the tinned variety. My dish had fish that stretched across a dinner plate. Other surprises were included in the evening meals. One owner gave us all a lovely drinking glass as a memento. He had each one engraved with our name on it before we left.

One evening we had a group of local singers and musicians serenading us as we ate. One song I really liked. A traditional air, it was very catchy. We were given a video of the island and when we got home and watched it, I was delighted this song was on it.

There was a lovely moment one evening when one of our number, Thelma, 'Pineapple', produced a commemoration cake she'd baked herself and brought from home. Everyone was very grateful for this. The proprietors of our evening café were especially pleased.

For four days we worked alfresco around and about, visiting hospitals and other selected places. One day was spent in a village that had arranged the whole day for us which included a procession through the village in the afternoon. They had stacked all our food in the village hall so we could live like Royalty during our stay. In the evening we were welcomed one by one onto a stage set up in the village centre and handed gifts and a specially made trophy to mark our visit. It was made of pottery and suitably engraved.

The procession was an eye opener. We were made part of an obviously annual event. The whole community was there. As we slowly meandered on our way, Deena and I did a roaring trade with the names. All ages, all shapes, one language, theirs, how we coped was something that will long remain with us. The weather was perfect and afterwards at bedtime each of us had not the slightest difficulty in getting off to sleep, of that, I'm pretty sure.

After three days of spreading ourselves all over the island on the last day, the Sunday, we were to give a gala performance in the town's theatre. It was an evening show and everybody was getting prepared. I had started long before this, mocking up an easel to do a lightning sketch act. I had brought my paper and chalks, but the easel was too large to bring on the plane.

During this whole venture Pezinho and his wife Maria had been cosseting us around, and a young student, Pedro, was helping out with the language problem. I now enlisted his help with my act. I would draw, he would speak. Sounds simple enough! I didn't know whether he had been on a large stage before. It can be quite daunting to some. Anyway, after a few dummy runs of the act during the afternoon, we awaited our fate. The show started very late, as was usual I was told.

When the actual time came we all did well. Deena helped by dressing the stage and taking my used papers from me. I had a couple of natives up on the stage and did their names. Pedro was a great help in explaining what I was about to the audience. We had a very good ovation when we went off, very relieved it had gone over well. Relaxing off stage we looked forward to enjoying the rest of the show.

All these performers I knew, but had not seen their acts before. The quality of the bits I saw made me very proud to have been a part of the whole. The variety of skills my friends displayed, no doubt in my opinion, enhanced the prestige of Clowns International well and truly, in the islands that make up The Azores.

The press next day gave us a very good write up. I noticed in the foyer of the theatre the Club's collection of clown eggs were on display. Each egg was decorated with the person's face and own clown make up on. These stretch back many years and include many famous faces of yesteryear. I hadn't had one made of me, I was always just waiting for the opportunity to make my own. I still haven't got round to it.

On the Monday half of our group returned home. The rest of us availed ourselves of a very kind offer from our hotel's owners for another four days at greatly reduced prices. We clubbed together and hired a minibus in which Bluey drove us about. We opted to re-visit some of the places we briefly saw on our initial tour. But first the men had a puncture to sort out.

Mobile again, we inspected greenhouses filled with rows of pineapples that dwarfed the ones we were used to seeing back home. Bathing costumes came to the fore a lot as our group enjoyed the excellent bathing beaches available. We then dined in the hotel. There was a nice bar to relax in afterwards.

One day we spent where Pezinho lived. A rocky wild sort of coastline that sent tingles down your spine. Especially, if like me, you don't take kindly to heights. Their house was quite a delight. The garden something else. Tropical plants and the first banana trees I had ever seen were eye openers to us from more temperate climes.

We sat down to an afternoon cuppa and enjoyed all sorts of goodies. This is where we made a big mistake. About an hour later we were told it was now time to eat! Going indoors again to a meal that couldn't be resisted. But where to put it? We did find a way in the end and so a fabulous day out came to an end with a bus ride back to Ponta. We all voted ourselves the luckiest of clowns to have come to this magical place, populated by such kindly people. To us a holiday never to be forgotten.

Chapter 40

Pain and More Travel

The Millennium was about to burst on us. We were passing the Tesco supermarket one Saturday and Deena was missing a couple of items, so we pulled in to rectify the matter. Our policy was always to use a shopping trolley. For so few items this time she held a wire basket instead. Lots of people were milling around caused her to stumble slightly and go off balance. Reaching out with a hand to steady herself, she grasped at an upright display stand and it moved away, causing her to fall.

Her shoulder took the brunt of it, dislocating itself in the process. She was in agony. An ambulance was called which took her to hospital. Over the next few months our lives literally came to a halt. She was in deep distress and constant pain. We had to sleep downstairs for weeks.

I examined the display stand situation. It was made entirely of cardboard and relied solely on the weight of the goods it displayed for its stability. Its narrow shelves held a variety of packets of sauces you mixed yourself with water when needed in the kitchen, or just added to dishes. It was not fixed to ground or wall. I was advised by the local Citizens' Advice Bureau of a solicitor to contact. We were accepted as a case against the supermarket on a no-win no-fee basis.

Later I was informed that I should have photographed the offending stand for evidence. This advice came too late. The corner of the store had been re-arranged which eliminated the evidence of it being within reach for her to have touched it. The store manager was less than truthful with his description of the event. They disputed liability.

Our representation was from a partnership with offices in Worthing and our man in Littlehampton. During the course of the next few months they split up. The Law Society stepped in and we were advised as to who would now have responsibility for our case. We met with the firm in Worthing and I got the distinct impression that they were not entirely happy with our situation and would rather withdraw. So it was. We were abandoned.

From the first meeting with our own man, I had complete faith in his integrity and ability. I never saw anybody from his partners' office. It was only this feeling of trust that persuaded Deena to take any action in the first place. She was not keen for any slanging match in court, but she was constantly assured by our solicitor that this would not happen. I don't know what caused their dispute, we were never told. Their offices closed down and I still feel we were hard done by events out of our control.

We lost a whole year in the garden, and have never really caught up. Deena had now to face her own physio and hospital visits. I suspect at our age things rarely return to where they were, and Deena agrees with me. These last few lines were written a few years after the fall. How right we were to think that way. The pain of lying in certain positions in bed are now highlighting the damage, caused by a free standing display cabinet, being used to display lightweight merchandise in a very busy supermarket lane. I wonder if that store manager ever reads this, will his conscience alter his recollection of what happened?

When I first spied some recycled note pads in our local stationers, I knew there was something in it for me. These A5 sheets, two hundred and fifty per pad, were of a paper texture that just suited the pens I used for my names, and they were only seventy five pence each.

In the Christmas work for Morants we did at the Chichester Cross, to attract shoppers, I had used A4 sized sheets, with a larger pen. It was like entertaining in the round, lots of eyes, lots of faces to put with names. It was the right size for the job. Later doing it sitting down at a table, this smaller size was now more than adequate.

It was whilst writing these pages it occurred to me that these drawings are probably scattered all over the place, but I'd never attempted a collection of my own. So I decided to do just that. Rather than a massive book I chose a size to show just twenty-four names. I had the ideal source for the job, in my own fun names order book. The vast magnitude of people's names is really staggering. Nowadays it's a nightmare the way even common ones are spelt differently. The rule now seems to be, 'there are no rules'.

We had enjoyed the Azores convention so much that when Leon Laurence organised a trip to Utrecht, Holland, for a Dutch hospital festival, we jumped at the chance. Bluey and Jenny again took all the strain away by getting us there.

No planes this time. When we alighted from the North Sea ferry we still had a fair journey to do by road. Our destination was a holiday home a few miles out of Utrecht. All very well organised with central heating, a well stocked refrigerator, and a book of suggestions on how to make our stay comfortable.

We never really got to grips with the heating but an electric fire did the trick anyway. After a good night's sleep we were ready to board the coach that was to take us each day to Utrecht. Here we met Leon and Margaret. They handed out our jobs for the day. Ours was to work in a shopping complex making up part of a day's show from a stage.

Deena hadn't enough Dutch to do all the translating for my stage act, but there were local helpers who agreed to try their hand at it. We were a mixed bunch of performers but we all gelled together to make a continuous stage show for a few hours. The businesses in the complex were our main sponsors for this part of the festival.

Afterwards, back to the hospital where we all dined in a large hall. The food was excellent and amidst the other bits and pieces contained in the hall was a piano. Joy of joys. After making a few enquiries as to the using of it, I was to play a bit each evening for the assembled eaters. They all applauded my efforts but to me playing was its own reward.

In another part of the hospital grounds was set up a circus tent. Any of our clowns who had something to offer in the ring for the circus programme did so. Leon was giving us all a change. Another day we were out visiting day centres, old folks homes and the like.

Most days we all met in another part of the grounds where we kept our clothes, make up and props, and had our lunch. Here we got to know who was who, what country they were from, and were generally able to let our hair down.

My camera was working overtime. I repeated something I did in Bognor all those years ago, systematically photographing all and sundry present. The light was excellent and my light meter didn't let me down. There were a couple of families with their children, all dressed up. These turned out to be marvellous subjects.

One of our lot, 'Smilie', Stephen Norman, saw the portrait I'd painted of the great Russian clown Popov, as a thank you for Bluey's kindness. He asked me to do one of him. Taking photographs of him in full motley, I was able to fulfil the request when I got back home.

One day Deena and I were part of a group allocated to entertain at a large watch manufacturer's party for the children of their employees. It was quite a do. The parents were there too, so there were a lot of people in the works canteen that day. I did a drawing spot, and then got comfortable at a table with Deena, drawing all their names. At the end of the day all our group were presented with wrist watches. Very good ones too! That evening a bar was opened in our holiday home site. Very welcome after a busy day.

Next morning back to the shopping complex, and in the middle of the day the fire alarm went off. The disruption it caused nearly ruined the rest of our working day.

We did have a few hours off one morning and walked into Utrecht's town centre for a shopping trip. There is such a lot of English spoken in Holland that the language never seemed a problem. On these occasions we both look out for postcards, Deena for inclusion in her scrapbooks or for mementos, me for subjects to paint. What luck this day. I found three postcard photographs of children, babies, that I have painted regularly since for selling back home.

One being bathed by Mum, another, all big blue eyes and dribbles everywhere, the third still in napkins and standing in Dad's shoes. Not knowing their photographers I do still take my hat, and wig, off to them for their skills.

For our last day off most of us decided we would a visit Amsterdam. The trains and motorways were all up to-the-minute and very impressive. On returning home I thought it was a shame that we couldn't seem to do as well, my personal feelings mind you.

The shops were breathtaking, however, when we went to pay for purchases our card was not accepted. Even now I don't know why. Had I not remembered my number correctly? It was early days for these practices and so there could have been a flaw in the system, or was it me?

Out in the streets again I had my first experience of professional street performers. I was fascinated by one silver clad figure striking poses. It was only his occasional blinking of the eyes that told you he was probably looking forward to egg and chips for supper after work. Would he have suffered severe rust problems should it shower, like the tin man in Dorothy's tale of Oz?

We opted for a boat ride on the canals and it was so restful gliding under the bridges. The banks of these canals were seemingly decorated with bicycles, mostly unmanned, leaning to their hearts content in large numbers, patiently waiting to ensure their owners don't have to walk far. I wondered how earlier generations had managed to pedal with clogs on!

It was on our return train journey, and hearing what the others had got up to, that my big disappointment came. I had not known that the fair city of Amsterdam housed the Van Gough museum. After all that I had read about the great painter, one of the greatest I think, it did not click that being a Dutchman he was bound to be honoured and his works housed in a principal city museum. I was watching bicycles instead of gazing at his paintings. The feeling of loss will never leave me, I'm sure.

After our Azores trip I was determined to make a present for Pezinho and family. The opportunity to present it was at a farewell party given us by the hospital for that year's presence of us clowns. I knew they would be there.

At an opportune moment we presented them with a pieces of my woodwork. A fun name for their daughter Marie, and a name sculpture for Pedro, which combined in its design his name and his favourite musical instrument, the guitar. For Maria, her name sculpture acknowledged her great skill as a cook, with a tiny mixing bowl and wooden spoon nestling in it.

For the chief himself I placed a clown figure astride an island holding his name Pezinho, above his head. The 'I' in his name was a rabbit, as he was also a conjuror, as well as being a singer with a fine tenor voice. I shaped the island he was astride of in the guise of the Island of San Miguel. His bit of the world out there in mid atlantic. I was so pleased they liked all our gifts, a present from Clowns International, Deena and me.

In our village of Middleton-on-Sea, we held our annual fete round about the first of August each year. I always did my bit whenever I could. From the very early years of us living there, they always knew where to find me. But it was in the latter years that I became a more regular contributor. Apart from so enjoying doing a show for the children, I am a keen believer in the 'if you can, then do it', sort of mentality. Don't be shy about joining in local events, whatever they are.

This approach is not thick on the ground. Every year the gallant doers and organisers would love to see their numbers increase and so lighten their work load. The reticence has something to do with shyness sometimes, so if this paragraph prompts a little bit more of the joining in feeling to abound, jolly good.

Looking down the year's happenings it's the regular dates that come to the fore. Littlehampton Regatta is one, Micheham Priory another. Both fair weather dates. Darker nights and with Christmas beckoning, more indoor stuff. One such date was Betty Lebron's playgroup party. They met in the Jubilee Hall in Middleton-on-Sea.

A week before the great day, I would go and entertain them all prior to the arrival of their red cloaked, white bearded visitor who was so kind with his gifts. Not very long ago their ages were from four to five, nowadays they include three year olds as well.

I used my Tufty show primarily, adding more goodies related to party time. I invented bits of business and many a game for this very young age group. The 'bird game' was one of these. Teaching these creatures to fly encouraged them to participate in no uncertain fashion. In the meantime I gently introduced them to clowns. Very seldom did we fail to get a happy acquaintance going, with thirty or forty young children present.

This number was made up by both morning and afternoon groups attending the party together. I didn't use make up on these occasions. Dressing up in front of them, I was only ever to briefly wear my red nose for a minute or so before hastily removing it. It pinched you see! I also had far more difficulty putting my coat on than they did. It seemed as if I had more arms than usual. Anyway, where these limbs got to produced guaranteed chortles from our young experts out front. Eventually I got my arms in my coat, and the show continued.

Galloping up over the horizon was my eightieth birthday. The family were determined to make it a memorable day. A marquee was booked to fit our garden. The apple tree had to slim somewhat by a couple of branches. A rose bush was moved for the celebration and never really recovered from its upheaval, otherwise the canvas structure fitted in very well. It was decked out with wooden flooring panels, and the hired circular tables and chairs enabled us to sit and feast in comfort.

Jim insisted we put up all my impressionist paintings as décor. So putting two large screw eyes in each frame, we hung them on the walls of the tent. It did my heart good to see so many being on display at once. It was an amazing sight too. I hardly think any museum would ever have shown such a variety of well known and loved paintings together. Being mostly full size copies, and not at all bad ones at that, all my friends were very impressed at the range of subjects.

For Van Gogh lovers was his 'Bedroom', 'Sunflowers', 'Café at Night', 'The Sower', 'Irises', 'Cornfield with Cyprus Trees', 'The Schoolboy', 'Zouave' and 'The Harvest'. Renoir was represented by 'The Two Circus Girls', 'The

Dancer', 'La Loge', 'Umbrellas', 'Girl with Watering Can', and 'The Luncheon Party'. For Manet admirers there were, 'The Bar at the Follies', 'At the Café', 'The Waitress' 'The Gypsy Girl', 'Jeanie', 'Nana', 'Berthe Morisot', 'On The Balcony', 'Flowers in a Vase', 'On the Beach', 'Plum', and four smaller portraits of women whose names I could never get my tongue around.

I always referred to them as 'The Blue Lady', 'Lady In Red'. I never really had a name for the person who had an imperious pose, and the one whose one breast was having a quick lookout from the dress she was wearing. I knew this one as 'The Bosom'. It's a good job I didn't have to catalogue them.

For good measure we also had 'The Absinthe Drinkers' by Degas, and Toulouse Lautrec's 'The Clowness', 'La Goulou', 'Doctor Gabriel', 'The Till Lady', 'The Brothel' and the 'Moulin Rouge Café'. The 'Bathers' by Seurat, and 'The Card Players' by Cezanne.

Jim's partners Alan and Dan were the music providers, and, when I asked 'could we have the piano in?', it was lifted, carried and placed right of stage, in a flash. The garden had been wired up to cater for seven or eight waterproof light points, so we had an area surrounding the marquee lit I in the manner you would expect from Leaderboard Ltd. Enchanting!

The hired diesel generator was not far away to keep us warm. We did have a hiccup just a few hours before the guests were due to arrive. The connector to the drum of diesel sprang a leak. It spilled over a ten foot patch of grass under the apple tree. The grass took more than a year to recover. The mechanics hastily came and put things right for us. It was February, and it felt like it too.

We decided to have the family come in the afternoon, most of whom had travelling to contend with. My lot lived in the home counties, Deena's family, of course, were from Wales. Other friends invited filtered in prior to sitting down to eat. Neighbours helped out with parking problems. Jim was M.C., Tina and Casey charming hostesses.

Our Michael, the younger son, was in charge of the bar. It was a difficult choice to make from the queues of volunteers. Michael's partner Hazel, and her two daughters Tina and Casey, came bearing the fruits of their labours in the kitchen. Hazel, a wonderful cook, did the hot dishes, making a wonderful spread when we sat down to eat.

Afterwards Jim surprised us by doing a 'This is your Life' on me. Projecting photographs of some of my bits and pieces onto a screen on the back canvas. I did my adult sketch act, then Jim and his group 'The Reunion Band' gave us some Irish music. It was a fantastic evening.

There was a clear plastic panel in the rear canvas and through it we could see the grass decorated with props and sculptures. Then in the garden lighting we saw large snowflakes descending. A touch of magic. We all trooped out to the front garden later for a fireworks display our boys put on. From being a private affair the whole works were being given to all and sundry as if November fifth had somehow got out of sync., and was giving a second show in February.

To end it all I played the piano for a massive quiz on songs from the Vesta Tilley era to the Beatles. When we turned off the generator, and all the folks had gone, whatever else had happened, it had been the most wonderful party any eighty year old could ever has wished for. Lucky me!

A few weeks after this I had quite a lot of trouble with my legs. A numbness was creeping over the outside of them but any slight tap revealed there was a lot going on in the inside. The tests I was put through were rather strange. Wired up on the feet with meters showing if there were any disconnected areas higher up. Bone density readings. All in all I was given the full treatment. It all failed to add to my understanding of what was going on. I survived though!

Joining in an exhibition of works by the over-sixties I got a certificate for my recycling entry. A small chest of drawers for the workshop, constructed out of cardboard. The drawers were actually plastic four pinta milk containers from the supermarket. With the stoppers glued shut and an entry hole cut in the top surface for storing small items like screws, washers and nails. I use these drawers all round my workshop, each with a number painted on the stopper. A workshop book tells what's in each one. The chest I got a gold certificate for in the crafts exhibition was pinched by Deena long ago to house her collection of buttons and knick knacks.

In subsequent years I put in my two clown collecting receptacles made from larger thin bleach bottles, and I also started entering paintings in the art section. I had another win with a portrait of my grandchild Oliver, being seen just observable in soap foam bubbles whilst he was being bathed. Later still I entered my cardboard dog sculpture, Boxer! The exhibition became a victim of local authority cuts to save money in 2006.

The September of that time saw a new activity added to attract visitors to Bognor in late season. Called the 'Sands of Time,' it was a grand sand castle making day, generally over a weekend. Paul Wells, a local councillor and shopkeeper who started the idea, sought my help in getting a procession through the town down to the pier, as a prelude to the moment when the tide went out. Then out would come the buckets and spades to start a day of digging and moulding the sand.

To encourage participation in the walk the council put up a fifty pound prize for the best entrant. During the weeks prior to this event I had been busy building a new fund collecting machine for Red Nose Day. It was a Colonel Blimp type figure astride a horse, mounted on a pram for ease of travelling. The horse was a 'Knights of the Round Table' type, named 'Trier' and his rider was 'Major Blunder'.

Another clown act had also been engaged to be there. It was Mr Woo of the Custard Clowns. I didn't see them on the day doing their act, I was busy wheeling our Major Blunder in the procession. My normal act on these occasions, with the large comb and feather duster, was given a rest. When, 'blow me down', it was announced over the loudspeakers that my prop had won the fifty pound prize. I hadn't even thought I would be considered for it. But there, a big surprise, and the cheque that accompanied the accolade was very welcome. 'Sands of Time' has prospered and grown into a popular annual event.

I'd earned another fifty pounds that week, entertaining at our local football club fund-raising event. Every year Bognor Rocks, as they're known, had a large firework display. I did a mix and mingle with the crowds before the main event.

My legs were playing up and I had trouble standing. To help me get through the three hours I'd altered my prop trolley to include a lift up lid which I'd upholstered for a bit of comfort. Nobody commented on the fact that the clown was sitting down more than usual! A good job too. The moans would have been much louder if said clown had failed to turn up at all.

Another red dot on my appointments list bore the legend 'visit health centre'. It was time for my flu jab. Anybody my age is advised to have one as a precaution against the flu virus. In my youth I saw how serious it could be, and these memories are not easily forgotten. Quite a bit different from when the army MO told me to drop them. No deep needles, hardly a scratch, but a potential life saver nevertheless.

Chapter 41

Making Alvine Comfy

Along with advice about getting inocculated against the flu was a kind letter from a government department calling itself 'Warm Front'. It asked, 'does your house leak warmth, and have draughts, un-insulated walls and roof space?' Yes, Yes, Yes, was my speedy reply. So a kind inspector came and inspected, to make sure I was not telling porkies. Porkies? Cockney rhyming slang for lies (pork pies).

It seems that as I was over eighty and lacking in assistance to keep warm over the cold months, I was eligible for help. They proposed installing central heating, insulating the walls and roof space and dealing with draughty doors and windows. I very nearly instructed my darling Deena to give the man a kiss. But seriously though, this was very good news to us both. Our cottage was a charming place, but with solid floors and only a couple of storage heaters, it was a killer in the winter.

In boot sales and charity shops I had managed to obtain a goodly supply of electric fires to supplement our open fires and heaters in the past. But they all only gave a fleeting service, and were very expensive to run, and from the government's point of view they in no way helped to conserve energy, the purpose behind the Warm Front's initiative.

Now we were to have a gas boiler supplying hot water to the radiators and hot water to the taps. We were to be allowed five radiators free, but you could pay the installer for extras if you wished. I opted to pay for three extra for the other two bedrooms, and my workshop. This meant the whole cottage would be heated. No longer would we need to make a swift exit from one room to another to keep the heat in!

The outside walls of the house were dealt with first. What I had considered to be an almost impossible job was dealt with in a properly modern way. When Les and I built our houses in Potters Bar, there wasn't the pressure to install insulation. As Les advanced up with the walls he would have installed the insulating material between the two layers of bricks which make up a cavity wall, as he built up. That's the modern way houses are insulated now.

Came the day and a one-man installer arrived with his lorry which carried all the warm insulating stuff and a blooming great drill. After he'd used the drill to bore holes in strategic places, through our cottage's outer skin of bricks, he then went on to the second stage of the job. With a long hose pipe connected up to a machine, he blew the warm stuff into the holes until the cavities were full. All clever stuff! After bunging up the holes afterwards, hey ho, the cottage has a woolly jumper on, buttoned up by technology and a spot of brute force. And the filler-upper drove off as happy as a sand boy.

Deena then stopped brewing up and making coffee to help him along, and realised with me that we'd just been insulated. What a difference a few years make. My natural inquisitiveness was also in full flood when the draughts man arrived to prevent 'Willy the wind' playing havoc through old doors and window frames.

With up-to-the-minute plastic strips, either pinned in position or being self-adhesive, stuck on, the job was soon accomplished. As I had boarded my roof space over with some insulation underneath, it was agreed not to disturb it. Then came the heating engineer, one plumber and his mate. This was to be a major enterprise as compared with the other work.

I have always admired plumbers and electricians, (good ones) for being able to do their jobs in the most difficult and trying circumstances. Putting all their pipes and wires mostly out of sight is not the easiest way of installing water or electricity services. Working under floors, baths, sink units, in ceilings and similar, is rather like the policeman in the Gilbert and Sullivan song, theirs is 'not a happy lot, tra la'.

The firm undertaking the work was called Quake. The workers and work done were of the highest quality. The three extra radiators caused them no trouble and made me a very happy man. The one in the workshop, my garage, especially so. When you see the state of it, it's no wonder I was worried. It's not a great big affair, but my van was too large for it, luckily, so my workshop problem was solved for me. With all its bits and bobs, the oil-stove and electric fire was not the safest way of keeping it warm.

We were told the system would be looked after for seven years under our Warm Front agreement. What happens next will be of great interest to me. I will probably be nearing ninety by then. I shall just love to be told the seven year agreement is up, to my face!

This business of heating water reminded me of a happening years earlier. Our hot water tank was a large galvanised affair heated by an electric immersion heater. It was very efficient and the airing cupboard in which it was installed was excellent for Deena and the washed clothes. The system had a snag. To put a new washer on a tap you had to drain the whole lot to do it. Jim and I had to install a new immersion element and thought it a good idea to drain and clean out the tank whilst it was empty.

On the front was a circular plate bolted on, the size of a saucer. We had buckets handy to collect anything left in the tank. Those last four words, 'left in the tank', heralded a Niagara-like gush of water that made us realise we should have asked someone about it beforehand. Like a Plumber! Most of it overshot our buckets and left an indelible mark on the ceiling below. Even when all the water above the level of the plate had gone, I still had about four buckets of lime scale from over the years to carry downstairs. Woe is the duo that thinks they know it all! Back to the harsh reality of old age. The Warm Front scheme gets my approval. Every winter it saves our lives as well as comforting us.

We had not really had holidays like other families since our boys were at school. We had had a week in Butlin's, Pwllheli, in the fifties, and regular visits to the family in Mumbles. After that for years the way we earned our living, and the places it took us to, seemed to suffice. Neither of us were 'laze on the beach' types. But when we withdrew from that lifestyle I fancied doing something completely different.

We thought to try a five-day all in winter break being trumpeted by the coach people Shearings. It was to be an all inclusive affair. We were to be picked up locally at Bognor Station and deposited back in the same place after the holiday. No money worries. Full board, free trips, and excellent coaches driving us to interesting places. Fine hotels and free drinks if wanted. The lot.

For our first venture we chose Port Madoc. The hotel was family-owned and when we arrived was enjoying a onceover in preparation for the coming summer season.

Port Madoc, North Wales, not far from Pwllheli, is a fine seaside resort. From the shops I stocked up with the pens I use for my fun names. They seemed considerably cheaper than at home. In a shoe shop I found a pair of carpet slippers that fitted beautifully, but one had a slight blemish, so the price was reduced. I don't think my tootsies ever noticed it.

Although we were supplied with a packed lunch from the hotel, we indulged once in a fish and chip meal. Our two seasons working for Butlin's had warmed us to the North Waliens. So with nice weather abounding what more could one want? Our coach trips saw us in a glass works of some repute, and a visit to Portmeirion, a fantasy town composed of bits of ancient buildings, of different styles, and exotic corners built on a forested slope in the Welsh countryside,

Returning about four o'clock to tea and biscuits back in the hotel, I found a piano in the lounge in very good condition. I asked if I would be disturbing anybody if I had a play. Nobody demurred. So playing anything from stage musical shows, recent hits, and some requests, an hour soon sped by. After a splendid dinner served by a staff of waiters that had amongst its accents the compelling Welsh lilt of local boys and girls.

In the evening there was a bingo spot, an entertainer, and drinks at the bar. No cash involved, for me any way, you just disclosed your room number to the barman. And so to bed, worn out. We loved every minute of it. Since then we have sampled Paignton, Llantwydd Wells and Ilfracombe. In 2007 we booked for Great Yarmouth. I don't know what caught up with me but my legs started to be a little unreliable. I had to give up driving, and also cancel the holiday.

It was costly too. According to the rules of the game I had to lose my deposit of a £100. It turned out to be more than £100. I never read the small print. Who does? I had to pay a further eighty pounds to extricate me from the booking regulations and cancellation fees.

There were a couple of downsides to these dream holidays. Neither Deena nor myself are shower takers. It was of little comfort to find there were no baths available in some hotels, only the stand up variety that can scald one minute, and freeze your socks off the next. And a bit of a slippy do when you're getting on a bit. I only came across one piano that I could get my hands on. Keyboards were sometimes about but its not the same to a piano lover.

But for enjoyability, cost and service, it was on par with the Butlin's experience when we worked there, except, in the camps, we had to hump our own luggage about! One of our excursions in the coach took us to Swansea. I had seen it after the bombing raids, and was a regular visitor for ten years whilst we lived in Mumbles, bringing our boys up.

No sign of the Swansea Empire now, where I was first given the opportunity to tread the boards of a gilded and plush entertainments venue. Only a short time before it seems we had watched Bruce Forsyth and Des O'Connor perform there, and were conned into giving two live shows for free to someone promising to see that I would be discovered on TV after doing so. What a lark it all was. The very stuff of life.

On our return journey to the hotel we passed through Mumbles and stopped for a short while. In the café's car park where we had stopped I could see the island with its lighthouse, where I had lived briefly at the war's end. With two cats, two guns, two tides that swept the linking causeway to the mainland to the steps that led up to the Pier Ballroom, where I first met Deena. In good time we had two sons. James David and Michael Anthony. Two good names each. It seems I'm getting all literal in my dotage.

Ilfracombe was chosen for one of our destinations because of childhood memories. Mum's sister Ann lived in Minehead with her daughter Elsie, and it was only a few miles down the Somerset coast to Ilfracombe. It was a favourite destination for Mum, Rene, Lil and me.

Down on the seafront was a building we would dearly have loved to have had at home in Bognor Regis. It was the tourist office and information centre plus an all-purpose concert hall. A modern concept of what the village hall of old used to be, for the whole community. When I told Jim about it, he declared that it was one thing that all his friends of a like mind had been striving towards for years. My own feeling about the situation is we are better off in Middleton-on-Sea than our parent town. We have our own Jubilee Hall. Although small, there is nothing quite like it in town.

There is a strange parallel to this next bit. It's from when the sound engineer of the film crew stopped filming when he said to the producer Jennifer, 'There's a noise'. I was being given a once over by my doctor when he declared, whilst wearing his stethoscope, 'you've got a murmur'. Being more used to a round of applause, I was intrigued by this lowering of appreciation, even though it was of an audience of one. There was no pain and I was quite well in myself, but to him there was a different slushing sound from one of my heart valves than he expected to hear.

So started a saga of tests, hospital visits, and close scrutiny by the heart department, to this indicator that something was amiss. After being seen by several consultants and having different scans, my first test was to be at Southampton General Hospital. Jim drove me there and then went off to work, arranging to pick me up in the evening after the procedure.

When I learned I could not be seen to that day, the hospital sent me home by taxi. The taxi driver was a poet. After the journey and over a cup of tea, Deena and I listened whilst he read some of his work. Afterwards Deena told me it was of a very high standard indeed.

Next day there was room for me on the list. My turn would come in the afternoon period. About six procedures a day I think. I was surprised how many hospital staff were needed to carry out the test. I remember being injected with a coloured fluid on the one side, then being turned and done again on the other. Now, though, I could see the television screen showing the progress of the fluid in the veins and arteries of my leg.

Thinking of it now it looked rather similar to my road map whilst travelling up north to the schools. There being no sedation for this procedure I can relate this now. Afterwards, and before Jim came to pick me up, I was told by the specialist I was in need of two by-passes to ensure a proper flow of the life giving red stuff, blood.

For my next test, this time in St Richards, Chichester, I was to be sedated. A probe was lowered through my throat to peek in at my discordant heart valve. It was not such a long procedure this time, and my memory only covers before and after my sleep. After all the information had been gathered I then came face to face with the consultant.

In very clear terms he told me what he advised I should have done to forestall any heart trouble in the future. I thought then, how lucky I was to have been picked up in time for this to happen, before any illness showed it was necessary. I agreed to having two by-passes and one heart valve replacement, performed as soon as possible. In the event of a certain time passing without an operation I could opt for having it done abroad.

This was not necessary and some weeks later I was summoned to Midhurst for the thing to happen. I was going to be treated in the King George's Hospital for Officers. Well, I do recall being for a short term, a local, unpaid, non-commissioned officer during my army days, but I never expected this. It's probably not what they meant either!

So with my bag packed and in Jim's car, off we went to the hospital. We met a surgeon who was there to explain what would happen to me in the next ten days or so. He also read out a risk list of the nasty bits that could also happen. Afterwards, I agreed with Jim that it sounded as though he was doing his best to get me to cancel and walk out! With a ten per cent risk here and a two per cent risk there of all the probabilities that could go wrong. I could imagine Tony

Hancock making a television sketch out of it. But then it was all over. We both enjoyed a cup of tea in the canteen and then Jim left me to it.

It turned out to be very satisfactory. Nice people and staff, good food, and a few of us awaiting our turn in a small ward, comfortable in bed. I had to get used to being called Harry by everybody. Hal the clown was left at home in Middleton-on-Sea.

It all seemed to happen very quickly. A 'nil by mouth' card was placed over my bed, then early the next morning I was given my pre-med, then I was wheeled away to somewhere or other.

I awoke back in the ward, a bit sore around my chest and also one leg. The surgeon who explained all the pitfalls of having my operation, had also explained that to enable them to repair bits of blocked veins they would be gathering the necessary tubing from my legs, seeking veins that were healthy and not varicosed. If none could be found they would search other parts for them instead. 'The mind boggles'!

I renewed my acquaintance with my fellow patients, some of whom had preceded me, others awaiting their turn. It wasn't long before I met the hospital physiotherapist. Helped out of bed, I was made to walk a little in short bursts.

I soon became aware of the post-operative routine. A bottle by the bed and an alarm button to press if I needed assistance. Mid morning, the surgeon's inspection entourage flowed by each bed in turn, discussing the latest stage of treatment required, with a ward sister taking notes.

The doling out of the medicine rounds. The periods when nurses were able to help with personal requirements. The list arriving for you to tick off your choice for the next day's meals. A hospital volunteer wheeling a comfort trolley around delivering newspapers and knick knacks. Visitors? I was not left for long before Deena walked in. Midhurst, being an hour's drive from Alvine Cottage, meant transport had to be organised, although there seemed to be no official visitor times.

The whole ambience of the hospital was very friendly. With a telephone by my bed, and other features about, it was clear that being in a private hospital accepting NHS patients like me, I was getting a very good deal indeed. I was totally unaware of any 'them and us' situations. Those who were paying privately and me, in there by the National Insurance contributions I paid every week for the stamp on my card.

I was coming to terms with my ablutions. The nurses were all angels in my eyes. Two names I remember, Alison and Karen. They both had a job combing their hair. It was their blooming halo getting in the way.

I had to sit down to shave and got quite skilled at it, secretly thanking the inventor of the safety razor. Standing for long periods was a problem at the time. It was the healing of my long leg wounds that delayed me getting out in the normal ten days. The scar in my leg where they had removed the vein was behaving in a less than helpful way. From heel to thigh it wandered, it took over a month to heal.

The nights were interesting. Every so often I went on the bottle, in a clinical sense mind you, and sitting on the side of the bed was a perfect time for pondering. Sometimes a nurse would pop in, see you awake and ask if you'd like a cup of tea. Heaven. Then it was six o'clock, and the night staff were getting ready for the change over to days. It was always a time for my eyes to act rebelliously and close, and in no time, I was fast asleep. Why they wouldn't do just that when I wanted it earlier, I never found out.

One rule of the ward I liked was an hour of quiet after lunch when the curtains were drawn and we all went to bed for an hour or so. Quiet, please! The food and service were excellent. I particularly liked being able to order soft boiled eggs for my breakfast. Without exception, every time I did so, they came just right. My soldiers could dip straight in and come out of the yoke again without spoiling their shape. No four minute eggs for me.

Shortly after, a different face appeared for a brief moment on the ward. She was a nurse named Bettie. She mentioned that she had met me before, and had also once painted me. Intrigued, I wondered if we had met at a painting class sometime. But no, there was no mystery, it was she who painted me with iodine prior to the operation. My orange period perhaps?

The residents of our ward soon got to know each other. I asked Deena to bring me in some art materials, and I started doing pencil portraits of anybody that would sit for me. I did about five of these. One night I awoke to find activity around one of the beds. The occupant was not there. When a nurse came over near me I jokingly said 'Where's so and so, has he gone walkabout?' Yes, he had. He'd just died. It suddenly descended on me like a ton of bricks that I was not in a place where they played games. Everything was for real. The poor fellow had been sitting for me, just hours before.

After I finished a drawing, I always gave it to the sitter to keep, asking that they would let me photograph it next day for the record. The following day the empty bed was made up and all effects cleared as well. I never met the family. I've often thought since then that if the drawing was discovered later, whether I'd done enough for him to be recognised. Poignant moments indeed.

A happier sort of thing that I enjoyed whilst being there was seeing my visitors. Mostly family, but some I rarely saw for years on end. When my niece Carol came with her husband, Gerry, she was a surprise for some of the staff too. Being a radiographer, she was recognised as a friend or previous fellow worker by two of the Midhurst staff.

You can guess it became no secret that I was a retired entertainer and could do funny things with people's names. I reckon I did the names of most of the people who worked there and some of their families too. I managed a bit of watercolour as well. A couple of the nurses claimed these.

The physio was also keeping me at it. As soon as I was walking well I explored the public parts of the hospital. I was looking for a piano, but without success. My treatment was paying off slowly, and instead of the normal period before being discharged, it was nearly a month before I left their care. There was some trouble also regarding an irregular heart beat. That did eventually right itself later. I was back in Alvine Cottage by that time but not before my blood thinning drugs included a short spell on warfarin.

Chapter 42

Start Warfarin

Now there's a word that evokes the past. In my youth that was the magic name for ousting unwanted guests such as rats. Most of the old terrace houses in Rackham Street and about housed a few mice, but this larger edition of rodent was not compatible with anybody I knew. I remember the wording on the poison label. 'Alongside the warfarin bait, place a saucer of water'.

Dad explained that the action of the bait, apart from having dire consequences for the furry target, was it made them thirsty. So instead of conking out under the floorboards and reminding you of their presence, in such a parlous state, they would come out to get a last drink. And hopefully to stay out until their demise, somewhere they could be seen, and also disposed of.

I wasn't on it for long. I was very glad to get my heart working properly again, and soon I was home. A little later I sent a colour photograph to Midhurst of me in my full regalia as Kerby Drill. I understand it was securely pinned to their notice board.

It was the beginning of my being left to recuperate, and get used to a routine of tablet taking that seems to have lasted to today. After the non driving period prescribed on my hospital release form was over, it said the Bognor Regis hospital physiotherapy department would require me to attend for a course of exercises designed to help me fully recover from the operation.

The size of the class surprised me. Mostly about the sixty age with some defect that was going to be helped by our three lovely girl instructors working with them. Before the start of each session a roll call led to a couple or more questions on our well-being, with responses being duly noted. Our heart rate was also recorded and compared to its rate after we'd finished. All very relaxed but thorough.

This carried on for a few weeks. Cycle machines with weighted cogs to drive around. Flights of two steps to simulate stairs. Walking machines. Exercises and trotting on the spot. Bouncing balls and press-ups. All good breathless fun!

Before leaving, a resting period of lying down comfortably with pillows and controlled relaxing exercises. Cold fresh water was on tap and throughout the whole procedure the girls were constantly encouraging and helping us to achieve the list of exercises, all numbered and displayed on the gymnasium walls

Around this period I was experimenting with a different kind of painting during my art group's sessions. I had the idea of a joint effort, them and me, for people who felt they were no good at art. Presenting them with a pencil and an A3 pad of paper, I asked them to make their mark or marks on the sheet. It was entirely up to them what was put down. A proper drawing or a few scribbles, whatever.

I then put in my pennyworth and without altering anything they put down, made a painting out of it. Their marks plus my imagination. I did this to all the twenty or so fellow members of our group, all my friends and relatives, in fact anybody that wanted to co-operate. The results were surprising. Excellent, according to most of the half artists that co-operated. They have a painting they recognise by their input, and I get a photograph for the record.

Recently I showed these photographs to a friend of mine who is a professional artists himself and who also owns an art gallery in Chichester. I could see he was quite impressed with them. So at the end of the physio sessions I asked the girls if they would like to have one of their own. They all agreed, made their marks, and I was very pleased to think of a small way of saying thank you for all their help in our recovery.

I must say the whole episode was a great success as far as I was concerned. It seems the new valve is doing its job. This is known as a tissue type valve. Others can be made of metal or plastic. I am told it was probably a gift from a pig. Since then I have given a lot of thought about a thank you painting in respect of this animal. Lots of other things like this writing, for instance, keeps me from finding time to solve the problem yet. Since then, the exercises that I now do every day, have been a great help in keeping me in good general health.

The same year as my heart business it seems I started attending the Bognor hospital fete. Over the years both Jim and I have had some sort of input into this event. Jim seeing to the microphones and public address systems and me doing the occasional show. This time I would only be sitting down at a table doing face names with a collecting box beside me. A friend of mine, Erik Jack, also a performer, in films, was always at the microphone, jollying the afternoon along.

We had worked well together in most of the public happenings in Bognor over the years. Now Erik giving out a gentle reminder to all those present about the wisdom of having me to do a little drawing for them. It always added a little more weight to my tin when it was emptied in the treasurer's room.

This was always an August do, and about that time I went for an eye check up. It seemed my steadily growing cataracts had reached a removable stage. The optician referred me to my doctor, to get into the system for another op. This was to be in St Richards, Chichester.

So now I started a round of visits to the eye department for the necessary preliminaries to take place. This involved my son again, getting me there, owing to the drops being placed in my eyes meant I was banned from driving a car. How people get on with no family support I don't know. My lot are a priceless part of my life. Of course the positions are reversed from when they were young and vulnerable. If there had to be a name given to the fuel that's driving this situation it must surely be called love. The basic cement of life.

These early visits were to confirm the optician's observations, and measure the lens to be implanted in the eye during the operation. In this situation I am constantly amazed at the wide variety of nationalities of the personnel seeing to our needs. Time for the op. No sedation, rather like a dentist's chair, but with a charming nurse holding my hand.

Should I have the urge to cough or sneeze, I must squeeze her hand to warn the surgeon of its coming. I notice I wasn't given the option of being able to skidaddle if I changed my mind about it all. There was no pain, just the very bright light the team had to do their work with. Afterwards, on being instructed how to use the eye drops at home, and sporting an eye patch, not at all like Captain Flint's, covering the post-operative site, we went back home.

Deena was to insert the drops in my eye for me. I learned that some people living alone had to learn how to do this themselves. I was lucky. One morning I took my patch off and gazed through my now unclouded eye. Revelation. I would go as far as saying 'magical'. Both my eyes needed the treatment, but it so happened this first one I had done, I had always considered to be my bad one.

It had an astigmatism, and this operation was not meant to rectify that. But now with the cataract gone, I could survey my domain, albeit still slightly distorted, far better than before. After the course of eye drops was finished, I was summoned to Chichester for a final check up. I could drive again.

A letter came from Rachel, in the library, whom I knew from being a member of a police initiative to help young people that had come to their notice. These children were a group that was being helped in a kind of mixture of social service and disciplinary procedures, in the charge of two young policewomen.

It was all very informal. Meeting in a Bognor youth club in the morning, after lunch we moved onto the grass in Hotham Park. My contribution was to tell them about being a clown and what I'd been up to. Just sitting there in motley, with my pocket gags and photos of my woodworking world. After that it was question, question, question.

I did all their names, and when it was time to go we all snaked back to the club and said our goodbyes. Later that year Rachel invited me to a get-together in the library, as an honoured guest. On display were the works done by the same group of boys and girls. It was a very happy gathering with people from the many disciplines that had had an input into the group.

It was also a bit of a learning curve for me. This by now very aged boy, who left school at fourteen, saw into a computer screen for the first time. One of these young people simply pressing keys, seemed to come up with the knowledge of the world. I realised I belonged to another age. Whether I shall ever become one of the new, or forever be one of the old, I am on the wrong end of the time scale, possibly, to know the answer.

There was an interesting development on the eye front too. I was told my second operation would probably be the next year, but now, a letter came in stating that a mobile surgery unit would be coming to Worthing very shortly. 'Would I like to be considered for treatment by this means?' A very quick 'yes' from me was sent off post haste.

The unit duly arrived and I reported for treatment. As soon as I'd entered its portals I noticed the staff were definitley not exuding one of the usual range of dialects associated with our fair isles. My friend and fellow craftsman Sam Fanaroff has a similar accent, which is quite distinctive. That's how I recognised it. The medical staff at the unit were from South Africa.

I was very impressed by the whole unit. It was sited in Shoreham hospital grounds, and once inside you could feel the amount of thought and design that had gone into its conception and construction. I could anyway. My niece Casey drove me there for the preliminaries and the operation a while later. Both of Hazel's girls are very pretty and I noted the male nurse taking an interest in my driver. It's what makes the world go round, so I'm told. However, she was already spoken for.

The preparation and actual operation were very similar to what had happened with my first eye. Casey picked me up later and the main difference between the two rides home was the colour of my eye patch. When at last both my eyes were freed from their unhelpful films, I was delighted. I really must construct a shrine, as would happen in other countries, to those three little letters, NHS, and all the people that work there.

On the first eye visit to St Richards, I had noticed how many walls would be perfect recipients for paintings. There were already some areas catered for but there seemed plenty left. When I came out after surgery I had determined to get a painting out of the experience. I managed two concepts. These were only A4 size and I had it in the back of my mind to produce a much larger version of one and offer it to St Richards' optical department.

I still had a chance to carry this out when I started painting again. Whether it will be received with open arms, I will have to wait and see. Whilst I was in Midhurst hospital, I floated the idea of them having one of my sculptures. I was not taken up on it. So far, my only success in these ventures has been the one in the Regis Centre foyer and a paper and card spinner we installed in the Flansham Park health centre that cares for me.

My own doctor McLoughlin said 'yes' when I offered the centre a spinner a couple of years ago. The centre was built around a small courtyard that could be seen through the windows of the waiting area. I hadn't made that one to last for posterity and the day came when the nylon cord from which it was suspended, broke. I replaced it in a better position to catch the wind. The replacement was made for more external use by having a fabric covering applied before decoration. It was painted in the bright colours of the rainbow and was very eye catching.

The courtyard was planted heavily with bushes that seemed to be designed to attack gardeners. They being ten times more spiteful than holly. Warily picking my way through to the place my ladder was up against the eaves, I managed to make a fixing to suspend the sculptures from. I had just finished, when from about six feet up, I slipped and fell flat on my back. Those bushes broke my fall. I don't remember blaming their spikes at the time. I had gone to put it up in the dinner hour, no-one was about, but apart from having the wind knocked out of me, I managed to get up straight away. Some people have been killed falling like that. I was lucky. It was ironic that I could not have been in a more suitable establishment to be injured in, except everybody was busy elsewhere at the time.

In January 2007, the Health Centre was rebuilt and enlarged, and I applaud the architects and builders for bringing us up to date with a fine modern centre. But when I went there recently it seems as though the gardeners enemy, the old spiky bush, is no longer around. For the short period of impact it was very much my buddy and served me well in a crisis. I have long forgotten my scratched and torn trouser legs.

A couple of years ago, I had some sad news about a founder member of the Super Sausage Squad, Howard Goldsmith, 'Goldie'. I visited him in hospital. Still the same irrepressible friend, except he was now minus a leg. A real tragedy for such an active person. After leaving the hospital, the business of sorting out an artificial limb began. It was a painful affair.

Often we discussed how we could help the situation by likening it to our prop making experiences of years ago. Grim humour, but that was one of the things we had in common, seeing humour where most people couldn't. Then his wife Bess died. This was so different.

A short time afterwards it was Howard's family who were determined to celebrate his eightieth birthday in style. It was truly a great surprise for him to meet his old navy shipmates and chums from his war service days. They had all kept in touch over the years. It was a great turnout and I did my bit for all the guests by drawing for them. It was a gentle reminder of his past connections with the entertainments game.

He and Bess with their puppet shows, me and him fighting the bungy blight. Howard died soon afterwards and I wrote expressing in the Joey what a loyal friend he'd been. Something all the other Joeys agreed with too. We had lost a talented entertainer and a great clown.

In Bognor there was a person who saw great potential in the making of an audio history section for the local library for future generations. I think it's rather like a 'getting on tape from the horse's mouth', whilst the old nag or gallant charger is still with us. Crudely but accurately put.

A Shirley Buck 'phoned me one day asking if I would like to record my war experiences, or clown work, for her sound archive. I said yes and did two recordings. My own thoughts on the subject have always been in line with the old dictum 'truth is stranger than fiction', and I might add, far more intriguing.

In a similar vein I spent an afternoon in a school where a few ex-service types were answering questions put to us by the young pupils, on the last war. It was very interesting too. I wondered if the children were as interested in us, as I was of them. Strange business this learning.

Later we, the audio subjects, were invited to a get-together in the lecture room of the Bognor library. With a glass of wine and nibbles, we were thanked by Shirley and her team for our co-operation. The recordings were to become part of the library henceforth.

It was here I met Louise Withington, the senior librarian. We talked about events held in the library and I told her of the showing of paintings a good few years ago by Matthew Hillier, a young local pupil still at art college. Later, four of us shared an exhibition in Chichester. I enquired about holding a similar show for me in the lecture room at Bognor Library. She very kindly said she would see what could be done.

Later she told me that in July there would be a vacant slot of a week's duration. 'Would I like it'? What luck. Earlier I had explained that I was no longer earning and now she had given me a free week's tenure and also set the date. The family was delighted and promised their full support. A solo show, and I was under no illusion how much work was to be done in preparation, but it was something I had always yearned for.

We went and had a close look at the lecture room, noted its size, and estimated how we could make the best use of its potential. A blackboard covered part of one wall, there were two lines of windows up above eye line, and two doors. A few years before, Deena had fancied a pine table, large enough to seat our family round. From a second hand wood yard I selected a few old boards that had excellent colouring and three very decorative large knots. I made up a table top from these that fitted on top of our existing table. It was not a permanent fixture.

I now saw this clear varnished colour and grain as a perfect showpiece surface for my wood sculptures, centrally placed in the room. I increased the height of my two saw stools so that with the pine top on them it was level with the library's table height. We were given permission to fix a baton at picture rail height on the walls. To help cope with the multitude of photographs I made, out of white card, hinged stands, rather like the smaller editions commonly seen outside newsagents showing the headlines.

These stood on tables amongst the exhibits. Over the entrance doorway I had a fair display of gala photographs. To represent my road safety work I had my school's easel with the Tufty quiz showing. The 'Play with this in safe places' ball, the Tufty puppet set-up, showing a Belisha crossing and flashing lights. A plastic foam flat fish decorated with black and white stripes, with a small beacon sticking out of its end. 'A safe plaice to cross', an adult gag.

The props from the Super Sausage Squad gala act included the unexploded sausage bomb from the last war. The detonator box. Giant frying pan come mine detector. My large entrance hat and clown boots. The sausage tree watering tap and the divining twig.

Props from the Boiled Egg Brigade act included the atomic egg, with a very patient chicken in a hatching position astride it, waiting to be blasted fifty feet up into the air for the big finale. The large brace and bit we used to drill for water for the chicken's drinkies, and the three differently-sized Ever Ready batteries used for our power supply.

When we were working with the model 'T', Pierre and I always had plenty of photos taken of us, and I had a selection of these up on display. My woodwork and sculptures looked beautiful on the pine table top. A collection of spinners and candle holders had pride of place also. Jig dolls I'd made for Jim. Two pieces of bent wood design coffee tables I was very proud of. Each was made up of only three components.

Then of course were my impressionist paintings. We used the same hanging procedure as in the marquee. They varied in size from Van Gogh's 'The Sower', to Renoir's 'The Umbrellas', the latter standing on the floor because of its size. Also represented, were Toulouse Lautrec, Manet, Cezanne and Degas. The 'Mother and Child' by Mary Cassett, made sure at least of one lady artist being included. Sixteen paintings in all, plus one of my own. A self portrait by Hal Brooks, of his other half, Kerby Drill the Road Safety clown.

My three larger sculptures, the Welsh Dragon, Clown, and Crane, were the final exhibits. I felt immensely proud of the collection and of our display. Jan Cosgrove, initiator of the Fun Bus company which provided a travelling collection of fun and learning for the young, housed in a double-decker bus, was someone for whom I'd done many favours for over the years. Now he was doing the same for me. He declared my exhibition open, in his capacity as Mayor of Bognor Regis at the time.

Loads of family and friends turned up and for a couple of hours it was party time. Tina, Casey and Deena were my hostesses, whilst I lorded it up. We kept a visitors' book, and over the week it attracted some lovely comments about the exhibition.

Deena and I attended each day with our packed lunches and flasks of tea, very reminiscent of the many times we had sat in previous arts or crafts shows. One big and most important difference though, in the one room there, Deena and I showed what we had got up to in our working life. But this time, absolutely nothing was for sale.

A month afterwards, the local newspaper, the Bognor Regis Observer, featured me in their weekly magazine. I had known Bill Shimmin, their photographer, for many years, and he took some fantastic photographs to illustrate a fine piece of journalism by Helen Husbands, who wrote the words. The front cover showed me with the biggest smile possible. I gave a copy to my dentist telling him 'he'll not get better publicity for his work than the smile the teeth produced'.

It really was a fine piece of work on me. I bought all the unsold copies from the paper for later use, things like this did not happen very often, not in my experience anyway. To have drawn our many and varied goings on into one publication was a real treat.

How quickly the old clock goes round. I noticed I attended my first check up from the cardiac department already. A year had slipped by and I had now to report for a scan to help the heart man gauge if my ticker was behaving itself, a year on.

The inevitable junior doctor or student were always there learning the ropes. How often I wished I'd had an apprentice watching my every move. It's called the learning route. Since I left the end of Dad's bench I've been very much a solo player. It would have been nice to have had another interested party learning through watching me sometimes, even if they had only been there to sweep up and make the tea, as I had done many times all those years ago.

Chapter 43

Rotary Art & Equity

There was a new innovation in Bognor in the shape of an open art exhibition being organised by the local Rotary Club. Seeing how short of exhibition halls we have of any size in Bognor town, they were mounting it in Felpham comprehensive college, at half-term. An excellent place with a nice hall, and plenty of parking.

These new ventures are always a gamble. The school was not within walking distance of Bognor Regis town, but was next to our leisure centre, so the area was well visited out of school hours, as well as by day. There was also a regular bus service.

I put in the amount of paintings allowed and the preview was very well attended. Clutching my glass of wine I surveyed all the works on show. I also noticed in the hall was a grand piano, and a volunteer was playing popular music. I was impressed with the hanging of the exhibits. The Rotary boys and girls had done a good job. It all augered well for the future. I wished them well and determined to give the event as much support as I could. I put in a couple of performances on the piano during the week.

At the preview I met up with Bill Lane, the artist who had in the past been a kind of mentor to me. He was the tutor at our evening classes when I did a self-portrait that I was very pleased with. Looking at it now I am amzed at how my style of painting has changed over the years. We had just moved from Mumbles to open up the Butlin's camp as Auntie and Uncle and children's entertainers in 1961. In those days my style seemed a lot smoother, less slap dash, less 'impressionist'.

Bill was then teaching art in Chichester College. His entries into the exhibition demonstrated the talents of the man were still very much alive and kicking. It was Bill who designed Kerby Drill's road safety certificate that I used for years. At the time he also gave me all the preliminary drawing and layouts he had done as ground work for the final certificate. I still have them.

We often met up with his wife at fairs, displaying her own talents with clothes. Why did I remember his tuition so well? It was my first attempt at painting in oil colours, and I found it extremely difficult to adapt to them. I really had to force myself to put brush to board in making a start.

It wasn't a new feeling. I'd been stuck on the bench for ages when starting building jobs. I never understood why. If Bill had just made a few marks to start me off I would have managed alright. I was too shy to ask. I never had this difficulty with my entertaining life. As soon as I stepped onto the stage I was in complete control, and wallowed in it. It was the same confidence I had in making up my designs in wood. Somehow a different me!

I sold two of my paintings at that first exhibition, and the Rotary decided it was a success and promised another the following year. Taking notice of some sculptures on show the previous year, I got permission to show my own three large sculptures, the Clown, Crane, and Welsh Dragon, at this show.

As a group they looked very good. It was a not-for-sale trio, just to add extra interest, (and show off!) In a previous show for the Bognor Art Society my painting was voted 'best painting in show' and I held the cup for a year. The painting was of an elderly French country woman cooking over a hob, laden with saucepans and pots, holding a spoon with very gnarled fingers. I called it 'An Old Hand'.

This was my only sale on that occasion. A downside always after making a sale is that afterwards 'you ain't got it no more (and you miss it)'. The third Rotary event was held in the Bognor Regis Music Academy. I'd known the principal, Sacha Levtov, for years. He always allowed me to use their private car park whenever I was working in town, such as at carnivals, and Christmas time. I had also done shows in the academy to raise money for the Birdman events. Sacha's domain had three pianos. Yummy yummy!

Once he had a full sized copy of Renoir's painting 'The Dancers at Bourgonville' hanging up. It was very good too. Someone else was also at it, like me. I never met the artist but I'm very sure he was using similar methods for gaining a likeness as I was, but just like my 'Old Hand', it had gone.

This year I had painted a portrait of Her Majesty Elizabeth II. It caused quite a stir so my Rotary friends told me, when I went to pick up my pictures afterwards. No sales this time.

Did I hear the sound of coming wedding bells, yes-yes-yes. Tina, our lovely

Tina, was marrying Chris, much to the wonder and delight of young Oliver, their son of a year or so. Tina, Casey, Hazel and Deena formed a giant 'getting it all ready' team.

Son Michael would be walking her down the aisle to Chris, and if I know anything, young Ollie would be watching to see if he could get close enough to influence the proceedings by getting in on the act. Tina had asked me to use my camera to capture the occasion in my own way. I had obliged previously on other family occasions.

The local Masonic Hall had been beautifully arranged to suit the occasion. I photographed the great spread of eats laid out on a line of tables all down the side of one wall. A bar was discreetly situated in another corner. All the teamwork of our band of ladies. On these family get-togethers my problem is always remembering names, faces and which bit belongs to who, and where from?

After the ceremony we all moved to a nearby park for photographs. The day was fine, and many smiles abounded amidst the clicking of a multitude of cameras. I took the opportunity to film important filling-in subjects for the final wedding album. The chauffeur of the wedding car for instance. I got a beaming shot of him. Next the children there. I wanted to pinpoint their looks and ages on the wedding day itself. They change so quickly whilst growing up in their own right.

Someone like me may be commissioned to paint a portrait based on my efforts. A snap is not much help in these cases. Although Tina had carefully placed a free throwaway camera on each table, she had absolutely no response from these, so my efforts at photography were very welcome.

Came the feast. Whilst dining, another chance to sort out who's who, starting with your table companions. Meal over and sinking back as full as an egg, the speeches. I couldn't quite catch all the nice things being said because of my hearing, but everybody's contribution was listened to and commented on in a variety of ways. A proper family occasion, enjoyed in a family way. Later, a competition of whose paper aeroplane went the furthest down the hall was gravely judged by some very biased participants. Although uproar was kept tightly under control, it was a near thing.

Deena and I finally gave up trying to keep up with the youngsters and beat a graceful retreat to our beds. On our departure, wife now, Tina, looking beautiful in her wedding dress, and well matched by her gallant husband Chris's outfit, wished us goodnight. It will be a good few years yet before Oliver will take as much care over his own looks. We can only hope for the trio, a happy and healthy life, to follow such a lovely day.

Only a few weeks after this happy episode of our lives, a terrible threatening cloud appeared on our horizon. It was on a normal Sunday after dinner, about 2pm, Jim and his friend Jane had dined with us and we were chatting away. Deena, without a sound, became limp in her armchair. We were so lucky that Jane was there. Amongst her many talents, she was also a nurse. She alerted us all to what she thought had happened and took charge. Deena had just had a stroke. Jim telephoned for an ambulance and within twenty minutes an emergency doctor had arrived by car. A little later an ambulance arrived and took Deena to St Richards in Chichester. We followed in Jim's car.

I must admit to my utter inability to have dealt with this on my own, at the time. She had made no fuss and it seemed as though she had just fallen asleep. When we reached the hospital she was in the emergency department. We learned that, yes, they thought she had had a stroke and was now being cared for. It was a week before she returned home again.

Talking to her later in 'recovery' she had no recollection of the frightful occurrence she had experienced. There were plenty of tests and checks needed to confirm the original diagnosis. With her medication established, I nursed her along with other medical staff, back to as near normality as can be expected in an eighty-year old.

From whoever had heard about the stroke, a constant question was asked, 'has it affected her movements in any way?' We were so fortunate that nothing major had occurred to her that restricted her mobility. Lots of time has gone by now, and I'm glad that my lovely girl is back to just being my lovely girl again.

On Monday 23rd January 2006, Equity was 75 years old. The actors' union was not able to cater for a vast celebration, so a few life members came up with the idea of a holding a party for them. Being one of them, I joined in. Anyone interested in helping was asked for a donation towards the cost. My effort didn't break the bank and I duly set off with son Jim in charge, to Bognor Regis railway station.

Neither of us fancied London traffic, what with parking and congestion charges, we plumped for the comfort of the train. I hadn't

been on one for years so I looked forward to it. The modern carriages were a treat to be in. We were travelling in off peak time so there was plenty of room.

I must admit the refreshment trolley did not materialise, as per schedule but never mind. Into Waterloo Station we alighted en route to the National Theatre, for the party.

Most of my life I had dealt with Paddington Station so the size of Waterloo surprised me. I had misjudged using the loo whilst on the train, so I was all eyes seeking relief. It was quite a walk. In that vast complex I only saw one toilet. I had grown up in a world where only women-folk had to fork out to go. In that world also we had separate places, this haven showed indicator signs of both trousered and skirted figures. We all went to the same pay in machine, a line of us clutching our twenty pence pieces. The tokens of relief!

The gate only allowed one person through per 20p, ('p' being an appropriate abbreviation). It was a multi-pronged arrangement that did not operate from a level position like traditional turnstiles used to. Rather, it was similar to a drunken windmill leaning against the wind. As I went through, the prong went down and I found myself astride it, with one leg in my space, and one leg in the space behind, which was occupied by a lady. I was stuck!

No way could my eighty-four year old torso be able to release me from its clutches. Consternation and delay. There may have been people behind me in the queue far more desperate than I. They were marginally better off. They could cross their legs, I couldn't. And the position of the prong had a tendency in me, a male, to prohibit discussion as to its whereabouts.

Fortunately there was an attendant at hand. The person behind, a lady of about seventy, was asked to offer up her token to release me. So in went her coin, and my leg was returned to me. I dryly commented to the said attendant that if I'd known I had been expected to do an assault course I would have had second thoughts. Whatever else lay before me at least now I could cross my legs.

When finally we were mobile again we proceeded to the National Theatre foyer where our party was to be held. Threading our way through the traffic I was very pleased to see a subway. Going underground we shortly surfaced in sight of the complex and of course the Thames.

Being born in North Kensington the few things that the noble river had come to mean to me was Putney for the boat race, Richmond for ice skating and honeymoon to boot, and the Royal happenings at Windsor Castle. To get cheaper fares we had come early. It was very cold. Looking around I spied three art students from a local art college. I'm not averse to barging in at times like these.

My mum when on buses always sat on the side seats by the conductor. Now lost to a new generation, the conductor was a person who collected fares, donged the bell and usually called out 'hold very tight please' as he did so. Very necessary if there were standing passengers.

In next to no time mum would be in conversation with anyone within earshot. Very seldom did people not respond. So, in like manner, I had a chat with the artists. All were interested in discussing their work. My suggestion that on days like these a couple of hot water bottles wouldn't come amiss, went down well.

The guests were drifting into the theatre foyer when I said goodbye to Jim. Only life members of Equity were allowed past a man with a check list. I was duly tagged with a neat badge, given a number for my coat and hat, and left to wander in. Jim had already decided to spend the next two and a half hours visiting the Tate Modern until 3pm, when I would be released back into his charge. This last sentence was to have been quite prophetic.

We were told there would be about four hundred attending the do. I already knew two attendees. These were clowns Sonny and Rainbow. Earlier I saw their brightly decorated van pulling into the car park. There was no doubting their names and profession from the excellent sign writing accompanying the colourful portraits of themselves all over the vehicle. On top of that, they arrived fully made up and dressed as befitted their task of entertaining us guests, in a mix and mingle way. When conjurors do it, they call it close-up magic.

I passed by the wine table picking up a glass of white. I tried a sip and it wasn't to my taste, so I asked for a drop of lemonade as a
sweetener. A search was made round the other tables, but no luck. I settled for a dash of orange juice which did the trick. The foyer was rapidly getting busy. There were lots of faces that you thought you knew but couldn't put a name to. Most folk there were around, and coming up to, my own age, so there was no shyness.

That we were all theatricals was in no doubt. What ran through my mind was that we'd all have been better off if our badges had also had our name on. I had suggested this to the top office on the 'phone but they weren't keen. My Butlins' days were coming to the fore here. You knew the name of each staff member in any conversation on camp. I can see the difficulty of wearing badges if you'd rather not be known, but my point was that having been in the profession for fifty years or more, faces change, girths may expand, and it could have been a long time since we may have worked together. Why not give ourselves more recognition points?

The afternoon wore on and I became more compliant with the wine. I was also aware there were not many chairs about. When I managed to sit down I kind of caught hold, conversationally of course, with anyone I thought would appreciate the intense value of my repartee! I found that the who-done-what and where theme of some was soon revealed in a well-rehearsed withdrawal technique.

In my own good time I found out there were lots of places and jobs I'd tackled, in a very minor way of course, so if someone did deem to converse, I could answer in a reasonably knowledgeable way. My business cards state quite firmly I am a clown, artist and woodworker, and had been around a bit.

By this tactic I met a lot of very nice folk from all branches of the business. I was really enjoying the wine now. Sitting down comfortably when the speeches started, I was aware that although I'd been a union man all my working life, it was not solely with Equity, the actors' union. I had been sick steward and branch chairman for the chippies' union, The Amalgamated Society of Woodworkers. A splinter group of the TUC you might say.

That's another reason why I felt a bit of an outsider on this sort of occasion. It was the same when filming at Shepperton for the circus film. I got the distinct feeling that the circus clowns also performing had pondered 'how did he get in here?' even though I'd well shed any leftover sawdust and shavings by then.

When I did a week's work at the now closed Collins Music Hall with my lightning sketch act, the bandleader looked at my dots he'd remarked 'this isn't the Albert Hall' and quickly reduced my pages of music to fit a smaller orchestra. Charlie on the drums, Alf on trumpet, and so on. The theatre fireman had also kept a close eye on me to make sure I didn't shed any loose sheets of paper from my easel onto the stage. You can gather from this I'd been on the fringe of many occupations in my working life.

I was really enjoying the wine now, as would a connoisseur with unlimited means. One lady I met was at the first Clown Convention in Bognor. My job of organising the school children and encourage them to join our procession through Bognor, meant I was busy elsewhere. Anyway, I never met her there. Her mode of entertainment was with performing dogs and I was very interested in her accounts of the trials and tribulations of running an animal act. Not with the dogs, but the people she had to deal with day by day.

Then I met someone I did know, Leon Lawrence. Once a clown and musician, now an agent. He'd had several clown presentations, one of which was a comedy car. Being a prop maker I had made two old-fashioned looking oil lamps for his vehicle, circa Victorian times. At a given moment he could fire these into the air. They had to be light but tough enough to withstand being blasted aloft at each performance. He also had a trick bicycle. For this prop it was the cycle lamp that was given the same role. A bang and off it went.

We were discussing the old days and about one agent in particular, Bert Layton of TB Phillips (Gloucester). He said that Bert had confided in him that my Super Sausage Squad routine was the most original and funny gala act he'd had on his books. I was very pleased to be able to relate this to son Jim on the way home, because he had also been a member of the squad.

In the letter saying how to get to the party was also contained details of what was planned. Drinks, speeches and refreshments. We were all welcomed by our newly appointed General Secretary, and afterwards a few words from one of the original lifers who's proposal it was to have the celebration. Film and TV actor, George Baker.

I had met George once, although I'm sure he would not have been aware of it. It was at the premiere of the circus film at the Plaza Cinema, London. Pierre, my business partner at the time, and I, were mixing with the invited audience in the foyer in full makeup and costume, to add a bit of flavour to the occasion. So although we may have rubbed shoulders I wasn't able to take part in all the chit chat that was going on amongst all the celebrated invitees.

After the speeches and the applause the food came round. And 'round' was the operative word. There were various trays of savouries being elegantly ushered about for our pleasure. These delicacies were vol-au-vents of various tastes, colours and textures, but all were round in shape and no larger than a fifty pence piece. It amused me to see what looked like a washer of ham being the basis for a meal. I could imagine an ancient toothless actor of many years' standing being thankful that they could be popped in whole. Which is what I did.

The wine by this time made an excellent lubricant. The various flavours of these delicacies made them very moreish. It was not until bed time that my wife pointed out, from a distance, that they must have had a fair smattering of garlic in them. I blamed the wine for not noticing. It must have been that liquid that kept the fires under control whilst we were stuffing ourselves.

My weekly intake of one pint of bitter shandy in the Elmer, my local pub, did not prepare me for the effects of this wine. I had become quite squiffy, and needed to lean on Jim quite heavily for the return journey to the station. But I was a very happy lifer. It was a long time since I had felt like this. Having to drive back after a celebration, held not in your own home, tempers the amount you can safely imbibe.

On this occasion with my reliable minder to hand, I enjoyed letting go. We got home safely to what is known in our family as a hero's welcome, and a slap-up meal. Bacon, tomatoes, mushrooms and eggs. I banked quite a few calories that day.

The following day I was sorting out some old newspaper cuttings that I had come across in a local newspaper requesting volunteers in the community. In the list of openings available was one for a piano player. As the date of the newspaper was over two years old I wrote to enquire fully expecting to be too late. However, next day I was telephoned and a meeting was arranged in the Tamarisk Centre, Littlehampton, about three miles away.

On arrival, Sue the person I had to see was not there, so I explained to her deputy, Debbie, that I was the pianist. I was received most cordially and I requested to see the piano. It was a beautiful upright instrument which I learned later cost over four thousand pounds. It was unlocked for me to have a go. I sat down and played 'I'm forever blowing bubbles', to everyone's satisfaction it seems.

There were two or three other people about. One, a lady approaching my age (although I wouldn't have dared to say so), was a singer and interested in seeing my repertoire. I was thankful to explain that I only played by ear, otherwise I'd have needed my arm stretched to cope with all the music!

Eve, for that was the lady's name, then let forth with a beautiful rendering of the song On the Street Where You Live from My Fair Lady. It was a touch of magic. She had a beautiful voice. It made me sound far more accomplished than I would have claimed. Afterwards, the gentleman that had unlocked the piano asked for a Nat King Cole tune. I half knew it so was able to fill in enough to put a beam on his face.

It turned out that I had come to show myself on an afternoon devoted to music. The rest of the class had gone home. And, you've guessed it, they'd no pianist. So I was booked to put in an appearance two weeks later, unpaid, but I had already been rewarded.

Chapter 44

Deena's Family

I know that as time unfolds its father, also sometimes referred to as 'the grim reaper', relentlessly clears the ground for new growth. And so it was he claimed Deena's elder sister Bettie. She and Coral had been brought up together by family, the Williams's. Deena by non-family, the Stocktons. Both had been very supportive of each other since the girls were orphaned at such an early age. Then, when grown up, the three girls continued in the same vein. Bettie, like Deena, was a teacher. She had moved to the Midlands after she married Ronald Acutt, a Birmingham man. They had two boys like us, Robert and Christopher. Son Chris had already died, tragically young.

Both girls had been put through college by their adoptive families. The determination of the Welsh towards education is something I have always admired. It couldn't have been easy for both families during the thirties. The hard times post first world war, were not yet past. Bettie went to Cheltenham, and Deena to Whitelands College, Putney, London.

Whereas Deena, after fulfilling her contractual obligations to the teaching profession, quit to look after Jim, Bettie carried on until retiring at the allotted time. Husband Ron was a very nice person and a highly skilled engineer. When he died, also tragically early, his popularity amongst his work mates was the cause of an unforgettable occasion. His hearse was diverted to pass his place of work, where the whole workforce, some hundreds, lined the pavements to bid him farewell.

Having two boys each of near parallel ages, Bettie kept our two supplied all during their schooldays with parcels of clothes. Whilst I was struggling at building and paying a mortgage, she was a most generous sister-in law. Deena always thought Bettie would have loved to have grown up in her own family, under her entertainer father's influence. She had a fine contralto voice and also a quiet style about her. A perfect advantage should you have an inclination towards the stage. Once when she was visiting us with her partner Gerald I played for them singing duets.

Bettie died in her native Tredegar, living near Coral. She was very generous to both sisters in her will. Her passing is still taking its toll on both girls, missing their lovely elder sister. Bettie was also a great traveller who always kept in touch by 'phone. When we heard her voice invariably our first question was 'where are you? The results of her preparations for Christmas always came early and together. One big parcel with nobody missed out. She was also a frequent visitor to the markets in Birmingham, sending us items that presented themselves to her, ahead of being exposed to our gaze in Bognor. She was like an artist's journeyman to me, with supplies. My paintings were always a part of her décor. I once did a portrait of her out in the garden. It wasn't a world-beater but it was graciously accepted and that pleased me.

There was some welcome news coming in on the Bognor home front, especially for residents who remembered the advent of the first clown convention in 1985. After some fifteen years the clowns were coming again in the Spring. Butlin's were to be our sponsors. The idea was to hold the activities to coincide with the camp opening for the new Summer season, although this meant the holiday camp would be at the hub of all the goings-on, not the town itself.

My position will be vastly different in these changed circumstances. No longer would my efforts to make a successful procession through town be to the forefront. Now very much an onlooker, I was working out how I could be a part of it at all. The longer route along the seafront ruled out walking. If I couldn't walk at all, I needed someone to push me. In keeping with my clowning and to justify my being wheeled I made myself a prop clown leg. Its foot was a little large, about size twenty-three I think, but it could be seen from a fair distance. In fact the big toe stood out, quite literally, suitably dressed up in a bandage environment but a little larger than life

My friend Tricky Nicky volunteered to push me in a Shopmobility wheel chair. They donated the chair free so I made two advertising placards to hang either side of this 'mobile invalid'. Nicky, who was a care assistant as well as a clown, did me proud. Outrageously dressed as 'nurse' Nicky, with bosoms going where no bosoms had gone before, and lips made up to out-do any madam of the movies. With a red nose and being over six feet tall, 'she' looked the perfect pusher of grown-up prams. You might have gathered he was also no shrinking violet. I don't think we looked out of place at all!

We had a fine day for the walk but it was very cold. With my big entrance coat on, gloved hands and red nose shielding half of my made up face, I survived the biting wind. My only warm area was under the false leg. The convention lasted four days and here I was able to contribute a little more. Sitting amongst the holidaying campers with pen and pencil at the ready I managed to cause much merriment by turning their written names into faces. Sometimes handsome and flattering, other times, well, that's where the humour comes in!

It was a very different experience from gallivanting about in the arena, but very pleasing still to be entertaining. With a collecting bucket by my side for donations to our clowns' benevolent fund, I pleased them with my free drawings. Some interested youngsters made full use of my services when it was clear there was no charge! Whole families of names, mates at school, sweethearts and so on. It was nice being back in harness again. My trousers were not so floppy around my waist as before!

On our last day we held our Annual General Meeting. It was very nice meeting up with old friends from all over the country again. When all the clown club business was concluded, we retired to a comfort station plus bar, for friendly chatter. I met our recent editor of the Joey, Marc Summers. He had taken over from our previous long-standing editor, Jenny Brattle. These two good folk have been instrumental in having these ramblings of mine put into print and published for over three years now It was Jenny who suggested I should contribute my past goings on to the journal. Starting modestly I now find each quarter I put four thousand words at their disposal. I was not told the shouts of 'enough' were loud enough to dare me to do any more, so like Topsy, my contribution 'just growed'.

Nearly coming now to the end of my saga, the question is what is to become of it? I realised my hand written offering needed to be 'computerised' to have any chance of going further. Realising that I had the time to put it into a word processor, I thought it was about time I learned how, so I looked up computer lessons in our local Adult Learning Services literature. Now carless, the nearest place of instruction was not easy to reach. No direct bus route. The local authorities came up trumps with help to get me there and back, so it was I booked into 'school' again.

I was impressed by the facilities and tuition provided. The only fault I could find was with this student. The language of the screen bore no resemblance to that of the bench. I have never had an aptitude for languages, and now it showed.

The computer speak just did not register with me. I realised this was to be no easy or quick undertaking.

Resorting to books from our fine mobile library alas shed no light on the problem. Me. After the course of six weeks I managed to glean enough to be able to transfer my written scrawl into beautifully understandable letters on the screen. To me the computer is a miracle. I am hoping to progress in its use because of its fantastic possibilities.

Carole, our art secretary has a sister Barbara who runs a partially sighted group in Littlehampton. I was booked to deliver a talk and play some music for her members, similar to tunes I played at the Tamarisk Centre. I took some props along and talked about earning my living as a clown. After tea and cakes I played for a singsong. It must have been well received as I got a further engagement a month later. This time I took some woodwork and small sculptures to talk about.

It was very interesting. I pondered how to deal with these club members who, with limited sight, would have to get to grips with my subject. In the end I arranged two rows of tables with a linking table at on one end. A sort of large 'U' shape. After talking and explaining about each piece I was holding up for them to see, I then put it down on the table to start its journey around to the other side. Each member had a chance to peer closely at it and feel its shape. A very tactile examination indeed. Afterwards another reward of tea and fine cakes, followed by my giving the ivories another tinkling.

It was a very successful afternoon, but it left me wondering what I would talk about when I returned on my third visit. How about my latest venture, writing my memoirs. Compiling a lifetime of memories. Speaking from my own experience I was finding the experience completely fascinating.

After my heart operation I had decided to sell some of my props. I placed a small ad in the Joey and some weeks later I received a telephone call. It was from a person in Wales who was interested in buying, but by now I felt fit again and had changed my mind about selling. I'd realised my props were too big a part of my life to let go.

At the next clown convention I met the interested party from Wales. It was Jonny Russell, clown name Chunkey Russell, a C.I. member from Pontardulais, near Swansea. That name Pontardulais brought back very early memories for me. It was in my old stamping grounds when Deena and I were doing our first children's parties.

Always on the lookout for new ideas and props, Chunkey told me about his theme park in Tenby, South Wales. Still not interested in parting with my own props, I offered him a compromise. I would duplicate my props for him. He said he liked the idea. I explained that this would be no dawdle, tomorrow like.

So for a year now my mechanic engineer friend, Ray Woolven, and I, have been struggling to remember how I made the original props, some forty years ago. The pop plant, with instant growth. The birthday cake with the capacity for 'lift off', mainly for indoor use at parties. A water loaded stand pipe tap, and a large brace and bit, both with an abiblity to produce an instant outpouring of water. I was right when I suggested it would be no dawdle. However calm has settled by now as I edit this.

The annual Bognor Birdman competition saw me and Deena doing a bit to help. It was surprising how many competitors and families got involved in this International event. It was amazing that we'd put all this on with only half a pier. Goodness knows what we could have managed if we'd had a whole one!

In a comfortable lounge on the pier we kept the competitors' children amused with games and names during the flying period. A large television screen kept us all informed of what was going on outside. It was very well received and organisers thanked us for the help.

Later that year, a party was put on in the Rosie Lee Café for everybody connected with the event. Deena and I had just celebrated our Diamond Wedding and we were welcomed to the event as honoured guests. It was a lovely evening, and to celebrate such an anniversary in this way, amongst so many friends, was the 'icing' on the cake. Not that there wasn't one baked especially for us, there was. It was delicious.

Pierre rang to say he had a job in Chichester with 'Chitty'. He didn't often get within visiting distance, so Jim took us in for a conflab. He was parked in a large newly-opened shopping complex, to attract customers to the place. He, like me, only bore a slight resemblance to our former active selves. If he had to stand the shock of going up in the old Model T's seat now, it would save a lot of trouble to have an ambulance there, at the ready!

He doesn't even have to drive the car, just be present. Dressed in appropriate costume, deerstalker and all, he certainly looks like a character in the film. Just like my writing, he's also found something he can still be doing from a wheelchair when ninety-plus. 'Tis strange, that as with our early antics with the Model T, and now with Chitty, the same situation is revealed. The cars are the real stars.

Hazel and Michael invited us for a holiday with them in France. It was some fourteen years ago that they started putting all the pieces together of their old and derelict farmhouse and barn. We were both looking forward to seeing the results of their efforts in the flesh. There was a hiccup at Southampton airport. Apparently our aircraft had developed a fault and so we had to vacate our plane seats and return to enter the departure lounge while repairs were carried out.

Whilst we were waiting, an Australian fellow traveller assured us that 'no news is good news' in these situations. Deena's supply of wine gums were running perilously low, when, three hours later, we were invited to board the same plane again. It seemed the new bit for the engine would work this time!

So it was farewell to the airport bus again, on seatbelts, a few cheery words from the pilot, and off we went, with my ears letting me know we were now high flyers. The comfortable journey was relieved by a tea trolley that dispensed its wares, via your pocket, and Typhoo tea, its sponsors. My first experience of budget airlines.

A soft and safe landing at Limoges Airport was livened up somewhat by our chasing the luggage around the unloading carousel, finally meeting our hosts Michael and Hazel. They had also endured the same period of waiting, punctuated only with 'no news' announcements from the loudspeakers.

Finally we were on our way to Couzou, in the department of Lot. In France a department is similar to a county in England. Arriving in the dark did not quell the excitement of seeing the farmhouse again. From wreck to palace was my immediate feeling of the house.

Getting the fire going and sitting down to Hazel's prepared meal was very welcome. She is a lovely cook. Plenty of chinwag, and so to bed. After a good night's sleep, waking by daylight, and the outdoors was revealed to us both. A wondrous place now to our eyes, after the earlier memories from all those years ago, when they decided they wanted to buy it.

When I said that I would like to paint while I was there, Hazel found two picture frames that were of an age that just suited their farmhouse, so I prepared a few boards of that size, to paint on, to be prepared. They were too big for us to fit in our suitcases, so Michael took them back to France with him on his return trip. Hazel wanted me to paint their buildings and field so I also had my subjects chosen for me. I had always yearned for a painting holiday, but expense was always a problem. They don't come cheap, so this was my chance.

A very famous residential learning establishment, West Dean College, catered for painting breaks only a few miles from where we lived. But although the man who founded it as a source of adult learning had admirable intentions, he forgot about the ability to pay. Deena and I could never afford the fees.

One or our first trips out was to visit Gramat, the nearest town. It had hardly altered to our eyes. We meandered around whilst Hazel did some business and then we nearly missed her. I hadn't adjusted my watch to French time and we were an hour out of sync!

One of the joys of the town was the bakers and their products. One particular kind of loaf was my favourite. Crusty, well baked, almost burnt in places, and to use a perfect word right out of my early days of reading comics to describe it, 'scrumptious'. What with Hazel's magnificent soups, and that bread, I could only guess where my waistline would be by the time we returned home. And that's not counting the main course!

Early on my first morning of painting, with a beautiful day to come, Michael had made me comfortable at an ample table where I wanted to sit. After I had set up he erected a large sunshade so I could keep out of direct sunlight. It was May and the sun was getting quite warm. I had remembered from my last visit how the heat used to hit you when coming out of doors. You realised you were in the south of France, and all that we English read into that phrase.

I started painting the farmhouse first. With its strangely angular shaped roof and walls to match, I realised very early on the exercise was was not going to do my ego much good. It was alright having ample confidence, but slowly the realisation dawns on you that you are not the 'clever clogs' you thought you were. So the struggle begins. By the end both mine hosts were pleased with the results and that consoled me a bit. It had been a long day.

Over the next few days I painted their garden which was at the front and end of the house bordering the road. The sunlight was very strong so the shadows, apart from being very intense, also produced very defining shadows. A great boon to the struggling artist, although their continuing movement didn't help much. Something else was on the move during the day. There was not a lot of traffic, but flocks of sheep were being moved by the local farmers to different fields. The tinkling and dinging of bells round the necks of their charges kept up the interest. A new sound to me.

The barn was next to be tackled. With most of its stone walls still standing, only the roof had collapsed. I treated the whole subject in the way I thought John Constable might have done. A threatening sky, as seen in his oil sketches. Very dramatic, with sombre undertones. After bringing it to what I thought was a satisfactory conclusion, I moved on to painting their field. The flint boundary walls and hedges were heightened by an outcrop of rock and poppies plumb in the middle. My lack of experience of doing landscapes was sorely put to the test.

The last effort was of the bread oven and garage, which Michael was working on at the time. The oven was more like small building itself, the size of a decent shed. He had rebuilt the interior and made it habitable enough for them to live in. Right at the beginning though, they made do with a caravan whilst making the whole place weather proof. Michael was a wonderful and prolific worker and it showed.

Seeing the four paintings together gave me a nice warm feeling. I felt that I had really done something in kind, to thank them for making us so welcome. In my mind's eye I thought I would be able to do something for them both in the house too, but I didn't manage it. I'm just not up to real work these days. My grip on tools is now sometimes insecure. And it doesn't do much for morale for big daddy to sit comfortably dishing out words of wisdom and not lifting a finger himself!

The department of Lot is hilly, if not mountainous, and three miles away from our small holding is Rocamadour, an unusual and popular place that is literally carved out of the steep countryside. A one street affair, it is a fascinating place. As you might expect for a popular visitor attraction the shops are mainly aimed at tourists. The shop windows were full of quality merchandise including arts, sculptures, woodwork bits and souvenirs to tempt cash from the gazing visitors' pockets.

One art shop took my eye. The artist had painted watercolours onto a very textured surface, and lit from the side, produced a kind of 3D effect. Most appealing. Asking the lady shopkeeper if she was indeed the artist she said she wasn't, but she spoke excellent English and was no slouch about the art business. We had a very friendly conversation and before I left I'd borrowed a sheet of paper and left my mark, her own face name. I'm getting quite cheeky in my old age! She was very impressed at the novelty. In fact a lovely day was had by all.

Chapter 45

Visiting Albi

An all time ambition of mine had always been to visit Albi and the Toulouse Lautrec Museum. On the map it seemed quite near to Couzou, but when Hazel and Michael kindly took us there one day, it was quite a long journey. It's a fact that I hadn't really got the size of France in perspective. I kind of forgot that from the channel coast to Couzou is about the same distance as Scotland is to Dover, and that puts us plumb in the middle of the country.

It was a beautiful day and after we'd dined well we sought out the museum which housed the great painter's works. With its many galleries the building was itself an impressive structure. I found myself vainly looking for my favourites until I realised paintings by Lautrec are scattered about the art galleries of the world.

But there was a large number of smaller paintings from his early days. Quite enough to establish his pre-eminence as a great artist. We've always been very grateful to Michael and Hazel for taking us there.

I still carried on with my writing whilst I was away. After the evening meal I managed to add a few more pages to move nearer to completion, whatever that means! As always when you are busy and enjoying yourselves time seems to accelerate. In no time it seemed we were saying our thanks and goodbyes for a lovely holiday. There was another delay leaving Limoges Airport, but when at last we arrived at Southampton, Hazel's daughter Tina was waiting patiently to drive us home.

A few years on and I awoke to a new reality. I had been engulfed in nerve pains from the waist downwards, and I could no longer trust my foot movements to control an automatic car. With just two pedals and already a lack of certainty that my feet would behave, I reluctantly had to give up driving. That in itself meant a major change in my life style. Up until then Deena and I could always make plans without hindrance to others. My darling wife never expressed any desire to drive. It was a great pity because she is such a talented person, and who knows where her interests would have led her if she had been an independent traveller in her own right?

An offshoot of these pains had a rather more serious consequence. After seeing my doctor about the swelling around the legs and ankles he prescribed a stocking of special weave and elasticity, that once on, helped by daring the legs to become swollen again. They were very good at their job. The operative words here being 'once on'.

Sitting on the side of the bed, with my heel resting six inches off the floor, on something like a flower pot, allowed me to threadle the garment over my toes. Bent double, it was the nearest I have ever got to self-inflicted torture, in my life. Puffing and panting, with my new pig's heart valve working overtime, I could only stay down for a few moments at a time, hardly enough to get a reasonable grip on the stocking tops.

Early days saw me getting them both on in half an hour. Later, gradually, I got this down to ten minutes or so. Viewing the task from my prop maker's experience, I decided I needed a guide to help me to get the heel of stocking to coincide with my own heel, instead of ending up to the left or right of the said leg.

Laying the stocking flat I marked a line down the instep side from toe to knee, with a permanent marker pen. It didn't do much to lessen the tugging and exertions needed but it could be watched whilst struggling, and lo and behold, the two heels met as though they were two lost friends. My visible line was obviously some help. After testing it for a few days I wrote to the manufacturers suggesting that for people similarly placed like me, it may be a big help to add a guide line whilst the stocking was being made.

I sent my letter to their customer care department. After a second class postage time had elapsed, a charming female voice thanked me over the telephone, for taking an interest in their products. She wasn't sure though whether my little gem of practical experience would be taken up. It was very similar to the sort of comment you would expect after an audition. 'Thank you, we'll let you know'.

It was after I saw the doctor a second time that I was prescribed painkillers to make me more comfortable. After my heart operation and subsequent procedures I was always given a few of these pills but I had never used them. However this time I did.

Shortly afterwards, my daily visit to the you-know-what, became an every two day event, then every three, then it stopped altogether. I realised I hadn't had any trouble before I took the painkillers. Reading the literature I noted a possible side effect, constipation. I was very fortunate to be having my feet seen to that day by Hazel, back home from France. Apart from being a chiropodist she is also a trained nurse.

The blockage in the one habit also upset the fluids department by cutting off any flow at all. I was increasingly in more distress. I think medical term is cessation. She recognised the dangers and ran me to the nearest A & E department at St Richards in Chichester. The six-mile drive did nothing to ease the discomfort. I cannot describe the feeling exactly. You know you are in pain. Busting isn't quite relevant, but I wouldn't wish the experience on anyone.

In the waiting area there were about six people before me. Hazel managed to get me straight into a room obviously equipped for rapid action. Oxygen and other services filled the end wall. I undressed to my socks and put on a hospital gown, the sort that let the draught in at the back. Up onto the bed. There was no comfort here. By now I couldn't lie down, sit down, walk about or do anything really that eased the intense discomfort.

I couldn't really say I was going to burst, although having all exits closed for seemingly hours now, it must have been on the cards. The real danger I was told afterwards was damage to the kidneys. A nursing sister, Sarah, was seeing to me, and nurse Sonia was also on hand.

Hazel, who hadn't left me, knew Sonia from her own nursing experience, so when Doctor Tundy appeared I thought relief wouldn't be long away. But then all sorts of considerations had to be taken into account, that is to say, of prime importance to the safety of me, the patient. I must admit I was getting past it all by now.

ACTION! Just like a film studio, a catheter was introduced, not only into the story, but into me as well. The poor doctor was unable to stand clear quickly enough, but I'm sure his gown caught the worst of the jet stream. The relief to me was immediate and so very welcome. After such fraught moments leading up to the happy release we all enjoyed the joke of the situation.

Doctor Tundy could have remarked that he'd always remember me whenever he went to a car wash, but he didn't, and became my friend for life by saying while he was about it, he'd also get the other encumbrance moving too. Sarah introduced the lubricant and then it was up to me. I can see the comedy in most situations and I was glad to be alone when finally I was rid of everything that could be got rid of. Then the good doctor told me that I might have to be taught how to wee again!

I had had a catheter whilst undergoing prostate surgery and I don't remember any difficulties afterwards. It seems as though I had just gone through a very traumatic happening to my bladder and that the two situations were quite different. After saying goodbye to our trio of nursing angels, Hazel drove me home again. It had been six hours or so since we left Alvine Cottage.

Deena and I seemed to bear charmed lives. Having Nurse Jane present when she had her stroke, and me having Nurse Hazel present to do battle for me. Now I found myself in the clutches of lovely community nurses who would steer me through the next bit, in case I did have to visit a specialist.

Yesterday Jim asked if I would like to be interviewed by a Worthing journalist, about the Clown's Convention in March. Also, would I please like to talk and explain to a playgroup that clowns are funny and not frightening, so as to allay any of the children's fears. Both dates to be fixed later. My knowledge of previous conventions would sustain me through the first interview, but what a task was presented by the second request!

One of the reasons I had to stop taking on children's parties was the mobility bit. Previously when bending down the mind had no cause to think about getting up again. Working on the principle of a spring you popped down and the second bit was automatic. You popped up again. Sadly now, I have to give prior consideration to returning to the upright position again! Not only the 'how', but the 'can I' when on my own? Now using a climbing frame, it becomes so time consuming, there's hardly any time for the funny bits. And, naturally, clients baulk at paying a full fee for half a show.

Just take one bit of business, 'nearly putting my jacket on'. First the wrong arm went in. Then the second arm can't get into an inside out sleeve, and so on. What caused the merriment to our young clients was the speed at which I could do it. This against the background of their own struggles of learning to dress! Now, in slow motion, would it be as funny?

The weekend offered Jim and me a chance to meet all my old clown mates at our awards dinner. Some of them staying over to visit the church for the Grimaldi service next day, in London. Being so spread out our clowns' club finds it difficult to arrange these sort of get-togethers. There is no simple solution. This time we were dining half way up the M1. So after extended chinwags over the dining table, speeches, being entertained by our talented colleagues, handing out the awards, and spending a very pleasant evening together, we depart, Jim and me, driving back to Bognor.

As I struggle to get these memoirs of mine from freehand to 'computer speak', it's pretty obvious I have to consider how to bring everything to an end. I've had such a lot of happenings to write about in the past that it's been comparatively easy for a non-academic like me to 'just put it down'. Now, no longer mobile, and being somewhat frustrated by an ageing mechanism, me, it 'no longer flows'. Now I'm being forced to come to terms with modern technology. Hurrah for adult education classes, but it's still very 'ard!

A very welcome visit from past road safety colleagues from Wales shone a light on how it was. Two of Walter Davies' officers came to see if Deena and I were 'still about'. John Jackson and Steve Baker, still 'road safetying' in Gwent, came and reminisced about old times.

Both were very complimentary about my routines for the school children in getting the message across. Steve related how indelibly my acts are implanted in his memory through having to sit through them so many times in school halls. Even today the echoes of them still abound, even being copied in some places. That was very nice to learn.

Both remarked how different it was to see me in the flesh, without make-up. Neither were un-gentlemanly enough to say 'albeit a little frayed around the edges'. Both expressed their wish to put me forward for an award from RoSPA, for my contribution to road safety education in schools. Steve sent me a copy of Inroads, the journal for road safety professionals, a little while later. His report of our meeting was contained in a lovely article about me in this latest edition. All very exciting stuff, this.

I'm very pleased to have gone up a notch in the mobility department, but the absence of a car rules out my visits as pianist to the Tamarisk Centre. I really do miss this 'chore'. I am still available but now any job I am asked to do carries the request of being picked up and returned afterwards. My new enabler now is what I call my 'Walkie'. It's a kind of pram without the baby. Perhaps I should rephrase that, as I often feel like a babe in arms, in these advancing years. Anyway this 'wheelie' has brakes and when they are applied, I can sit down in it. The little seat also lifts up to reveal a small space for any shopping. So now the village is within reach again.

I can also get down to attend my art group again. Another permit has arrived that helps with parking, the Blue Card. Friends and relatives who kindly give me a lift anywhere can stop a little nearer our destination now. With our free bus pass at the ready we are contenders for a seat on the buses too. Another plus, it puts me in touch with our mobile library van. In fact the excellent service of this facility has also helped this little writing venture of mine. Books about the computer and allied subjects, selected by a devoted team of librarians, for us out in the country.

It has just entered my head that I'm so up to date now that if I carry on much more I'll be in the business of forecasting the future rather than writing about the past.

I must say its been a most intriguing and fascinating experience getting it all down. Rather like living it all again. A second life sort of thing. Haven't I been lucky?

www.halbrooks.me